Pirkei Avot

Pirkei Avot

A SOCIAL JUSTICE COMMENTARY

Rabbi Dr. Shmuly Yanklowitz

HEBREW TEXT EDITOR
Rabbi David E. S. Stein

FOREWORD BY
Ruth Messinger

CCAR
Press

CENTRAL CONFERENCE OF AMERICAN RABBIS
New York · 2018/5778

This book is written in honor of my parents, Mr. Stephen Yanklowitz and Mrs. Sandra Yanklowitz, who have always been rocks of love and support for me and to whom I'm eternally grateful. —*Rabbi Shmuly Yanklowitz*

Library of Congress Cataloging-in-Publication Data
Names: Yanklowitz, Shmuly, 1981- translator, writer of added commentary. | Stein, David E. S., 1957- editor.
Title: Pirkei Avot : a social justice commentary / Rabbi Dr. Shmuly Yanklowitz ; Hebrew text editor, Rabbi David E.S. Stein.
Other titles: Mishnah. Avot. | Mishnah. Avot. English.
Description: New York : Central Conference of American Rabbis, 2018 = 5778. | Item includes newly edited Hebrew text, new English translation, and original commentary in English. | Includes bibliographical references and index.
Identifiers: LCCN 2018006973 (print) | LCCN 2018007878 (ebook) | ISBN 9780881233230 | ISBN 9780881233223 (pbk. : alk. paper)
Subjects: LCSH: Mishnah. Avot--Commentaries. | Social justice--Religious aspects--Judaism.
Classification: LCC BM506.A23 (ebook) | LCC BM506.A23 P59 2018 (print) | DDC 296.1/234707--dc23
LC record available at https://lccn.loc.gov/2018006973

Interior designed and composed by Scott-Martin Kosofsky, The Philidor Company, Rhinebeck, NY. www.philidor.com
Printed in the United States of America.
10 9 8 7 6 5 4 3 2 1

CCAR Press, 355 Lexington Avenue, New York, NY 10017
(212) 972-3636 · www.ccarpress.org

Contents

About the Hebrew Text

Rabbi David E. S. Stein

ALL RABBINIC TEXTS have come down to us in variant versions. There is no authoritative "original" of *Pirkei Avot*. Inevitably, then, a publisher must make editorial choices about which variants to include.

In editing the Hebrew text that appears herein, I took as a starting point several prior Reform movement publications. I then modified that Reform "tradition" in light of the Israeli scholar Shimon Sharvit's masterful critical edition of *Pirkei Avot* (2004), and of his monograph on this tractate's grammar, lexicon, and style (2006). Where a material discrepancy was evident, I gave the greatest weight to the majority reading of the five relatively early Mishnah manuscripts that Sharvit collated. I also considered the readings that he found in Cairo Geniza fragments, early siddurim, and the discussions of medieval rabbinic commentators. (I did not address the considerable variance that exists in the paragraph divisions within each chapter. In that respect, in accord with Rabbi Dr. Yanklowitz's preference, we have followed the Artscroll edition edited by Rabbi Nosson Scherman.)

Compared to a typical recent rendition of *Pirkei Avot*, this edition's expressions, spellings, and grammatical forms are more in line with actual Rabbinic (rather than Biblical) Hebrew. At the same time, our text adapts Rabbinic Hebrew practice by adding punctuation in order to aid the contemporary reader in parsing the text.

A word of acknowledgment: I thank Michelle Kwitkin for calling my attention to Shimon Sharvit's scholarship. And let me thank The Rabbinical Assembly for graciously sharing a pre-publication copy of editorial notes on the Hebrew text in its new commentary on *Pirkei Avot*. My work benefited from Rabbi Dr. Martin S. Cohen's instructive observations in those notes.

Foreword

Ruth Messinger

THIS IS TRULY a contemporary "guide to the perplexed," and it arrives when many of us feel deeply the need for some guide as to how to work in the world. Rabbi Yanklowitz has taken the preeminent ethical teachings of Judaism as these are laid out in *Pirkei Avot*, and he has brought his own wisdom and that of others to considering what these teachings mean and—most important—how we might think about applying them in our own lives in the twenty-first century.

Whether the question is care for the homeless, or how to be a welcoming congregation, or how to organize to fight climate change, there is wise guidance for all of us in *Pirkei Avot*, and Rabbi Yanklowitz teases it out. Along the way he shares what brilliant teachers from Pete Seeger to Maimonides, from Jeremiah to Eleanor Roosevelt, from ancient rebbes to Rabbi Jonathan Sacks have to teach us about how to live ethical lives. Rabbi Yanklowitz reads widely, and he is eager for us to glean from him how very different people have looked at and spoken about these issues. He hopes that we will not only read but act, that we will choose to walk in some of the footsteps he lays out for us.

There is a brilliant focus in these commentaries on the core importance of living an ethical life. The author makes it clear that we must care about and pay keen attention, first, to knowing ourselves and, then, to developing our relationships with others and with God, because these are essential to our being able to make a difference in the world. This is an insight too often neglected in texts and courses about how to be an activist, and it is powerful to have it be so central in this "guide."

This is particularly the case in the present moment. There is a great deal going on that is legitimately distressing to people; and as a result, too many of us—wanting to respond—are pulled from issue to issue, acting in ways that may make us feel good in the moment but lack discipline and focus. The result is that we then feel overwhelmed and are not able to work in coherent and effective ways.

What this book does is remind us of the importance of focus, connect up our activist interests to a deeper sense of spiritual drive, and lay out for us that we will be able to do more and do it more effectively if we approach our work with an appreciation for the past experience and the wisdom of others.

We are indebted to Rabbi Yanklowitz for helping each of us find not only intellectual but also spiritual inspiration from these ancient maxims; for guiding us to open our hearts to receive this inspiration; for encouraging us to apply it to developing our own individual characters and ensuring that we are present and effective throughout our lives—and that we work as we can to make the world better for all its inhabitants.

Acknowledgments

THIS BOOK is in memory of Rose (Rachel) Davis ("Babi") ל״ז, after whom we were so honored to name our first child. May Babi's spirit continue to live through Amiella Rachel's good deeds. It is also in memory of Betty and Mitch Janowski, Harold and Beulah Yanklowitz, Martin Davis, and David and Magda Stein. May all their memories be a blessing and may their souls soar in the heights of the heavens.

In the time I have worked on this book, I have been blessed to have had so many wonderful people by my side. Though the process was long, it was undoubtedly worthwhile and spiritually edifying. I am grateful to my publisher, CCAR Press, for providing me the opportunity to add my words and ideas to an esteemed catalog of inspiring Torah and Jewish thought. Its history as a leading publisher of Jewish works left me humbled. I am truly grateful for everything CCAR has done for me. Many thanks to the delightful (and insightful!) Rabbi Hara Person for being my guiding light at CCAR and to (now) Rabbi Andrue Kahn for his editing insights. I am grateful to proofreader Rabbi David E. S. Stein for his thoughtful edits, suggestions, and wisdom. His attention and diligence to the small details elevated this book immensely. Thanks to Scott-Martin Kosofsky for his design and production acumen. I'm also grateful for the marketing expertise of Ortal Bensky and the whole CCAR Press team, including Debbie Smilow, Sasha Smith, Rabbi Dan Medwin, Carly Linden, Rabbi Beth Lieberman, and CCAR chief executive Rabbi Steven A. Fox for all of their support.

I'm so thankful for the diligent editing work of Abraham J. Frost, who spent countless hours editing drafts, offering constructive feedback, and providing support. I'm also grateful to Suzanne Bring, who steadily added enormous insight with her contributions and editing acumen. Their assistance was invaluable as I wrote this book.

Most importantly, this book would not have been possible without the everlasting love of my beautiful and brilliant wife Shoshana, and our wonderful children, Amiella Rachel, Meir Lev Kook (MLK), and Maya Neshama, as well as our foster children. Whenever I found myself in need of deep inspiration, I thought of my family. Thank you for all the joy and light you share with me on a daily basis. I love you.

Finally, I thank the Creator—the One True God—for giving me life, for giving me hope, and for giving me the ability to pursue a life of holiness.

Introduction

WHAT DOES *Pirkei Avot* mean? Literally, it means *The Chapters of the Fathers* or, as some translate it, *Ethics of the Fathers*. The Hebrew word *avah* (of which *avot* is plural) is found in Proverbs 1:30, meaning "to lead through advice."[1] Therefore, another way to understand the title of this work is *The Chapters of Advice*. *Avot* can also mean "first principles," so another translation may be *The Chapters of First Principles*. Further, some have suggested that *avot* doesn't mean "fathers" so much as it does "archetypes." The words of the Sages are words to live by, rather than being direct explications of ritual or exegetical minutiae.

Initially, *Pirkei Avot* was composed of only five chapters of wisdom. At some later point in history, a sixth chapter was added (taken from *baraitot*, Rabbinic teachings that were not included in the Mishnah, but were from the same era). This sixth chapter came to be called *Kinyan Torah*, "the acquisition of Torah," because most of the content concerns itself with engaging in Torah study. Some have suggested that the sixth chapter was added because there are six Shabbat afternoons between Passover and Shavuot.[1a] The last would be about Torah study, which is central to the holiday of Shavuot.

Many of the *mishnayot*, the early Rabbinic literature in the Talmud, deal with rituals, sacrifices, and points of nuanced theology. *Pirkei Avot*, however, is unique in that it draws upon the Jewish ethical tradition and expands these teachings in simple and clear ways. Each teaching in *Pirkei Avot* is called a *mishnah*. The Sages who are credited with the teachings emphasized how important it is to study continuously and to work to fulfill the teachings found within *Pirkei Avot* (BT *Bava Kama* 30a).

It is remarkable that *Pirkei Avot* is free of the study of religious procedures, as most Jewish texts from the era are primarily concerned with ritual and legal practices. The objective is not to focus on studying religious rules. Instead, this is a work that consists purely of timeless life wisdom. Each of the Talmudic Sages had multiple points of wisdom to share, but only one or a handful of their teachings were recorded in *Pirkei Avot*. It is humbling to think that after a life teaching profound wisdom, one's existence may be remembered through only one sentence.

For my commentary, I decided to draw and weave from commentators both historical and contemporary. My commentary is heavily informed by the mystic and philosopher Rabbi Judah Loew ben Bezalel, known as the Maharal of Prague (Bohemia, early 1500s–1609), as well as by Rabbi Y'hudah Aryeh Leib Alter, the S'fat Emet (Poland, 1847–1905). From more modern thinkers, I've been inspired by the commentaries of Rabbi Samson Raphael Hirsch (Germany, 1808–1888) and Rabbi Abraham Isaac HaKohen Kook (Poland, then Mandatory Palestine, 1865–1935); and two contemporary thinkers, Rabbi Irving (Yitz) Greenberg and Rabbi Binyamin Lau. For some commentators, such as Maharal, S'fat Emet, and S'forno, I have used my own translations of their original works for this book. These sources form the core of my commentary here. But the sources in this volume go far beyond these six. Unfortunately, the only full commentaries on *Pirkei Avot* have been written by men, so whenever possible I have worked to include women's voices from other, more contemporary sources.[2]

In his commentary on *Pirkei Avot*, my teacher Rabbi Yitz Greenberg writes that he has

> long loved the rabbinic sages—not only for their great teachings and their role in transmitting Judaism, but also because they break the model of either/or. Thus, they simultaneously transformed the tradition and brought it along *in its entirety*. They avoided the arrogance of the modernists who dismiss many elements of the past as obsolete or primitive. The sages understood that the whole of Jewish tradition is sacred.[3]

He continues:

> *Ethics of the Fathers* should also serve as an inspiration and a challenge to our generation to follow in the footsteps of the sages— to offer new wisdom, to uncover new revelation, to unite past,

present, and future, and to help the Jewish people and all of humanity find their way through the next phase of the covenantal journey toward a perfected world.[4]

I used to think inspiration could be found anywhere, but I learned there are indeed bad books, pointless movies, and invitations that are best declined. These compose the cold zone. They take energy from you, in contrast to the hot zone: the people and activities that leave you with greater energy. Our task is to fine-tune our spiritual antennae to detect the hot zones that charge us.

Our bodies naturally transfer food into energy. But we must learn how to intentionally transfer inspiration into energy. Otherwise, that energy remains mere entertainment and not nourishment for the soul. Thus, the art of inspired living is to learn how to keep our inspiration full enough that we do not burn out, yet drawing enough from it that we stay charged with holy fire. Indeed, our end goal is neither to be perfectly rested, nor to exist on an artificially high plane. The goal of the inspiration seeker is to do good works, pour out positive energy, and share inspiration wherever we go. Just as we need food to keep our bodies going, we need inspiration to fuel the embers in our souls to keep it burning.

We run between movies and books, counselors and houses of worship, without ever feeling spiritually satiated. But with deep human inspiration that truly touches and changes us, we leave each experience spiritually overflowing. I'm inclined to be inspired by human stories of triumphant people—those who overcome obstacles and commit their lives to serving others, looking to extend the limits of human possibility, and to achieve self-transformation and love. When I was a young man and spent time in developing parts of the world, I was inspired by a woman named Margarita, the leader of a movement to support the poor in rural Argentinean villages. As an inspiration seeker, I found myself writing down every word she shared about how she would work for the redistribution of wealth.

I would identify three primary types of inspiration: moment-inspiration, encounter-inspiration, and soul-inspiration. In moment-inspiration, given the conditions of one's life at that moment, one understands a truth more deeply. In encounter-inspiration, one experiences an event that is transformative. The most powerful is soul-inspiration, in which one does not need a particular moment or experience to have a deeply inspiring moment. Rather, it is self-cultivated. One has gained the tools to experience self-discovery and self-motivation without external stimuli.

At one time, the Jewish people relied solely upon God for inspiration. The prophets would be filled with *ruach hakodesh* (divine inspiration) and the ability to understand higher truths. But the Rabbis also teach that this type of inspiration ended with the deaths of the prophets Haggai, Zechariah, and Malachi (BT *Sanhedrin* 11a). The root of inspiration is spirit, and in Judaism this spiritual process also has a connection with respiration. God breathed the first breath into humanity to provide the capacity for deeply internal inspiration. Today, we must take it upon ourselves to open our hearts and allow ourselves to be inspired each and every day by infinite possibility.

When you find environments and people who inspire you, hold them close. We learn to generate our own inspiration wherever we are if we maintain the proper outlook on life. When you find that you just cannot get enough of these meaningful experiences, you will know that you have become an inspiration addict. And from this inspiration, we achieve a level of worldliness. Through experience, we achieve wisdom. We should seek wisdom wherever we can find it. *Pirkei Avot* is a key motivator to advance us on the journey through our Jewish sources of wisdom.

The Sages of our tradition not only inspire us, but can provide spiritual light when we're in darkness. The martyred Hannah Senesh, in her poignant poem "*Yeish Kochavim*: There Are Stars," reminds us of the power of memories illuminating our path forward.[5]

> There are stars up above,
> so far away we only see their light
> long, long after the star itself is gone.
> So it is with people that we loved—
> their memories keep shining ever brightly,
> though their time with us is done.

But the stars that light up the darkest night,
these are the lights that guide us.
As we live our days, these are the ways we remember.

Working through this commentary on *Pirkei Avot* has been personally meaningful for me. It helped me realign my thoughts toward the relationship between humanity and the Divine as well as interpersonal relationships between individuals. One of my most important life shifts in emerging adulthood was realizing that my life question should not be "What do I want to receive?" but "Who do I want to be?" I realized that what mattered more than acquisition was character development. That spiritual awakening gave me a heavy moral charge, but also released the stress that accompanied the often futile rat race of contemporary society. I wanted to be more reflective about my moral and spiritual choices and to strive to live wisely. I wanted to feel the burning challenge every day to strive for intellectual, spiritual, relational, religious, and moral growth. *Pirkei Avot* became the work that continues to keep me focused on this journey. And I hope that my commentary inspires you to find that place within yourself to propel the world toward reconciliation and spiritual enlightenment.

Many blessings to you.

Chapter 1

I:I

מֹשֶׁה קִבֵּל תּוֹרָה מִסִּינַי וּמְסָרָהּ לִיהוֹשֻׁעַ, וִיהוֹשֻׁעַ לִזְקֵנִים,
וּזְקֵנִים לִנְבִיאִים, וּנְבִיאִים מְסָרוּהָ לְאַנְשֵׁי כְנֶסֶת הַגְּדוֹלָה.
הֵם אָמְרוּ שְׁלֹשָׁה דְבָרִים: הֱווּ מְתוּנִים בַּדִּין, וְהַעֲמִידוּ
תַלְמִידִים הַרְבֵּה, וַעֲשׂוּ סְיָג לַתּוֹרָה.

Moses received the Torah from Sinai and transmitted it to
Joshua; and Joshua to the Elders; and the Elders to the
Prophets; and the Prophets transmitted it to the Men of
the Great Assembly. They [the Men of the Great Assembly]
said three things: Be deliberate in judgment; develop many
students; and make a fence for the Torah.

THIS FIRST PASSAGE of *Pirkei Avot* presents to us the foundational
document of Jewish ethics. It begins by establishing the Sages' unin-
terrupted authority back to the Sinaitic Moment—when the heavenly
conception of the Jewish people as ideal become an earthly reality.

This first mishnah does not state directly that God gave the Torah
to the Jewish people. Instead, it begins with Moses receiving the Torah
from "Sinai," rather than with the story of communal divine revelation. By beginning in this manner, mishnah 1:1 describes the Torah's
primary focus on human relationships. Were this mishnah to focus on
God first, then ethics—which are matters between human beings—
would necessarily be considered second. Ethics become the foundation
for a covenantal relationship with the Divine.

The Sages impart this message from the start. The entire Torah
enterprise requires *relationship*. To embrace tradition, one does not
hide away in the library or the sanctuary, but instead engages in face-
to-face encounters. Indeed, it is these face-to-face encounters that are
central to the ethics of Emmanuel Levinas (twentieth century, France)
and Martin Buber (nineteenth–twentieth century, Austria/Israel) and
that help inform a modern reading of the ancient text. Consider these
meta-commentaries:

LEVINAS: "The face to face is not a modality of coexistence . . . but is the primordial production of being on which all the possible collocations of the term are founded."[6]

BUBER: "The great achievement of Israel is not so much that it has told man of the one, real God, the origin and goal of all that exists, but rather that it has taught men that they can address this God in very reality, that men can say Thou to Him, that we human beings can stand face to face with Him, that there is communion between God and man."[7]

Furthermore, to take part in such an intellectually rigorous tradition, the Maharal teaches that people must strengthen three components of the human intellect: *chochmah* (wisdom), *binah* (understanding), and *daat* (discernment), which he aligns with the three pieces of guidance that end this mishnah. He also aligns these teachings respectively with *mishpatim*, laws that enable society to function justly; *mitzvot*, religious mandates of the Torah; and *chukim*, laws that are less based on common sense and societal order and more on our character development and relationship to God. The Mishnah encourages us to be more careful with *din*, our judgment. Such lessons pertain to both our *dinei mamonot*, monetary decisions that affect others' property, and *dinei n'fashot*, decisions that affect others' lives.

To exercise this inherent intellect, every generation is responsible to render safe passage to the tradition. And to do so, each generation must transmit the teachings in such a way that they are stronger than when they were received. Rabbi Abraham Isaac Kook teaches that to do this is to "expand the palace of the Torah."[8] Every generation has new insights based upon the changing times, and when we add those contributions to the wealth of the previous transmissions, we strengthen our heritage. We must embrace discomfort at times, challenge dogmas, and question outdated assumptions that no longer further the Torah enterprise nor the whole of the human enterprise.

Today, we see danger to the Torah enterprise from two places. There are those who want to distort the tradition so radically that our ancestors would no longer recognize its essence at all. On the other hand, there are those who seek to freeze the tradition, so that its relevance can scarcely be grasped by our contemporaries. The Sages of *Pirkei Avot* caution against both destructive approaches and seek new measured understanding. Consider the Talmud's story that imagines God showing Moses the teachings of Rabbi Akiva in the distant future. In this telling, Moses is at first distressed because those teachings do not resemble what he himself knows; but he is assured by the claim that this, too, is authentic Torah linked through an eternally continuous chain (BT *M'nachot* 29b). The sacred goal is not merely the survival of the tradition (as that would be quite a low bar). Instead, tradition flourishes because each successive generation has sufficient independence to pursue the transformational interpretations of tradition, within the context of their own time and place.

While we always engage in our own private text analysis and personal reflection, relationships with others should never be relegated to an afterthought. We are fascinated—naturally—by older generations but are most compelled by the concept of *halachah k'batrai*, following not the ways of the ancients but the ways of the generation immediately preceding our own; it is a multifaceted learning experience, watching one's community, learning from one's parents and grandparents, and embracing a teacher.

Why does this mishnah teach that Moses "received" (*kibeil*) the tradition, but then state that he "transmitted" (*m'sarah*) the tradition? Rabbi Judah Loew ben Bezalel teaches in a commentary that "received" implies an imperfect communication, whereas "transmitted" implies that all was fully given over. Thus, we start to explore the *challenge* of revelation. In God's infinite wisdom, it is impossible for any human to comprehend the entirety of Torah completely. Moses, the greatest prophet in Jewish history, received as much as was possible. Yet, the perfect Divine will could not be grasped. The fact that the amazing revelation we have been gifted is imperfectly received should humble us: it should make us pause when we are tempted to think we know the truth. This reminds us that Torah teaching and learning are ethically rich. Even where Torah was "transmitted," there were oversights. The Rabbis teach that much of Torah was lost during the thirty-day mourning period after Moses's passing (BT *T'murah* 16a), although they suggest that Otniel ben Kenaz, the first biblical judge, restored it. Handing over teachings is through *mosar*, a word related to *musar*, or the practice of ethical and spiritual development. What matters is not merely that the information is received and understood, but that the encounter itself is refined and internalized for inner spiritual awakenings and growth.

This revelation was not privately conveyed to Moses, nor are we asked to invest our blind faith in Moses. Rather, the Torah is clear that the masses heard and saw the revelation (Exodus 19:9; Deuteronomy 5:19–24). It is our task to ensure that this singular moment of revelation—the spark of Jewish life and learning—is kept alive and relevant for the generations to come.

The closing advice of this first passage is critical, not only to understand the passage in isolation, but also as a metonym for the general ethos of Judaism. To improve oneself ("be deliberate in judgment"), to strengthen others ("develop many students"), and to strengthen the tradition ("make a fence for the Torah") are the decisive factors when approaching the text; one needs all three accountings (*cheshbonot*) to cultivate a more completed understanding of the universe:

> Am I learning in a fashion that has integrity, self-awareness, rigor, and passion?
> Am I engaging others in learning Torah, spiritual growth, and performing mitzvot?
> Am I guarding our core values and preserving them while elevating them?

Although we learn through relational transmission, we must hold ourselves each spiritually and intellectually accountable to the collective holy enterprise of transmitting Torah to the next generation.

1:2

שִׁמְעוֹן הַצַּדִּיק הָיָה מִשְּׁיָרֵי כְנֶסֶת הַגְּדוֹלָה. הוּא הָיָה אוֹמֵר:
עַל שְׁלֹשָׁה דְבָרִים הָעוֹלָם עוֹמֵד: עַל הַתּוֹרָה, וְעַל הָעֲבוֹדָה,
וְעַל גְּמִילוּת חֲסָדִים.

Shimon the Just was among the survivors of the Great
Assembly. He used to say: The world stands on three things—
on Torah study, on service [of God], and on kind deeds.

THE AUTHOR of the apothegm in this mishnah, Shimon the Just, was
known for his unique righteousness, as well as for an influence that
extended beyond the Jewish people; even Alexander the Great was
impressed by his deeds and wisdom (BT *Yoma* 69a). Shimon the Just
served as *Kohein Gadol*—High Priest—of Israel, but he lived in an era
after most of his contemporaries, the other sages of the Great Assembly, had already died. He was one of the last sages connected to that rich
past. He was indeed a survivor, one with a unique perspective on both
what sustains the world and what passes from the world.

This mishnah's concrete lesson could well have served as the first
teaching of *Pirkei Avot*. However, the rabbis who compiled the mishnah taught it second, purposely placing it after the first mishnah. Here
they are emphasizing that in addition to constantly striving for moral
and spiritual growth, our lives should be suffused with holiness—
k'dushah—and that our adoption of religious systems will serve to
sustain and bolster our ethical commitments.

Torah study, service [of God], and kind deeds are like a three-legged
stool, and like that stool, knocking out any single leg causes collapse.
Each leg is not merely one-third of the whole stool's support; each is
100 percent necessary—none can stand without all in place. Comprehending and internalizing each of these three elements of Judaism are
essential. Judaism requires the development of one's intellectual capacity through Torah study, emotional capacity through cultivating the
service of God, and performative capacity through kind deeds. These
constitute the cognitive, affective, and behavioral aspects of one's whole

being; indeed, Torah asks for the *whole self*. When we recite the *Sh'ma*, it is with reverence that we utter, "With all your heart, with all your soul, and with all your might" (Deuteronomy 6:5).

Yet, we are challenged by our individual proclivities. One variety of person loves to volunteer but can't sit still to read a book. Another loves the solitude of the library but is shy or anxious around other people. Some can open their hands to volunteer at a homeless shelter but not their hearts in intimate relationships.

The world of Judaism, the world described by Shimon the Just, requires that all three religious activities inform one another through the routine of study, prayer, and giving. They are completely entwined, though different eras and cultures may have different priorities. For example, the Chasidic rabbi Elimelech of Lyzhensk (eighteenth century, Poland) teaches that the world is primarily sustained through acts of kindness, for it says (Psalm 23:6), "Only good and kindness shall pursue me all the days of my life, and I shall dwell in the house of God for length of days."[9] Our subsequent obligation is to grow in an intellectually mature fashion, while always learning to become more emotionally intelligent, and to give more of ourselves to others. Indeed, as it is written in Psalms, "The world is built on kindness" (89:3).

When we, either as individuals or as a community, fail to uphold the good deeds and the three activities required of us, it is as if the tenets of Jewish faith have become void of true meaning. *The stool collapses*.

In his commentary on this mishnah of *Pirkei Avot*, Rabbi Samson Raphael Hirsch distinguishes between the language of this mishnah and that found in a parallel formulation in mishnah 1:18:

> The difference in meaning between the term *omeid* as is used in this verse and *kayam* in mishnah 18 seems to be as follows: *omeid*, lit. "stands": that on which something "stands" or "is based" constitutes its foundation; if it loses that base or foundation, it will fall. *Kayam*, on the other hand, denotes a "standing up" or "enduring" through time; i.e. stability or permanence. If a thing loses that on which it depends for stability or permanence it may continue to exist but it will not endure.

This mishnah states that the world (*olam*) depends on these three articles, and the Jewish commentators taught that *olam* derives from the same root as *he-elem* (hiding).[10] Thus, *tikkun ha-olam*, repairing the world, hints at *tikkun he-elem*, repairing that which is concealed, whether from our thoughts or from our heart. Our job is not just to repair the world, but to make what is hidden visible and repair that, too. This includes the suffering of invisible people—those vulnerable people who go through life without the concern of the broader populace—while also combatting the pernicious and hidden forms of injustice, below-the-surface oppression, and scarcely seen brokenness that silently affect millions.

Undertaking this task reinforces the purpose of human creation and our human essence. Rabbi Obadiah ben Jacob S'forno (sixteenth century, Italy) writes in his commentary on Genesis 1:26 that "through Torah and kind deeds Israel fulfills the intent of the verse 'Let us make human beings in our image, after our likeness.'" Our *tzelem Elohim* (human dignity) is directly connected to our potential to have an impact on the world. Both the Maharal and Rabbi Hirsch teach that Torah, *avodah*, and *g'milut chasadim* guide all our relationships. Torah is about development of the self. *Avodah* is about the development of our relationship with the Divine. Practicing loving-kindness—*g'milut chasadim*—is about developing our relationships with others. By doing and being good to all—God, people, self—we justify that creation is actually "good" (BT *B'rachot* 6b). At the least, we validate God's continued investment and sustenance of all human existence.

The alternative is terrifying. The Maharal teaches in his commentary on this mishnah that the Flood destroyed the world precisely because the three pillars were violated during the antediluvian period. Even further, the Talmud teaches that if ordered by authorities to publicly violate a Torah prohibition under pain of death, one should do so except in cases of idolatry, sexual immorality, and murder (BT *Sanhedrin* 74a). Strikingly, the Maharal teaches that these three misdeeds align exactly in opposition to our mishnah's priorities of *avodah*, Torah, and *g'milut chasadim*. Serving God requires rejecting idolatry, embracing a Torah of ethical conviction requires rejecting harmful sexual relationships, and embracing the mandate to act kindly requires one to reject all forms of oppression.

But Creation is also about seeing what is and what can be. Rabbi Mira Beth Wasserman writes about the normative task of progress that creation sparks within us: "Creation is not merely making new things, it seems; creation also means contending with what is, rearranging materials that are already there."[11]

To follow the Sages' blueprint, we must invest faith in the importance of all acts. Imagine if someone came to you and offered to give you $86,400 every day for the rest of your life. The only condition is that you had to spend every penny each day and that you wouldn't be able to save a dime. This is what God has given us: 86,400 seconds each day, not one of which can be recovered. Each moment counts. Indeed, Maimonides teaches that we should view our next decision as if there is a scale and that our next act will tilt the world toward redemption or destruction.[12]

As humans, we are to strive for continual spiritual cultivation. The Sages teach that behind every blade of grass is an angel whispering, "*Grow!*"[13] If this stands true for every blade of grass, imagine how many angels must be standing in solidarity behind each and every human being.

This sustains each of us, the entire world.

All of existence.

1:3

אַנְטִיגְנוֹס אִישׁ סוֹכוֹ קִבֵּל מִשִּׁמְעוֹן הַצַּדִּיק. הוּא הָיָה אוֹמֵר:
אַל תִּהְיוּ כַעֲבָדִים הַמְשַׁמְּשִׁין אֶת הָרַב עַל מְנָת לְקַבֵּל
פְּרָס, אֶלָּא הֱווּ כַעֲבָדִים הַמְשַׁמְּשִׁין אֶת הָרַב עַל מְנָת שֶׁלֹּא
לְקַבֵּל פְּרָס. וִיהִי מוֹרָא שָׁמַיִם עֲלֵיכֶם.

Antigonus, leader of Socho, received [his Torah] from Shimon
the Just. He used to say: "Don't be like servants who serve
their master for the sake of receiving a reward; instead be like
servants who serve their master with the understanding that
they will not receive a reward. And let the awe of heaven be
upon you."

ANTIGONUS, a third-century Talmudic sage (with a notably non-
Hebraic name), lived during a period of profound Hellenistic influence
on Jewish culture. The inclusion of this Jewish man with the Greek
name in the canon attests to Judaism's ongoing and complicated interaction with a dominant, non-Jewish culture—be it Hellenistic, Ottoman, Christian, or secular. Antigonus, and his Greek name, reminds
us that we dare neither embrace nor reject all truths of the surrounding
culture. He judiciously filtered Greek values and maintained the absolute integrity of his Torah scholarship. Nor was Antigonus unique in
this approach. The Sages permitted the embrace of Greek language,
cultural norms, and names when these choices did not contradict
immutable Jewish values and practice. We are expected to live in two
worlds, yet remain completely loyal to our holy Torah.

This mishnah describes the moral yoke clapped upon the Jewish people: We are not to follow religious teachings blindly in search of some
sort of material reward. Our task—as individuals and as a people—is
to share the burden as well as the opportunity to show moral leadership to a broken world. Through this rigorous ethical structure, we can
grapple with difficult truths honestly and embrace the complexity of
the moral tasks.

What were the implications of this moral yoke then? What are the implications now? Then, as now, we have been guided from an anthropocentric worldview toward a theocentric worldview. Humans are not the center. God is. Therefore, neither our human reputations nor our longevity nor any other reward for good behavior matters. Rather, we matter when we invest in the eternal. When we love good, when we do good, good is its own reward. *The eternal is its own reward*—that's what Antigonus means when he says, "And let the awe of heaven be upon you."

Through this mishnah, the Sages deal with the complicated issues that underlie tangible religious motivation. Lawrence Kohlberg, the late psychology professor at Harvard University and founder of the academic field of moral development, suggests there are six stages of moral development.[14] Elucidated through many academic pieces during his career, Kohlberg's thesis evolved over time but kept the same basic three-part structure. In the earliest stages, one is concerned with reward and punishment. In middle stages, one is most concerned with adhering to the law and following cultural norms. In the actualized, final stage of moral development, we live by principled conscience and universal ethics. As we mature, our motivations develop toward means that go beyond the personally selfish and toward the (broadly) egalitarian and communal. This is the stage that Antigonus describes here.

It is striking that the mishnah here refers to us as "servants." The Renaissance-era rabbi S'forno teaches that this theological concept of *avadim*, or servants to God motivated by fear or awe, contrasts with *ben*, the child, who is driven by love.[15] When we serve God from *yirah* (awe, fear), we are part of the less-actualized cycle of reward and motivation. When we serve God from love, we do not seek reward.

Neither, however, is it religiously empty to consider reward and punishment. In fact, a later mishnah in *Pirkei Avot* tells us, "Calculate the cost of a mitzvah against its reward" (2:1). There is a place for self-interest, which can sometimes guide and motivate. But it should not *overtake* us. The Sages say that one can do righteous acts when motivated by some reward:

If one says, "(I donate) this money to charity in order that my son
will live" or "in order that I will merit life in the world-to-come,"
that person (remains) fully righteous. (BT *Bava Batra* 10b)

The story of Antigonus is also closely linked to the emergence of the
Sadducees, a Jewish sect that originated around the second century
BCE. According to legend, the Sadducees were created based upon a
translation error by Tzadok and Boethus, students of Antigonus. They
broke from tradition by denying the authority of the Oral Law (what we
now call the Talmud) and the concept of life after death. They taught
that God does not provide rewards at all.[16]

The last line of this passage reminds us that even living in our current
era, which so privileges reason and conscience, we would do well to
hold the "awe of heaven" in our consciousness. This awe, this spiritual
awareness, reminds us to go beyond the zealous arrogance of certainty
to the productive humility of doubt. In our lives, we should remember
how unintentional errors have real consequences—and even reinforce
from time to time that we live in a world of justice, where all will be
accounted for. These steps can inspire deeper faith as we strive to be
our best on challenging days.

1:4

יוֹסֵי בֶּן יוֹעֶזֶר אִישׁ צְרֵדָה וְיוֹסֵי בֶּן יוֹחָנָן אִישׁ יְרוּשָׁלַיִם קִבְּלוּ
מִמֶּנּוּ. יוֹסֵי בֶּן יוֹעֶזֶר אִישׁ צְרֵדָה אוֹמֵר: יְהִי בֵיתְךָ בֵית וַעַד
לַחֲכָמִים, וֶהֱוֵי מִתְאַבֵּק בַּעֲפַר רַגְלֵיהֶם, וֶהֱוֵי שׁוֹתֶה בְצָמָא
אֶת דִּבְרֵיהֶם.

Yosei ben Yoezer, leader of Tz'reidah, and Yosei ben Yochanan,[17] leader of Jerusalem, received [their Torah] from him.
Yosei ben Yoezer, leader of Tz'reidah, says: Let your house be a
meeting place for sages; sit in the dust of their feet; and drink
in their words thirstily.

YOU CAN LEARN a lot about a family's values when you walk into their
home. What are the objects you see when you enter a house? Perhaps
there are shelves of beautifully bound but well-thumbed Jewish texts,
ritual objects, family pictures, and other items of religious value and
personal meaning. One's home is to be a *makom kadosh*, a "holy place,"
to which you invite guests, especially scholars and teachers who can inspire others with their wisdom and support those in need.

In his commentary on this mishnah, Rabbi Y'hudah Aryeh Leib
Alter—known as the S'fat Emet—interprets the passage to mean that
we should make places of learning into homes, rather than merely
inviting scholars into our homes. We should find that we are such
regulars at the *beit midrash*, the place of learning, that we feel fully at
home there. Then, because we've fostered an environment where learning is heartily welcomed, we'll grow intellectually and spiritually. We'll
drink in the words of the scholars and teachers "thirstily," working
continually to renew this thirst for deeper engagement and knowledge.

Maimonides teaches that one cannot fulfill *simchat yom tov*, "the joy
of a holiday," through *simchat kereiso*, "joy of the stomach." Rather, by
inviting those who are struggling—financially, emotionally, or with
low self-esteem, for example—to sit at one's table, one can more fully
realize the cardinal spirit of *simchat yom tov* and thus transmit the wide

breadth of Torah wisdom.[18] The home can be an even more powerful site of learning than the synagogue or yeshivah, because the intimacy of sharing personal space fosters communal relationships and societal trust.

Our current era so values equality that it sometimes dismisses merit, even perhaps overlooking great talent. We are uncomfortable acknowledging the higher spiritual or moral quality of a truly meritorious individual, but the Sages tell us to do so anyway. When we meet a person who lives rigorously by a code of high moral principles and possesses considerable insight and wisdom, we are obliged to pursue them and imbibe their holy wisdom.

Yet, this teaching comes with a caution. We are not to be overzealous in following those who have wisdom, and we must guard against unhealthy dependency on their teachings. We should seek out teachers and spiritual guides who encourage the development of our own critical thinking and moral improvement, rather than furthering their own influence, control, or power.

According to the Talmud, even "the [mundane] conversation of Torah scholars is worthy of study" (BT *Sukkah* 21b). If we are to "sit in the dust of their feet," we can absorb the deeper truths beneath their ordinary conversation. Drinking in their words—what a powerful image for internalizing their ideas! The Jewish people's engagement with Torah is not to be merely cognitive, but also affective and spiritual.

Filtering out unhelpful ideas and ideas that do not seem correct to us is imperative. We also need the ability to internalize and truly accept ideas containing essential truths. Our thirst is more than physical. We pursue inspiration. We do not have to rely only upon biological forces to be "thirsty." Instead, we run after inspiration, enjoying the insatiable thirst for learning.

1:5

יוֹסֵי בֶּן יוֹחָנָן אִישׁ יְרוּשָׁלַיִם אוֹמֵר: יְהִי בֵיתְךָ פָּתוּחַ
לָרְוָחָה, וְיִהְיוּ עֲנִיִּים בְּנֵי בֵיתֶךָ, וְאַל תַּרְבֶּה שִׂיחָה עִם
הָאִשָּׁה. בְּאִשְׁתּוֹ אָמְרוּ, קַל וָחֹמֶר בְּאֵשֶׁת חֲבֵרוֹ. מִכַּאן
אָמְרוּ חֲכָמִים: כָּל הַמַּרְבֶּה שִׂיחָה עִם הָאִשָּׁה גּוֹרֵם רָעָה
לְעַצְמוֹ, וּבוֹטֵל מִדִּבְרֵי תוֹרָה, וְסוֹפוֹ יוֹרֵשׁ גֵּיהִנָּם.

Yosei ben Yochanan, leader of Jerusalem, says: Let your home
be open wide; treat the poor as members of your home; and
do not talk excessively with a woman. They said this even
about one's own wife; surely it applies even more to another's
wife. Consequently, the Sages said: Anyone who talks excessively with a woman causes evil to himself, dismisses words
of Torah, and will eventually inherit *Geihinam*.

FIRST: "Let your home be open wide." This passage tells us to be neither closed-minded nor closed-gated to those outside our immediate
circle of friends and family. When we open our home, we are to be intellectually, spiritually, and socially inclusive and engaged. If we include
those who do not already have a place within the sanctum of our private
lives, it will foster our own internal and interpersonal growth. This is
distinct from how we may conduct ourselves in public, at work, or on
the street, where we may be more guarded.

Rabbi Binyamin Lau proposes that both Yosei ben Yoezer and Yosei
ben Yochanan are responding to Hellenism's pressure on ancient Jewish communities. Yosei ben Yoezer wanted Jews to close out external
forces and turn inward; to fill our houses with scholars and block out
Hellenistic influences. Conversely, Yosei ben Yochanan advocated for
opening our homes to guests and engaging others, meeting Hellenism
in open contest without fear.[19]

Second, the phrase "treat the poor as members of your home" has
lent itself to multiple interpretations. Rabbeinu Yonah, the thirteenth-
century Spanish sage, says that this means that if you employ workers

and they remain poor, you must make them members of your home.[20] And S'forno, the sixteenth-century Italian commentator, on the other hand, explains that this means that if you meet someone poor, you must employ him or her. Today, either interpretation challenges us to reconsider the boundary between the private realm and the public sphere.

Indeed, hospitality to the poor is a type of openness. A simple reading of the term *r'vachah* (widening), as seen in this mishnah, means exactly that: opening or widening up one's domain to another. In his commentary on this mishnah, Rabbi Hirsch writes, "In Exodus 8:11, the term *r'vachah* is used to denote 'relief,' literally a 'widening' or 'loosening' of the bonds of want and distress."

Furthermore, Hirsch quotes Rabbi Yosei:

> Let your home be open always to those who suffer and seek relief, and even if you are not able to eliminate all want and distress, be ready at all times to ease and relieve suffering to the best of your ability. . . . When you extend your hospitality to the poor, treat them as you do members of your own household.

Again, hospitality as responsibility blurs the boundaries between family and community, between the private and the public.

So too, we should consider the psychological needs of guests. The Kotzker Rebbe, Menachem Mendel of Kotzk, writes that we should show our guests their bed before we invite them to the meal, so they can enjoy their meal more fully, knowing that they need not then worry about having a place to sleep (quoted in S'fat Emet's *Pirkei Avot* commentary). The Talmud reminds us of how holy an act it is to show hospitality to others: "Rabbi Y'hudah said in Rav's name: 'Hospitality to wayfarers is greater than welcoming the presence of the *Shechinah*, for it is written, "And he [Abraham] said: My lords, if I have found favor in your sight, please do not pass your servant by" (Genesis 18:3)'" (BT *Shabbat* 127a). As can be discerned from this passage, the reason that Abraham's actions are religiously revolutionary is that he values welcoming his guests over his communion with God. Thus it is more important, according to the Rabbis, to create space in our home for others in need than it is to connect to God.

Third, those of us who are men are cautioned against excessive talk with women. In his commentary on this mishnah, Rabbi Hirsch explains that "the sayings of the Sages are replete with maxims stressing the high esteem in which womanhood should be held, the respect and honor due one's wife and particularly the great importance that a husband should attach to the views, opinions and counsel of his wife." Rabbi Hirsch further states that "*sichah* [in this context] does not mean serious conversation but merely idle talk and gossip."[21] A husband who truly respects his wife should strive to offer her more than just trivial talk and idle chatter.[22] He will want to discuss with her the serious concerns of life and will derive enjoyment from the resulting mutually respectful exchange of views and counsel.

It is inevitable that many readers will view this mishnah through a lens of misogyny. While not a defense, Rabbis Jonathan Sacks and Marc D. Angel interpret the reasoning behind the inclusion of the troubling language found in the verse: "The rabbis assumed, based on the reality of their time, that most women were not versed in Torah. Thus, a man who conversed with a woman was invariably wasting time that should have been spent on Torah study."[23]

Rabbi Shlomo Ephraim Luntschitz—known as the Kli Yakar (sixteenth century, Prague)—teaches that the well of water stopped flowing because the Israelites didn't cry or even eulogize when Miriam died (as the Torah tells us that they did when Moses and Aaron died). They needed to be taught how great of a person they had lost. How did they miss this? How do we learn to celebrate the accomplishments of women the way we do for men? How do we learn to properly appreciate those humbly providing "the water" in our lives?

Rabbi Irving (Yitz) Greenberg comments that within the sociocultural context in which this mishnah was written, "men and women were socially isolated from each other. . . . Excessive socializing and talk between men and women could lead to improper thoughts and actions."[24] Today, however, given "the extraordinary entrance of women into contemporary society and their rise to the dignity of public activity in the last century,"[25] the caution has shifted. All of us, men and women, are required in public and private to exercise self-control in each other's presence, and thus uphold modesty, morality, and correct behavior. This *tikkun*, a spiritual repair, redresses the consequences of the first recorded divine command (Genesis 2:16–17), in which Adam and Eve transgressed the boundaries of holy space and sinned. Judaism has no problem with men and women talking together, let alone a problem with talk between husband and wife. Rather, in this mishnah the Sages were inveighing against the type of inappropriate and excessive speech that could lead to wrongdoing.

Judith Plaskow, professor emerita of religious studies at Manhattan College, is among the vanguard of feminist Jewish thinkers who subvert the teachings presented in this mishnah. But even more so, she provides us with a critique about the need for dissent within Jewish tradition when certain ancient norms simply cannot pass muster with contemporary sensibilities. She writes:

> The need for a feminist Judaism begins with hearing silence. It begins with noting the absence of women's history and experiences as shaping forces in the Jewish tradition. Half of Jews have been women, but men have been defined as normative Jews, while women's voices and experiences are largely invisible in the record of Jewish belief and experience that has come down to us. Women have lived Jewish history and carried its burdens, but women's perceptions and questions have not given form to scripture, shaped the direction of Jewish law, or found expression in liturgy. Confronting this silence raises disturbing questions and stirs the impulse toward far-reaching change. What in the tradition is ours? What can we claim that has not also wounded us? What would have been different had the great silence been filled?[26]

The Jewish ethos and discourse must be adamant about embracing feminism and women's equality. On that topic, U.S. Supreme Court justice Ruth Bader Ginsburg remarks, "Women will only have true equality when men share with them the responsibility of bringing up the next generation."[27] While Justice Ginsburg was primarily talking about child-rearing, her larger point is that the social paradigm of a women's role—whether as paragons of domesticity or as innovators in the working world—is undervalued, to society's detriment. Through this lens, we see that women can choose to be stay-at-home mothers but also that equal opportunities provided to women who choose to be in the workplace must be present and accounted for. Justice Ginsburg continues, "I said on the equality side of it, that it is essential to a woman's equality with man that she be the decision-maker, that her choice be controlling."[28]

The fluidity of gender roles is a modern phenomenon, certainly one that the Sages would never have considered in their lifetime. But now, with the deconstruction of which gender is suited for any particular activity, there is a Jewish imperative to think broadly about how we relate to one another. Consider Hannah Greenebaum Solomon, an early twentieth-century social reformer and founder of the National Association of Jewish Women, who remarked, "Who is this new woman? She is the woman who dares to go into the world and do what her convictions demand. She is the woman who stays at home in the smallest, narrowest circle, forgoing all the world may offer to her, if there her duty lies."[29]

Warren Buffett, one of America's most successful businessmen, once remarked that one of the real reasons he was so successful is because he was competing with only half of the population.[30] Perhaps this is why many men naturally reject women's leadership: fear of competing with women or losing ground to women. Sheryl Sandberg, the chief operating officer of Facebook, writes:

> Of the 195 independent countries in the world, only 17 are led by women. Women hold just 20 percent of seats in parliaments globally. In the United States, where we pride ourselves on liberty and justice for all, the gender division of leadership roles is not much better. Women became 50 percent of the college graduates in the United States in the early 1980s. Since then, women have slowly and steadily advanced, earning more and more of the college degrees, taking more of the entry-level jobs, and entering more fields previously dominated by men. Despite these gains, the percentage of women at the top of corporate America has barely budged over the past decade. A meager twenty-one of the Fortune 500 CEOs are women. Women hold about 14 percent of executive officer positions, 17 percent of board seats, and constitute 18 percent of our elected congressional officials. The gap is even worse for women

of color, who hold just 4 percent of top corporate jobs, 3 percent of board seats, and 5 percent of congressional seats.[31]

Sandberg shares a 2011 McKinsey report that notes that men are often promoted based on their potential, while women are often promoted based on past accomplishments.[32] This double standard is unacceptable. To the extent that we are committed to continuity in our holy tradition, we must also be committed to spiritual repair of those parts of the tradition that still embody gender bias and reject egalitarianism. Some of our Jewish communities have been comfortable moving quickly in adapting those traditions. Others have moved more slowly. We can respect different paces of evolution provided that there is a commitment to ultimately reaching the end goal of equality, dignity, and respect for both women and men equally. We have not adequately kept the teachings of Jewish women alive. Religious teachings (like all ancient teachings) recorded the voices of men. Anita Diamant writes in her novel *The Red Tent*, "The other reason women wanted daughters was to keep their memories alive."[33] We must double down on our efforts to ensure that the voices of women are not silenced but amplified.

The three statements in this mishnah are interrelated. Cultivate openness of the mind and exercise hospitality in one's home. Behave generously toward guests, especially the poor, so that it is as if they are one's own family. But respect the worth of one's closest relations, including one's partner, and treat them with high-minded regard. The home—the actual *and* symbolic locus of the private—is where propriety most matters, especially when we allow what's outside inside.

1:6

יְהוֹשֻׁעַ בֶּן פְּרַחְיָה וּמַתַּי הָאַרְבֵּלִי קִבְּלוּ מֵהֶם. יְהוֹשֻׁעַ בֶּן
פְּרַחְיָה אוֹמֵר: עֲשֵׂה לְךָ רַב, וּקְנֵה לְךָ חָבֵר, וֶהֱוֵי דָן אֶת כָּל
הָאָדָם לְכַף זְכוּת.

Y'hoshua ben P'rachyah and Matai of Arbel received [their
Torah] from them. Y'hoshua ben P'rachyah says: Make a
teacher for yourself; acquire a friend for yourself; and judge
everyone favorably.

WE LIVE ineffably alone in this world. The first existential dilemma
in the Torah, and central to the first chapters of Genesis, is *lo tov heyot
haadam l'vado*, "it is not good that the man be alone" (Genesis 2:18). We
may not think of ourselves as alone, because we may be surrounded
by family, friends, and community. But consider that each of us has
millions of thoughts daily that no one else can ever truly know or understand. In response to humanity's internal depth, complexity, and,
ultimately, the loneliness that wells inside even the most extraverted of
our fellows, we need God. In this loneliness, no one knows or understands me except for *Yodei-ah Machashavot*—the Knower of Thoughts. I
am not alone in my head, my heart, and my soul.

Today, we consider independence a great virtue. "I can take care of
myself!" "I am self-reliant." Perhaps, even, "I don't need teachers or
friends." Instead of showing our maturity as a society, this overvaluing
of independence reveals a deep flaw. We now have a culture of excessive
competition and egomania. Consider this analogy: A man buys the
brightest flashlight to show everyone that he has the brightest light.
But once the sun starts to shine, the light of flashlights is irrelevant.
When we collaborate, we are like the sun. The individual with his powerful flashlight is not even noticeable under the sun's bright light of day.

Our idea of what constitutes friendship has been drastically altered
through the widespread use and prominence of social media. Digital
companionship is now the go-to substitute for flesh-and-blood relationships; "friends" are never more than a mouse click away. People

are proud to collect hundreds, even thousands, of social media friends, connections, or followers. As a society, what have we to gain by this commodification of friendship? Has the goal of accumulating these friends disrupted long-standing definitions of human relationships? This question strikes at the heart of the contemporary human condition: Are our relationships reducible to abstracted pixels on a computer, or are they still about individual contact, interpersonal development, and growth? Our existential quest, then, is to transcend the distractions of meaningless digital ephemera that have become our companions and to regain the virtues of true friendship.

From the beginning of existence, humans have been not only physically alone, but also emotionally isolated and spiritually alienated. Perhaps the biblical figure of Joseph was the loneliest: "A man happened upon him as he was wandering in the countryside. The man asked him: What are you looking for? He said, 'I'm looking for my brothers'" (Genesis 37:15–16). This problem continues today. We are constantly seeking our "brothers."

Rabbi Abraham Isaac Kook articulates the Jewish responsibility to seek our fellow for partnership and friendship. Discussing the centrality of these relationships in human development, Rabbi Kook writes about finding companions within community, even amid disagreement of views:

> Part of the characteristic of Torah is that it recognizes the need for a social life with friendships, which bring to the world a good life within society. This is particularly rewarding when one's social group consists of good and scholarly people. Separation from other people and extreme asceticism—which is the approach of a significant portion of those people who, of their own, have sought closeness to God—is a foreign idea to the Torah. For that reason, if one wants to acquire knowledge of Torah, he will succeed specifically by joining together with a group of learners, which shows the gains of avoiding isolation.[34]

Formal teachers are important, but friends who know us deeply can support and challenge us much more meaningfully. "I have learned much from my teachers, but from my friends more than my teachers"

(BT *Taanit* 7a). Indeed, Maimonides, who understood friendship (and most of his ontology) in the Aristotelean context, in which partners for the development of reason and cultivation of virtue are essential, says that "people require friends all their lifetime."[35]

Friends are needed not only for good times and growth; we require friendship to help us persevere and survive. Rabbi Joseph B. Soloveitchik (twentieth century, United States) values both "a *chaver lid'agah*, a person in whom one can confide both in times of crisis, when distress strikes, and in times of glory, when one feels happy and content," and "a *chaver l'dei-ah*, a friend in whom he or she has absolute trust or faith."[36] Rava, a renowned fourth-century Talmudic sage, says simply, "Either friendship or death" (BT *Taanit* 23a).

Rava may be correct. Studies have shown that people with the most friends (and not just relatives or children) live significantly longer than those with few friends. The companionship that many couples experience also has demonstrated health benefits. A study of 3,700 British couples ages fifty and older, published in *JAMA Internal Medicine* in 2015, found that individuals in relationships promoted and sustained healthful behaviors in each other. For instance, individuals were more than six times as likely to quit smoking if their partner also tried to quit. Companionship matters.

For a Torah scroll to be kosher, it must have not only the perfect black ink of the words but also the perfect prescribed white spaces. Likewise for the text of our personal lives: the spaces—what we might call the context—are as crucial as the text. The context is created through building relationships, through rigorous devotion to the ideas of those who have come before, and through breaking down the barriers of interpersonal connection. It is the warmth of the collective spirituality and the feelings that surround these revelations that engenders human growth, quite to the contrary of secular values studied in isolation.

"A righteous person falls seven times and rises seven times" (Proverbs 24:16); falling is essential to the enterprise of gaining wisdom. Without the fall (maybe we call this "experience"), we can never rise up stronger than before; we must stumble in our learning and growth. The Talmud says, "No person can really learn unless one has stumbled first"

(BT *Gittin* 43a). If we are to stumble, we need others who can support us and lift us back up.

This mishnah reminds us that Torah cannot be truly learned in an environment of pure isolation or complete independence. We need teachers and friends to guide us, support us, and, most importantly, challenge us. We have the normative obligation to greet everyone warmly, for each may end up becoming a teacher or a friend. Treating each encounter as a moment to find either learning or friendship fulfills the mandate to view everyone as created in the image of God. But to replicate godliness, we always need to consider the needs of humanity. Rather than judge another harshly, we judge others favorably and explore together how our lives are tied up with one another.

S'forno writes that we are to "judge everyone favorably because without this trait friendship will not endure. For the majority of statements, the listener can judge a speaker in a negative light. And this [attitude] will unquestionably annul all friendship."[37]

The Talmud teaches that even Jesus was a student of the author of this mishnah. According to this Talmudic tradition, Y'hoshua ben P'rachyah pushed Jesus away for his bad behavior. After seeing the growing movement around Jesus, Y'hoshua felt great sorrow and thus expressed that we should never push anyone away completely; this would be an abdication of his pedagogical obligations. Rather, as this lapse in judgment displays, we should be gentler and accepting. Rabbi Binyamin Lau notes that Y'hoshua taught this point in this mishnah because of the failure to act to his fullest potential. Total condemnation of another has consequences that are too great. Therefore, the mishnah says *kol haadam*, that we should judge "the whole person" favorably.[37A] There will be aspects of every person that we won't judge favorably, but we should not reject the entirety of a person.

The Talmud teaches that if we judge others favorably, God will judge us favorably as well (BT *Shabbat* 127b). In fact, the connection is even more immediate. When we are judging another, what we find irritating in that individual is often something we dislike about ourselves. The other's shortcoming holds a mirror to our own. We should use the inclination to judge another as an opportunity to be reflective and corrective about our own character and actions.

Finally, the mishnah says "make" for yourself a teacher. This is because a teacher is indeed "made" by one's students. But then it says "acquire" a friend. Why "acquire" and not "make"? The use of "make" teaches that more active involvement is required of you, with regard to your teacher.

I:7

מַתַּי הָאַרְבֵּלִי אוֹמֵר: הַרְחֵק מִשְּׁכֵן רָע, וְאַל תִּתְחַבֵּר
לְרָשָׁע, וְאַל תִּתְיָאֵשׁ מִן הַפֻּרְעָנוּת.

Matai of Arbel says: Distance yourself from a bad neighbor;
do not associate with a wicked person; and do not despair of
retribution.

THE PREVIOUS MISHNAH was centered around the importance of
developing relationships and bringing people closer. By contrast, this
mishnah focuses on when to push people away.

Rabbi Binyamin Lau suggests that Y'hoshua ben P'rachya (the subject of the previous mishnah) and Matai (the subject of this one) offer
distinct approaches to the growing schism between the Maccabees,
who were traditionalists, and the Hellenists, who favored accultura-
tion or assimilation. While Y'hoshua suggested that we invite others
in and develop relationships, Matai suggests that we exercise caution,
cutting people off when necessary. The successive placement of these
two *mishnayot* is intentional; we are to seek balance between conflicting
positions.

This passage's rhetorical construction is through negative phrasing—these are actions *not* to take. Yet the lesson is that one must take
personal responsibility for one's actions.

A common Chasidic teaching states that the biblical figure Noah was
a *tzaddik im peltz*, a "righteous person in a fur coat."[38] This means that
when he got cold, he put on a coat to stay warm, but he didn't light a
flame to keep others warm. When God chose to flood the world and
cleanse it of sin, Noah was unable to persuade anyone else to change
and unable to save humanity from itself. He was a righteous man, but
not much of a leader. As Jews, we are asked to emulate part of Noah's
model, that of being simply faithful. But unlike Noah, we must also
lead others toward righteousness.

Like Noah, we have to protect ourselves, our bodies, our minds, our
hearts, and our souls. As we go out into the world to effect change,

any lingering air of negativity can threaten our work. When this pessimistic aura permeates outward from ourselves, it jeopardizes the entire human enterprise. While we may need to help others who are mean-spirited, we can never allow their character to penetrate our own emotions. We must always keep a healthy distance from those who seek to bring down our holy work.

Perhaps we should not befriend a wicked person, but is it perhaps okay to conduct business or align politically with them? Here the mishnah is clear: "*Do not associate.*" We are not merely utilitarian thinkers who sell out for long-term gain. The process by which we move forward matters. The character we develop along the way matters. We may embrace an activist partner on one issue even though we disagree on others, but we exercise restraint and do not embrace someone who we feel is wicked through and through.

That we do battle or at least enact firm boundaries might seem an extreme reading, but it is one that fits within the ethical framework of *Pirkei Avot* as a whole. When we build emotional and spiritual boundaries, we ensure our continuous spiritual growth. We cannot "despair of retribution"—that certain individuals will come and hurt us in our righteous tasks. We should embrace others and foster inclusion, while exercising discernment to filter out negative influence. Knowing what is right and what to peacefully avoid protects the soul, while allowing others to live their lives in harmony.

"Do not despair of retribution!" Some fear that they will miss out if they don't join the liars and cheaters who seem to be winning. The mishnah reminds us that the honest and faithful will win, both in this world and in the world-to-come.

The S'fat Emet, in his commentary on this mishnah, writes that "distance yourself from a bad neighbor" means that one must distance oneself from the evil within. Before judging another for a negative character trait, search and uproot the evil within oneself.

‏ח:א

יְהוּדָה בֶּן טַבַּאי וְשִׁמְעוֹן בֶּן שָׁטַח קִבְּלוּ מֵהֶם. יְהוּדָה בֶּן
טַבַּאי אוֹמֵר: אַל תַּעַשׂ עַצְמְךָ כְּעוֹרְכֵי הַדַּיָּנִין. וּכְשֶׁיִּהְיוּ בַּעֲלֵי
הַדִּין עוֹמְדִים לְפָנֶיךָ, יִהְיוּ בְעֵינֶיךָ כִּרְשָׁעִים. וּכְשֶׁנִּפְטָרִים
מִלְּפָנֶיךָ, יִהְיוּ בְעֵינֶיךָ כַּצַּדִּיקִים שֶׁקִּבְּלוּ עֲלֵיהֶם אֶת הַדִּין.

Y'hudah ben Tabai and Shimon ben Shatach received [their
Torah] from them. Y'hudah ben Tabai says: [When serving
as a judge] do not make yourself into a lawyer; and while the
litigants stand before you, consider them both as wicked; but
when they are dismissed from you, consider them as innocent
persons who have accepted the judgment upon themselves.

SOCIETY WITHOUT ORDER is physically and spiritually dangerous.
The Rabbis of the Talmud were committed to fostering a rigorous
system of justice; one can find both integrity and deep wisdom in the
Jewish judicial system. Consider, for example, the fascinating Talmudic principle of *kulo chayav zakai*, which teaches that if all of the judges
agree in a capital case that the defendant is guilty, then the defendant
must be acquitted (BT *Sanhedrin* 17a). Unanimity is considered dangerous for Jewish intellectual and spiritual integrity. Rather than work
toward unanimity, the Rabbis preferred that the majority wins the case.
Indeed, it is possible that half of the judges may consider the other half
to be accomplices to murder, when they reconvene to argue on the
next case (an extreme example, to be sure). For the Sages, this would
be better than unanimity. Such intelligent people could not possibly
all agree, so there may well be a flaw here—a unique injustice found
among intellectual giants operating in unanimity. Even if there is not
an unjust flaw, the problem is that if all the judges agree, then there is
no one still arguing for the defendant. (In the rabbinic legal system,
there are no attorneys to prepare and submit briefs.) This lack of legal
representation is an adequate reason to dismiss a conviction.[39]

Looking closer to home, the American judicial system holds

sacrosanct the presumption that a person charged with a crime is deemed innocent until proven guilty. Fairness is compulsory, even while the litigants engage in rigorous efforts to uncover the facts. The full truth of any case will never be known by anyone but God, but individual courts nonetheless have the obligation to do all they can with imperfect facts to sustain resolute justice in society.

Let us look at the first crime in the Bible. It is difficult to understand how the eating of fruit in the Garden of Eden was a sin. Should not humans have been encouraged to eat from the Tree of Knowledge of Good and Evil? Surely we would have yearned to learn the boundless secrets of infinite moral consciousness. Even at this rudimentary stage of their moral development, perhaps Adam and Eve already intuited the distinction between good and evil, but they sought certainty within an amorphous, newly created world teeming with potential. What they sought was what only God knows and what only God *can know*: they sought to evade the complex ambiguities of moral life and access the clear truth. So, in their quest to attain a level playing field with God, Adam and Eve erred. They sinned by dismissing the moral complexity needed to ground humanity in a newly formed world.

We cannot shy away from argument in our quest to promote the most just society. Modern society has been clever at creating new ways of enabling destruction and death, but we have not been nearly as innovative in fostering new models for peace, equity, and justice.

Today, American society can be unforgiving of people who have made grievous mistakes. One's reputation can be tarnished forever after the spotlight is shown on one's moral failing. But this mishnah instructs us to "consider them both as innocent" after a case is resolved. Rabbi Hirsch writes, "For there are disputes in which even the best person may be wrong and the worst person may be right." Y'hudah ben Tabai himself wrongly sentenced someone under dubious political circumstances, after which he committed to acting only in partnership with Shimon ben Shatach (BT *Makot* 5b). But, to be sure, Shimon ben Shatach also erred and needed partnership. Living amid the religious upheavals of first-century Judea, Shimon experienced firsthand the conflict between the Sadducees, who denied the Oral Law, and the Pharisees, who were the progenitors of our modern Rabbinic Judaism. Shimon's brother-in-law was the Hasmonean king Yanai, a Sadducee who brutally persecuted the Pharisees, and Shimon envisioned a rabbinic justice system that instead embodied integrity (JT *Sanhedrin* 6:3, 6:6).

Understanding the system of justice in ancient Judaism is illustrative to us. We should always demand reason and evidence and never merely rely upon the piety or wisdom of the authorities. Every person has intellectual challenges, as well as psychological blind spots. To treat both parties in a conflict equally is a matter of justice that requires us to be aware of our biases. We must admit that we all—even unconsciously—judge based on appearance, age, race, intellect, and so on. Understanding these biases is the first step.

1:9

שִׁמְעוֹן בֶּן שָׁטַח אוֹמֵר: הֱוֵי מַרְבֶּה לַחֲקוֹר אֶת הָעֵדִים, וֶהֱוֵי
זָהִיר בִּדְבָרֶיךָ, שֶׁמָּא מִתּוֹכָם יִלְמְדוּ לְשַׁקֵּר.

Shimon ben Shatach says: Interrogate the witnesses exten-
sively; and be careful with your words, lest they learn to lie.

OUR THOUGHTS, speech, and deeds can have life-or-death consequences. This mishnah continues the previous passage's focus on the
legal system. But the Rabbis are speaking about something beyond
that, too: speaking evil of another and bringing shame on the person is
akin to murder; this concept is found regularly in the Talmud (e.g., BT
Bava M'tzia 58b). Distancing oneself from what is false and honoring
what is true are of utmost importance, but this commitment must be
more than internal; it must show in our speech, too. We learn from this
that the Torah is adamant that "you shall not commit a perversion of
justice" (Leviticus 19:15). The S'fat Emet, in his commentary, suggests
that in this mishnah, *eidim*, "witnesses," mean both one's *yetzer tov*,
"good inclination," and one's *yetzer hara*, "evil inclination." Each person must search inside, lest one fuel the evil inclination to lie to one's
deepest self.

The Rabbis are clear that we must "interrogate" to determine the
truth, rather than shy away from confrontation. Each step matters: in-
vestigating deeply, reflecting on one's inner self, and considering one's
speech.

Rabbi Shimon was renowned for his integrity, as depicted in the
following story: One day, the disciples of Rabbi Shimon presented him
with a donkey that they had purchased from a gentile merchant. After
receiving the donkey, Rabbi Shimon removed its saddle and discovered
within a costly jewel (usually described as a pearl). The students were
joyous! They told their master that he might now cease toiling, since
the proceeds from selling the jewel would make him wealthy (Rabbi
Shimon, though a business owner, was quite poor). A Talmudic legal
formula of the sale ("When we pay you, this donkey and everything

that it carries is ours") meant that the jewel was now his legal property. Rabbi Shimon replied that although his students had interpreted the law to the letter, they had misunderstood its deeper meaning. He had no intention of keeping the jewel, just as the seller had no intention of selling it. Later, Rabbi Shimon, with his students in tow, returned the jewel to the gentile merchant, who exclaimed, "Praised be the God of Rabbi Shimon ben Shatach!" (JT *Bava M'tzia* 2:5).

The Sages were real people, influenced by personal calamities as well as political realities. Based on false testimony, Rabbi Shimon's own son was condemned to death (JT *Sanhedrin* 6:3), and this might well have influenced Rabbi Shimon's fervor for honesty. But even if he were not influenced by this, his inherent moral compass was true. In this mishnah, we are cautioned against encouraging others to lie through ambiguity in our own speech. Not only is one to be honest, one must also use one's speech to foster honesty in others, and one must transcend narrow self-interest in doing so. We are to give the best of ourselves, even if it would seem to run counter to our personal bottom line. It is all too easy to stretch the meaning of our words and actions to gain a client, to gain a friend, to gain favor. This is a vital and difficult teaching of *Pirkei Avot*, but one that has sustained Jewish communities around the world for centuries.

1:10

שְׁמַעְיָה וְאַבְטַלְיוֹן קִבְּלוּ מֵהֶם. שְׁמַעְיָה אוֹמֵר: אֱהַב אֶת
הַמְּלָאכָה, וּשְׂנָא אֶת הָרַבָּנוּת, וְאַל תִּתְוַדַּע לָרָשׁוּת.

Sh'mayah and Avtalyon received [their Torah] from them.
Sh'mayah says: Love work; despise positions of authority; and
do not become overly comfortable with the authorities.

THE TWO AUTHORS of this mishnah were noted to be converts or
descendants of converts (BT *P'sachim* 66a; BT *Yoma* 71b). In either case,
they were publicly respected (BT *Yoma* 71b), which is an example of
the value that Judaism places on embracing fully those who embrace
Judaism. Indeed, once converted, an individual is no longer considered
a convert, but merely a Jew, as fully capable of becoming a leader in our
community as any individual of Jewish birth.

The Talmudic dyad of Sh'mayah and Avtalyon are clear: The goal
of Jewish life is *not* to find nirvana in solitude, nor is it to retire to rec-
reational pursuits. No, the essential elements for a good life include
working to support family and community, performing physical labor,
and making contributions to society. By being productive, we contribute to society, grow in character, and support our communities. While
we should make the most of our professional lives, we should do so
neither from avarice nor from lust for power.

We are to guard ourselves from the inclination to seek prestige
through professional position. It is not worth the burden of internal
and external stress. One would best keep away from the whole culture
of competition for power. One should strive not for authoritative leadership, but for inspired leadership. We never want a "bully pulpit" for
the sake of coercion, but rather we seek to cultivate sincere relationships that enhance the good life for everyone.

Let's be clear. We should not despise power. Power can be used to
achieve so much good on a large scale. Rather, we despise the temptations of money and fame, which often accompany power. We must turn
our backs on power that is abused for self-gain.

In another Talmudic passage, Sh'mayah teaches how people should engage with others in the public realm:

> Heaven should be beloved through you. A person should study the Written and Oral Law, and apprentice to scholars; they should speak gently with people. Their purchasing and business dealings should be pleasant; they should conduct their business in good faith. What do people say of such a person? "Fortunate is the one who learned Torah! How beautiful are their ways, how proper is their conduct!" (BT *Yoma* 71b)

The Rabbis encouraged creating spiritual and societal change not primarily by pushing for alterations outside ourselves but, first and foremost, by refining our inner world. They even suggested that it is a healthier way to live. As is stated in another Talmudic tractate, "Woe to authority, for it buries those who hold it; there is not a single prophet who did not outlive four kings" (BT *P'sachim* 87b). To be sure, there is nothing wrong with gaining influence or political position. Indeed, if no one of virtue were willing to run for positions, we would only have scoundrels for public leaders. Rather the goal is to be deeply cautious in one's leadership.

We can look to the example of Joseph, one of the preeminent figures of biblical leadership and spiritual wisdom. Joseph presents a curious case. He lived a life filled with triumph and despair. At his lowest, Joseph was rejected and abandoned by his brothers: "Joseph dreamt a dream [one time], and when he told it to his brothers, they hated him all the more" (Genesis 37:5). Yet, after his familial banishment, Joseph rose to power as a powerful seer and advisor for the Pharaoh, and he became wealthy and nearly peerless in the process. When his brothers came before him to plead for their well-being, Joseph could have rejected them. Instead, he welcomed them with open arms. For such a mitzvah one would think that Joseph would have outlasted his brothers and been blessed with long life. Yet, despite this (and being the second youngest of twelve sons), Joseph was among the first to pass away. This leads to an interesting question, which the Talmud also answers: "Why did Joseph die before his brothers? Because he conducted himself in a position of authority" (BT *Sotah* 13b).

What are we to glean from this passage? We learn that at best, one will enjoy more life if one prioritizes relationships and helping others over gaining positions of authority.

In his commentary, Rabbi Hirsch writes, "It seems that the purpose of these three maxims of Sh'mayah is to counsel us to preserve our personal independence," lest one "becomes a slave to one's position." In this way, Rabbi Hirsch emphasizes how important it is to have freedom in life. Indeed, freedom is central to the religious ethos, but it can only be actualized when embraced with concomitant responsibility.

I:II

אַבְטַלְיוֹן אוֹמֵר: חֲכָמִים, הִזָּהֲרוּ בְדִבְרֵיכֶם, שֶׁמָּא תָחוּבוּ
חוֹבַת גָּלוּת וְתִגְלוּ לִמְקוֹם מַיִם הָרָעִים, וְיִשְׁתּוּ הַתַּלְמִידִים
הַבָּאִים אַחֲרֵיכֶם וְיָמוּתוּ, וְנִמְצָא שֵׁם שָׁמַיִם מִתְחַלֵּל.

Avtalyon says: Scholars, be careful with your words, lest you
incur the penalty of exile and be banished to a place of toxic
water. The students who follow you there may drink and die,
and the Name of Heaven will be desecrated.

THE PARADIGMATIC *chilul HaShem* (desecration of the name of God)
is a Jew acting dishonestly in business dealings with a gentile (BT *Yoma*
86a). Many of us spend the majority of our lives at work. In this environment, in constant interaction with people outside our typical social
sphere, we are given the ability to cultivate our character and demonstrate our true values to the public. Here we have the chance to put our
highest values into action and to go beyond what's merely passable,
legal, and socially acceptable. Yet taking the low road is far easier.

This mishnah returns to the theme of mishnah 1:9—caution with
one's words is of utmost importance. What we feel in our minds and
hearts and what we allow from our mouths (and computer keyboards)
can have immense and immediate effect on the greater world.

In this mishnah, Avtalyon cautions scholars specifically. Then, as
now, scholars and their scholarly production, which are really nothing
more than words arranged into argument, have the potential to cause
damage. If not exceedingly careful, scholars have the potential to lead
students, and perhaps anyone, astray. Scholarly commentary on Torah
is not exempt from this caution; rather, one must be especially cautious
with such scholarship, lest we alter the divinely created system and desecrate the Name of Heaven. With increased education comes increased
responsibility.

"The students who follow you there may drink and die." Teachers
can take students to unforeseen places (that is their job, after all), but
there can also be a danger in such places. While scholars help us see the

world in new ways, that new vision makes it difficult to return to other ways of understanding. Immersing oneself in the postmodern philosophers, for instance, makes it challenging to see the world according to their predecessors, the modern thinkers. Some could study the classics and only view the world through the lens of ancient philosophy. While these ideas have stood over time, it is up to our individual conscience to determine how we act upon our thoughts and feelings.

A Jew may dabble in other religions, but imbibing too freely of those teachings runs the risk that the centrality of Judaism is lost. While learning the plurality of thought and philosophy that the world has to offer is itself a worthy virtue, delving too deeply into an ecology that poisons the mind (racism or political extremism, for example) is to be avoided at all costs.

Acting rashly rather than thinking deeply is like banishment: forced exile into a place of evil waters. The neurotransmitters of our brain can cultivate automatic reactions and memories that direct us away from our spiritual foundation. Learning when to refrain and when to speak up is vital to the human psyche and our spiritual, moral development. We often must transcend our personality type, a unique challenge for each of us.

It is our sacred duty, then, to reject these false notions and work to attain something much greater than ourselves.

1:12

הִלֵּל וְשַׁמַּי קִבְּלוּ מֵהֶם. הִלֵּל אוֹמֵר: הֱוֵי תַּלְמִידוֹ שֶׁל
אַהֲרֹן: אוֹהֵב שָׁלוֹם וְרוֹדֵף שָׁלוֹם, אוֹהֵב אֶת הַבְּרִיּוֹת
וּמְקָרְבָן לַתּוֹרָה.

Hillel and Shammai received [their Torah] from them. Hillel
says: Be a disciple of Aaron, loving peace and pursuing peace,
loving people and bringing them closer to the Torah.

IN THE MODERN AGE, with every vice but a click away, it is easy to
become cynical. We have finite energy and resources, so we may also
come to believe in the finitude of love and compassion. But when we
open our hearts, we tap into the miraculous reality of infinitude. We are
invited in this mishnah not merely to love those like us but all *b'riyot* (all
humans—and, indeed, all creatures).

The ethics of peace are foremost on the minds of the Rabbis as the
means to reconcile their philosophy with a greater, and oftentimes
violent, world. After reminding us of the value of peace, Hillel teaches
us to love people. How difficult could these precepts have been for the
followers of Hillel's thought after the destruction of the Temple in
70 CE and the subsequent destruction the Jewish people witnessed at
the hands of enemies? And even more so, at the hands of Jewish co-
religionists during the time of revolution, defeat, and, ultimately,
millennia-long exile? For even in this moment, the presence of the
Divine is clear. Centuries later, Chasidic philosophy explicates that
human beings shall follow this path not because God commanded it,
but because we discover God through it.[40]

This raises an interesting point: Why does the mishnah conclude
rather than start with the imperative to "bring them closer to Torah"?
This is because peacemaking is not merely a pragmatic necessity for a
safe and stable society, but also a spiritual endeavor. Torah will reinforce
this holy interpersonal enterprise. Ovadiah ben Avraham of Bartenura,
the Renaissance-era sage, on his commentary on this mishnah, shared
Aaron's unique approach to bringing others closer to Torah. When

Aaron would see another err, he would not rebuke that individual, but rather would become friends. Through a warm relationship, he would help to steer the errant person back to the moral path. Pursuing peace precedes bringing others closer to Torah. Only once we embrace peace and good character traits in general does Torah work to achieve its goal (*derech eretz kad'mah laTorah*).

Indeed, peace is so central to the Jewish tradition that it assumes one of the names of God—the name *Shalom*. Consider how the Chafetz Chayim (Israel Meir Kagan) teaches this value:

> Seek [peace] for your loved one and pursue it with your enemy. Seek it in your place and pursue it in other places. Seek it with your body and pursue it with your material resources. Seek it for your own benefit and pursue it for the benefit of others. Seek it today and pursue it tomorrow. With reference for "seek it tomorrow," it teaches that one should not despair, thinking that one cannot make peace, but rather one should pursue peace today and also tomorrow and on the day afterwards, until one reaches it.[41]

The mishnah instructs us not only to "love" peace but also to "pursue" peace, an emotional imperative for our inner world and a behavioral imperative regarding our outer world. Maharal explains in his commentary that "loving peace" is about preventing new disputes from arising, whereas "pursuing peace" is about resolving existing disputes. We don't give the ultimate priority to truth (e.g., "I'm right, so why should I initiate conversation?"), but rather to peace. The Midrash itself teaches that peace triumphed, in the creation of the world, over truth.[42]

Consider the teaching of Rabbi Yerucham Levovitz, a twentieth-century *musar* (Jewish ethics) teacher:

> Why was the Torah given in the wilderness at Mount Sinai and not in the calm and peacefulness of Israel? This is to teach us that true peace of mind doesn't come from physical comforts, but from an awareness of one's ultimate life goals. When you focus on this, you are constantly traveling toward your goal and will never be overly disturbed or broken.[43]

There are, of course, times when conflict is necessary, through litigation, arbitration, or military defense. Even strength and force sometimes must be used. But, peace should always be the first approach and the ultimate value. The Sages consider bringing peace between people to be a virtue that brings reward both in this world and in the world-to-come (BT *Shabbat* 127a).

Hillel was a remarkable personality. He grew up poor and became a woodcutter. He became interested in Torah but could not afford admission to the study hall, so he climbed onto the roof of the hall and lay on the skylight, trying to watch and listen to the teaching. He almost froze to death but was rescued (BT *Yoma* 35b). He went on to become one of the greatest sages in Jewish history. In addition to his novel insights, he was known as a model of humility. "The harshness of Shammai threatened to remove us from the (eternal) world, while the humility of Hillel brought us under the (sheltering) wings of the Divine Presence" (BT *Shabbat* 31a). One mark of his school's humility is that they would quote Shammai's teachings along with their own and even mention them before mentioning their own (BT *Eiruvin* 13b). Further, Hillel was capable of bold innovation, such as when he responded to the quickly changing economy by establishing the *prozbol* in which rabbis could essentially override the biblical imperative to cancel debts during the Sabbatical year through new legal mechanisms (BT *Gittin* 36a).

Hillel was not an ivory-tower scholar, and he believed that the ethical dimension of Torah was not parochial but rather about all facets of life. For example, he felt that taking a bath was itself a mitzvah, because we are created in the image of God, and it is important to show respect to our bodies, which represent God.[44] He also took a notably inclusive approach to receiving converts. He engaged a person in Jewish learning by teaching its precepts with simplicity: "That which is hateful to you, do not do to others; that is the entire Torah, everything else is its commentary; now go and study" (BT *Shabbat* 31a). Rather than push away someone with a simple question, he offered up the very heart of Torah to encourage others' interest.

Our emulating Hillel's peacemaking and love-sharing requires a real focus on our purpose.

1:13

הוּא הָיָה אוֹמֵר: נְגַד שְׁמָא אָבַד שְׁמֵהּ, וּדְלָא מוֹסִיף יָסוּף,
וּדְלָא יָלַף קְטָלָא חַיָּב, וּדְאִשְׁתַּמַּשׁ בְּתָגָא חֲלַף.

He [Hillel] used to say: One who seeks renown loses one's
reputation; one who does not increase decreases; one who
refuses to teach deserves death; and one who uses the crown
of Torah [for self-interest] shall fade away.

RELIGIOUS FERVOR has the potential to lead to overconfidence and a
sense of ill-deserved self-importance. Religious life requires fostering
self-awareness, self-growth, and self-sacrifice; the individual must simultaneously challenge one's obsession with the self with the Chasidic
teaching of *bitul hayeish*, nullification of the self (i.e., the sublimation of
the ego and the mundanity of our everyday lives).

This mishnah teaches healthy balance. One is cautioned about
self-absorption and arrogance but is still required to teach and put
oneself forward. One doesn't stop teaching and leading for the mere
sake of embracing humility. Rather, one is to work hard to ensure that
leading a morally expansive life—wherein one is dedicated to others,
rather than one's self—remains a vital focus. The S'fat Emet teaches
that self-promotion to further holy means is not the concern, but
rather that self-promotion as an end in itself is a problem: "One who
seeks honor, honor will flee from them."[45]

In his commentary on this mishnah, the Maharal takes a more mystical approach, suggesting that when a purely physical object emerges
from a spiritual entity, it cannot continue to exist. A person who seeks
and retains Torah wisdom (a spiritual entity) cannot desist from keeping its teachings for purely personal gain. When a person behaves in
such a way, one becomes a purely physical being more concerned with
material rewards and thereby becoming devoid of a deeply rooted and
meaningful spiritual actualization. This is akin to death, as if one ceases
to exist before one's time is up.

When the mishnah states that one who refuses to deeply engage and contribute to the richness of the Torah enterprise "deserves death," Hillel is teaching that to spiritually die is akin to physical death. We need our moral and spiritual source of life to truly live with passion and meaning. As Viktor Frankl teaches, it is our ability to make meaning and live with purpose that enables us to survive and ultimately to thrive.[46]

1:14

הוּא הָיָה אוֹמֵר: אִם אֵין אֲנִי לִי, מִי לִי? וּכְשֶׁאֲנִי לְעַצְמִי, מָה
אֲנִי? וְאִם לֹא עַכְשָׁו, אֵימָתַי?

He used to say: If I am not for myself, who will be for me? And
if I am for myself, what am I? And if not now, when?

PEOPLE CANNOT ACHIEVE transformation overnight. There are
changes we wish to make in our lives, but we don't feel we can achieve
them at present. Rather than dismiss them, we must keep them alive.
Let them simmer for some time—days, weeks, years, if need be—in the
back of our consciousness. It is essential to the integrity of the soul to
embrace courageously that which is true and good, even if we feel the
inadequacy of not yet being able to achieve consistent practice. Keeping the dream alive sustains our endeavors. Gloria Steinem remarked,
"Without leaps of imagination, or dreaming, we lose the excitement of
possibilities. Dreaming, after all, is a form of planning."[47]

The passage presented is among the most powerful and oft cited in
all of Jewish thought. Because human beings have been bestowed with
the unique gift of self-awareness, we can heed the complexity of this
mishnah. Rabbi Hillel's words continue to resonate through the millennia—their beauty and meaning are enhanced by their brevity. In this
brief passage, we read the raison d'être of Judaism laid bare.

Hillel reminds us that it is challenging to find the proper balance
between religious self-preservation and self-sacrifice. In our spiritual
journeys we must be gentle with ourselves. There is no need for self-
blame. We can exchange any worries about our inner qualities for honest, gentle, and nonjudgmental curiosity. We will, however, experience
more pain by avoiding introspection than we will in engaging in difficult spiritual work. Carl Jung writes, "There is no coming to consciousness without pain."[48] Further, he writes, "People will do anything, no
matter how absurd, in order to avoid facing their own soul. One does
not become conscious by imagining figures of light, but by making the
darkness conscious."[49]

The essence of Jung here is simple: Our darkest demons can also lead us into the brightest light. Our inner struggles, once discovered and realized for what they are, can become allies in our journey to find out our true selves. And while today, as in the past, religion can encourage arrogance in the overly certain person, it doesn't always have to be that way. To be sure, Hillel is directing us to do otherwise, telling each of us to ask: Will I realize my moral responsibility and spiritual potential? It is difficult to speculate, but still, I must learn to be me. Paradoxically, to learn to be me, I must also look outside of myself, which requires humility. Indeed, a primary goal of religion is to inspire humility, especially when challenged by life's seemingly unanswerable mysteries.

Once having transcended (as best we can) or channeled self-concern and the might of our ego, we gain clarity about our place in the world. We must be ourselves regardless of social pressure toward conformity and desire for approval. The Kotzker Rebbe, Menachem Mendel of Kotzk, teaches (as quoted by Martin Buber), "If I am I because I am I, and you are you because you are you, then I truly am I, and you truly are you. If, on the other hand, I am I because you are you, and you are you because I am I, then I am not I, and you are not you."[50]

We may feel despair. We may feel that we are likely to end up taking more than we give. But this is the great gamble of the human enterprise. The Rabbis debated whether humans should have been created at all. There is a spirited discussion elsewhere in the Talmud about this seemingly nihilistic supposition:

> For two and a half years, the school of Shammai and the school of Hillel debated. The former said that it was better for humankind not to have been created than to have been created. The latter said that it was better for humankind to have been created than not to have been created. They voted and concluded: It was better for people not to have been created than to have been created, but now that they have been created, let them search their deeds. (BT *Eiruvin* 13b)

Judaism is about radical impatience. When we know what is just and good, we must act immediately. While we do not expect the world to change overnight, we nonetheless still act with alacrity against injustice and all forms of evil. In our fervor to eradicate wickedness for the perpetuation of righteousness, we should not be afraid to operate from self-interest. The mishnah teaches that we must act now; time is fleeting. Jedaiah ben Abraham Bedersi, the Provençal philosopher who lived some 700 years ago, says that "the past is now gone, the future is yet to arrive, and the present passes like the blink of an eye."[51] Indeed, "if not now, when?"—given that this moment is all we have.

Rabbi Yitz Greenberg writes on the topic:

> World revolutionary movement such as Communism and Maoism attacked the family as "bourgeois" and as a source of selfishness. They succeeded only in weakening the natural bonds of love and affection for one's closest relatives. This degraded people's humanity and made them less humane to others as well. Starting with one's own interest and then reaching outward often leads to greater good than "idealistic" approaches that dismiss loyalty to oneself as selfish. Proof for this is that people working for themselves under capitalism out-produced and liberated more people from poverty than people working under communism, whose ideological goal was defined by ending poverty and providing economic equality for all . . . the key to moral behavior is balance: self-interest, yes; self-centeredness, no.[52]

We cannot say conclusively if humans are doing more good than bad in this world. But now that we are here, we should search our souls and our ways and improve all that we can. We are obliged, however, to pray, and even cry, about our situation. The Rabbis teach that the heavenly Gates of Prayer were locked, but the Gates of Tears were not (BT *Bava M'tzia* 59a). When we open our hearts, and truly feel our inner pain and vulnerability, we are closer to the heavens than we can ever otherwise be. To keep our inner fire lit, we must keep adding fuel to it. We must learn to keep our soul alive and growing, because there is no task more holy than cultivating our inner light. It inevitably shines on others.

1:15

שַׁמַּי אוֹמֵר: עֲשֵׂה תוֹרָתְךָ קֶבַע, אֱמֹר מְעַט וַעֲשֵׂה הַרְבֵּה,
וֶהֱוֵי מְקַבֵּל אֶת כָּל הָאָדָם בְּסֵבֶר פָּנִים יָפוֹת.

Shammai says: Make your Torah study a fixed practice; say
little and do much; and receive everyone with a friendly face.

LEARNING HOW TO FOCUS and listen to what other people are saying in front of us (and to us) requires us to break from mindless, idle
chatter. The Rabbis reminded us to open our hearts to everyone we
come across in our lives. A life of pure contemplation makes it difficult
to offer proper attention to the people we encounter and the human
reality in which we exist. Just as the Rabbis taught us to go inward, they
were sure to remind us that we must also send love and joy outward.

However, consistency is difficult. The rapid fluctuations of modern
society don't support steady spiritual growth. Some communities follow the practice of reciting the Six Remembrances, cornerstones of
Jewish thought that foster a singular Jewish identity, at every prayer
service. These Six Remembrances—the Exodus from Egypt, the revelation from Mount Sinai, the attack on the vulnerable people of Israel
from the Amalekites, the sin of the Golden Calf, the chastisement of
Miriam for her negative speech, and remembering the Sabbath[53]—are
what inform Jewish individual and collective identity. The Six Remembrances commemorate core historical events and concomitant principles—namely that of constant awareness of where the Jewish people
have been and how far we still need to go; the importance of these
remembrances should be present in one's consciousness even if they
are not on one's mind at every moment.

It requires much discipline to maintain spiritual growth. And even
more so, it requires the careful cultivation of traits to enhance and
supplement the central process of gaining clarity into one's full self.
To achieve such enlightenment, there are crucial tasks that one should
undertake, including the following general *musar* approaches:

Hatmadah—a commitment to finding daily consistency
K'viut—a time set aside each day for honing tasks
Chazarah—repetition of those tasks
Mahalach—embracing one's spiritual path

Normally, the popular conception of Shammai is that he is not a friendly figure; perhaps he is offering a rebuke to himself when he says to "receive everyone with a cheerful face." Some of the most powerful Torah we teach to others is that which is closest to our own hearts. This is why this mishnah says *Torat'cha*, "your Torah." What matters most is that we're not living our parents' Judaism, or our teacher's model of religion, or our friend's truths. Rather, we should become intimate with our own personal Torah, one that we own, cultivate, and cherish. Merely continuing our parents' Judaism is not continuity, but laziness. Our charge is to discover our own Torah, one that fires us up to actualize the unique potential of our individual lives. In being taught to smile to everyone, we are reminded that Torah teaches that everyone and everything matter. How we engage with society, community, family, friends, colleagues, and even strangers passing by in the street matters. No aspect of life is too small to be made holy.

When we learn Torah, we have the ability to become kinder and more broad-minded in our life pursuits. This is what it means to "say little and do much": we are to observe and digest what we learn, with the hope that we do not impede the ways of the world with our growing knowledge. Humility is the key lens to understanding this precept. Indeed, what matters most is how our learning translates into an improved life and the actualization of our unique potential. Some people pick up books when they're in the mood, others attend synagogue when invited or pray when needed or in need, and some may find the time to meditate when the opportunity strikes. But leading a spiritual life requires much more than defining oneself as "spiritual" when convenient. If we are not learning and moving forward at a consistent pace, we risk falling backwards in our spiritual journeys. If our inner selves are truly a priority, then it is vital that we dedicate regularly scheduled time to cultivating our inner light—our mind, our heart, our soul—to face the outside world.

‏1:16‏

‏רַבָּן גַּמְלִיאֵל הָיָה אוֹמֵר: עֲשֵׂה לְךָ רַב, וְהִסְתַּלֵּק מִן הַסָּפֵק,‏
‏וְאַל תַּרְבֶּה לְעַשֵּׂר אֲמָדוֹת.‏

Rabban Gamliel used to say: Make a teacher for yourself and remove yourself from doubt; and do not give excess tithes by estimating.

THREE DIFFERENT MEN named Rabban Gamliel lived in the period that this mishnah was written. The one referenced here is Rabban Gamliel the Elder, the *nasi* (head of the Sanhedrin) and grandson of Hillel. He led during the first century CE, a time of unprecedented turmoil. Rabbi Marc Angel writes about this period:

> He is the first sage identified with the title Rabban (our Rabbi). This title was conferred on sages of the coming generations who were also descendants of Hillel. The only non-Hillelite to have this title was Rabban Yohanan b. Zakkai, the leading sage during the period immediately following the end of the Judean State in 70 CE. Prior to Rabban Gamliel, sages were simply known by their names, without having titles such as Rabban, Rabbi, or Rav.[54]

Following that thought, Rabbi Yitz Greenberg writes about the significance of Rabban Gamliel's leadership during this chaotic era:

> Rabban Gamliel exercised strong leadership despite the increasing civil unrest and clashes with the Romans. He strengthened the procedure of declaring the new month by the Sanhedrin, thus preserving an area of religious autonomy in the face of growing Roman control of national life. He also showed strong, courageous leadership in protecting women's dignity and rights. When there were situations where a husband's death could not be established by two witnesses (see Deut. 19:15), he ruled that one witness was sufficient, so that his wife would not be trapped for life and unable to remarry (BT *Yevamot* 122a). Similarly, he ruled that a husband could not write or cancel a *get* (bill of divorce) in the absence of his wife, in order to stop an abuse whereby husbands would cancel a

> *get* after writing it, leaving their wives chained to the marriage and/
> or delegitimizing their children from a later marriage which they
> had innocently entered into, thinking that they had been freed by
> divorce from the first marriage (*Gittin* 32a).[55]

This passage shows Rabban Gamliel's wisdom and his significant position in Jewish philosophy. When dealing with life-and-death matters, approximation is insufficient. Whether we're tithing or providing for the immediate needs of the vulnerable through other means, we must be sure to address such needs exactly and in full. Pressing moral issues are often demanding, which is why, perhaps, Rabban Gamliel teaches that we need a teacher on whom we can rely to provide critique as well as guidance. Also, we must be sure to achieve moral clarity and remove barriers—doubts—that block us from taking necessary action. Many centuries later in his commentary, Rabbi Samson Raphael Hirsch (nineteenth century, Germany) teaches that to avoid being intellectually and spiritually lazy, we are to be thoughtful rather than taking an excessively strict, pietistic approach.

The most common doubt that prevents people from taking meaningful action is the shortsighted perspective that our little actions do not matter. Torah tells us over and over in different ways that every act of kindness matters, every step to fulfill a positive commandment matters, and that even minute sparks of light can expel darkness from the deepest recess. The late historian and commentator Howard Zinn expresses crisply and forcefully the power of small acts:

> The essential ingredients of struggles for justice are human beings
> who, if only for a moment, if only beset with fears, step out of line
> and do something, however small. And even the smallest, most
> unheroic actions add to the store of kindling that may be ignited
> by some surprising circumstance into tumultuous change.[56]

Embracing spiritual partners—be they family, friends, or indeed even teachers—who support and challenge us can significantly help the long-term success of the moral enterprise called *life*. Removing ourselves from doubt does not mean that we should embrace certainty. To the contrary, it is healthy to embrace skepticism, have concern, and recognize the ambiguities that life presents before us. Once we have a modicum of clarity, we can remove lingering internal doubt that blocks us from acting on what we know to be good and true.

After the fact, the moral enterprise demands that we feel challenged by the choices that we could not make, even if we feel we made the right choice. We do the best we can with the knowledge we have. Sometimes the results are in our favor, sometimes not. Yet, when we remove doubt to act, we can still come to re-embrace it during times of reflection. The necessity to remove doubt is an intellectually rigorous principle that asks us to spend more time and effort gathering data, reflecting, and consulting with experts.

I:17

שִׁמְעוֹן בְּנוֹ אוֹמֵר: כָּל יָמַי גָּדַלְתִּי בֵּין הַחֲכָמִים וְלֹא מָצָאתִי
לַגּוּף טוֹב מִשְּׁתִיקָה. וְלֹא הַמִּדְרָשׁ עִקָּר אֶלָּא הַמַּעֲשֶׂה.
וְכָל הַמַּרְבֶּה דְבָרִים מֵבִיא חֵטְא.

Shimon, his son, says: All my days I have been raised among
the Sages and I found nothing better for oneself than silence;
not study, but practice is the main thing; and all who talk
excessively bring on sin.

WHAT WOULD the world look like if every human being paused for
five minutes of intentional silence a day? Rabbi Kook teaches, "Some
silence means cessation of speech. Another silence means cessation of
thought. That silence arrives together with the most hidden, beautiful,
and exalted thought."[57]

In this mishnah, we have the son of a sage—someone who must have
learned from some of the greatest minds of the classical world, and one
who said about himself that he was *g'dalti bein hachachamim*—raised
among scholars. Yet, this person advocates silence. Why? Perhaps
Shimon felt uncomfortable, inarticulate, or intellectually inferior
around such great minds. Another way to understand Shimon's reti-
cence, however, is to reinterpret what it means when he described himself as *gadalti* among scholars. Rather than having been "raised" among
the scholars, he was "made great" (*gadol*) among the scholars. This is a
subtle way of saying that greatness is achieved neither in isolation nor in
independence, but within intellectual community and interdependence.

Professor Michael Fishbane of the University of Chicago writes:

> There are two kinds of silence. One of these is natural silence, and
> is characterized by the absence of noise. It is a modulation, a di-
> minishment, a negative valence. The other kind of silence is spiri-
> tual, and is characterized by potentiality and anticipation.... With
> respect to deliberate speech, silence conveys the ethical potential
> of words; for it sharpens the transition from inwardness to worldly
> expression. Prayer may also stand at this juncture of silence and
> speech.[58]

This mishnah indicates that practice takes priority over study. As Jews, we are committed to mitzvot—good deeds of the heart—which are achieved in their highest form not through text study, but through converting the mandates of those texts and the mandates of the soul into action.

Rabbi Marc D. Angel and Rabbi Jonathan Sacks, commenting on this verse, write, "A rabbinic teaching claims that the Torah has seventy 'faces,' i.e., can be interpreted in a variety of ways. A Hasidic rabbi taught that one of the seventy 'faces' is silence."[59] One of the most profound ways to grasp Torah and come close to God is through intentional silence. By approaching the world with deliberation of the mind rather than the mouth, great feats can be achieved.

Rabbi Hirsch, in his commentary on this mishnah, writes:

> Let the speech of men and their discussions center on spiritual and moral concerns. Indeed, there is nothing more offensive than the pompous gusto with which men converse about the merits of food and drink. As a matter of fact, there are limits to the usefulness of speech even in the teaching and inquiry associated with things moral and spiritual; deeds and accomplishments count the most.

Additionally, the Sages teach *kol hamosif gorei-a*—those who add too much to truth subtract from it (BT *Sanhedrin* 29a). The aphorism that less can be more applies to this passage, as well. How important is the capacity for speech, anyway? Is it constitutive of the human enterprise from a Jewish perspective? Rabbi Obadiah ben Jacob S'forno writes:

> In spite of the importance [of the gift of speech], it is not the expression and exposition of [a person's thoughts] that is of paramount importance and [humanity's] ultimate goal and purpose, but the deeds which result from it as they affect society and the intellectual pursuit of knowledge. And even in those [noble endeavors], it is best to use words sparingly and be concise in one's studies, for "one who talks excessively brings on sin." For [excessive words] promote uncertainties and errors of forgetfulness.

Wisdom originates in the mind but is serviced by the heart. Finding the time to seek silence and listening to the prudence of others can only encourage and support inner soul-seeking. At least once a day, it would be wise to retreat to an intentional space for silence, solitude, and listening to what is stirring in our hearts. As the pace of the world increases, this necessity, even if for a moment, cannot be last on our daily tasks. No one can be too busy to turn inward. Exploring the inner self supports the outer self, giving people clarity and a forthrightness to proceed during the day. Intentional silence, at its best, promotes humility and cultivates awe.

1:18

רַבָּן שִׁמְעוֹן בֶּן גַּמְלִיאֵל אוֹמֵר: עַל שְׁלֹשָׁה דְבָרִים הָעוֹלָם
קַיָּם: עַל הַדִּין וְעַל הָאֱמֶת וְעַל הַשָּׁלוֹם, שֶׁנֶּאֱמַר: אֱמֶת
וּמִשְׁפַּט שָׁלוֹם שִׁפְטוּ בְּשַׁעֲרֵיכֶם (זכריה ח:טז).

Rabban Shimon ben Gamliel says: The world endures on
three things—justice, truth, and peace, as it is said: "Truth
and the verdict of peace is what you shall adjudicate in your
gates" (Zechariah 8:16).

THERE ARE THREE proscribed categories of misdeeds in Jewish law—
murder, idolatry, and sexual wrongs—for which a Jew should choose
to be killed rather than publicly transgress the Torah prohibition. (The
category is known as *yeihareig v'al yaavor*.) For instance, a Jew offered
the choice of death or pork must choose the non-kosher food. A Jew
offered the choice of death or idol worship, however, should choose
martyrdom. These three prohibitions align with the three values in this
mishnah. Murder aligns with its opposite, justice, or the prohibition of
murder. Truth contrasts with idolatry, its opposite. Peace is in opposition to the sexual misdeeds that destroy marriages, families, and trust
within community.

The Maharal, in his commentary on this mishnah, teaches that the
three virtues in the mishnah align with the three parts of the self. One's
physical possessions match justice (concerned with fair distribution),
one's spiritual possessions match truth (concerned with intellectual
integrity), and finally, one's actual self matches peace (bringing one's
full self forth with equanimity). These three virtues sustain the world
because they sustain human existence.

These three values are also ways of being in the world. We are to cling
to "justice, truth, and peace" and incorporate them into all of our relationships and ways of being. This is hard work. The Alter of Novarodok,
a nineteenth–twentieth century rabbi and educator in Eastern Europe,
once remarked, "The trouble with people is that they want to change

overnight and have a good night's sleep that night, too."[60] If we are to do our part to ensure that "the world endures on three things," then we must have daily spiritual practices to ensure we combat injustice, falsehood, and unrest both inside of us and outside of ourselves.

Rabbi Yitz Greenberg writes:

> Robert Cover [the late professor of law from Yale Law School] interprets Rabban Shimon's words: The world is *sustained*, meaning it continues to exist, being upheld by the operation of these three principles. Drawing on an interpretation by Rabbi Joseph Karo, he suggests that the pillars articulated by Shimon the Righteous [or: Shimon the Just] (Torah, divine service, and acts of loving-kindness) are the building blocks in the creation of a society. Rabban Shimon's three principles (truth, law, and peace) were central to the preservation of the post-Destruction[61] Jewish community. The values paramount to building a new world are different from those of insuring the continuity of an ongoing communal life.[62]

How to balance different values is not an easy matter. The Sages taught that one may, in a necessary situation, revise truth to preserve the higher value of peace (BT *Y'vamot* 65b). Rabbi Greenberg continues to wrestle with the tensions between competing values:

> Truth is not always identical to justice, and it is often incompatible with peace. Think of the daily white lies and unspoken criticism which protect peace in the family or the workplace. The ideal society will reconcile all three principles. For the sake of peace one may yield some aspect of justice or, for the sake of justice one may override some aspect of peace. The key to a just and harmonious society lies in balance and limits. If an individual or group pursues one principle to the exclusion of the others, then there will be serious trouble. "Peace above all" leads to appeasement and the loss of peace. Justice, when pursued relentlessly, while sweeping aside compromise for the established interest in others, may well lead to conflict, tyranny, or worse.[63]

Similarly, Rabbi Ben-Zion Meir Chai Uziel, the great Sephardic Chief Rabbi of Mandatory Palestine and Israel (1939–1953), taught that legal rulings must not only be intellectually correct, but also morally good.[64] The Talmud teaches, "Where there is strict justice, there is no peace; and where there is no peace, there is no strict justice!" (BT *Sanhedrin* 6b). Rather, the Rabbinic preference is to reach for compromise. Rabbi Marc Angel writes:

> The Talmud reports a tradition that when King David rendered a legal decision, he would acquit the innocent and condemn the guilty. However, when he saw that the condemned party was poor, he paid the damages on behalf of the poor person. Thus, David upheld truth by awarding damages to the plaintiff; and he upheld peace and charity by providing the poor defendant with the means of paying what he owed.[65]

Inner spiritual work is essential to the health and well-being of the soul, as is outward-directed work essential to sustain our families, communities, society, and world. Balancing forthrightness with an understanding that the world presents multiple temptations encourages a person to seek the most just path, not the easiest one. Traveling this path requires both patience and self-doubt, both learning and spiritual growth. It is an essential part of flourishing spiritually in a time that seems to demand attention only for the material realm. In this journey, we are to center our lives around "justice, truth, and peace."

Chapter 2

2:1

רַבִּי אוֹמֵר: אֵיזוֹ הִיא דֶרֶךְ יְשָׁרָה שֶׁיָּבוֹר לוֹ הָאָדָם? כָּל
שֶׁהִיא תִפְאֶרֶת לְעֹשֶׂהָ וְתִפְאֶרֶת לוֹ מִן הָאָדָם. וֶהֱוֵי זָהִיר
בְּמִצְוָה קַלָּה כְּבַחֲמוּרָה, שֶׁאֵין אַתָּה יוֹדֵעַ מַתַּן שְׂכָרָן שֶׁל
מִצְוֹת. וֶהֱוֵי מְחַשֵּׁב הֶפְסֵד מִצְוָה כְּנֶגֶד שְׂכָרָהּ, וּשְׂכַר עֲבֵרָה
כְּנֶגֶד הֶפְסֵדָהּ. הִסְתַּכֵּל בִּשְׁלֹשָׁה דְבָרִים וְאֵין אַתָּה בָא לִידֵי
עֲבֵרָה. דַּע מַה לְמַעְלָה מִמְּךָ: עַיִן רוֹאָה, וְאֹזֶן שׁוֹמַעַת,
וְכָל מַעֲשֶׂיךָ בַּסֵּפֶר נִכְתָּבִין.

Rabbi [Y'hudah HaNasi] said: Which is the proper path that
a person should choose for oneself? Whatever is a credit to
oneself and earns one the esteem of others. Be as scrupulous
in performing a minor mitzvah as in a major one, for you do
not know the reward given for the respective mitzvot. Calculate the cost of a mitzvah against its reward, and the reward of
a sin against its cost. Consider three things and you will not
come into the grip of sin—know what is above you—an Eye is
watching, an Ear is listening, and all of your deeds are being
recorded in a book.

WHEN THE MISHNAH states, "Know what is above you," the S'fat
Emet interprets this passage, in his commentary, as "Know that *what
is above you* (da mah l'maalah) is from you (mim'cha)." In this manner,
he taught that the actions of heaven are affected by the behaviors that
take place on earth. As earth looks to heaven for guidance, so do the
angels look down on earth's moral inhabitants and learn from their
hopes, dreams, and fears. The *Zohar* teaches that with every mitzvah
performed on earth, an angel is created above to defend us.[66]
So how does knowing this affect our daily existence? Let's look at it
this way: Reflecting upon how the classical Rabbis viewed our death
and subsequent divine judgment can inspire us to lean toward acts of
repentance, self-repair, and growth (usually rendered in Hebrew as

t'shuvah). Furthermore, reflecting on such divine judgment (whether literal or spiritual) also puts our lives into perspective; although we are indeed small when compared to the infinities of the Divine, we are not so insignificant that our deeds are meaningless.

Such thoughts necessarily make us think of aspects of our existence that are unpleasant. The knowledge that we will someday no longer walk this earth is extraordinarily sobering. For example, consider how James L. Kugel, a scholar of Hebrew Bible exegesis at Harvard University, describes how humbling it is to watch the lowering of a casket: "The smallness of the freshly dug, open holes you see here and there in the cemetery grounds. Can a whole human being fit in there, a whole human life? Yes. No problem."[67]

It is not that we behave as children would, acting only in anticipation of reward or punishment. Rather, we are good for the sake of being good, attuning our hopes toward moral order in the world, an order that works for everyone—ourselves included. We are aware when our motives may not always be pure, and this is acceptable. We help others because it is good, but also because we feel good by doing so.

We need not feel shame about that. Something would be wrong with moral life if we didn't feel good when we did good. Rather, we are to channel our blessings to assist others who are vulnerable. The eighteenth-century Italian rabbi Moshe Chayim Luzzatto writes in his seminal text on *musar*, Jewish ethics, that our blessings or advantages are sacred obligations:

> One who is wealthy may rejoice in one's lot, but at the same time they must help those in need. If one is strong, they must assist the weak and rescue the oppressed. . . . In truth, there is no place for pride here.[68]

In seeking the "proper path," Reb Simchah Bunim (late eighteenth century/early nineteenth century, Poland) teaches that we should hold a pluralistic orientation,[69] being receptive to new ideas and outside perspectives. Each of us will have our unique path in serving God; rather than judge others, we should learn to appreciate the beauty of this diversity.

Spiritually, morally, we should act as though we *are* being watched. Evolutionary psychologists-anthropologists Kevin J. Haley and Daniel M. T. Fessler have shown in their research that drawing watchful eyes on a surface facing other people will affect behavior.[70] When people feel—even irrationally—that they are being watched, they are more likely to act morally.[71]

Torah teaches that there *are* real consequences for all our choices. Rabbi Hirsch identifies two levels of reward and punishment: the objective level and the experiential level. He writes in his commentary on this mishnah:

> The other recompense is spiritual in character and it comes to us immediately; it is inherent in the good deed or in the sin itself. The immediate reward of any Divine command scrupulously performed is a sense of moral elevation, an increase in our moral strength, and the awareness, most blissful of all, that we are worthy of the nearness of God because we have faithfully carried out our duty toward God.

Maimonides (twelfth century, Spain) also teaches that reward is not immediately tangible:

> When a person appropriately performs any mitzvah of the 613 mitzvot, without any ulterior motive other than the love of God, they will merit a portion of the world-to-come on the basis of this one mitzvah alone (Commentary on the Mishnah, *Makkot* 3:16).

So, why does this mishnah tell us to consider "the esteem of others"? Because this is how we practice humility. The text does not say *b'riyot*, average people, but rather *adam*, refined people. We should seek the counsel and wisdom of those who live with great ethical intent. As our Sages taught, "A person is unable to recognize their own weaknesses" (Mishnah *N'gaim* 2:5). We have blind spots and need others to help us see.

In our mishnah above, Rabbi Y'hudah HaNasi (Judea, second century CE), the son of Rabban Shimon ben Gamliel and the redactor of the Mishnah, poses one of the eternal questions asked by every great philosopher over the millennia: What is the good life? What is the virtuous path? The prerequisite to living a good life is actually asking the question itself—and not once, but continually. The Chafetz Chayim broadly suggests that we ask ourselves throughout the day, "What benefit will I have spiritually or physically from the words I am about to speak or the action I wish to perform?"[72]

This power is in our hands. In the High Holy Day liturgy, we recite that our signature will be on the document decreeing our fate. We are the ones in control of our moral and spiritual lives.

Balancing our altruistic selves and our self-interested selves is a paradox of the human spirit. Can we inhabit both roles? Is there inherent worth to doing so? How do we know which is the correct path to follow? There is no clear answer, which is why we must dedicate our whole selves to understanding the gravity of our choices. Just as there is no "minor mitzvah," so too there are no minor choices when it comes to pursuing a moral existence.

Everything is recorded in the Book of Life, because *all life* matters. Each moment matters. The world is altered by every human action, and this should give us pause. What matters is not which mitzvot to prioritize, but the wisdom to discern the proper, special moment in which to engage in mitzvot. That is where our true potential is made tangible.

2:2

רַבָּן גַּמְלִיאֵל בְּנוֹ שֶׁל רַבִּי יְהוּדָה הַנָּשִׂיא אוֹמֵר: יָפֶה
תַלְמוּד תּוֹרָה עִם דֶּרֶךְ אֶרֶץ, שֶׁיְּגִיעַת שְׁנֵיהֶם מְשַׁכַּחַת עָוֹן.
וְכָל תּוֹרָה שֶׁאֵין עִמָּהּ מְלָאכָה, סוֹפָהּ בְּטֵלָה וְגוֹרֶרֶת עָוֹן.
וְכָל הָעֲמֵלִים עִם הַצִּבּוּר, יִהְיוּ עֲמֵלִים עִמָּהֶם לְשֵׁם שָׁמַיִם,
שֶׁזְּכוּת אֲבוֹתָם מְסַיְּעָתַן, וְצִדְקָתָם עוֹמֶדֶת לָעַד. וְאַתֶּם,
מַעֲלִים עֲלֵיכֶם שָׂכָר הַרְבֵּה כְּאִלּוּ עֲשִׂיתֶם.

Rabban Gamliel, the son of Rabbi Y'hudah HaNasi, says:
Torah study is good together with an occupation, for the
exertion of them both makes sin forgotten. All Torah study
that is not joined with work will cease in the end and lead
to sin. All who exert themselves for the community should
exert themselves for the sake of heaven—for then the merit
of the community's forefathers aids them, and their righteousness endures forever. Nevertheless, as for you, as great a
reward will be bestowed upon you as if you had accomplished
it [on your own].

THROUGHOUT JEWISH TRADITION, the Sages extolled the virtue of
hard work. Human existence is meaningful because of our responsibility to build and improve the world that we have been lent; this brief
stewardship of an eternal universe is an enormous task to bear. As it
says elsewhere in the Talmud, "One who inspires and causes others to
do good deeds and to fulfill their duty has even greater merit than one
who does the same good with one's own resources" (BT *Bava Batra* 9a).

This mishnah teaches, "All Torah study that is not joined with work
will cease in the end and leads to sin." A Torah life requires work, and
Torah does not stop when work begins. The whole enterprise of Torah
is actualized through work: we are required to have a God-based
consciousness in the forefront of our minds; strive to uphold proper
business ethics; bring spirituality to the workplace; work with integrity. What we study is made tangible when we bring the best ethics and
practices into the workplace.

In this mishnah, we are introduced to the concept of pairing Torah study together with an occupation (*Torah im derech eretz*); the phrase *derech eretz* is often translated as an "occupation." Rabbi Samson Raphael Hirsch interprets Rabban Gamliel's notion of *Torah im derech eretz*—Torah in the modern world—as being much more than modernity simply "working" alongside "Torah." For Rabbi Hirsch, one is to be culturally engaged and intellectually growing; a public citizen, in addition to being a Jew. Rabbi Hirsch notes in his commentary, "This term—*derech eretz*—includes the means by which humans make a livelihood, one's national citizenship, the courtesy, sensitivity, rectitude, customs and manners of the milieu in which one lives and all the forms—cultural, personal, general, and national—of society generally."

Rabbi Yitz Greenberg also emphasizes the complementary value of work to the study of Torah:

> Among the Talmudic sages, we are told that Hillel was a wood-chopper and Shammai was a construction worker. Other professions of sages included tailors, carpenters, blacksmiths, well-diggers, surveyors, and beer and whiskey distillers. In the Middle Ages, Maimonides famously worked as a doctor at the court of the Sultan of Egypt. He had to give religious guidance and write books late at night, when he was exhausted. Nevertheless, he persisted in the work and strongly upheld the ruling that sages and teachers should support themselves with their own labor.[73]

But Greenberg contrasts these values with contemporary practices:

> In modern times, especially in the State of Israel, a counter-cultural traditional public support for full-time Torah students was developed. The outcome is that in our day and age, sixty percent of all *chareidi* adult males in Israel are full-time students of Torah, substantially supported by government stipends. . . . Some degree of return to Torah study with worldly occupation seems unavoidable.[74]

As we read in mishnah 1:10, Sh'mayah teaches the concept of *ehav et ham'lachah*, the notion that one is to love work. A primary parental responsibility is to teach children a trade (BT *Kiddushin* 29a). Rabbi

Shimon ben Elazar also teaches about the importance of work to the human condition:

> Great is work, because even Adam did not taste food until he had performed work, as it is said, "So God Eternal took the man, placing him in the Garden of Eden to work it and keep it" (Genesis 2:15). Only then do we read, "God Eternal then commanded the man, saying, "You may eat all you like of every tree in the garden" (Genesis 2:16).[75]

Work is not only desirable but also a commandment, a divine marker of human dignity. How do we come to that conclusion? The Rabbis say that we need only look to the commandment to observe the Sabbath, which not only designates the day of rest, but also implies that we are to work the other six days.[76] Rabbi Joseph B. Soloveitchik, who wrote about the intersection between traditional Jewish life and modernity, argues that human work was at the core of our dignity and sanctified purpose: "When God created the world, He provided an opportunity for the work of His hands—man—to participate in His creation. The Creator, as it were, impaired reality in order that mortal man could repair its flaws and perfect it."[77]

Rabbeinu Bachya, a Spanish rabbi of the thirteenth and fourteenth centuries, writes:

> Apart from the period of [the Israelites'] wandering in the wilderness, and other times of miraculous intervention, there is no manna from heaven. This active participation of people in the creation of their own wealth is a sign of spiritual greatness. In this respect, we are, as it were, imitators of God.[78]

The Chasidic rabbi Levi Yitzchak of Berditchev interpreted Rabban Gamliel's mishnah as saying that we can learn Torah while working in commerce. Whenever we have opportunities to make ethical decisions in business, it is a Torah-learning opportunity. Torah learning is to be used in our daily lives, not segregated in the house of study. After all, the Sages taught that at the gates of heaven we'll be asked, "Did you deal honestly?" (BT *Shabbat* 31a).

With all these perspectives in mind, let's think about how Jews are to bring Torah values into the general, secular world of work. Surely, contemporary labor is far different from ancient agrarian society. Are we to separate ourselves from people of other groups and look out only for other Jews? Or, are we to look more broadly at how our economic interactions affect greater society?

Torah is committed to the creation of a just society and individual lives of responsibility. These obligations reject anarchy. This is seen in biblical history, during the turbulent period that incubated the *shof'tim*, "judges." "In those days there was no king in Israel; every person did what was proper in their own eyes" (Judges 17:6, 21:25). In such a culture, many charismatic leaders attempted to lead but possessed no moral foundation on which to stand. Lack of leadership meant that society festered, and matters were settled without recourse to law. Today, we risk doing what's right merely in our own eyes, potentially risking the well-being and lives of countless others.

Ultimately, the individual balance between the desire to grow in the ways of Torah and career determines one's personal path and one's role in the grand scheme of the universe. Maimonides, who in his time imagined only men learning Torah, writes:

> Anyone who decides to study Torah and not work [for a living] but live off of charity desecrates the Name [of God] and disgraces the Torah and extinguishes the light of religion. He causes evil to himself and deprives himself of the world-to-come because it is forbidden to gain this-worldly benefit from Torah. All Torah that is not accompanied by work is ultimately annulled and leads to sin. The end of such a person [who studies but does not work] is that he will steal from others [to sustain himself].[79]

Jewish thought from Bible to Talmud to modern Jewish philosophy supports the acquisition of wealth but demands that wealth and its power are cultivated righteously, used justly, and allocated deliberately. Taking without giving is a grievous misuse of the faculties afforded to humankind by the Divine. Thus, work is necessary and holy. By understanding that the consequences of hard work and intellectual growth are conjoined, we are better equipped to fulfill humanity's economic, moral, and spiritual needs.

2:3

הֱווּ זְהִירִין בָּרָשׁוּת, שֶׁאֵין מְקָרְבִין לוֹ לָאָדָם אֶלָּא לְצֹרֶךְ
עַצְמָן. נִרְאִין כְּאוֹהֲבִין בְּשָׁעַת הֲנָאָתָן, וְאֵין עוֹמְדִין לוֹ
לָאָדָם בְּשָׁעַת דָּחְקוֹ.

Beware of those in power, for they bring people close only to
fulfill their own needs; they act friendly when it benefits them,
but they do not stand by someone in the time of their need.

THIS PASSAGE offers advice for Jewish survival. Rabban Gamliel believed that Roman authorities were motivated by nothing more than
selfishness and corruption in their ruling over Israel. But for Jews to
survive and even thrive under such despotism presented the Sages with
an ethical dilemma: should one obey or rebel?

This mishnah also hints at the distinction between power and leadership. King David, treasured in Jewish tradition as our greatest monarch and the progenitor of our eventual redemption, is represented
as having had both. David was skilled, kind, and devoted to serving
the best needs of the public. His leadership, as well as much of Jewish
thought, seems to point toward monarchy as Judaism's preferred type
of government. As it says: "You shall be free to set a king over yourself,
one chosen by the Eternal your God" (Deuteronomy 17:15). But kings
have their own limitations. They are generally not accountable toward
their public (toward God, perhaps, but not toward the people). They
have the power to stifle individuals for their own personal gain. Placing
trust in a single figure is a gamble, especially if the monarch is vindic-
tive, vainglorious, vapid, or all three.

Even with its weakness and wickedness, Rome originated many of
the common functions of legislative democracy; the expansive model
of democracy, in which individuals are entitled to participate in the political process, was a huge step in worldwide societal progress. Roman
modes of debate and philosophy, refined from the earlier—and no less
unkind—Greeks, inspired enlightened minds, ultimately shaping what
became the American democratic experiment. In a poetic twist of fate,

American democracy and tolerance saved some of the Jews escaping from political and religious violence in Europe.

Democracy has its own set of drawbacks. Majority rule can inflict untold damage on unprotected minorities. When the majority chooses an unfit leader, there can be dire consequences. One can have authority without the true qualities of leadership. Those who seek formal authority and rely upon it as their primary mode of management often get trapped by becoming seduced by the attractions of power. To keep their authority, they climb over others to get ahead. Constant vigilance and participation in the system are the only safeguards.

Martin Buber offers a critical spiritual elucidation of these models in his magnum opus *I and Thou*. In his work, Buber teaches that there is a tripartite system that defines human relationships:

- The *I-It* relationship is defined by its Machiavellian qualities: We treat others only as a means to an end: What can the other give me? Such were the rulers discussed in this mishnah.[80]
- The *I-Thou* relationship is one in which we treat others as an end in themselves. We see the inherent value in others, rather than seeing them for their potential benefit to us. This model encourages humility in interpersonal relationships, because we see all others as equal to ourselves, fostering a more egalitarian mode of interaction. We can rationalize better and empathize with others because we strive to see the world through their eyes. This is a formidable reminder that human beings inhabit an equal station in the world, where no one is greater than anyone else.[81]
- The *I–Eternal Thou* relationship is our individual human relationship with the Divine. By developing a relationship with the incorporeal substances of the universe, we are clearly able to see the interconnectedness of all beings. Indeed, others are not *others* at all; from the grander perspective, we are all one. Within the intersubjectivity of every person is the Creator in the heavens, and the many conscious bonds blend and transmute into a singular connection with all that was and all that will be.[82]

Wherever we see people in society objectified and oppressed, we must bring both the I-Thou and the I–Eternal Thou understanding with gentle force. We can avoid the pitfalls of empowering I-It relationships on the societal level as well.

This mishnah requires us to be wary of authority's motives, but not beholden to them. We should turn inward and develop character, and trust what we learn there. Without knowing the workings of our inner world, we may be doomed to harm the outer world in unexpected and myopic ways. Wherever possible, we need to give more and love more, shifting our primary orientation from the self toward the I-Thou and the I–Eternal Thou relationships that are foundational to a sustained, just, and peaceful society.

2:4

הוּא הָיָה אוֹמֵר: עֲשֵׂה רְצוֹנוֹ כִּרְצוֹנֶךָ, כְּדֵי שֶׁיַּעֲשֶׂה רְצוֹנְךָ
כִּרְצוֹנוֹ. בַּטֵּל רְצוֹנְךָ מִפְּנֵי רְצוֹנוֹ, כְּדֵי שֶׁיְּבַטֵּל רְצוֹן אֲחֵרִים
מִפְּנֵי רְצוֹנֶךָ.

He used to say: Treat God's will as if it were your will, so that
God will treat your will as if it were God's will. Nullify your
will before God's will, so that God will nullify the will of
others before your will.

THIS SIMPLE MISHNAH is vital to comprehending, even a little, the
awe-inspiring, humbling, and terrifying partnership that God has established with humanity. This passage nudges us to ask monumental
questions: What are we most concerned about in the world? Is it acquiring wealth? Or perhaps obtaining nirvana? Do we care about creating
a legacy, or are we content with living in obscurity? The quest to lead a
fulfilling life has stymied the best of human philosophy for millennia.

At the crux of this mishnah is the intangibility of the universe. Of
course, we can never view the expanse of the universe with anything
near the divine perspective. Yet, by awakening that sense of awe and
humility in the face of infinity, we can see the moral problem invoked
by this ancient passage, and we can allow the supernal to invigorate our
conscience.

Jewish law says that it takes sixty times the quantity of kosher food
to render meaningless a bit of nonkosher contaminant. Applying that
as an analogy to our own will, we are to be other-focused and Other-
focused sixty times more than our self-interest would normally allow.
This phenomenon was described by Scottish philosopher David Hume
when he suggested that we are more concerned with the stubbing of
our own toe than we are with a death on the other side of the world.
Keeping self-regard in modest proportion to our caring for the wider
world is challenging. It is unrealistic to think that we can do so immediately, but we can strive to shift the balance.

One of life's spiritual goals, then, is to bring our human will closer to the divine will. How to achieve this is one of those central mysteries. We must seek answers for ourselves.

Nevertheless, moral decision-making is difficult and delicate. We might not know every minute detail, and yet we must act. This is in contrast with God, who at any one moment can see the totality of the universe from the smallest atom to the most massive galaxy; the human brain can never compare. When we make decisions that include a moral dimension, we must ask ourselves, "What would God say about this?" Of course, none of us will ever know the true inner workings of the mind of God. We can only approximate responses based on studying the ancient texts, our intuition, and opening our hearts to the winds of the spirit.

The pertinent question is: can we attune ourselves to the whispers of the Divine? It never hurts to try. And try we must. Rabban Gamliel suggests so right here in this mishnah. People are meant to grow into their best selves, rather than prostrate needlessly before the idols of perfection. Humbling ourselves to see the biggest possible perspective, while still living within the limits of our bodies, is our mandate. It is part of the bargain of accepting the burden of free will.

Listening to our inner voice—that quiet voice that calls out to us to do right—is most important, for it is that one that originates from the heavens. How we respond to it is our test and our destiny. We are temporal beings who have been blessed by a spark of the Divine within our souls. Meditative practices such as mindfulness and separation from the material world can help us transcend our self-interest and access a grander vision for all of humanity—indeed, all of Creation. Being self-aware is but one way to move toward this. This is how we grow in our potential to create the change we want to see in the world.

2:5

הִלֵּל אוֹמֵר: אַל תִּפְרֹשׁ מִן הַצִּבּוּר. וְאַל תַּאֲמֵן בְּעַצְמָךְ עַד
יוֹם מוֹתָךְ. וְאַל תָּדִין אֶת חֲבֵרָךְ עַד שֶׁתַּגִּיעַ לִמְקוֹמוֹ. וְאַל
תֹּאמַר דָּבָר שֶׁאִי אֶפְשָׁר לוֹ לְהִשָּׁמֵעַ, שֶׁסּוֹפוֹ לְהִשָּׁמֵעַ. וְאַל
תֹּאמַר לִכְשֶׁאֶפָּנֶה אֶשְׁנֶה, שֶׁמָּא לֹא תִפָּנֶה.

Hillel said: Do not separate yourself from the community; do
not believe in yourself until the day you die; do not judge your
fellow until you have reached their place; do not say something inappropriate, for it will then be appropriated; and do
not say, "When I am free I will study," for perhaps you will not
become free.

PURSUING YOUR HEART'S DESIRE is a precarious proposition in a life
of unrelenting commitments. All too often, we hear people say they're
waiting for the proper time to go out and do something worthwhile.
We hear students say they are waiting until graduation, professionals
say they are waiting until they have enough money, or nearly everyone
say they're waiting until they're less busy. This is tragic and self-defeat-
ing. What should be the most important aspects of our lives—family,
spiritual growth, kindness, and learning—cannot be put on hold until
later. Rather, we must live our priorities now. They cannot wait.

We are taught to "not judge your fellow until you have reached their
place," but the truth is that we never reach anyone's place. One's *makom*,
"place," includes upbringing, genes, experiences, and unique spiritual
development. We can never really judge another because another's
consciousness is so fundamentally different from our own. This is not
moral relativism. We can judge actions as good or evil, but we cannot
judge the whole person, the being in his or her entirety. As the Sages
teach, no two people are alike (JT *B'rachot* 5:9).

Refraining from judgment is not just charitable; it's also prudent.
Rabbi Menachem Meiri, the fourteenth-century Provençal Talmud
scholar (more widely known by his surname only), teaches that someone

new to a community may present himself as more righteous and pious than he is.[83] Therefore, we cannot always place trust in someone's outer appearance. Knowing what is in someone's heart is the telling of their true character. Therefore, we should be careful not to judge a person within a community's false context. Instead, we should assess every person by his or her actions and kind deeds.

Still, there is potential danger in how one understands and applies this mishnah. One may understand this teaching as requiring submission, obedience, conformity, and acquiescing to dogma. But this cannot be the case, since the essence of being a Jew is cultivating oneself to swim *against* the tide. We must be a people of protest, rather than a people of submission. We must be individuals of struggle rather than people of simple acceptance. Nonetheless, we cannot be anarchist or libertarian. Judaism requires that we build communities and societal systems to support one another. Furthermore, we must find time away to be alone and grow in private, to complement our communal and societal activities.

Maimonides discusses the idea behind Hillel's mishnah:

> One who separates oneself from the life of the community—even if he did not commit any transgressions—is one who stays separate from the congregation of Israel and does not fulfill commandments among them, and does not share in their sufferings nor fast on their fast days. They act as though they were a member of one of the [other] nations, as though they were not an Israelite: they have no place in the world-to-come.[84]

We cannot achieve the goal of building a cohort of like-minded individuals through suspicion and skepticism about other people's hearts. Therefore, we are instructed not to separate from community; we need the support and challenge of community. For the community to be healthy, we should "not judge our fellow" and not try to speak above others' heads ("do not make a statement that cannot be easily understood"). Rather, we prize honest communication that values the dignity of all. This, of course, requires humility. It requires the knowledge that we must go beyond our pettiness and reach out to others, even when it seems uncomfortable to do so.

The Chasidic masters explain that the biblical passage "She joyfully awaits the last day" (Proverbs 31:25) describes the souls of the righteous, which can finally celebrate their moral victories. Having stood up for the downtrodden, shown respect to all kinds of people, and acted ethically in business dealings, they can now believe in themselves on the day of death. They have lived, for the most part, as beings created in the image of God. Daily, we need to make concrete such abstract notions.

Rabbi Yisrael Salanter (nineteenth century, Lithuania) was once asked: If I have only one hour in the day to study, should I study Talmud or should I study *musar* (reflective, ethical, and spiritual development literature)? He answered, "Study *musar*, because it will inspire you to find the second hour to study Talmud."[85] When we invest in the soul, we will have more time to do so.

Certainly, when Hillel here instructs us to "not believe in yourself until the day you die," he is not calling for self-disparagement or a lack of confidence. Rather, we should never believe in ourselves to the extent that we think we are a finished product. We should never feel complete with our achievements or growth. That is what life is for. With this humility, we will realize our need for community.

2:6

הוּא הָיָה אוֹמֵר: אֵין בּוֹר יְרֵא חֵטְא, וְלֹא עַם הָאָרֶץ חָסִיד.
וְלֹא הַבַּיְשָׁן לָמֵד, וְלֹא הַקַּפְּדָן מְלַמֵּד. וְלֹא כָל הַמַּרְבֶּה
בִסְחוֹרָה מַחְכִּים. וּבַמָּקוֹם שֶׁאֵין אֲנָשִׁים, הִשְׁתַּדֵּל
לִהְיוֹת אִישׁ.

He used to say: An ignorant person cannot be fearful of
sin; an unlearned person cannot be scrupulously pious; the
bashful person cannot learn, and the quick, impatient person
cannot teach; anyone excessively occupied in business cannot
become a scholar; and in a place where there are no leaders,
strive to be a leader.

THIS MISHNAH lays out the normative response—or, more accurately,
what one shouldn't do—to prepare for moments when our leadership
is required. We are told to be refined, learned, courageous in scholarship, and patient and not to prioritize career and money over values.
Indeed, in his commentary, the Maharal saw this mishnah as dealing
with the actualization of the intellect, soul, and body. We must take
precautions in each of these realms to ensure we can meet our potential
to learn, grow, and serve.

The obvious biblical parallel in the mishnah's use of the word *ish*
(which in the context of leadership can mean "leader") is the episode in
Exodus involving a young Moses. When Moses saw an Egyptian beat-
ing a Hebrew slave, the verse says Moses "turned this way and that and,
seeing no one (*ish*) about, he struck down the Egyptian and hid him
in the sand" (Exodus 2:11–12). Commentators on this biblical verse
have interpreted the deeper meanings of Moses's seemingly confus-
ing actions. Moses looked both ways to be sure no one was watching,
so that he would not get caught in his violent deed. Moses, however,
was also acting on "where there are no leaders, strive to be a leader."
Moses, in this critical historical moment, saw that there was no leadership and knew that he must intervene personally. To be sure, an act

of violence cannot serve as our paradigm for moral leadership, but the decision-making process involved is one we might emulate.

How could it be, though, that Moses saw "no one (*ish*) about," when countless Israelite slaves were no doubt all around him, working simultaneously to build Egypt's grandeur? Moses, who was raised in the Egyptian royal court, still considered himself as a person of power and privilege, and he dignified neither the Israelites around him nor the Egyptian he struck with the status of *someone who counts*—that is, who can be labeled as "one" (*ish*). In this earlier stage of his spiritual journey, he dehumanized others to the point of not seeing the humanity in those who were right before his eyes.

When no one is looking—especially at such times—we should strive to live our best. Today, it seems that every good deed must be seen on social media, shared with the world, or added to one's résumé; and that can be toxic. At worst, such deeds are self-aggrandizing, used in a way to advance oneself in a ruthless, competitive marketplace. The Sages were certainly not against self-advancement, but rather, they urged us to be the same person in private as in public. They urged us to embrace the holy and not to see every encounter, person, and moment as simply a means to an end.

But what is the most effective mechanism for growing in one's leadership? A leader must be measured and reflective. This requires courage, patience, and, most crucially, critical thinking. Today, too many leaders are immersed solely in their self-referential world of superficial action and ego. In contrast to this shallow understanding of leadership, the Jewish model requires a leader's ongoing immersion in study, healthy self-doubt, and reflection. That is what separates those who are merely in charge from those who take on the sacred mantle of leadership.

This presents us with another question. What do the Rabbis mean that "an ignorant person cannot be fearful of sin"? At first glance, this statement seems condescending. To be ethically sensitive, however, one cannot be ignorant. One must pay deep attention to trends, norms, and ideals. To be attuned and sensitive toward others requires emotional intelligence, even more than it requires regular intellect. Sensitivity toward others is not an inborn trait, but a cultivated ethical practice.

Indeed, to be pious means to go above the letter of the law to fulfill the deepest intention of the tradition. "An unlearned person cannot be scrupulously pious." If one does not develop a nuanced understanding of the tradition, one risks becoming too strict in some observances and too lax in others. This comes at the expense of truly investing in the richness of Jewish spiritual and ethical engagement, which accompanies understanding what is most significant. Rabbi Hirsch writes in his commentary:

> One may attach significance to things which are actually without value; on the other hand, one may regard as unimportant matters which, in fact, should be viewed as most significant.

A common confusion is the belief that ritual is an end in itself rather than a mechanism for deeper ethical actualization. Rabbi Menachem Mendel of Vorka (nineteenth century, Poland) describes an *am haaretz*—the "unlearned person" mentioned in this mishnah—as one who blames the *aretz* (their environment) for who they are at their present moment. We are free to evolve, and so to use our environment as an excuse will stunt our ability to grow. On this teaching, still, the Kotzker Rebbe teaches the reverse: Anyone who is afraid of doing wrong will not remain ignorant.[86] Indeed, how could we desire to be ethically and spiritually sensitive and yet not seek out learning and growth?

This leads to another, broader inquiry: Why can't a bashful person learn? Or, more precisely, why does the person who is less able and willing to go out of one's comfort zone struggle with facilitating a real connection to community learning? Real learning is about being uncomfortable, about opening up and letting oneself become vulnerable. We need to leave the comfort zone of what we know, and venture into a new territory of the unknown, to more deeply understand. Consider what Brené Brown writes about on the subject of vulnerability:

> Shame resilience is key to embracing our vulnerability. We can't let ourselves be seen if we're terrified by what people might think. Often "not being good at vulnerability" means that we're damn good at shame.[87]

Perhaps, as this mishnah teaches, those highly engaged in business cannot become scholars because they lack the orientation. Making money is a tangible outcome, while religious scholarship is precisely the opposite; it is holy, non-instrumental. There is no attempt to gain money, fame, real estate, or political access through deepening religious insight. This may well be the greatest religious challenge in our time—that so many in our community are more concerned with material gain than with spiritual growth.

If we wish to learn about our true selves, we must be willing to be laughed at. The Maharal taught in his commentary on *Pirkei Avot* that the Torah is referred to as "fire."[88] Such imagery suggests that anyone truly seeking the bright light of the fire will be pulled from their bashful nature to come out to learn. This said, we must be sensitive in our communities and classrooms to different personalities. For some, this task is much more difficult than it is for others. It is not our place to judge them, but to meet them where they are. This is the true meaning of striving to be the best leader one can be.

2:7

אַף הוּא רָאָה גֻלְגֹּלֶת אַחַת צָפָה עַל פְּנֵי הַמָּיִם. אָמַר לָהּ:
עַל דַּאֲטֵפְתָּ אַטִיפוּךְ, וְסוֹף מְטִיפַיִךְ יְטוּפוּן.

He [Hillel] also saw a skull floating on the water; he said to it:
"Because you drowned others, they drowned you; and those
who drowned you will be drowned eventually."

THIS IS a singularly odd passage for *Pirkei Avot*. Situated among
more benign, enlightened nuggets of wisdom, the parable of the skull
is brooding, brutal, stark, and a ferocious contrast with the relatively
warm-hearted idea that we have of the Sages. This grave juxtaposition
of tone offers a profound message.

Why such a harsh passage, especially in a book dedicated to ethical
teachings? Jewish mystics understand this passage to be representative
of Jewish karma. While karma is not often associated with Judaism,
this passage shows the concept to be part of normative Jewish epistemology. Jewish rationalists understand that humans engage in acts of
cruelty and revenge, and punishment should be expected for the perpe-
trators of evil. Mystics understand that divine justice may punish per-
petrators and reward the innocent in this world, the next world, or in a
different incarnation (*gilgul*) entirely.[89] Anyone who works in a pastoral
or therapeutic capacity knows the importance of neither blaming the
victim nor suggesting that the reason for suffering is known.

This teaching can be seen as a pedagogical tool to cultivate empathy.
Indeed, one can see this passage as the inverse of the globally understood Golden Rule. We shouldn't do to others what we don't wish done
to ourselves. *How would you like to be drowned? Not at all, thank you very
much!*

This applies to every piece of minutia concerning ethics, of course,
and not just to murder and other barbarities. Ordinary rules of a just
society require that people treat both neighbors and strangers with
decency, in part because the respectful treatment of others guarantees
that they are ensured freedom to reach full potential without undue

suppression of their true selves. This is easier to say than do, but that is part of our spiritual challenge in this world.

Another manner by which we read this passage is by understanding the limits of mass punitive incarceration. As a society, we still focus on indulging the collective id—our base instinct—in meting out supposed justice. Both instinct and norms of fairness seem to incline us toward measure-for-measure justice. If someone does something wrong, we believe in just deserts, payment of debt to society, and correctional measures. But our criminal justice, corrections, and prison systems today have run amok. America, admired worldwide for its precepts of liberty and equality, has, of any nation, the highest proportion of its population incarcerated.[90]

We should not wish or pray for the death of others. Rather, we should wish that those causing harm do *t'shuvah* (repentance) and change their ways. We learn a fascinating insight from the great Talmudic matriarch B'ruriah about this:

> There were some boors in Rabbi Meir's neighborhood, who caused him great distress. Rabbi Meir would pray that they would die. His wife B'ruriah said to him, "What are you thinking?" [He responded,] "Because it says, 'Sinners will cease' (Psalm 104:30)." [She responded,] "Does it say 'sinners'? 'Sins' is what it says [End the evil, not evildoers]. Furthermore, go down to the end of the verse: 'The wicked will be no more.' Since their sinning will stop, will there 'no longer be sinners'? Rather, you should pray that they repent, then 'they will be wicked no more.'" [Rabbi Meir] prayed for mercy upon them, and they repented (BT *B'rachot* 10a).[90a]

Here, the Sages communicate an uncomfortable psychological reality: human beings can be trapped by their baseness. The human tendency toward violence is often met with more violence. But the Sages ask us to pause. The skull in the water—a symbol of the fragility of life—is the marker for elementary empathy. No matter how cruel a person is, he or she can change. No matter how depraved a society becomes, it can repent and turn toward what's right. The blessing of free will allows such changes.

Certainly, we should seek outcomes that leave society safer, as well as outcomes that allow those who have erred to fulfill their potential to learn, repent, and rebuild moral character. Rather than implement outdated versions of an "eye for an eye," individuals and communities dedicated to righteousness should structure rehabilitation and reconciliation so as to counter retribution. We should work for changing today's climate of exceptionally callous punishment. We should pray to open our hearts and allow mercy to pour into all of our sinews. It is difficult, but it is just.

2:8

הוּא הָיָה אוֹמֵר: מַרְבֶּה בָשָׂר, מַרְבֶּה רִמָּה. מַרְבֶּה נְכָסִים,
מַרְבֶּה דְאָגָה. מַרְבֶּה נָשִׁים, מַרְבֶּה כְשָׁפִים. מַרְבֶּה שְׁפָחוֹת,
מַרְבֶּה זִמָּה. מַרְבֶּה עֲבָדִים, מַרְבֶּה גָזֵל. מַרְבֶּה תוֹרָה, מַרְבֶּה
חַיִּים. מַרְבֶּה יְשִׁיבָה, מַרְבֶּה חָכְמָה. מַרְבֶּה עֵצָה, מַרְבֶּה
תְבוּנָה. מַרְבֶּה צְדָקָה, מַרְבֶּה שָׁלוֹם. קָנָה שֵׁם טוֹב, קָנָה
לְעַצְמוֹ. קָנָה לוֹ דִבְרֵי תוֹרָה, קָנָה לוֹ חַיֵּי הָעוֹלָם הַבָּא.

He used to say: The more meat, the more worms; the more possessions, the more worry; the more wives, the more witchcraft; the more maidservants, the more lewdness; the more manservants, the more thievery. [On the other hand], the more Torah, the more life; the more study, the more wisdom; the more counsel, the more understanding; the more charity, the more peace. One who has gained a good reputation has gained it for their own benefit; one who has gained himself Torah knowledge has gained himself the life of the world-to-come.

THIS MISHNAH does not discuss activities forbidden in Judaism. Instead, it explores activities that are permitted, yet wrong. Nachmanides (thirteenth-century, Spain) taught that it is possible for one to be a scoundrel with the permission of the Torah (*naval birshut haTorah*).[91] On the outside, this scoundrel looks like any other observer of the tradition, but this person lives by the letter, never going beyond the minimum expression of normative righteousness. This is tragic, because such an individual never explores her or his true potential.

The Maharal of Prague, in his commentary on this mishnah, teaches that just as the Ten Commandments are divided—half touching spiritual matters, half touching physical matters—so too is this mishnah. Physical matters are impermanent, but the spiritual is eternal. It is easy to get distracted by the allure of gaining material possessions at the expense of building up spiritual capital within oneself. Instead, meditate on the fact that each of us will die, and at the moment of death, all that will remain is whether or not we lived a righteous life. When this mishnah teaches that increasing Torah means increasing life, it does not necessarily mean one's lifespan in *this* world. Rather, in embracing a *Torat chayim*—a Torah most committed to affirming the fullness of the sanctity of one's earthly life—one enjoys the deeper spiritual rewards of living in line with a great moral mission, a life committed to service and giving.

The theological principle in this passage is that human beings are endowed with free will. One would think that free will is self-evident and universally understood. Not so. Three Jews whose philosophy shaped modernity made the case against free will: Karl Marx argued that we're determined by our socioeconomic (material) status; Sigmund Freud argued that we're determined by the imprint of early childhood experiences; Baruch Spinoza argued that we're determined by our internal makeup (later expressed as our genetic inheritance).[92]

Even acknowledging the considerable contributions of these three thinkers to modern thought, we yet reaffirm that we possess free will. It is in our hands to choose worry or joy. It is our choice to live a life of integrity and kindness or its opposite. It is up to us to support or destroy another person. Viktor Frankl teaches that what is fundamental to our core humanity is the ability to embrace the brief moment between a stimulus and a response.[93] Deliberation allows us to exert choice and go from stimulus to a new moral response, breaking away from our normal instinctual response.

This mishnah teaches that the more charity in the world, the more peace in the world. This is a net positive, and it speaks volumes to how we think about international conflicts and diplomatic bridge-building. It is common for radicalism's violence to emerge where there is deep poverty and desperation. Rather than going to war, we might think about addressing the physical needs, through charity, to create the desired spiritual result, peace. We'd be wise to reflect on the words of Lillian Wald, an early twentieth-century nurse, humanitarian, and author: "Women more than men can strip war of its glamour and its out-of-date heroisms and patriotisms, and see it as a demon of destruction and hideous wrong."[94]

The first teaching in the mishnah is allegorically rich and unsettling. Read plainly, if one eats more meat, there will be more worms, more death. The Sages intuited something here that wouldn't be known until millennia later: not only is killing animals for pleasure wrong, but we now know that overconsumption of animal products is linked to common, deadly diseases, like cardiovascular illness. The Torah requires us to guard our souls and our bodies.

Rabbi Kook teaches that even a "fear of God" could cause moral confusion:

> A person's fear of God [*yirat shamayim*] should not displace natural morality, since then it ceases to be a pure fear of God. The sign of a pure fear of God is when it aids natural morality, which arises from the human being's upright nature, to attain an even higher level, higher than it could attain alone. However, if fear of God is depicted as hindering the person's effectiveness and capacity to perform beneficial actions for the individual and the community, and as causing fewer activities to be undertaken, then that fear of God is invalid.[95]

In addition to just living with religious virtues (like the fear of God), we must cultivate moral conscience, so as to inform our other virtues. Rabbi Kook says that natural human morality crucially aids us in living an ethical life:

> The manifest natural morality needs to be clarified before the soul can reach a higher fundamental morality. Only by encouraging a firm, basic foundation in this way can we build the structure whose summit reaches heaven. The more extensive the oak tree's roots, and the deeper and more deeply rooted they are, the fresher, stronger and more fertile its branches will be and its leaves will not wither.[96]

We must have the larger consciousness to cultivate moral character beyond what religious traditions mandate. One could believe in God and the Torah, profess fidelity to Jewish law, show kindness to one's friends and local community, and live fully within the Jewish laws and still be a scoundrel, all the while hating refugees, shunning immigrants, oppressing women, or neglecting the poor. All terrible acts of callousness subvert the holiness that religion is meant to imbue in the world.

Beyond Judaism, religious communities should never be afraid of drawing from moral wisdom from outside the canon, even if such wisdom might seem to contradict a traditional or literal reading that's within the canon. Religious people should not try to escape responsibility by dismissing hateful texts within one's particular tradition as un-Jewish, un-Christian, un-Buddhist, or un-Islamic. Such myopic apologetics should be countered by asking how such ideas entered our traditions and then by responding to problematic texts through reinterpretation that is committed to the dignity of all.

It is important to address root causes in our lives. One may wish to be learned, one may wish to excel above the rest, but wishes alone will not bring worldly intelligence. One can yearn to be honest with colleagues and friends, but simply yearning is empty. The choices one makes—positive over negative, deliberation over haste—have consequential implications for one's character. Ultimately, whether we achieve spiritual heights in this world (and the next) rests upon each choice that we nominate to actualize. Living creatures have been given the blessing of free will; but if we don't exercise it, it will atrophy.

2:9

רַבָּן יוֹחָנָן בֶּן זַכַּי קִבֵּל מֵהִלֵּל וּמִשַּׁמַּאי. הוּא הָיָה אוֹמֵר: אִם
לָמַדְתָּ תּוֹרָה הַרְבֵּה, אַל תַּחֲזִיק טוֹבָה לְעַצְמָךְ, כִּי
לְכָךְ נוֹצָרְתָּ.

Rabban Yochanan ben Zakkai received the tradition from
Hillel and Shammai. He used to say: If you have studied much
Torah, do not take credit for yourself, because this is what you
were created to do.

IT IS IMPORTANT to distinguish between privileges and accomplishments. One's birthright as a Jew—whether as a Jew-by-birth or as a
Jew-by-choice—is access to the vast expanse of Torah knowledge. This
access is truly a privilege. But more so than a privilege, it is a humbling
gift. We are blessed to have contact with this wisdom that reaches back
millennia. But simply studying and memorizing the ancient words and
moral lessons are not, in and of themselves, accomplishments. Indeed,
studying like that is a barrier to the internalization of the scholars' precepts; it stymies the ability to bring their light into the world. Taking
the time to learn and translate the words is meaningless unless one
responds by going out into the world to perform good works. Turning
study into positive change in society is holy work.

We all know that some Jews treat Torah learning as a badge of
honor and as a way to gain authority, in spite of this mishnah. Perhaps
this person memorizes difficult tractates of Gemara (Talmudic debate)
and midrashic minutiae, as if knowing the most obscure fragment of
information will transform one into a seer of ultimate truth. This is
an abuse of the Torah, altering its beautiful privilege into something
grotesque.

Responding to the vanity of such a phenomenon, Rabbi Yisrael
Salanter founded the modern era of *musar*, which focuses on spiritual
and ethical development in Judaism. *Musar* stresses that value is not in
the amount of information that one absorbs, but in the richness of the
tradition that one gains. As one teaching goes, what matters more than

how many times you've gone through the Talmud is how many times the Talmud has gone through you. Meditative practices and inner reflection are part of *musar*'s means of aiding self-improvement. In studying *musar*, we move truth from our mind to our heart; and from there outward, to emanate from every fiber of our being.

Rabban ("our Rabbi") Yochanan ben Zakkai argues that we no longer need a Temple with animal sacrifices. Instead, we can seek atonement through acts of kindness.[97] Our motive may still be to fulfill the psychological need for purity and removal of guilt, but we help others in the process. Self-interest and a broader interest toward others can be combined toward a productive life.

For Rabban Yochanan ben Zakkai, the arduous but essentially rewarding work to perfect the world consists almost entirely of little acts that comprise the broader whole. Commentators on the Talmud tell us that nobody ever initiated a greeting to Rabban Yochanan ben Zakkai—because he was always the first to greet them. They note this on a passage that concludes with the words *v'afilu nochri b'shuk*, which means that one should greet even an unknown gentile in the public market. What is the purpose of such a pronouncement, especially for an encounter of seemingly little consequence? The ability to greet and engage others warmly is at the core of Jewish virtuous living. When approaching someone for the sake of meeting or greeting, we need not have a great intellectual master plan for conversation. On the contrary, we can merely offer a smile and warmth.

While Rabban Yochanan ben Zakkai focused on life's small acts, it is also because of him that *all* of Judaism survived (BT *Gittin* 56a–b). When the Romans defeated the Jewish defense and destroyed the Temple in 70 CE, they ended that historical period of Jewish sovereignty. Under Governor Vespasian, Rabban Yochanan ben Zakkai gathered the Sages in Yavneh and ensured the survival of Torah.

This is an important lesson, for otherwise we might take Torah for granted. Who knows what could have happened had it been lost to Roman cruelty? By living Torah values, we preserve the memories of those who were martyred and thus unable to fulfill their mission in the world. We must focus on the moment, whether it is the tree we're planting, the person we're speaking with, or the time with someone we love. We must scope the big picture: perfect the world, ensure the survival of our holy Torah, and make its concomitant moral mandates flourish. Our intellectual conversations about grand ideals are important, but the talk we have in the hallways and streets can be just as important, if not more, in defining us as individuals and as community.

This is perhaps why we've been blessed with bodies, the souls' conduit to the temporal world. Maintaining the body for the good of the soul is paramount, something people "were created to do." One should not exercise for the sake of honor, but to use one's body for good acts. So, too, one's mind requires learning, to bend it toward pondering the depths of God's Creation and toward helping others. Still, we should not take credit for our knowledge, because we should remember how little we really know. Yes, contrasted with children or those who aren't invested in intellectual pursuits, we may feel self-satisfaction. Compared with the greatest intellects and spiritual giants of our time and prior, we are humbled.

Our work to heal the brokenness in the world is never done, even when it seems that redemption has come. As it says in an ancient commentary to *Pirkei Avot*: Rabban Yochanan ben Zakkai used to say: "If there is a sapling in your hand when they say to you, 'Behold, the Messiah has come!' complete planting the sapling, and then go and welcome the Messiah."[98] The redemptive process makes sense only if we continue the work. Once we stop planting for the future, that path toward redemption is lost forever.

2:10

חֲמִשָּׁה תַלְמִידִים הָיוּ לוֹ לְרַבָּן יוֹחָנָן בֶּן זַכַּאי, וְאֵלּוּ הֵן: רַבִּי אֱלִיעֶזֶר בֶּן הֻרְקָנוֹס, וְרַבִּי יְהוֹשֻׁעַ בֶּן חֲנַנְיָה, וְרַבִּי יוֹסֵי הַכֹּהֵן, וְרַבִּי שִׁמְעוֹן בֶּן נְתַנְאֵל, וְרַבִּי אֶלְעָזָר בֶּן עֲרָךְ.

Rabban Yochanan ben Zakkai had five [primary] disciples. They were Rabbi Eliezer ben Hurkanos, Rabbi Y'hoshua ben Chananya, Rabbi Yosei the Kohein, Rabbi Shimon ben N'taneil, and Rabbi Elazar ben Arach.

2:11

הוּא הָיָה מוֹנֶה שִׁבְחָן: רַבִּי אֱלִיעֶזֶר בֶּן הֻרְקָנוֹס – בּוֹר סוּד שֶׁאֵינוֹ מְאַבֵּד טִפָּה. רַבִּי יְהוֹשֻׁעַ בֶּן חֲנַנְיָה – אַשְׁרֵי יוֹלַדְתּוֹ. רַבִּי יוֹסֵי הַכֹּהֵן – חָסִיד. רַבִּי שִׁמְעוֹן בֶּן נְתַנְאֵל – יְרֵא חֵטְא. וְרַבִּי אֶלְעָזָר בֶּן עֲרָךְ – מַעְיָן הַמִּתְגַּבֵּר.

He used to enumerate their praises: Rabbi Eliezer ben Hurkanos is like a cemented cistern that doesn't lose a drop; Rabbi Y'hoshua ben Chananya, praiseworthy is she who bore him; Rabbi Yosei the Kohein is a scrupulously pious person; Rabbi Shimon ben N'taneil fears wrongdoing; and Rabbi Elazar ben Arach is like a spring flowing stronger and stronger.

As DESCRIBED in the last chapter, Rabbi Yochanan is perhaps the pivotal reason why Jews still study Torah. What, though, is the pedagogical purpose of dedicating all of mishnah 2:10 to naming his disciples?

Let's step back for a moment. It is all too easy for a teacher to become critical of one's students. Criticism of effort and character too often accompany unrealistic expectations of what students should be. Each new class of students suffers the same censure: they are lazy, not clever, not as good as the previous generation. This critique, in Jewish theology, is typically called *y'ridat hadorot* (decline over the generations).[99]

Both 2:10 and 2:11 remind the reader, by distinguishing Rabban Yochanan ben Zakkai's disciples, not to criticize students needlessly. An effective teacher loves and admires one's students. If not so, then what is the point in dedicating countless hours to mentorship and support? Indeed, offering counsel is as important as teaching subject matter fundamentals.

We learn from these *mishnayot* that Rabban Yochanan ben Zakkai's students are great not because they are *his* students, but because each is virtuous in his own right. None are alike, but each has a spiritual virtue. In this way, Rabban Yochanan ben Zakkai embraced—centuries before it was elucidated in the academy—a concept called multiple intelligences. As proposed by Harvard's Howard Gardner in his book *Frames of Mind: The Theory of Multiple Intelligences*, this theory says there are many ways to learn, many ways to interact, and varying paths to greatness. A teacher also has multiple avenues on which to lead students to fulfill their potential. Individuals' differences mean that there are untold avenues toward greatness.

This is important when considering how to direct the next generation toward ethical, meaningful leadership. When one views being a teacher as a calling rather than an occupation, one can transcend mere pedagogy and move into the realm of the spiritually important. This is key to the transmission of knowledge to future generations of leaders and thinkers.

When a teacher takes on the teaching of students as a spiritual responsibility, then that teacher must stand with those students, see their strengths, and encourage them to grow in their talents. The Sages teach that one should not go over the top in one's praise for anyone, because this will prompt a critique from others (BT *Arachin* 16a). Given this Talmudic approach, in 2:11, Rabban Yochanan ben Zakkai must either believe he is giving basic praise for students who are far more talented than described or believe he is only teaching this to lovers of Torah who will truly appreciate learning from these different models of virtue and not critique them amidst his praise.

When we look back at our lives, we tend to have warm memories of the teachers who believed in and guided us, encouraged us when no one else would, and gave us the spark to dig deeper when the world didn't make sense. When these *mishnayot* discuss Rabban Yochanan ben Zakkai's students, they are lauding his kindness toward his students as much as his erudition and skill.

Each of us should strive to seek new teachers and maintain contact with mentors. These shouldn't be gurus we unquestioningly follow, but individuals who challenge us to look deep into our souls. Because each of us has so much to learn and so much to teach in our brief time in this world, we shouldn't squander a single opportunity for growth. Often, our students are our best teachers.

In a meta-sense, anyone who picks up *Pirkei Avot* is a student of Rabban Yochanan ben Zakkai; he is the great equalizer. In this context, 2:10 and 2:11 make perfect sense. Whether we learn from sages who lived two millennia ago or we await what tomorrow will teach, we are obligated as students to absorb the lessons from our teachers, think deeply about challenges in our lives, and consider challenges around the world. By thinking about these problems together, we can make progress and launch the next human innovation.

2:12

הוּא הָיָה אוֹמֵר: אִם יִהְיוּ כָל חַכְמֵי יִשְׂרָאֵל בְּכַף מֹאזְנַיִם
וֶאֱלִיעֶזֶר בֶּן הֻרְקָנוֹס בְּכַף שְׁנִיָּה, מַכְרִיעַ אֶת כֻּלָּם. אַבָּא
שָׁאוּל אוֹמֵר מִשְּׁמוֹ: אִם יִהְיוּ כָל חַכְמֵי יִשְׂרָאֵל בְּכַף
מֹאזְנַיִם וְרַבִּי אֱלִיעֶזֶר בֶּן הֻרְקָנוֹס אַף עִמָּהֶם, וְרַבִּי אֶלְעָזָר
בֶּן עֲרָךְ בְּכַף שְׁנִיָּה, מַכְרִיעַ אֶת כֻּלָּם.

He used to say: If all the sages of Israel were on one pan of a
balance-scale, and Eliezer ben Hurkanos were on the other,
he would outweigh them all. Abba Shaul said in his name: If
all the sages of Israel, with even Rabbi Eliezer ben Hurkanos
among them, were on one pan of the balance-scale, and Rabbi
Elazar ben Arach were on the other, he would outweigh
them all.

2:13

אָמַר לָהֶם: צְאוּ וּרְאוּ אֵיזוֹ הִיא דֶּרֶךְ טוֹבָה שֶׁיִּדְבַּק בָּהּ
הָאָדָם. רַבִּי אֱלִיעֶזֶר אוֹמֵר: עַיִן טוֹבָה. רַבִּי יְהוֹשֻׁעַ אוֹמֵר:
חָבֵר טוֹב. רַבִּי יוֹסֵי אוֹמֵר: שָׁכֵן טוֹב. רַבִּי שִׁמְעוֹן אוֹמֵר:
הָרוֹאֶה אֶת הַנּוֹלָד. רַבִּי אֶלְעָזָר אוֹמֵר: לֵב טוֹב. אָמַר
לָהֶם: רוֹאֶה אֲנִי אֶת דִּבְרֵי אֶלְעָזָר בֶּן עֲרָךְ מִדִּבְרֵיכֶם,
שֶׁבִּכְלַל דְּבָרָיו דִּבְרֵיכֶם.

He said to them: Go out and discern which is the proper way
to which a person should cling. Rabbi Eliezer says: A good
eye. Rabbi Y'hoshua says: A good friend. Rabbi Yosei says: A
good neighbor. Rabbi Shimon says: One who considers the
outcome of a deed. Rabbi Elazar says: A good heart. He [Rab-
ban Yochanan ben Zakkai] said to them: I prefer the words of
Elazar ben Arach to your words, for your words are included
in their words.

In a famous Talmudic debate known as *tanur shel achnai*, Rabbi Elazar ben Arach's view, within an argument, is confirmed by a heavenly voice, a *bat kol* (BT *Bava M'tzia* 59b). Yet, we learn that the Sages reject his position, because the majority opinion of sages matters more than a heavenly voice. This is a religiously subversive notion. How so? Because, there is an assumption that if an edict of religious importance comes down from the heavens, then it must be immutable in all its forms. Yet, despite the centrality of the Divine in Jewish intellectual endeavors, there is also the precept of *Torah lo bashamayim hi*, namely that the "Torah is not in heaven." What is the significance of this operating principle? At the elementary level, the idea of *Torah lo bashamayim hi* means that human beings, in the totality of all their earthly wisdom, must take responsibility to interpret the Torah in our unique time and not look to the heavens for the answers. The Rabbis similarly teach that a sage is preferable over a prophet for this reason (BT *Bava Batra* 12b). Rather than look to the heavens for answers, we are to engage our divinely gifted innate (and cultivated) human capacities.

People are blessed with the ability to cherish many values simultaneously, without needing to sacrifice some for others. In our spiritual practice, however, we are to cultivate moral decision-making. Rabbi Elazar, favored in both of these *mishnayot*, suggests that what's most central is a good heart. While others suggest that the "proper way" is found in something external (eye, friend, neighbor, outcomes), Rabbi Elazar favors what's internal, the heart. Rabbi Elazar is teaching here that to do the messy work of our outer world, we must first do the messy work of our inner world. When we have not done so, we are ill equipped to handle the complexity of the outer world.

In his commentary on these verses, Rabbi Hirsch explains that the word *lev* means more than just "heart":

> The term *lev* denotes a typically Jewish concept, the wellspring of every emotion, every aspiration, every endeavor, the source of every moral and spiritual impulse and tendency, even of all thought and character. Hence *lev* denotes the root and source of every endeavor and every achievement.

It can be hard to keep our heart open. Doing so requires us to acknowledge our own vulnerability and inner pain. C. S. Lewis explains about the virtue of love, within a religious personality:

> To love at all is to be vulnerable. . . . Lock [your heart] up safe in the casket or coffin of your selfishness. But in that casket, safe, dark, motionless, airless, it will change. It will not be broken; it will become unbreakable, impenetrable, irredeemable. To love is to be vulnerable.[100]

Collectively, such vulnerability would serve society well. Expressing moral distress is difficult to do; it's not considered culturally acceptable to show one's heartfelt anguish at the state of things, but it can be healthy when done in the proper environment. On this topic, University of Chicago Law School Martha Nussbaum, a moral psychologist, says:

> What I am calling for . . . [is] a society that acknowledges its own humanity, and neither hides us from it nor it from us; a society of citizens who admit that they are needy and vulnerable, and who discard the grandiose demands for omnipotence and completeness that have been at the heart of so much human misery, both public and private.[101]

We don't have to feel alone in this struggle to let our truest inner feeling. Parker Palmer of the Center for Courage and Renewal writes about the connection between the health of society and the health of one's inner world:

> Democratic institutions are not automated. They must be inhabited by citizens and citizen leaders who know how to hold conflict inwardly in a manner that converts it into creativity, allowing it to pull them open to new ideas, new courses of action, and each other. That kind of tension-holding is the work of the well-tempered heart: if democracy is to thrive as that restored prairie is thriving, our hearts and our institutions must work in concert.[102]

Rabbi Kook describes how people need to embrace holy moments to ensure that their hearts are transformed:

When you experience a strong desire to be good to all, realize that an illumination from the supernal world has come to you. How fortunate you will be if you prepare a proper place in your heart, in your mind, in the acts of your hands and in all your feelings to receive this exalted guest, which is greater and more exalted than the most noble of this earth. Take hold of it and do not let go!

Do not allow any delays and obstacles—whether physical or spiritual—that hinder you from acting on this holy inspiration. Fight for everything. Rise in your strength. Lift your consciousness to the far reaches and imitate the qualities of God, who is good to all and whose compassion encompasses all God's creatures.[103]

If our hearts are filled with hate, jealousy, and fear, we cannot go out into the world and achieve our moral, spiritual mission. But, if the heart is filled with pure love, pure compassion, and pure generosity, every aspect of our lives can be transformed for the better. We can learn what provokes us and gain control of our lives. Still, we should never allow the perfect to be the enemy of the good; and we should embrace the complexity of self-awareness, self-mastery, and self-growth as a lifelong project never to be fully completed. The Kotzker Rebbe interprets "a pure heart create for me, O God" (Psalm 51:12) as meaning that anyone who already thinks she or he has a pure heart actually does not.[104] As Rabbi Adin Steinsaltz, one of the great modern scholars of Torah, teaches, if you think you've arrived, you're lost.[105]

It is all too easy to get stuck in our own hearts and not exist empathically within community. James Baldwin once said, "You think your pain and your heartbreak are unprecedented in the history of the world, but then you read."[106] The opening of hearts is actualized not in moments of pain and concern, but when we realize that we are all entwined in this grand human enterprise together.

2:14

אָמַר לָהֶם: צְאוּ וּרְאוּ אֵיזוֹ הִיא אֵיזוֹ דֶרֶךְ רָעָה שֶׁיִּתְרַחֵק מִמֶּנָּה
הָאָדָם. רַבִּי אֱלִיעֶזֶר אוֹמֵר: עַיִן רָעָה. רַבִּי יְהוֹשֻׁעַ אוֹמֵר:
חָבֵר רָע. רַבִּי יוֹסֵי אוֹמֵר: שָׁכֵן רָע. רַבִּי שִׁמְעוֹן אוֹמֵר: הַלּוֶֹה
וְאֵינוּ מְשַׁלֵּם. אֶחָד הַלּוֶֹה מִן הָאָדָם כְּלוֶֹה מִן הַמָּקוֹם,
שֶׁנֶּאֱמַר: לוֶֹה רָשָׁע וְלֹא יְשַׁלֵּם, וְצַדִּיק חוֹנֵן וְנוֹתֵן (תהלים
לז:כא). רַבִּי אֶלְעָזָר אוֹמֵר: לֵב רָע. אָמַר לָהֶם: רוֹאֶה אֲנִי אֶת
דִּבְרֵי אֶלְעָזָר בֶּן עֲרָךְ מִדִּבְרֵיכֶם, שֶׁבִּכְלָל דְּבָרָיו דִּבְרֵיכֶם.

He said to them: Go out and discern which is the evil path
from which a person should distance oneself. Rabbi Eliezer
says: An evil eye. Rabbi Y'hoshua says: A wicked friend. Rabbi
Yosei says: A wicked neighbor. Rabbi Shimon says: One who
borrows and does not repay; one who borrows from another
is like one who borrows from the Omnipresent, as it is said:
"The wicked borrow and do not repay, but the Righteous One
is gracious and gives" (Psalm 37:21). Rabbi Elazar said: A wicked
heart. He [Rabban Yochanan ben Zakkai] said to them: I
prefer the words of Elazar ben Arach to your words, for your
words are included in his words.

IN THE NINETEENTH CENTURY, Johann Wolfgang von Goethe, the
German statesman remembered best for his dramatic work *Faust*, remarked, "One must *be* something in order to *do* something."[107] Inad-
vertently it seems, Goethe articulated one of the most potent aspects
of *Pirkei Avot*'s pedagogical ethos. Rather than simply focusing on what
we could be doing in the world, we need to be concerned with who we
are for the benefit of others. Our external actions emanate from our
inner being, and these actions are cultivated through careful and deliberate study, reflection, and a commitment to the good.

To cultivate one's own virtue, one cannot merely turn toward the
good. One must also shun what is destructive. Once again, following

the lessons from the previous mishnah, which described the positive attributes people should seek, Rabbi Elazar points learners not to aspects of life that are externally dangerous, but to aspects that are internally dangerous. Each of us, no matter our creed or station in life, feels toxic emotions that we must learn to manage and expel. Consistent and attuned spiritual behavior is at the foundation of the ethical practices that allow us to look to our inner selves and see what needs to be improved and strengthened. But this is no mere New Age theology. Indeed, we find that Torah thought itself emphasizes and guides us in the quest toward integrating *musar*—ethical practices—as a matter of course for our daily existence. The Musar movement, quite radically, introduced the idea that the center of our study should not be the Talmud but rather our character traits. Each day, we are to study, reflect, and engage in rigorous exercises to improve our *midot* (character traits). Rabbi Hirsch, in his prominent commentary, writes about the individual "who borrows and does not repay":

> Whatever we receive from this world—and indeed, the entire Universe makes countless contributions to every breath we take on earth—is only a loan granted us to help us strive for and bring about those goals by means of which we advance the welfare of God's world in accordance with God's will as revealed to us in God's Law. . . . The righteous human [*tzaddik*] is not so. Because people place duty above all else and devote their whole lives to its fulfillment, striving solely to "do justice" to God and to God's world, it is the world that owes these holy people a debt of gratitude. And the fewer the good and pleasures these holy people have received from the world, the more does the world owe them; and it is usually as a major "creditor" that the [*tzaddik*] departs from the earth.

Similarly, Oscar Wilde defines a cynic as someone "who knows the price of everything and the value of nothing."[108] If we were to live as cynics, we would squander what makes us unique in the divine scheme of existence. Indeed, acknowledging that our short lives are a gift is the first step toward venturing into the broader universe. We owe a great debt for our existence that we should seek to repay. Paying it forward is more than a social meme; it is a quest. The opportunities to get ahead at the expense of others are everywhere, but when we focus on the gift of life and the debt we owe, we can ground ourselves in our mission. When we do not focus on the gift of life and the debt we owe, when we are ungrateful, we are cynical, which is considered the one of the most dangerous of Jewish sins. Rabbi Yirm'yah bar Abba teaches that a cynic is not able to welcome the Divine Presence (BT *Sotah* 42a).

The heart itself is a potent instrument. Its spiritual and empathetic attributes must be exercised in conjunction with spiritual growth. Therefore, Rabbi Elazar reminds us that before we can distance ourselves from others whom we find troubling, we must first look inward. For that is where our greatest strengths are cultivated.

As we grow older, our knowledge and, thus, our debt to the universe only increase. Susan B. Anthony remarked, "The older I get, the greater power I seem to have to help the world; I am like a snowball—the further I am rolled the more I gain."[109] As we add wisdom in our lives through daily living, we gain much more than years. We develop a sense of the world and what needs to be accomplished. Going through life is a challenging path, tumbling as if through gulches, valleys, plateaus, and nadirs. Yet, through this journey, we cannot forget that we were placed on this earth for a simple purpose: to act humbly and perform deeds of kindness.

2:15

הֵם אָמְרוּ שְׁלֹשָׁה דְבָרִים. רַבִּי אֱלִיעֶזֶר אוֹמֵר: יְהִי כְבוֹד
חֲבֵרְךָ חָבִיב עָלֶיךָ כְּשֶׁלָּךְ וְאַל תְּהִי נוֹחַ לִכְעוֹס. וְשׁוּב יוֹם
אֶחָד לִפְנֵי מִיתָתָךְ. וֶהֱוֵי מִתְחַמֵּם כְּנֶגֶד אוּרָן שֶׁל חֲכָמִים,
וֶהֱוֵי זָהִיר בְּגַחַלְתָּן שֶׁלֹּא תִכָּוֶה – שֶׁנְּשִׁיכָתָן נְשִׁיכַת
שׁוּעָל, וַעֲקִיצָתָן עֲקִיצַת עַקְרָב, וּלְחִישָׁתָן לְחִישַׁת שָׂרָף,
וְכָל דִּבְרֵיהֶם כְּגַחֲלֵי אֵשׁ.

They each said three things. Rabbi Eliezer says: Let your
fellow's honor be as dear to you as your own and do not anger
easily. Repent one day before your death. And warm yourself
by the fire of the sages, but beware of their glowing coal lest
you be burnt—for their bite is the bite of a fox, their sting is
the sting of a scorpion, their hiss is the hiss of a serpent, and
all their words are like fiery coals.

ONE OF THE MOST formidable ontological questions of Jewish existence is this: How can we repent one day before our death if we don't
know when that day will be? Perplexing, which is precisely the point.
We must be in a continual state of self-repair, *t'shuvah*, to ensure that
we are doing all we can to improve ourselves, our relationships, and
the state of the world. Each day, we repent for our mistakes and resolve
them. Each day, we strive to fortify personal intent and strategic rigor
to actualize our unique potential. *T'shuvah* means "to return," to return
to one's most true self.

If someone stole something and that object has been unaltered,
then according to the Torah, the thief must return that stolen object.
If someone stole something but fundamentally altered it (like turning
a stolen piece of wood into a beam holding up a house), however, we
allow the thief to pay back the value of what was stolen rather than the
specific altered stolen object (BT *Bava Kama* 110a). It is prohibited in
Jewish law to prevent someone from doing *t'shuvah* (changing their
ways); we want to be sure to make it possible for people to correct their

mistakes, and so we make it even easier for them to do so. Maimonides teaches that after people have repented, we may not remind them of their mistake or of the type of life they used to live.[110]

In the previous mishnah, Rabbi Eliezer taught that a "good eye" is the central virtue for living a good life. Now he elaborates on the ethical implications of this. Indeed, this requires acknowledging the infinite dignity of every person. In this passage, Rabbi Eliezer hints at three components central to Judaism: the self, the other, and the Divine. Dealing with the self, we learn to control our emotions (anger in particular). Dealing with the other, we learn to honor others. Dealing with the Divine, we learn to remind ourselves of our mortality and the divine bonfire to which every spark will ultimately return.

Anger is the most toxic emotion that can overtake a person. Its ability to influence mood and dictate action makes a person unpredictable and full of misgivings. Anger has the potential to bring about one's downfall. Rabbi Shimon ben Lakish teaches, "Anger deprives the sage of wisdom, the prophet of vision" (BT *P'sachim* 66b). The Sages see the person who lives in a state of anger as a dangerous person, a liability to the community; they eloquently discuss the destructive power of anger:

> Rabbi Yochanan said, "All kinds of *Geihinam* [hell] dominate one who gets angry." Rabbah bar Huna said, "Even the Divine Presence is not important to one who gets angry." Rabbi Yirm'yah said, "One [who is angry] forgets Torah studies and increases in foolishness." Rav Nachman said, "It is certain that one has many sins." (BT *N'darim* 22a)

In this mishnah, the Sages are wise to connect dishonoring others with anger. It is difficult to care about the honor of another as much as we care about our own. Human defense mechanisms ensure that we're constantly in survival and self-preservation mode. Nevertheless, we should do all we can to balance moral commitments to self and to others. At the least, we should never gain honor at the expense of others. We need to ensure that we go out of our way to honor others, as they wish to be honored. Gaining control of our emotions is important to treating others with dignity, even when we experience challenging moments.

In a seminal treatise about the challenges of Judaism's relationship with modernity, Rabbi Joseph B. Soloveitchik writes:

> To recognize a person is not just to identify him physically. It is more than that: it is an act of identifying him existentially, as a person who has a job to do, that only he can do properly. To recognize a person means to affirm that he is irreplaceable. To hurt a person means to tell him that he is expendable, that there is no need for him. The *halachah* equated the act of publicly embarrassing a person with murder.[111]

The Sages of the Talmud were not alone in speaking to this idea. The later era of the kabbalists believed that when one becomes angry, one's soul departs.[112] It is only human to feel a full range of emotions, and we should not suppress them, but we are taught to use self-control, especially over emotions and consequent actions that can harm others. In his commentary on this verse, Rabbi Hirsch thinks deeply about how we should reverse our inclinations toward anger: "Rather than feeling anger at your friend's conduct, think of your own shortcomings and work unceasingly at the improvement of your own character." Likewise, the fifteenth-century Italian rabbi Obadiah ben Abraham Bartenura explains why honoring others is juxtaposed in our mishnah with controlling our anger: because each is the prerequisite to the other.[113]

Although this mishnah warns us about the Sages, they are not and should not be thought of as dangerous. Sadly, there are countless stories of rabbis shaming their rabbinical students in order to uphold the highest intellectual standards, but in so doing causing injury and scars that carried into the professional lives of those students once they themselves became rabbis. Rabbi Eliezer, the author of this mishnah, was excommunicated by the Sages, not because he wasn't brilliant in his own way, but because he refused to submit to the will of the majority. His influence as one of the most esteemed Torah minds of his era was not enough to shield him from the swift retribution for not following along with the stated opinions of his colleagues. Thus, this teaching about being burned and bitten, which is so pained in its rendering, likely emerged from Rabbi Eliezer's psychological struggle between hubris and acceptance; these internal scars never properly healed.

Though the teachings of the Sages may seem caustic to our modern sensibilities, they are presented to us as challenges so that we can improve ourselves. The Sages neither sugarcoat their words, nor protect the egos of learners. We must get close to our teachers and leaders who hold onto ancient wisdom, so that they can guide us and let us grow. We should also be cognizant that the closer we get, the higher the likelihood that they will challenge us beyond our comfort zone. This is essential to development of the human(e) being.

2:16

רַבִּי יְהוֹשֻׁעַ אוֹמֵר: עַיִן הָרַע, וְיֵצֶר הָרַע, וְשִׂנְאַת הַבְּרִיּוֹת
מוֹצִיאִין אֶת הָאָדָם מִן הָעוֹלָם.

Rabbi Yehoshua says: An evil eye, the evil inclination, and
hatred of other people [all] remove a person from the world.

THIS MISHNAH PRESENTS us with a direct challenge: What most negatively influences us? There is a real existential danger that evil will creep
into our lives, and this assumes that evil can be objectively known. Nonetheless, we must protect ourselves from influences that would stain our
souls should we act upon them. We must exercise a cautious eye and neither heed the voice of anger from within nor feel hatred for others. We
will never achieve heavenly peace in this world if we do not subdue these
negative forces and redirect them toward acts of charity and kindness.
Rabbi Moshe Cordovero, a sixteenth-century kabbalist who lived in the
mystical city of Safed, teaches, "All souls are united with each other since
they all stem from the first person's soul. To love another is to love oneself!"[114] Rabbi Cordovero's teaching has remarkably relevant modern-
day applications. We have all been witness to the schismatic nature of
contemporary society, where political or social classifications matter
more than individual character. There are individuals in power whose
only wish is to divide us, to make us unequal, and to make us afraid of
one another. Resisting their hatred preserves our souls.

When we are unable to resist, we remove ourselves from the world.
What does this mean?

"Removal from the world" suggests that we no longer live to achieve
our potential. We are no longer "alive" in the spiritual sense. When
we devolve into pure negativity or get dragged down by our negative
perception, we can no longer see objectively. We can no longer fulfill
our purpose of emulating the Divine through acts dedicated to love
and kindness. To counter this self-absorption that removes us from
the world, we must focus on the other. Elie Wiesel, of blessed memory,

writes, "To say, 'I suffer, therefore I am' is to become the enemy of man. What you must say is 'I suffer, therefore you are.'"[115]

Following Wiesel's line of thought, Mother Teresa comments that the suffering of others needs to be felt to be considered tangible:

> It is not enough for us to say: "I love God, but I do not love my neighbor." Saint John says that you are a liar if you say you love God and you don't love your neighbor. How can you love God whom you do not see, if you do not love your neighbor whom you see, whom you touch, with whom you live?"[116]

The Ari-zal, Rabbi Isaac Luria (sixteenth century, Safed), teaches that before we declare our love for God in prayer, we must look around and feel love for the human beings who are present with us.[117] God is not interested in our professions of love if we hate or lack love for God's creations. We are obligated to resist the thought that everyone is out to get us. We are more than that part of the subconscious that reacts at the basest level. We are transcendent beings, capable of reaching marvelous heights when we stave off the base part of ourselves that is most influenced by the evil eye. It is easy to succumb to its temptation, but virtuous to repel it.

We will never eliminate the scourge of wickedness from the world if we fight evil with evil, hate with hate, rage with rage. Judea Pearl, father of *Wall Street Journal* writer Daniel Pearl, who was murdered by Islamic terrorists in 2002, was asked why he was still willing to work toward reconciliation between Muslims and Jews. He responded by saying, "Hate killed my son. Therefore, I am determined to fight hate." And, most poignantly, Dr. Martin Luther King Jr. wrote, "Darkness cannot drive out darkness; only light can do that. Hate cannot drive out hate; only love can do that."[118]

2:17

רַבִּי יוֹסֵי אוֹמֵר: יְהִי מָמוֹן חֲבֵרְךָ חָבִיב עָלֶיךָ כְּשֶׁלָּךְ. וְהַתְקֵן
עַצְמְךָ לִלְמוֹד תּוֹרָה, שֶׁאֵינָהּ יְרֻשָּׁה לָךְ. וְכָל מַעֲשֶׂיךָ יִהְיוּ
לְשֵׁם שָׁמָיִם.

Rabbi Yosei says: Let your fellow's money be as dear to you as
your own. Apply yourself to Torah study, for it is not yours by
inheritance. And let all your deeds be for the sake of heaven.

AN UNFORTUNATE by-product of a good education is that the student
who has attained it can become arrogant. People like this boast about
their grades or their degrees, or where they went to college, or they
purposely use words others will not understand. People boast about
their Jewish education, too; students might brag about their grasp of
the minutiae of obscure laws or teachings from the Sages. The focus on
the status of the learning—rather than the learning itself—is anathema
to the humility that Jewish learning is meant to cultivate. That is exactly what is going on in this mishnah. Here, Rabbi Yosei says that we,
as perpetual students, should be humble. We should not take Jewish
wisdom for granted as a deserved "inheritance," but we should find the
conscientiousness to strive with a humble and curious spirit.

Even the Sages' children are not guaranteed an "inheritance" in
Torah. Moses, the greatest prophet in Judaism, had a grandson who
became a pagan priest (Judges 18:30; BT *Bava Batra* 109b). Perhaps
because of the pressure to keep up appearances as the child of a rabbi or
preacher, it can be more difficult to remain committed to an inherited
Torah and to always perform at the highest levels that others demand
(i.e., one can suffer from what has come to be called "preacher's kid
syndrome").

Rabbi Yosei applies the value of humility to various realms: the public
realm (financial matters and how we project ourselves to the world), the
private realm (Torah study and how we project ourselves to our family
and friends), and our inner realm (acting for the sake of heaven and unseen forces of eternity). In each case, there is the danger of focusing too

much on ourselves, rather than our effect on others. We might focus on money, we might feel smug in our Jewish knowledge but not develop emotional intelligence, or we might act merely for self-advancement. Rabbi Yosei pushes us to see the bigger picture.

Feelings of competitiveness, envy, or inadequacy should not block our basic inclination toward human solidarity with others. In his commentary on this verse, Rabbi Hirsch writes:

> Even as we take care to preserve our own wealth and to increase it, so, too, it is not enough merely not to be envious of the wealth of our fellow-man or to view it with unconcern; we should be happy when another prospers. . . . We should rejoice at any opportunity we may have to help another improve their lot.

Natalia Ginzburg, an Italian anti-Fascist anarchist, describes the link between money and self-worth: "Being moderate with oneself and generous with others; this is what is meant by having a just relationship with money."[119] How we spend money indicates core values and is as much a social/political act as taking to the streets. But we rarely consider this because of the mechanized nature of spending. We spend several dollars on a drink or t-shirt, not thinking about the people on the other side who manufactured, transported, designed, or grew the components needed to make the product. Understanding even the smallest parts of the ethics of money, spending, and consumption will develop our empathy—that part of ourselves that cares for people whom we will never meet.

"And let all your deeds be for the sake of heaven." To account not only for self-interest but also for other-interest requires humility. Many centuries after the great Sages, Maimonides wrote about humility in leadership:

> One should be gracious and merciful to the small and the great, involving oneself in their good and welfare. One should protect the honor of even the humblest of people. When one speaks to the people as a community, one should speak gently, as in "Listen, my brothers and my people . . ." [King David's words in I Chronicles 28:2]. Similarly, I Kings 12:7 states, "If today you will be a servant

of these people. . . ." One should always conduct oneself with great humility. There is no one greater than Moses, our teacher. Yet, he said, "What is our part? Your grumbling is . . . not against us!" (Exodus 16:8). One should bear the nation's difficulties, burdens, complaints, and anger "as a caretaker carries an infant" (Numbers 11:12).[120]

Humility stands at the center of our private lives. But it is also the foundation of public leadership. It is not self-deprecating but empowering, as we expand ourselves by expanding our consciousness toward others. C. S. Lewis has been attributed with the notion that humility is not about thinking less of oneself but about thinking of oneself less.[121]

In whatever we pursue, all our deeds should "be for the sake of heaven." Some might think that because they're moving toward just ends, we can get there through any means. Yet the Torah teaches us, *Tzedek tzedek tirdof*—"Justice, justice, you shall pursue" (Deuteronomy 16:20)! The word "justice" is repeated here to emphasize that moral means must be used to get to the just end.

It is easy to sequester religion to the sanctuary. But Judaism is meant to be lived in the streets, in the offices, in the schools, and in the privacy of our homes. Why does this teaching on the importance of motives appear next to one focused on concern for others' money? In order to highlight that our business ethics and the cultivation of a compassionate marketplace, which on the surface appear to be essentially mundane aspects of human life, are actually crucial components to living a holy life.

2:18

רַבִּי שִׁמְעוֹן אוֹמֵר: הֱוֵי זָהִיר בִּקְרִיאַת שְׁמַע וּבִתְפִלָּה,
וּכְשֶׁאַתָּה מִתְפַּלֵּל אַל תַּעַשׂ תְּפִלָּתְךָ קֶבַע, אֶלָּא רַחֲמִים
וְתַחֲנוּנִים לִפְנֵי הַמָּקוֹם, שֶׁנֶּאֱמַר: כִּי־חַנּוּן וְרַחוּם הוּא,
אֶרֶךְ אַפַּיִם וְרַב־חֶסֶד, וְנִחָם עַל־הָרָעָה (יואל ב:יג). וְאַל תְּהִי
רָשָׁע בִּפְנֵי עַצְמָךְ.

Rabbi Shimon says: Be meticulous in reading the *Sh'ma* and in
prayer. When you pray, do not make your prayer a set routine,
but rather [meditate on] compassion and supplication before
the Omnipresent, as it is said: "For God is gracious and
compassionate, slow to anger, abounding in kindness, and
repents of the evil" (Joel 2:13). And do not judge yourself to be a
wicked person.

ACCORDING TO THE TALMUD, "God does not act tyrannically toward God's creatures" (BT *Avodah Zarah* 3a). God is merciful. God is
just. God exists in the universe so that everything can be suffused with
holiness. While Jewish truths branch off toward both the general and
the esoteric, this truth is central: we are to emulate the Divine and, in
turn, become beings of holy compassion. This requires rigorous prayer,
study, and discipline. For any person, being spiritually attuned is a difficult pursuit. Yet, the rewards—be they spiritual, communal, or personal—are immense. Cesar Chavez, the twentieth-century Latino and
immigrant worker-rights organizer, teaches, "We must understand
that the highest form of freedom carries with it the greatest measure
of discipline."[122]

In this mishnah, Rabbi Shimon sets up the ideological framework
for compassion. He believed that prayer makes humans more compassionate and that by being engaged actively in prayer, people can become
more like God (whose compassion stretches across the expanse of the
universe). The quintessential approach to Jewish spirituality is to emulate the ways of God, which is foremost expressed through compassion

and kindness to others. Cultivating an understanding of ourselves as considerate and caring people—especially to strangers and the vulnerable—heightens our relationship with the Divine.

The declaration of *echad*—One—in the *Sh'ma* can be understood in several ways: (1) there is only one God; (2) God is unified (is one); (3) God is everything (the entirety of oneness). For the Jewish people, these aren't simply religious statements. Indeed, these are also ethical principles. How so? Because these constituent pieces of the *Sh'ma* define the manner by which Jews understand our metaphysical relationship with the Divine. Even though we may not comprehend exactly what this means, we are nonetheless gifted the intellectual tools to decipher these intangible qualities of the universe.

On the other hand, such thoughts lead to another question: What does the phrase "Do not make your prayer a set routine" mean? Aren't the repetitive structure and scheduled timing of prayers routine? Maimonides teaches that "any prayer uttered without mental concentration is not prayer. If a service has been recited without such concentration, it must be recited again devoutly."[123] While prayer needs "set routine" to achieve consistency and growth, this mishnah suggests that overemphasis of such routines strip prayer of meaning by rendering it rote. We should not make stagnant our opportunity for divine contact.

In ancient Platonic theology, the concept of multiple gods implies multiple sources of heavenly authority and morality (what we might call moral relativism). Embracing one God means there is but one moral truth, since there is only one moral authority. Here theology and ethics intersect. Within Judaism, this singular entity is the moral authority that holds the cosmos together.

Offering supplication to this Moral Authority is a difficult concept. How many of us know people who attend services only because they feel compelled, or because it is mere habit? That is not to say they are simply going through the motions, but rather that gratitude, introspection, joy—everything that should be meaningful in prayer—are secondary to the habit of the ritual.

Rabbi Abraham Joshua Heschel's vision for prayer goes beyond the notion of ritual for the sake of ritual:

> Prayer is meaningless unless it is subversive, unless it seeks to overthrow and to ruin the pyramids of callousness, hatred, opportunism, falsehoods. The liturgical movement must become a revolutionary movement, seeking to overthrow the forces that continue to destroy the promise, the hope, the vision.[124]

This revolutionary liturgical movement should awaken us to the urgent needs of other human beings. If we embrace the radical ontological notion that every human is created in the image of God, then it is our obligatory honor to show deference to the infinite dignity in every person. Treating others with kindness and dignity, no matter their class, their actions, or station in life, is commensurate with the building of a just, equitable world.

This is not a peripheral point to the Torah. Rabbi Akiva taught that the great principle of the Torah is to love one's fellow as oneself.[125] Implied is that one must love oneself. As a Chasidic teaching goes: In our era, more important than believing in God is believing that God believes in us.

In our effort to connect with the Divine, we will make mistakes. But in doing so, we should not get down on ourselves. S'forno writes, "And do not judge yourself to be a wicked person . . . if you do err, you should realize that rectification is possible, and repent in a state of remorse over the evil."[126] Rabbi Hirsch demonstrates in his commentary on this mishnah that one should not be "crushed by guilt" and should not believe "that it is solely through the gracious intercession of another that one can gain control over evil and be delivered from the burden of their sin." One must instead believe in oneself, one's potential, and one's actual goodness.

Praying as Rabbi Shimon suggests is our eternal task. If through prayer we allow the ethos of compassion to enter our ecosystem, we will gain the capacity to alter the great mountains and bend the mighty rivers toward the pursuit of justice.

2:19

רַבִּי אֶלְעָזָר אוֹמֵר: הֱוֵי שָׁקוּד לִלְמוֹד מַה שֶּׁתָּשִׁיב
לְאֶפִּיקוֹרוֹס, וְדַע לִפְנֵי מִי אַתָּה עָמֵל, וּמִי הוּא בַּעַל
מְלַאכְתָּךְ.

Rabbi Elazar says: Be diligent to study how to answer a heretic. Know before Whom you toil. And know whom you work
for and who pays your wages.

THIS MISHNAH presents stark power dynamics: holy versus heretical,
God above human, and employer in relationship to employee. What is
the deeper meaning? Why should we "know what to answer a heretic"?
Knowledge is not meant to exist in a vacuum, nor should it be used
merely to refute those who do not grasp Jewish theology or any other
theology. Rather, by engaging with those who reject the truths that we
hold dear, we show our true inner power, our wisdom. We are never
to turn away from intellectual diversity and ideological pluralism. We
should know how to answer, because we must always be considering
the counter-argument.

There may be a Jewish imperative to study ideas that we consider
heretical. Consider this from Rabbi Kook:

> The basic thrust of this kind of tolerance is to find a place for every
> form of illumination, of life, and of spiritual expression. It knows
> that there is a spark of light in everything and that the divine spark
> of light shines in all the various belief systems, as so many different
> pedagogics for the culture of humanity, to improve the spiritual
> and material existence, the present and the future of the individual
> and of society. . . . Therefore, instead of rejecting every pattern of
> ideas from which the tiny elements of good have begun to sparkle
> . . . a task which is bound to fail, it is for us to enhance the original
> light. It is for us to disclose the breadth and the depth, the compre-
> hensiveness and the eternity that is immanent in the light of the
> faith of Israel. It is for us to clarify how every spark of the good that
> is manifest in the world stems from its source and is linked within

a natural bond. Then will all the sparks newly made manifest add light and life to the soul of the people mighty in its spiritual vitality, in its divine potency. . . . This type of tolerance is bound to spread so that the human spirit will be able to find the divine spark hidden in everything, and to automatically discard all dross.[127]

Thinking critically and openly, rather than blindly following authorities and texts, is an imperative. Avoiding enriching, honest disagreement is folly. Jewish values dissuade us from blindly outsourcing interpretation and meaning-making to teachers and authorities. This would be the fallacy of accepting authority. Rabbi Chayim of Volozhin ruled that it is forbidden for a student to accept his or her teacher's words without understanding them fully.[128]

Rabbi Elazar modeled the proper teachings of faith. This is not an easy task. For Rabbi Elazar, maintaining faith in an ever-evolving, complex world requires three elements:

1. Being prepared for external challenges
2. Keeping ever conscious of the Divine
3. Remembering that there is a God of justice who is in control of the universe

To accept this, however, we must move beyond ideas that sustained previous generations but do not sustain our own. The renowned philosopher Isaiah Berlin explains, "The history of thought and culture is, as [Georg] Hegel showed with great brilliance, a changing pattern of great liberating ideas which turn inevitably into suffocating straitjackets."[129] And indeed, redemptive Jewish ideas can become stale and irrelevant in a new era. Rabbi David Hartman comments that "a sacred text is a text that haunts me all the time—but it doesn't paralyze me."[130] Ideas that shake us out of the torpor of everyday mediocrity, even those with which we vehemently disagree, are worth at least a cursory glance. We *should* have trepidation in the process of reinterpreting texts, but we need courage to face them when the opportunity arises.

Rabbi Elazar's three principles are sensible given society's drift away from reflection and critical analysis. Indeed, since lack of self-reflection and an increasing indifference toward ethical truths are real threats to civilization, we should train the cognitive faculties toward eternity's great questions. It is too easy for one to be pulled away from inspired faith and purpose-directed living. Other truths emerge, and the path becomes a labyrinth, making it a challenge to focus on the truth.

The enterprise of pursuing truth requires an important hermeneutical qualification. One can look at the world and see only evil and suffering. One could also see only miraculous beauty. We should follow the advice of folksinger-activist Pete Seeger: "The key to the future of the world is finding the optimistic stories and letting them be known."[131] This is about us. Only us. As Marcel Proust explains, "The voyage of discovery consists not in seeking new landscapes but in having new eyes."[132] One can look and see the rampant violence and vanity and forget that there is a Creator who breathes life into us and is present at every moment. Here, the cosmological implications of our being become tangible. This is where faith is born, developed, and understood.

Like every teaching, Rabbi Elazar's comes from a personal place. Rabbi Elazar moved away from the Sages to live in greater comfort and so he focused less on spiritual ideals (BT *Shabbat* 147b). There, he declined spiritually and intellectually. When he is reminding us to "be diligent in the study of Torah," he is teaching from his personal experience, having slipped away from a rigorous routine committed to intellectual and spiritual growth.

To sustain this commitment, one needs friends. Once, Rabbi Tarfon (who was known as a wealthy man) approached his friend Rabbi Akiva and asked him to invest a substantial amount of money for him. Rabbi Akiva instead donated the money to vulnerable people in the community. When Rabbi Akiva showed Rabbi Tarfon the impact this had, Rabbi Tarfon gave him even more money to "invest."[133] This anecdote raises the critical point that one of the most powerful strategies to reach the highest standards of personal excellence and growth is to surround ourselves with others who help to raise us up.

2:20

רַבִּי טַרְפוֹן אוֹמֵר: הַיּוֹם קָצָר, וְהַמְּלָאכָה מְרֻבָּה, וְהַפּוֹעֲלִים
עֲצֵלִים, וְהַשָּׂכָר הַרְבֵּה, וּבַעַל הַבַּיִת דּוֹחֵק.

Rabbi Tarfon says: The day is short, the task is abundant,
the laborers are lazy, the wage is great, and the Master of the
house is insistent.

THIS MISHNAH is remarkable in the Jewish philosophical canon. In
the economy of a single sentence, Rabbi Tarfon lays out a Jewish apothegm of a life dedicated to hard work in a hard world. And certainly,
a critical Jewish task is to become a person who values the remarkable
nature of time. Every day, people rush from urgency to urgency because
of feelings of deep responsibility. But it is a spiritual art to be in a state
of rush, accomplishing as much as possible as effectively as possible,
while also remaining focused and calm. We are divided, consumed by
an overabundance of commitments, and yet we are to be present, focused, and attentive. We are to sprint, while remaining aware of every
footfall. While we continue to act and lead, we also must reflect deeply
about the nature of our leadership and our purpose in the world.

Our days are short. Our lives are busy. We have obligations to meet:
work, family, health, recreation, and attending to our spiritual needs.
Balancing these disparate aspects of life is difficult. But we must find
balance; it is commanded of us. Rabbi Moshe Chayim Luzzatto, in his
eighteenth-century magnum opus on the cultivation of Jewish virtues,
The Path of the Just, teaches:

> Alacrity consists of two elements: one that relates to the period
> prior to the commencement of a deed, and the other that relates
> to the period that follows the commencement of a deed. The for-
> mer means that prior to the commencement of a mitzvah a person
> must not delay [its performance]. Rather, when its time arrives, or
> when the opportunity [for its fulfillment] presents itself, or when it
> enters his mind, he must react speedily, without delay, to seize the
> mitzvah and to do it. He must not procrastinate at this time, for

no danger is graver than this. Every new moment can bring with it some new hindrance to the fulfillment of the good deed.[134]

Some changes in life happen quickly, and others take a long time. Consider how Michael Walzer, professor emeritus at the Institute for Advanced Study in Princeton, New Jersey, explains the biblical journey from slavery in Egypt to redemption in Israel:

> Physically, the escape from Egypt is sudden, glorious, complete; spiritually and politically, it is very slow, a matter of two steps forward, one step back. I want to stress this is a lesson from the Exodus experience again and again.[135]

Dionne Brand, a Canadian poet and essayist from Trinidad and Tobago, explains:

> Revolutions do not happen outside of you, they happen in the vein, they change you and you change yourself, you wake up in the morning changing. You say this is the human being I want to be. You are making yourself for the future, and you do not even know the extent of it when you begin but you have a hint, a taste in your throat of the warm elixir of the possible.[136]

While not every person is meant to be a revolutionary, taking on the mantle of leadership and creating local change are within reach for those who choose. Embracing this mission while "the day is short" means that we must "taste . . . the warm elixir of the possible." Social change can happen quickly when a president signs a new law or when a new nation declares independence. Events can spiral in unintended directions at the behest of a small but vocal group. But spiritual and cultural changes take a long time to shift. Slavery was prohibited in America, but more than a century and a half later, we're still dealing with the racial injustice that the practice of slavery set in motion.

And to be sure, the fact that injustice continues to fester shows that the work to improve the world can never cease. We must engage deeply in the issues that affect countless people and propel the world toward justice.

2:21

הוּא הָיָה אוֹמֵר: לֹא עָלֶיךָ הַמְּלָאכָה לִגְמֹר, וְלֹא אַתָּה בֶן
חוֹרִין לִבָּטֵל. אִם לָמַדְתָּ תוֹרָה הַרְבֵּה, נוֹתְנִין לָךְ שָׂכָר
הַרְבֵּה. וְנֶאֱמָן הוּא בַּעַל מְלַאכְתָּךְ שֶׁיְשַׁלֶּם לָךְ שְׂכַר
פְּעֻלָּתָךְ. וְדַע שֶׁמַּתַּן שְׂכָרָן שֶׁל צַדִּיקִים לֶעָתִיד לָבֹא.

He used to say: You are not required to complete the task, yet
you are not free to desist from it. If you have studied much
Torah, they will give you great reward; and your Employer
can be relied upon to pay you the wage for your labor, but be
aware that the reward of the righteous will be given in the
world-to-come.

As CHAPTER 2 of *Pirkei Avot* closes, it leaves learners with an admonition: *There is much work still to be done.* We cannot withdraw from this
work, even when we know we might not win. There are so many barriers to acting on our core values. "Wisdom is knowing what to do next.
Virtue is doing it," explains David Starr Jordan, the founding president
of Stanford University.[137] The capacity not only to inculcate virtue, but
also to expend it daily, requires quiet courage, wise discernment, a little
bit of chutzpah, and a lot of heart. These ingredients are the recipe for a
virtuous society and for an animated soul. "Without courage we cannot
practice any other virtue with consistency. We can't be kind, true, merciful, generous, or honest," says Maya Angelou.[138]

This mishnah helps us understand Judaism's eternal role as the spiritual beacon that enables us to develop empathy and compassion. It
is easy to excuse ourselves from hard communal work because it feels
as though our contribution can be insignificantly minimal. A litany
of questions arises: In the aggregate, what could one person do? Why
donate hard-earned wages? Why sign a petition? Why start an advocacy
group? Why show up to a rally? Why vote? I'm but one person; what
could my role possibly be in an ocean of other interests? But the Rabbis teach that our act may be precisely the one that tips the scales. As a

matter of central principle and faith, Jews must never desist from active participation in society and communal concerns.

Maimonides expounds on this. He suggests that people should embrace the thought experiment that our next act might be the one that tips the universal scales, either toward the destruction of the world or toward its redemption.[139] Unfortunately, we will never know which acts tip the scales; this knowledge is not obtainable by humans. Nonetheless, it should be enough to spark action.

The following Talmudic passage reminds us that we don't ultimately strive for the perfection of the world in our lifetime. Rather, our contributions are aimed at providing a better life for the next generation.

> One day he [Choni the Circle Drawer] was journeying on the road and he saw a man planting a carob tree; he asked him, "How long does it take [for this tree] to bear fruit?" The man replied, "Seventy years."
>
> He then further asked him, "Are you certain that you will live another seventy years?" The man replied, "I found [ready grown] carob trees in the world; as my ancestors planted these for me, so I too plant these for my children." (BT *Taanit* 23a)

At the same time, one must embrace humility. To accept that we will not be the ones to complete the world's most important work, we should learn the mystical concept of *tzimtzum*. By embracing *tzimtzum*, we can emulate the divine capacity to step back from control over the world and let action take its course. Every creative act requires both exertion and contraction. The Rabbis teach that we learn this from the creation of the world:

> Rabbi Y'hudah said in the name of Rav: When God created the world, it expanded and continued to extend itself like two threads of a loom's warp, until God rebuked it, and stopped it, as it says, "The pillars of the heavens trembled [moved], and were astonished [into a standstill] by God's rebuke" (Job 26:11). And this is what Reish Lakish said: What is the meaning of the verse "I am El Shaddai" (Genesis 35:11)? [It means] I am the One who told the world "enough." (BT *Chagigah* 12a)

Going forth into the world to promote change and seek harmony is a sacred task. We are to embrace the potential to change the world, while embracing the impermanence of our lives and all things. We are to learn to attach, but also to detach. To learn, but also to unlearn. To grow in our knowledge, but shrink in our humility. Mastering such human traits and becoming a more well-rounded person are beyond desirable. These skills are essential.

As chapter 2 concludes, our task becomes less ambiguous. We are to act. We are to be involved with the affairs of the world, no matter the difficulty of the task. No matter how much we want to resist taking the mantle of spiritual leadership, it is in our interest to pursue holy work. This doesn't mean we all have to become rabbis or join the clergy. Instead, our task is to take the inherent gifts we have and actualize them in the world. Wherever we may be on our Jewish journey, there is always another step to take. We are to treat every moment and every action as enormously significant in the long arc of the universe. Even the smallest action has the potential to send ripples across the great beyond to affect countless others, as well as others who have yet to be.

Chapter 3

3:א

עֲקַבְיָא בֶּן מַהֲלַלְאֵל אוֹמֵר: הִסְתַּכֵּל בִּשְׁלֹשָׁה דְבָרִים וְאֵין
אַתָּה בָא לִידֵי עֲבֵרָה – דַּע מֵאַיִן בָּאתָ, וּלְאָיִן אַתָּה הוֹלֵךְ,
וְלִפְנֵי מִי אַתָּה עָתִיד לִתֵּן דִּין וְחֶשְׁבּוֹן. מֵאַיִן בָּאתָ – מִטִּפָּה
סְרוּחָה. וּלְאָן אַתָּה הוֹלֵךְ – לִמְקוֹם עָפָר רִמָּה וְתוֹלֵעָה.
וְלִפְנֵי מִי אַתָּה עָתִיד לִתֵּן דִּין וְחֶשְׁבּוֹן – לִפְנֵי מֶלֶךְ מַלְכֵי
הַמְּלָכִים, הַקָּדוֹשׁ בָּרוּךְ הוּא.

Akavya ben Mahalalel said: Consider three things and you will
not come into the grip of sin: Know where you came from, to
where you are going, and before whom you will give justification and reckoning. "Where you came from?"—from a putrid
drop; "to where you are going?"—to a place of dust, worms,
and maggots; "and before Whom you will give justification
and reckoning?"—before the Ruler of Emperors, the Holy
One of Blessing.

MOVING INTO the third chapter of *Pirkei Avot*, we have read the philosophical foundations for Judaism's ethical practices. Over time, the application of these practices flourished. Today, we recognize the modern
rendering of these ancient teaching as *musar*, the movement of spiritual
and ethical development that emerged and flourished in the nineteenth
century. The two primary schools of thought in *musar* are Novarodok
and Slobodka, each named after the place where it matured, each stressing distinct types of personal development. The Novarodok academy
emphasizes the lowliness of the self, while Slobodka emphasizes the
self as repository for human nobility.[140] This mishnah fits neatly within
the philosophy of the Novarodok school, emphasizing that our physical
body will decay. If we embrace impermanence, why do we obsess about
our physical appearance? Who doesn't struggle today with insecurity
about their body, the projection of self that yearns to conform to the
normative notion of beauty? It is a sad challenge, endemic in our time.
Kabbalah, on the other hand, instructs us to dismiss these concerns,

teaching that each of our bodies is a unique representation of the Divine. A crooked nose? A bigger body type? Large ears? They are all part of the divine manifestation in the world. We are created in the image of God. You are. I am. All of us are. We can cherish the body we've been given and connect more deeply with the eternal soul housed within the body we've been gifted; indeed, we can start a body-image revolution. Or we can ignore these and pursue a life of cheap ostentation and material emptiness. The choice is ultimately ours.

However, standing at a graveside, staring down into the black hole into which the body will be lowered, who is not humbled by the lowliness of the self? Virtually no one will remember our names after our deaths. Realizing our own relative insignificance can bring us to despair. Or to hedonism—*just eat, drink, and be merry, for tomorrow we die*. But the religious response in this mishnah is the exact opposite. Rather, we can do *t'shuvah* to engage in self-transformation to return to our fundamentally good selves, our inner divine spark. This return to God can inspire awe in us mere mortals and a desire to become our best selves.

The Rabbis explain how the three remembrances from this mishnah are derived from the word for Creator:

> There are three variations: *boreicha* [your Creator], *borcha* [your pit], *b'eircha* [your well]. "Your well" refers to the putrid moisture; "your pit" refers to worms and maggots; "your Creator" refers to the King of kings, the Holy One of Blessing, before whom you will give judgment and reckoning.[141]

What gives us a sense of permanence is our attachment to the Eternal. Rather than seek external gain as the highest reward, we can seek to do what is right, regardless of who is watching. When Moses first went up on Mount Sinai to bring down the Ten Commandments, there was the sound of a shofar blasting, thunder, and lightning. Everyone heard the voice of God. But those tablets were broken. Then, his receipt of the second set of tablets occurred in silence, without attention or publicity. Rabbi Yaakov Culi—the MeAm Loez, an eighteenth-century Turkish Bible commentator—points to this story to demonstrate how good acts done privately have a more lasting impact than good acts done publicly.

We know the opposite can be true, as well. Often, when good acts are done publicly, they can encourage others to follow suit. We are to engage in both private good acts and public good acts. The key is to be the same in private as we are in public.

It makes sense that Akavya ben Mahalalel is the one teaching us to zoom out from our current context to see the bigger heavenly picture. He is a Talmudic hero who exemplified intellectual courage. When pressured to accept majority views, he would not capitulate. Offered a prestigious position if he would retract his views, he refused. When told he would be deemed a fool if he didn't accept the position, he responded, "It would be better for me to be called a fool all my life rather than be wicked in the eyes of God for even one moment" (Mishnah *Eduyot* 5:6). Yet, on his deathbed, he advised his children to follow the majority view rather than his, because he didn't believe others were bound by his own convictions, not even his children (Mishnah *Eduyot* 5:7).

We are encouraged, perhaps shallowly, to follow our dreams and reach for the stars. But often, such guidance presents a distorted view of destiny. Just because we dream of attending an Ivy League school, finding our one true love, changing the world, or pursuing the most fulfilling work doesn't mean that these will happen. No, it takes more than the stuff of fairy-tale magic to see our dreams come to life. We have to embody our dreams, to make them real. We have to work toward making them become tangible. It is not a simple path. Where we come from, where we end up—these are part of the continuum of a divine plan unknowable to the human mind. But should we have the determination to avoid the pitfalls of despair, our innermost hopes will spring forth at the least expected moments. When our incorporeal selves gaze upon our gravestones, they won't focus on the numbers that represent the years of our life. Instead, they will focus on the dash in between our birth date and death date, for those are the years when our lives—and all of our hopes, dreams, and triumphs—truly happened.

3:2

רַבִּי חֲנִינָא סְגַן הַכֹּהֲנִים אוֹמֵר: הֱוֵי מִתְפַּלֵּל בִּשְׁלוֹמָהּ שֶׁל
מַלְכוּת, שֶׁאִלְמָלֵא מוֹרָאָהּ אִישׁ אֶת רֵעֵהוּ חַיִּים בָּלָעְנוּ.

Rabbi Chanina, the deputy *Kohein Gadol* [High Priest], says:
Pray for the welfare of the government, because if not for
people's fear of it, we would have swallowed each other alive.

So far in our *Pirkei Avot* journey, the teachings have focused on
cultivating the inner self to serve the broader world. This mishnah,
however, focuses on society's elites, rather than its vulnerable. Rabbi
Chanina compels us to ponder the social constructs, power dynamics,
and ethical responses to those who may not live up to society's ideals.
No simple task, considering the danger for often powerless Jewish
communities living under hostile governments.

According to Brandeis University historian Jonathan Sarna, Rabbi
Chanina is referring to the leaders of Rome.[142] Rome's cruelty scarred
the Jewish psyche; the Jewish people have never quite recovered from
the Romans' destructive impact on Judaism. Despite the burning hatred for Rome, outright revolt is not called for in this mishnah. Why
the self-restraint?

Let's step back and ask another question. Why should Jews, as a holy
nation, pray for the welfare of any government? Don't we assume that
inhospitable governments and their officials would act counter to the
interests of the Jewish people and counter to the most cherished of
Jewish values?

It's complicated. The prophet Jeremiah said that we are to "seek the
peace of the city into which I have caused you to be carried away cap-
tives, and pray to God for it; for in its peace shall you have peace" (Jeremiah 29:7). We are obliged to pray for government officials because this
is how to keep peace—through at least the appearance of respectful
deference to the leader when Jewish self-rule is not attainable. Is this
the best method? Debatable. But it is preferable to seem openly impo-
lite toward a government with all the power.

Absent Jewish self-determination, our people's historical relationship to multiple governing powers has been complicated—including many periods in which Jewish life under gentile governments has been made nearly unbearable by cruelty, mass deportations, baseless bigotry, and genocide. During periods of relative calm, Jews were often subjected to harsh tax penalties and limited mobility within social, economic, and religious structures. We were second-class citizens at absolute best.

Why, then, should Jews "pray for the welfare" of governments we know are corrupt, violent, and filled with evil people? Because the alternative to government is anarchy. Anarchy is something that the Sages were loath to accept. Nonetheless, sometimes regimes are too unjust or even evil to be prayed for. Rather, our response should be resistance and civil disobedience. One prays in vain if it is for the welfare of the Nazi regime, for Stalin, or for contemporary dictators who murder the innocent.

Thankfully, in contrast with the brutal regimes of Europe's czars, monarchs, and despots, the United States has been a bastion of religious tolerance, freedom, and opportunity for Jews and others. Jews flocked to the shores of America to lead lives free from the cruel whims of Russia's ruler (the line from *Fiddler on the Roof* sums up this view cheekily, "May God bless and keep the czar . . . far away from us!"). American rabbinical leaders wrote prayers to honor the United States' commitment to allowing religious communities to worship as they wished. (Many of these prayers invoke the need to "Grant our leaders wisdom and forbearance," requesting: "May they govern with justice and compassion."[143])

In most of these prayers, there are subtle hints of subversion, as no individual person is the focus of the invocation. Rather, the prayer is far more oblique, focusing on "the office of the president" or "the sitting congressmen." The subtle focus of the prayer is for the mantle of leadership, rather than for the specific officeholder. Many different versions of this prayer for the government and its leaders have been introduced through various siddurim.

We pray for the welfare of the American government and civil governments around the world because our individual destinies and that of the Jewish community are entwined in their success or failure. Reading this mishnah through the lens of two thousand years of the Jewish Diaspora, we see that even when our community's relationship with the ruling authorities was miserable, we still desired, even prayed, for improvement.

It is possible to believe that a government can be a vehicle for progress, yet still think it ineffective in meeting its obligations to its constituents. If operated correctly and efficiently, government has the capacity to reduce violence and to ensure that all people are treated equally under the law. Even more, government is responsible for maintaining stability, providing regulations, and protecting the vulnerable. If there are weaknesses in government action, it is the duty of every citizen to advocate for improvement. In the United States, at least, involving ourselves in electing leaders who best represent our interests, and the interests of the nation as a whole, carries tremendous significance. Neglecting this basic duty runs counter to our moral mandate to improve the world.

When we pray for the government, we should try to focus away from petty partisanship and toward a unifying redemption. While we can never expect everyone to get along simply for this purpose, our foremost concern is improving relations between people for the benefit of a just society. It is our goal, then, to lift up leaders and hope they succeed in developing their inner selves. Thus, they will be better able to serve their nation and all who wish to see the world become a better place.

3:3

רַבִּי חֲנַנְיָה בֶּן תְּרַדְיוֹן אוֹמֵר: שְׁנַיִם שֶׁיּוֹשְׁבִין וְאֵין בֵּינֵיהֶם
דִּבְרֵי תוֹרָה – הֲרֵי זֶה מוֹשַׁב לֵצִים, שֶׁנֶּאֱמַר: וּבְמוֹשַׁב לֵצִים
לֹא יָשָׁב (תהלים א:א). אֲבָל שְׁנַיִם שֶׁיּוֹשְׁבִין וְיֵשׁ בֵּינֵיהֶם דִּבְרֵי
תוֹרָה – שְׁכִינָה שְׁרוּיָה בֵּינֵיהֶם, שֶׁנֶּאֱמַר: אָז נִדְבְּרוּ יִרְאֵי יְיָ
אִישׁ אֶת־רֵעֵהוּ, וַיַּקְשֵׁב יְיָ וַיִּשְׁמָע. וַיִּכָּתֵב סֵפֶר זִכָּרוֹן לְפָנָיו,
לְיִרְאֵי יְיָ וּלְחֹשְׁבֵי שְׁמוֹ (מלאכי ג:טז). אֵין לִי אֶלָּא שְׁנַיִם. מִנַּיִן
שֶׁאֲפִלּוּ אֶחָד שֶׁיּוֹשֵׁב וְעוֹסֵק בַּתּוֹרָה, שֶׁהַקָּדוֹשׁ בָּרוּךְ הוּא
קוֹבֵעַ לוֹ שָׂכָר? שֶׁנֶּאֱמַר: יֵשֵׁב בָּדָד וְיִדֹּם, כִּי נָטַל עָלָיו
(איכה ג:כח).

Rabbi Chananyah ben T'radyon says: If two sit together and
there are no words of Torah between them, it is a session of
scorners, as it is said: "In the session of scorners the praiseworthy person does not sit" (Psalm 1:1). But if two sit together
and words of Torah are between them, the Divine Presence
rests between them, as it is said: "Then those who fear God
spoke to one another, and God listened and heard, and a book
of remembrance was written before God for those who fear
God and give thought to God's name" (Malachi 3:16). From this
verse we would know this only about two people; how do we
know that if even one person sits and occupies oneself with
Torah, the Holy One determines a reward for the person? It
is said: "Let one sit in solitude and be still, for they will have
received [a reward] for it" (Lamentations 3:28).

3:4

רַבִּי שִׁמְעוֹן אוֹמֵר: שְׁלֹשָׁה שֶׁאָכְלוּ עַל שֻׁלְחָן אֶחָד וְלֹא אָמְרוּ
עָלָיו דִּבְרֵי תוֹרָה – כְּאִלּוּ אָכְלוּ מִזִּבְחֵי מֵתִים, שֶׁנֶּאֱמַר: כִּי
כָל־שֻׁלְחָנוֹת מָלְאוּ קִיא צֹאָה בְּלִי מָקוֹם (ישעיהו כח:ח). אֲבָל
שְׁלֹשָׁה שֶׁאָכְלוּ עַל שֻׁלְחָן אֶחָד וְאָמְרוּ עָלָיו דִּבְרֵי תוֹרָה –

כְּאִלּוּ אָכְלוּ מִשֻּׁלְחָנוֹ שֶׁל הַמָּקוֹם, שֶׁנֶּאֱמַר: וַיְדַבֵּר אֵלַי,
זֶה הַשֻּׁלְחָן אֲשֶׁר לִפְנֵי יְיָ (יחזקאל מא:כב).

Rabbi Shimon said: If three have eaten at the same table and have not spoken words of Torah there, it is as if they have eaten of offerings to the dead idols, as it is said: "For all tables are full of vomit and filth, without the Omnipresent" (Isaiah 28:8). But if three have eaten at the same table and have spoken words of Torah there, it is as if they have eaten from the table of the Omnipresent, as it is said: "And he said to me, 'This is the table that is before God'" (Ezekiel 41:22).

(*See page 135 for 3:5 and page 139 for 3:6. Mishnah 3:4 is connected here with 3:7, as they are thematically linked.*)

3:7

רַבִּי חֲלַפְתָּא בֶּן דּוֹסָא אִישׁ כְּפַר חֲנַנְיָה אוֹמֵר: עֲשָׂרָה
שֶׁיּוֹשְׁבִין וְעוֹסְקִין בַּתּוֹרָה – שְׁכִינָה שְׁרוּיָה בֵּינֵיהֶם,
שֶׁנֶּאֱמַר: אֱלֹהִים נִצָּב בַּעֲדַת־אֵל (תהלים פב:א). וּמִנַּיִן אֲפִלּוּ
חֲמִשָּׁה? שֶׁנֶּאֱמַר: וַאֲגֻדָּתוֹ עַל־אֶרֶץ יְסָדָהּ (עמוס ט:ו). וּמִנַּיִן
אֲפִלּוּ שְׁלֹשָׁה? שֶׁנֶּאֱמַר: בְּקֶרֶב אֱלֹהִים יִשְׁפֹּט (תהלים פב:א).
וּמִנַּיִן אֲפִלּוּ שְׁנַיִם? שֶׁנֶּאֱמַר: אָז נִדְבְּרוּ יִרְאֵי יְיָ אִישׁ אֶת־
רֵעֵהוּ, וַיַּקְשֵׁב יְיָ וַיִּשְׁמָע (מלאכי ג:טז). וּמִנַּיִן אֲפִלּוּ אֶחָד?
שֶׁנֶּאֱמַר: בְּכָל־הַמָּקוֹם אֲשֶׁר אַזְכִּיר אֶת־שְׁמִי, אָבוֹא אֵלֶיךָ
וּבֵרַכְתִּיךָ (שמות כ:כא).

Rabbi Chalafta ben Dosa, leader of K'far Chananya, says: If ten people sit together and engage in Torah study, the Divine Presence rests among them, as it is said: "God stands in the assembly of God" (Psalm 82:1). How do we know this even of five? For it is said: "God has established God's bundle upon earth" (Amos 9:6). How do we know this even of three? For it is said: "In the midst of judges, God shall judge" (Psalm 82:1). How do we know this even of two? For it is said: "Then those who fear God spoke to one another, and God listened and heard" (Malachi 3:16). How do we know this even of one? For it is said: "In every place where I cause My name to be mentioned, I will come to you and bless you" (Exodus 20:21).

RABBI CHANANYAH (mishnah 3:3) saw beyond the surface not only during his life, but also during the moment of his death. In perhaps the most famous death in the Talmud, Rabbi Chananyah was wrapped in a Torah scroll, set aflame, and executed by the Romans. As the flames rose above him, he called out to the students, "I see the parchment burning, but the letters are floating in the air" (BT *Avodah Zarah* 17b). Even during his torture and execution, he sought to discuss Torah with his students. He looked beyond himself and into the souls of others. Although he was neither the first nor the last to have such a remarkable end-of-life experience, such a standard could never be expected of others.

This grouping of *mishnayot* prescribes righteous thought during meals, whether there are several at the table or just one. Righteous thought is even more important in solitude, when one is free of social pressures. When we believe no one is watching, we truly define who we are, solidifying not only self-perception but eventually how others perceive us when our privately cultivated character emerges in public spaces.

Yet, what does it mean to "engage in Torah study"? The meaning seems self-evident, but perhaps it's more complicated. Rabbi Hirsch explains in his commentary on these verses:

> We believe, therefore, that the meaning of *divrei Torah* [studying words of Torah] would include not only the actual teaching contained from the Torah for the fashioning of human affairs, as well as anything that is shaped in accordance with the Torah's teachings and is fulfilled in accordance with the spirit of the Law of God.

Indeed, any of our activist discourse about social change and improving the world is "Torah" when discussed compassionately and for the sake of raising up others. This can be a refreshing framework for how to view "religion" and "religious learning." It is both theology in action and text study through face-to-face moral discourse.

This leads to another question: Why is Torah study so central to meal times? Aren't the distractions of eating counter to the sacred nature of text study? No. Because we bless our food before eating, we make our meals holy. And, if we're in a group of three or more Jews, we add the ceremony of thanks (*zimun*) to the Blessing after Meals (*Birkat HaMazon*)—another way of adding holiness out of the most banal of instances. What's more, animals (and some people) that are driven by instinct view others as rivals for food, rather than seeking to share in harmony. By eating together, we not only share in the enjoyment of good food, good ideas, and warm company, but also we break the instinct to isolate ourselves from others to hoard scarce resources.[144]

Like our meals, our shared conversation should be more than instrumental or for material gain. It must be relational and also warm, honest, and open. Writing in 1947, Martin Buber explains:

> There is genuine dialogue—no matter whether spoken or silent—where each of the participants really has in mind the other or others in their present and particular being and turns to them with the intention of establishing a living mutual relation between himself and them. There is *technical dialogue*, in which two or more men, meeting in space, speak each with himself in strangely tortuous and circuitous ways and yet imagine that they have escaped the torment of being thrown back on their own resources.[145]

A disciple of Rabbi Akiva, Rabbi Shimon bar Yochai (see mishnah 3:4), like Rabbi Chananyah, looked for the substances beneath the surface, be they physical or spiritual. Likewise, he is viewed to be among the founders of the Jewish mystical tradition. We learn from his experience that spiritual isolation can be quite dangerous. After criticizing the ruling Roman government in the Holy Land, Rabbi Shimon hid in a cave and, while there, studied Torah for twelve years. When the emperor died, the decree was annulled, and he emerged from his self-imposed exile. He saw Israelites working the field. He couldn't believe that they would spend their time engaged in such mundane activity when they could be engaged spiritually, so his mere glance became destructive to them: "Every place they [Rabbi Shimon and his son, who had gone into the cave with him] turned their eyes to—was immediately burned." His harsh outlook led to a heavenly voice instructing him to return to the cave (BT *Shabbat* 33b–34a).

Rabbi Shimon's teachings reveal both his former self—critical of those who were not religiously engaged—and his transformed self, which is now socially engaged with others during meals. Often, leaps in personal piety have the ability to make one more judgmental of those who are less so. This is common among those who find solace in religious practice. This mishnah says that we need not focus so much on others' observance. Rather, to temper certain negative attitudes, we must proactively engage with others as they progress in their spiritual journey. A broad reading of this mishnah is that it delivers an egalitarian message: We don't sit only with scholars, but rather we all come together in the greater spirit of Torah.

The Talmud says, "Welcoming guests is greater than greeting the Divine Presence" (BT *Shabbat* 127a). Here, we are not just engaging with folks who happen upon each other in the marketplace. We are also doing the mitzvah of welcoming guests, known as *hachnasat orchim*. Abraham is the paragon of this ethical ideal in Jewish thought. His warm welcome of the three angels in Genesis 18 exemplified divine hospitality. But he did much more:

> Abraham . . . would go forth and make his rounds, and wherever he found travelers, he would bring them to his house. To the one who was accustomed to eating wheat bread, he gave wheat bread to eat. . . . To the one who was accustomed to drinking wine, he gave wine to drink. Moreover, he built stately mansions on the highways and left food and drink there so that every traveler stopped there and thanked God. That is why delight of the spirit was vouchsafed to him. And whatever one might ask for was to be found in Abraham's home.[146]

This passage says that hospitality has enormous value in Jewish ethics. But being hospitable is even more meritorious when we go beyond our comfort zone to invite the vulnerable and downtrodden into our homes. It's not enough to create a Jewish home that is isolated from the broader world. One must build a nurturing environment that supports intellectual and social growth.

When we see others as ends in themselves, there is honor. When the relationships we pursue are relational rather than transactional, there can be holiness. We honor the dignity of the other and bring holiness to our time together, by offering elevated ideas to the conversation. When we speak in the language of Torah with others, in its broadest, most universal sense, we show others that they matter to us and that our lives and relationships are guided by the most upright values. People are meant to be together and learn from each other, and through those relationships, they grow toward spiritual heights and develop their inherent ethical strengths.

3:5

רַבִּי חֲנִינָא בֶן חֲכִינַי אוֹמֵר: הַנֵּעוֹר בַּלַּיְלָה, וְהַמְהַלֵּךְ בַּדֶּרֶךְ
יְחִידִי וּמְפַנֶּה לִבּוֹ לְבַטָּלָה – הֲרֵי זֶה מִתְחַיֵּב בְּנַפְשׁוֹ.

Rabbi Chanina ben Chachinai says: One who stays awake at
night or who travels alone on the road, but turns one's mind
to idleness, indeed bears guilt for one's soul.

WE ARE CAUTIONED against engaging with the dark (whether by stay-
ing awake in the dark or by traveling in the dark). Why was darkness
—indeed, the idleness often experienced with darkness—understood
to be so dangerous by the Sages?

In the Book of Exodus, the penultimate plague is a complete, envel-
oping darkness upon the land of Egypt. The placement and essence
of this plague are fascinating, both as displays of divine power and as
radical pedagogical construct. What is it about this plague that makes it
so heartrending and mystical? After all, don't we all experience roughly
half of each day cocooned by darkness? Why should anyone continue
to be afraid of the dark? The answer is a stark one. Darkness, in all its
many forms, represents the infinite gap between the self and the other.
There is no measurement for space or time in the dark—merely endless
solitude and despair.

Night is a symbol for spaces and times of strange, undiluted darkness. So is traveling to a foreign place, metaphorically speaking. We
may feel alone, alienated, desperate. It is easy when in times of darkness—literal or metaphorical—to be pulled into the realms of idleness
and vanity. Rabbi Moshe Chayim Luzzatto teaches, "The dark of night
has two effects upon us. We either see nothing at all or mistake one
thing for another."[147] It is precisely for these times that we must be most
prepared. Moments of direct revelation are fleeting, like a lightning
bolt that illuminates the darkness for a moment. In those remaining
moments of darkness, we can live based upon the vision we saw when
the world was briefly illuminated. This is what it means to have faith, to
trust in those moments of clarity, and to be cautious and guarded when
we struggle to see beyond the lingering darkness.

A midrash in *Sh'mot Rabbah* explains that the darkness that sank into Egypt was not natural. Rather, it was formed from the metaphysical depths of *Geihinam* (hell).[148] Thus, this darkness is inherently evil; it is felt throughout every sinew. Rabbi Levi ben Gershon (known as Ralbag or Gersonides) teaches that this darkness is tangible fear and suffering, an early explication of existential angst.[149] Likewise, Midrash *Tanchuma*, a collection of aggadic exegesis, understood the darkness mentioned in this Torah portion as relational.[150] After all, the literal reading—*p'shat*—of the verse states that no one could see anyone else, nor could they leave their homes for three whole days.

Still, there is an inspiring message here. Torah thought teaches us that it takes a miracle, or, in this case, an anti-miracle—one of the ten devastating plagues—to create a world where individuals were not able to see each other. It is light, and therefore love, that is the natural default in our world.

After the plague of darkness, Pharaoh cries, "Be gone from me! Take care not to see me again!" (Exodus 10:28). When one cannot see another, one seeks to break all relationships—even those that offer complete redemption. Pharaoh knew for certain by this point that he needed Moses for his salvation. Nevertheless, he failed to seek that salvation and sent Moses away. Retreating from seeing another, the breakdown of relationship, is the ultimate defeat.

We should have hope: In this story, Israel is preserved in light, and nothing less than divine intervention keeps the Egyptians from seeing each other. The plagues are the inverse of blessings; indeed, they are subverted blessings oriented toward human redemption, that is, blessings via plagues. By this, it is meant that the plagues remind us that people contain an innate, holy capacity to see the souls of others with compassion, but that is not apparent with the amount of cruelty in the world. When there is total darkness, we all stumble. We can only see one another clearly in the light.

Although darkness is ever-present in the world and in our personal lives, we are equipped to see one another vividly. We do so when we acknowledge the blessings of human love, empathy, and transcendental encounters that occur during our time on earth.

The first step in dispelling the darkness in our world is seeing it within us. Pema Chödrön, a Tibetan Buddhist monk of American extraction, writes in her book *Comfortable with Uncertainty: 108 Teachings on Cultivating Fearlessness and Compassion*:

> Compassion is not a relationship between the healer and the wounded. It's a relationship between equals. Only when we know our own darkness well can we be present with the darkness of others. Compassion becomes real when we recognize our shared humanity.[151]

Indeed, one of the great paradoxes of kabbalistic thought is that light and darkness, as well as good and evil, are interwoven with each other, undulating like waves in a never-ending metaphysical typhoon:

> When God came to create the world and revealed what was hidden in the depths and disclosed light out of darkness, they were all wrapped in one another. Therefore, light emerged from darkness, and from the impenetrable came forth the profound. So, too from good issues evil, and from mercy issues judgment; and all are intertwined: the good impulse and the evil impulse.[152]

Our obligation in this world is to separate the darkness and the evil from the light and the good. The first step is to see both within ourselves and in the broader world. Being out in darkness or traveling in a foreign land are this mishnah's examples of dangerous situations, but their very foreignness should strengthen our inner resolve. In these situations, we must focus more toward God and our innermost moral values; these are moments for faith and conviction. It is easy to stumble. We must get back up, stronger than before, to overcome challenges.

When darkness descends, we lose the ability to see one another. Metaphorically, when darkness extends, humanity loses the ability for compassion. When it gets dark, people stay home. They'd prefer not get up and leave the comfort of their current existence. They'd rather build a society based on their individual whims rather than the needs of all. Indeed, when the times gets tough and rough, and people seek the security of what they once knew, they can only see sorrow around them. Nothing is what is used to be. But such thinking resides in misplaced nostalgia; this is the plague that undermines the moral fabric of society. Perhaps the primary covenantal task is to bring light wherever we see darkness. So, indeed, let us not "travel alone on the road" in the darkness of night, but travel together, travel in light.

3:6

רַבִּי נְחוּנְיָא בֶּן הַקָּנָה אוֹמֵר: כָּל הַמְקַבֵּל עָלָיו עוֹל תּוֹרָה –
מַעֲבִירִין מִמֶּנּוּ עוֹל מַלְכוּת וְעוֹל דֶּרֶךְ אֶרֶץ. וְכָל הַפּוֹרֵק
מִמֶּנּוּ עוֹל תּוֹרָה – נוֹתְנִין עָלָיו עוֹל מַלְכוּת וְעוֹל דֶּרֶךְ אֶרֶץ.

Rabbi N'chunya ben Hakanah says: If someone takes upon
oneself the yoke of Torah—the yoke of government and the
yoke of worldly responsibilities are removed from the person.
But if someone throws off the yoke of Torah from oneself—
the yoke of government and the yoke of worldly responsibilities are placed upon the person.

IN A LIFE suffused with meaning, one strives to achieve balance. Being
involved with community, going to school, raising a family, enjoying
precious moments away from work, engaging with friends, contributing to society, growing spiritually—all must be balanced. No one can
give full attention to every facet of life, so we make hard choices. This
mishnah says that we must be firmly planted somewhere. At times, this
is in Torah and Jewish communal life. At times, this means larger societal undertakings. We don't have to feel guilt when we prioritize where
to focus our attention if we are fully committed to the vision of a more
just society.

The Sages held such ideas, but they were pragmatists who understood human limitations. Rabbi Meir ben Raphael Plotzky (nineteenth
century, Poland) explained the exemption from engaging in a mitzvah
while doing another mitzvah, or *oseik b'mitzvah, patur min hamitzvah*:

> For this rule—that persons engaged in one mitzvah are exempt
> from another—is because while they are engaged in one mitzvah
> they have no obligation to carry out another one. But this is the
> case only with regard to a mitzvah [in the category known as] "be-
> tween humanity and its Maker." But we have not heard that this
> would exempt anyone from a mitzvah [in the category known
> as] "between one person and another," for the ultimate end that
> would serve that other person cannot be pushed aside because one
> is engaged in a mitzvah directed towards one's Maker.[153]

In choosing where to commit, we reflect on what is most important to our spiritual growth. Each of us has one life, and we must take ownership for it. We need authenticity. Lifestyle coach and prominent consultant/speaker Barbara Sher writes:

> Einstein needed to formulate theories of physics, Harriet Tubman needed to guide people to freedom, and you need to follow your original vision. As Vartan Gregorian said, "The universe is not going to see someone like you again in the entire history of creation." Each of us is one of a kind. Every living person has a completely original way of looking at the world, and originality always needs to express itself.[154]

This mishnah alludes to distinct ways to interact with government. In advocacy, there is often a tension between insiders and outsiders. The insiders are sure that they create change from within the system and resent the radical, rabble-rousing activists. The outsiders are sure they create change in their own way and resent the sell-out, conformist insiders. But we need both insiders (think of Esther, wife of the king, agitating from within to protect her people) and outsiders (like Mordechai, a prominent figure using his influence to effect change through pressure-applying tactics and proactive organizational methods) in a collaborative relationship.

Our commitments change through our lives. When one is twenty years old and single, one engages the world in ways quite distinct from that of a working parent. And again, a retiree might have a different capacity for engagement than the parent of three young children. The question is not "Who do I need to be?" but "Who do I need to be right now?" This guides us as we pursue our journeys and explore our unique potential.

(*For 3:7, see page 130.*)

3:8

רַבִּי אֶלְעָזָר בֶּן יְהוּדָה אִישׁ בַּרְתּוֹתָא אוֹמֵר: תֶּן לוֹ מִשֶּׁלּוֹ,
שָׁאַתָּה וְשֶׁלְּךָ שֶׁלּוֹ. וְכֵן בְּדָוִד הוּא אוֹמֵר: כִּי־מִמְּךָ הַכֹּל
וּמִיָּדְךָ נָתַנּוּ לָךְ (דברי הימים א, כט:יד).

Rabbi Elazar ben Yehudah, leader of Bartota, says: Give God
from God's own, for you and your possessions are God's. And
so has David said, "For everything is from You, and from Your
Own we have given You" (I Chronicles 29:14).

A RADICAL JEWISH TEACHING: We humans subsist in spiritual debt.
Even the object that one clings to most, the body, is not truly one's own.
The physical space our hearts and minds inhabit is but a bequest from
the Divine. We cannot own anything, because the Creator is the true
owner of all—our lives included. To say that we are not entirely in possession of our physical bodies should inspire untapped humility and
modesty. One's goal should not be to amass money or property, nor to
attain beauty. All of that will fade after this life. Our life.

Jewish tradition certainly does not instruct us to forsake pleasure
or embrace asceticism. That would be too extreme, even for the most
pious. Jewish law instructs donating at least 10 percent of one's income
(immediately when it comes in), but no more than 20 percent. Tithing,
maaseir, is not just about generosity, though that's a by-product. Rather,
it is about acknowledging the spiritual truth that the money was never
really our own. We thus symbolically communicate that our fortunes
are enmeshed with those of the world by immediately taking care of
others with the money we have earned.

Further, the Rabbis teach that any food we acquire is not ours, but
God's. Before one savors a meal, be it snack or feast, one expresses
thanks before the Creator for being in the position to eat. Only after
the blessing and acknowledgment that God is the source of food may
one consume it. Otherwise, the mere act of eating is considered sacrilegious and, in some interpretations, akin to stealing. And afterward,

once every morsel has disappeared from our plates, we say thanks that God "gives food to all flesh, for [God's] kindness is everlasting" (BT *B'rachot* 35a).

Contemplate the premise that the only currency we ever own eternally is what we give away to help others. It is both an intimidating and a liberating idea, because it helps us realize that life's object isn't only centered around the concept of happiness (maybe this thought can be rendered as personal prosperity), but something higher. A holy life is about service to others, even when it makes us uncomfortable; we merely have to choose how to be of service. At its most radical, let us consider that the only organs we "own" eternally are the organs that we have donated to save lives; that the only income we claim goes to those who struggle to escape poverty; that the prayers we dedicate go to those who cannot speak for themselves; and that the mitzvot we perform in the world leave lasting legacies for future generations to discover, markers for when we finally leave this world. Our sacred contributions in this life become intertwined with the eternity of all existence. And while performing mitzvot in isolation from other tasks will not leave traces in the physical world, the fact that we took the opportunities to fulfill the most radical of opportunities to save others can remain with us through our journeys in the universe. This is eternity. This is the eternal potential of the human being.

Now, giving up ownership is not only altruistic. It is also deeply rewarding to prioritize life experience over petty pleasure. Indeed, who among us wishes to be wondering at the end of our life whether or not we have truly lived to our fullest potential? At best, we wish to leave a positive mark on human civilization, on our communities, and on those we love. And even more so, we wish to leave a positive impression on our eternal souls—the part of our existence that transcends the body and the transience of this earth. We don't want to have merely passed through life unconsciously without truly embracing the richness and depth of human existence. As the Pulitzer Prize–winning poet Mary Oliver writes: "I don't want to end up simply having visited this world."[154a]

We don't want to look back to say that we've "visited this world."

We want to exist and make our mark, leaving a legacy of goodness and kindness. How we approach such lofty ideals is left to us, though we have Jewish thought to guide us. Considering that we should give ourselves over to our higher calling by interweaving our existence with all existence is a good start. Yet, we can do more. We should challenge ourselves to think broadly about our actions. Whenever we go into the world, we should pause and consider how our choices led us to that point. Nothing is as mundane as it seems. Any everyday activity, like a trip to the grocery store or the commute to work can be suffused with holiness. But only when we begin to realize the vastness of our potential to do good in the world can we grasp the monumental weight that our souls bear on us during our life.

3:9

רַבִּי יַעֲקֹב אוֹמֵר: הַמְהַלֵּךְ בַּדֶּרֶךְ וְשׁוֹנֶה, וּמַפְסִיק מִמִּשְׁנָתוֹ
וְאוֹמֵר: מַה נָּאֶה אִילָן זֶה, מַה נָּאֶה נִיר זֶה – מַעֲלִין עָלָיו
כְּאִלּוּ מִתְחַיֵּיב בְּנַפְשׁוֹ.

Rabbi Yaakov said: One who walks on the road while review-
ing [Torah] but interrupts the review and exclaims, "How
beautiful is this tree! How beautiful is this plowed field!"—it is
reckoned as if one bears guilt for one's soul.

ONE PARTICULARLY TRANSCENDENT midrash taught that God used
the Torah—physically and conceptually—as a blueprint for the creation of the world and that Torah preceded physical Creation.[155] This is
neither temporal explanation nor scientific theory, but a lesson about
priorities: It tells us that in Judaism, ethics preceded nature. Purpose
preceded content. In this mishnah, ethical and spiritual duties precede
our encounter with the natural world. Torah and science—related but
distinct—are in service of one another. But we know that we choose the
"ought" over the "is." We embrace nature but seek to transcend it.

There is value in admiring beauty whenever we see it. Whether we
admire a natural wonder or a piece of art, pausing for such aesthetic
pleasure is rare in a society that floods our consciousness with images.
Rabbi Abraham Joshua Heschel taught that people should practice
"radical amazement"[156] and experience each moment with renewed
excitement and gratitude. While the world offers plenty of beautiful
vistas, rolling hills, and soaring seas, these are not enough to ensure
spiritual fortitude.

Maimonides taught that nature is a spiritual pathway. He asked,
"What is the way to love and fear God?" He answers:

> When a person contemplates God's wondrous and great works and
> creations, and sees in them God's infinite wisdom, immediately
> one loves and praises and exalts and yearns with an overwhelming
> yearning to know God's great name.[157]

It is tempting to be drawn excessively by the external world's allure—pleasure, enjoyment, and virtually every possible material distraction. In this mishnah, Rabbi Yaakov nudges us to ignore the noise and to seek respite in our peaceful inner worlds. It is all too easy to get caught in the spiritual malaise of a vacuous life. If one is working through an important life issue, or a Torah lesson, or a spiritual matter and becomes distracted by the external world, one is in danger of never manifesting intrinsic spiritual potential.

Rabbi Yitz Greenberg writes about this mishnah:

> It is a mitzvah to admire nature and even to say a blessing over beautiful, natural phenomena such as a rainbow, or when the trees first blossom in the spring, or when tasting a fruit. However, here the sin is to break off from Torah study in order to appreciate beauty, thus pitting God's beautiful revelation against God's beautiful nature. There are two books of revelation—Torah and nature ("The heavens tell the glory of God and the firmament proclaims God's handiwork" [Psalm 19:1]). The two do not contradict each other since they have one Creator. Each should be accorded its own respective study in its own time.[158]

Every part of our essence is divided between the world we see and the world we dream. In Jewish practice, we also tend to bifurcate our proclivities between the tangible and the intangible. We learn both from external revelation (texts) and from internal revelation (natural morality). We do not dismiss moral intuition when it appears to conflict with sacred text. Rabbi Abraham Isaac Kook taught that to dismiss one's moral conscience when in tension with tradition is to diminish one's fear of heaven—yirat shamayim. For Rabbi Kook, natural morality is fundamental to living a religious life.[159]

Jewish mysticism believes that everything on earth, whether a tree, ice cube, piece of granite, piece of paper, is imbued with divine spirit. Everything is created for a purpose, and its related utility derives from acknowledging the special holiness that resides within. When Rabbi Heschel taught about radical amazement, he was challenging us to go beyond what our corporeal vision observes to imagine the metaphysical aura that surrounds every aspect of the world. As leaders or as ordinary people, this is how we should live.

But another way of looking at the relationship between the mystical and the mundane is that they are linked by an inherent thread of divinity. In this conception, there isn't so much a division between the two, only an altered perspective. Consider how Evelyn Underhill, a Christian mystic, writes on this thought in her 1930 book:

> It is in the "inclusive" mystic, whose freedom and originality are fed but not hampered by the spiritual tradition within which he appears, who accepts the incarnational status of the human spirit, and can find the "inward in the outward as well as the outward in the inward," who shows us in their fullness and beauty the life-giving possibilities of the soul transfigured in God.[160]

Every day, we are blessed with limited time to make a difference in the world. We can expend our spiritual capital in any way we see fit. But following a directive to be the change we want to see in the world, we should seek both the purpose and spiritual obligation of the task. It might not come naturally to all, but it is something that is essential to the preservation of the delicate balance that divine forces have given us to tend. Indeed, what emerges from experiencing nature is the urgent Torah imperative to preserve creation and a pressing example that natural morality resides within the spiritual DNA of every person (even if he or she might not realize it). The Rabbis teach that an environmental charge and moral caution were given right at the beginning of Creation:

> When God created Adam, God took Adam and led him around all the trees of the Garden. And God said to Adam, "Look at my creations! How beautiful and amazing they are! And everything I made, I created for you. Be careful that you don't spoil or destroy my world—because if you do, there is nobody after you to fix it."[161]

We cannot even begin to understand aspects of our complex interconnected ecosystem. The Rabbis encourage us to maintain wonder and reverence:

> Our Rabbis said: What is this "And the advantage [*yitron*] of the land in all things" (Ecclesiastes 5:8)? Even things you see as superfluous [*m'yutarin*] in this world—like flies, fleas, and mosquitoes—they are part of the greater scheme of the creation of the world, as

it says (Genesis 1:31), "God then surveyed all that [God] had made, and look—it was very good!" And Rabbi Acha bar Rabbi Chanina said: Even things you see as superfluous in this world—like snakes and scorpions—they are part of the greater scheme of the creation of the world.[162]

This mishnah teaches that encountering nature's beauty merely for its own sake is a distraction from Torah. But it is not a distraction when Torah elevates this encounter, reminding us of our moral duty to preserve creation for our children and generations to come.

Wasting of natural resources (*bal tashchit*) is a Torah violation (Deuteronomy 20:19–20) that is pervasive in America (indeed, the entire world) today. Rabbi Abraham Joshua Heschel suggests that Shabbat can be a corrective to wasteful lifestyles:

> To set apart one day a week for freedom, a day on which we would not use the instruments which been so easily turned into weapons of destruction, a day for being with ourselves, a day of detachment from the vulgar, of independence of external obligations, a day on which we stop worshiping the idols of technical civilization, a day on which we use no money, a day of armistice in the economic struggle with our fellow human beings and the forces of nature—is there any institution that holds out a greater hope for human progress than the Sabbath?[163]

3:10

רַבִּי דוֹסְתַּאי בְּרַבִּי יַנַּאי מִשֶּׁם רַבִּי מֵאִיר אוֹמֵר: כָּל הַשּׁוֹכֵחַ
דָּבָר אֶחָד מִמִּשְׁנָתוֹ – מַעֲלֶה עָלָיו הַכָּתוּב כְּאִלּוּ מִתְחַיֵּב
בְּנַפְשׁוֹ, שֶׁנֶּאֱמַר: רַק הִשָּׁמֶר לְךָ וּשְׁמֹר נַפְשְׁךָ מְאֹד, פֶּן־
תִּשְׁכַּח אֶת־הַדְּבָרִים אֲשֶׁר־רָאוּ עֵינֶיךָ (דברים ד:ט). יָכוֹל, אֲפִלּוּ
תָקְפָה עָלָיו מִשְׁנָתוֹ? תַּלְמוּד לוֹמַר: וּפֶן־יָסוּרוּ מִלְּבָבְךָ
כֹּל יְמֵי חַיֶּיךָ (דברים ד:ט). הָא אֵינוּ מִתְחַיֵּב בְּנַפְשׁוֹ עַד שֶׁיֵּשֵׁב
וִיסִירֵם מִלִּבּוֹ.

Rabbi Dostai of the House of Yannai says in the name of
Rabbi Meir: Whoever forgets anything of their Torah learning, the Torah considers it as if they bear guilt for their soul,
for it is said: "But beware and guard your soul exceedingly lest
you forget the things your eyes have seen" (Deuteronomy 4:9).
Does this apply even if [one forgot because] one's studies were
too difficult for them? [This is not so, for] Torah teaches, "And
lest they be removed from your heart and all the days of
your life" (Deuteronomy 4:9). Thus, one does not bear guilt for
one's soul unless one sits [idly] and removes them from one's
consciousness.

A REFLECTIVE LIFE matters to religiously sensitive people. Acquiring
the fortitude to engage in action requires constant learning, as well as
the ability to review one's values through a system of basic morality. The
expansion of the mind, let alone the soul, is essential for growth. How
tragic it is to learn and forget. So many truths we hold are simple, but
many are not at the forefront of our minds; they elude us when needed.
Through this mishnah, Rabbi Dostai of the House of Yannai teaches
us not to treat memory as a passive operation, but to take an active role
in shaping our memories to ensure that the central tenets of our lives
guide us toward propriety of action and thought.

Developmental constructivist psychology today suggests that memory is not a storage bank where old data lingers, to be accessed as we left

it.[164] Memory is built and is in various states of reconstruction. As we evolve, so do our memories. This is why we must be active in holding and shaping our human capabilities.

In Jewish studies, we value re-learning—known as *chazarah*—even more than we value learning. If we only retain what we learn as children, we'll hold a basic, if not infantile, approach to Judaism. If we return to text, holidays, or ritual with big questions, we have the impetus to learn anew. Indeed, repetition is ascribed enormous religious value in Talmudic thought: "One cannot compare a person who reviews their learning 100 times with a person who reviews their learning 101 times" (BT *Chagigah* 9b).

Several mitzvot are associated with remembering. Fourteen times in Deuteronomy, Moses cautions the Israelites against forgetting. Jewish continuity relies not upon history (at least, not exclusively), but on memory. The Baal Shem Tov is reported to have said that "exile is forgetting." History is studied from books. Memory is passed down, experienced, internalized. Sustaining positive memories and creating new ones are key to Jewish pedagogy and progress. Consider this: During the *Havdalah* ceremony that commemorates the end of the Sabbath day and the embrace of a new week, we smell spices because the sense of smell reportedly has the greatest capacity to trigger memories or, perhaps, the effect of raising our faculties to experience something novel. Even more so, the reset of Shabbat causes us to unload the baggage from the prior week and renew our minds to absorb fresh ideas in the new week.

It is tragic to forget, but it can also be a virtue. Why? Because we can forget how others have wronged us, forget outdated information, and forget unimportant ideas. We can selectively construct reserves of memories that serve us in positive, judicious ways. In Jorge Luis Borges's short story "Funes el memorioso," a man suddenly cursed with the ability to remember everything reflects that "to think is to forget."[165] Dwelling too deeply on a negative thought only squanders our potential to learn and move on from the experience. Remembering too much, we forget our essence.

The focus of this mishnah helps us remember the isolated elderly people in our communities. The most tragic form of forgetting, however, is one that is cruelly forced by nature: dementia. Confused and isolated, disoriented and unwanted, one can feel lost and alone in one's own mind as precious memories slip away. As Mother Teresa explains in *A Simple Path*, "The greatest disease today is not leprosy or tuberculosis, but rather the feeling of being unwanted. We can cure physical diseases with medicine, but the only cure for loneliness, despair, and hopelessness is love."[166] Here, she describes something felt not only by those with dementia; she is describing the feelings of those whose lives are untouched by others' compassion. (This theme runs throughout *Pirkei Avot.*) Accordingly, one of the greatest modern epidemics is loneliness. Sometimes remembering family, community, and past relationships can make current relationships more painful. Yet, they can also be sources of comfort. While it can be difficult for some people to interact with older people or with those struggling with ailments of the mind, communities should do more to invest in and care for seniors and those suffering from depression, those suffering from dementia, and all who feel socially isolated or spiritually alone.

Acknowledging that memory is a winding path and not a straight line helps us trust that we should imbibe material that nourishes the soul as much as the brain. Idle learning distracts from true, experiential learning. And while memory's utility is itself a mystery, the fact that there is an element within us that allows to us to gaze into our past is a formidable tool for developing into our best selves. But even more so than forgetting passages of Torah or Talmud, forgetting how to engage other people in the world is a problem of the highest order. If we forget who we are—as individuals, as a people, as a society—then we cannot bring wisdom to make the world a better place. René Descartes writes, "So blind is the curiosity by which mortals are possessed, that they often conduct their minds along unexplored routes, having no reason to hope for success, but merely being willing to risk the experiment of finding whether the truth they seek lies there."[167]

Engaging in any form of study—Torah or physics, cosmology or agriculture, mysticism or mathematics—is a worthy objective. Seeking out learned people creates an ecology of erudition and memory production. It is more important than ever to seek out such people, because the world is constantly becoming more complex. How we fit into an ever-changing ecosystem of new technological systems is overwhelming. But that is where the desire to learn fits itself neatly into the epistemologies of the future.

And while sustaining memory, including the memories of our spiritual journeys, is an integral part of producing a good society, there is always more for us to accomplish. Our task in life is not only to learn and discover who we are as actualized individuals, but also to ensure that the accumulation of knowledge throughout history continues to have a place to reside: the mind.

3:11

רַבִּי חֲנִינָא בֶּן דּוֹסָא אוֹמֵר: כָּל שֶׁיִּרְאַת חֶטְאוֹ קוֹדֶמֶת לְחָכְמָתוֹ – חָכְמָתוֹ מִתְקַיֶּמֶת. וְכָל שֶׁחָכְמָתוֹ קוֹדֶמֶת לְיִרְאַת חֶטְאוֹ – אֵין חָכְמָתוֹ מִתְקַיֶּמֶת.

Rabbi Chanina ben Dosa says: Anyone whose fear of sin takes priority over their wisdom, the wisdom will endure; but anyone whose wisdom exceeds their fear of sin, their wisdom will not endure.

3:12

הוּא הָיָה אוֹמֵר: כָּל שֶׁמַּעֲשָׂיו מְרֻבִּין מֵחָכְמָתוֹ – חָכְמָתוֹ מִתְקַיֶּמֶת. וְכָל שֶׁחָכְמָתוֹ מְרֻבָּה מִמַּעֲשָׂיו – אֵין חָכְמָתוֹ מִתְקַיֶּמֶת.

He used to say: Anyone whose good deeds exceed their wisdom, their wisdom will endure; but anyone whose wisdom exceeds their good deeds, their wisdom will not endure.

(See page 156 for 3:13. Mishnah 3:22 is connected here with 3:12, as they are thematically linked).

3:22

הוּא הָיָה אוֹמֵר: כֹּל שֶׁחָכְמָתוֹ מְרֻבָּה מִמַּעֲשָׂיו, לְמָה הוּא דוֹמֶה? לְאִילָן שֶׁעֲנָפָיו מְרֻבִּין וְשָׁרָשָׁיו מֻעָטִין, וְהָרוּחַ בָּאָה וְעוֹקַרְתּוֹ וְהוֹפַכְתּוֹ עַל פָּנָיו, שֶׁנֶּאֱמַר: וְהָיָה כְּעַרְעָר בָּעֲרָבָה וְלֹא יִרְאֶה כִּי-יָבוֹא טוֹב, וְשָׁכַן חֲרֵרִים בַּמִּדְבָּר, אֶרֶץ מְלֵחָה וְלֹא תֵשֵׁב (ירמיהו יז:ו). אֲבָל כָּל שֶׁמַּעֲשָׂיו מְרֻבִּין מֵחָכְמָתוֹ, לְמָה הוּא דוֹמֶה? לְאִילָן שֶׁעֲנָפָיו מֻעָטִין וְשָׁרָשָׁיו מְרֻבִּין, שֶׁאֲפִלּוּ כָּל הָרוּחוֹת שֶׁבָּעוֹלָם בָּאוֹת וְנוֹשְׁבוֹת בּוֹ, אֵין מְזִיזוֹת אוֹתוֹ מִמְּקוֹמוֹ, שֶׁנֶּאֱמַר: וְהָיָה כְּעֵץ שָׁתוּל עַל-מַיִם,

וְעַל־יוּבַל יְשַׁלַּח שָׁרָשָׁיו, וְלֹא יִרְאֶה כִּי־יָבֹא חֹם, וְהָיָה
עָלֵהוּ רַעֲנָן, וּבִשְׁנַת בַּצֹּרֶת לֹא יִדְאָג, וְלֹא יָמִישׁ מֵעֲשׂוֹת
פֶּרִי (ירמיהו יז:ח).

[Rabbi Elazar ben Azaryah] used to say: Anyone whose
wisdom exceeds their good deeds, to what are they likened? To
a tree whose branches are numerous but whose roots are few,
then the wind comes and uproots it and turns it upside down;
as it is said: "And they shall be like an isolated tree in an arid
land and shall not see when good comes; they shall dwell on
parched soil in the wilderness, on a salted land, uninhabited"
(Jeremiah 17:6). But one whose good deeds exceed their wisdom,
to what are they likened? To a tree whose branches are few but
whose roots are numerous; even if all the winds in the world
were to come and blow against it, they could not budge it from
its place; as it is said: "And they shall be like a tree planted
by waters, toward the stream spreading its roots, and it shall
not notice the heat's arrival, and its foliage shall be fresh; in
the year of drought it shall not worry, nor shall it cease from
yielding fruit" (Jeremiah 17:8).

WISDOM IS MEANINGLESS without a constructive purpose. Elsewhere in the Talmud, the sage Rava teaches, "The goal of wisdom is
repentance and good deeds" (BT *B'rachot* 17a). It is this notion that is
reflected in these related passages of *Pirkei Avot*. The objective of acquiring knowledge must not be acquisition alone. Ethical development
would be stunted if this were the case. Rather, the pursuit of knowledge
must merge the teachings of the great thinkers, mathematicians, sci-
entists, religious scholars, and artists into one vessel—the mind—and
put them into service to the world.

Throughout the Jewish world, there is laudable emphasis on public service and social justice. Every denomination of Judaism does its
part in ensuring that the next generation is educated in the values and
ethics of Judaism while also approaching the ancient texts with varying

methods of internalization and exposure. While there will always be debates about the best manner to model Jewish values in the world, every denomination feels the same meaningful push to go out into the world and perform acts of charity and kindness. Yet, at the same time, the focus on external service can come at the expense of more reflective practices. From an institutional standpoint, the practical needs of financial security and continual access to precious resources means that some values are prioritized over others. But sometimes that need to maintain this commitment to improving the world comes at the expense of evocative Jewish learning, transformative ritual, and engagement with tradition. In certain parts of the Jewish world, especially the greater Orthodox community, there is commendable attention paid toward learning, ritual, and observance, but these communities can become isolationist, removing themselves from the great moral challenges of our day. Such stances are myopic. Rather than existing on poles, we ought to learn from one another and grow toward the fullness of our spiritual and ethical potential. Each type of Jewish community can learn from others.

Shortly before he passed away, Rabbi Aharon Lichtenstein *z"l* (1933–2015) wrote about a peculiar incident that illustrates the tragic paradox when some forms of religious learning prevent moral action. One day, while walking near his home in Jerusalem, Rabbi Lichtenstein encountered an Arab man in dire need of assistance. Not too far from this Arab man was a group of young ultra-Orthodox boys, deliberately ignoring the Arab man and failing to come to his aid. Commenting on the situation, Rabbi Lichtenstein observed that these boys were neglecting their spiritual obligations:

> The question came up as to how to help him [the Arab man]; it was a clear case of . . . helping one load or unload his burden. There were some youngsters there from the neighborhood, who judging by their looks were probably ten or eleven years old. They saw that this merchant was not wearing a *kippa*. So they began a whole *pilpul* [debate], based on the *gemara* in *Pesachim* (113b), about whether they should help him or not. . . . My feeling then was: Why . . . must this be our choice? Can't we find children who would have helped

him and still know the *gemara*? Do we have to choose? I hope not;
I believe not. If forced to choose, however, I would have no doubts
where my loyalties lie: I prefer that they know less *gemara* but help
him.[168]

Where did these boys err? Weren't they religious individuals, at least
externally? Didn't they dress the part of pious Jews? In their desire to
debate the merits of helping a stranger, they failed to see the moral opportunity in front of them.

Jewish life is a moral enterprise, not a purely academic pursuit. To
live an ethical life means gaining understanding of the world as it is.
Such understanding cannot be gleaned from books; it is experiential.
Cultivation of our character traits, *midot*, and our good deeds, *maasim
tovim*, are central to Jewish spiritual development, and wisdom is a complement to action, rather than detached from action. It is not through
armchair reflection alone that wisdom is mastered, but through the
world of action, the realm of giving. Failure to act is akin to failure to
learn from the world. When it seems as if there is too much occurring,
or if there is a psychological block to taking action, we might consider
alternative models of participation, to help our soul's nourishment.

Wisdom is the means to an end, not the end itself. Wisdom itself
aspires to take the best elements of the world and turn them back into
points of spiritual light. Whether this means charity or activism, community involvement or philanthropy, is up to the individual. What is
essential is that knowledge is used positively, with the intent to create a
better, more righteous world. Justice is a direct corollary to wisdom—
and when we forsake one or the other, the system collapses. Strengthening both not only gives succor to the vulnerable, but also inoculates
the soul against cynicism and baseless hate. These truths are what
should spark our commitment to safeguard strangers and those who
could fall victim to humanity's worst proclivities.

3:13

הוּא הָיָה אוֹמֵר: כָּל שֶׁרוּחַ הַבְּרִיּוֹת נוֹחָה הֵימֶנּוּ – רוּחַ
הַמָּקוֹם נוֹחָה הֵימֶנּוּ. וְכָל שֶׁאֵין רוּחַ הַבְּרִיּוֹת נוֹחָה
הֵימֶנּוּ – אֵין רוּחַ הַמָּקוֹם נוֹחָה הֵימֶנּוּ.

[Rabbi Chanina ben Dosa] used to say: If the spirit of one's
fellows is pleased with them, the spirit of the Omnipresent
is pleased with them; but if the spirit of one's fellows is not
pleased with them, the spirit of the Omnipresent is not
pleased with them.

AN ASPECT of Jewish spirituality is seeking and seeing the essence of
God that resides within other human beings. This can be difficult for
anybody because we are all susceptible to prejudice. For the Jewish people especially, we need only look back at the tragedy and despair that
has befallen us throughout history. Nevertheless, when, in the spirit of
our tradition, we honor others as creations in the image of God, we are
likely to encourage their best qualities. Doing this is neither fast nor
easy. Through rigorous practice, training of the mind, and text study,
one can develop this holy attribute and thus feel God's presence in each
person. Only then can the presence of God be felt fully.

At the outset, it should be noted that this mishnah is not calling for
a popularity contest. On the contrary, its purpose is to expound on the
profound relationship between ethics and spirituality. Consider this elementary example: If one is not a kind person known for being gentle
and giving, then God is distanced. If one is a giver who is appreciated
by others for one's contributions, then God is brought closer. Indeed,
the reality of our character can, as one measure, be tested by the perception of our character. This simple precept is one of the most important
found in *Pirkei Avot* and one that continues to guide the expansion of
Jewish social consciousness.

Dr. Rivkah Blau once said that the ethos with which she was raised
by her parents was one of acting on behalf of others and of "think for
yourself."[168a] This teaching, to think for ourselves yet do for others, is

at the center of this mishnah. We are neither to become conformists nor isolationists, but to seek our own path in the world. We should follow our hearts, even if that means that people will disapprove of our opinions or choices. As Martha Nussbaum remarks, "To be a good human being is to have a kind of openness to the world, the ability to trust uncertain things beyond your own control that can lead you to be shattered."[169] Learning to embrace faith and trust in process requires a balance of both self-control and relinquishing control.

In Jewish thought, the biblical figure Mordechai is an example of one who took a risk based upon his religious convictions. He was not willing to conform, especially if conformity was to be forced upon him by iniquitous scoundrels. The story of Mordechai told during Purim is a testament to his conviction:

> And all the king's servants, who were in the king's gate, knelt, and bowed before Haman, as the king had commanded concerning him. But Mordechai would not kneel nor bow before him. Then the king's servants, who were in the king's gate, said to Mordechai, "Why have you disobeyed the king's order?" (Esther 3:2–3)

Mordechai risked his life when he refused to bow to Haman, the corrupt adviser to the king. Some commentators suggest it was because of an idol that Haman wore and to which he insisted that Jews bow, to mock their proscription against idol worship. Because the Jews were powerless, Haman thought he could bully the king's Jewish subjects into supplication. It might be assumed that the Jews would ignore Haman's order; still, many thought they should obey to preserve their lives. That is probably the reason for the rebuke from the "king's servants." And who were "the king's servants" who challenged Mordechai referenced in this passage? Midrash explains this fascinating discrepancy:

> "The King's Servants"—These are the rabbinic judges. . . . And Mordechai did not bow nor prostrate himself; they [the judges] said to him, "Be aware that your actions will cause [Israel] to fall by the sword. Why would you defy the decree of the king?" He responded, "Because I am a Jew!"[170]

According to this midrash, who was challenging Mordechai? The

Jewish leaders! And his response to them is that he cannot conform because he is a Jew—that Jews do not conform when socially pressured to stray from their ethical and spiritual commitments. Nonetheless, we should be pleasant with others, because our relationship with humans precedes our relationship to God.

According to the eighteenth-century rabbi Pinchas Eliyahu Hurwitz of Vilna, this mishnah is specifically tailored toward the betterment of interfaith relations. As he writes about the use of the term rendered as "fellow," he explains that the Rabbis use the term to refer

> not to the members of one's own nation, [but] in order to include all humanity, whether from one's own people or from another people.... Our Rabbis have clearly stated that there is no difference ... between Jews and gentiles.... The essence of neighborly love consists in loving all mankind of whatever people and whatever tongue, by virtue of their identical humanity.[171]

Every day we interact with people in the most banal of ways. Yet, in these moments, we must also set boundaries and limits based upon our values, to ensure that we live with integrity, rather than living to seek praise and acceptance.

3:14

רַבִּי דוֹסָא בֶן הַרְכִּינָס אוֹמֵר: שֵׁנָה שֶׁל שַׁחֲרִית, וְיַיִן שֶׁל
צָהֳרַיִם, וְשִׂיחַת הַיְלָדִים, וִישִׁיבַת כְּנֵסִיּוֹת שֶׁל עַמֵּי הָאָרֶץ –
מוֹצִיאִין אֶת הָאָדָם מִן הָעוֹלָם.

Rabbi Dosa ben Harchinos said: Late morning sleep, midday
wine, children's chatter, and sitting with the unlearned remove
a person from the world.

ON THE VERSE "Let us make human beings" from Genesis 1:26, the
Chasidic master Israel Baal Shem Tov taught that because humanity
is a partner with God in God's Creation, humanity must ensure that
God's Creation was not in vain. We are meant to be more than passive
observers of the wonders of the world; we are to be agents of action in
improving it. Though God is the metaphysical definition of perfection,
those made in God's image are far from perfect, linking the heavens
and earth in the always swirling ether of the unreachable ideal.

We are to do our part to mold the world into a perfected state. Like
the later Chasidic conception of serving God through expressions
of joy, this mishnah describes blessings that evoke joy. Sleep is a gift
that replenishes us. "Wine" has the same numerical value in Hebrew
as "secrets" (lending a knowing gravity to the aphorism *nichnas yayin
yotzei sod*, "[when] wine goes in, secrets come out"), which hints that a
slight alteration of perception can not only be relaxing, but also inspire
insight when used lightly and responsibly. Children are the greatest
blessings in our lives. Joining in community, even with those who are
"unlearned" (and in this context, it could be understood in regard to
the minutiae of tradition), provides great satisfaction.

The problem that Rabbi Dosa ben Harchinos elucidates in this mishnah is not the blessings themselves, but their misappropriation. We
should lift children up, rather than merely engage them in insubstantial
talk. We should lead groups (or, for those who'd rather not lead, be pro-
active participants in groups that align with our values), rather than be
content merely to sit among them. We should sleep at the proper times,

but not indulge in our slumber when there is so much work to be done. Of course, we should drink in moderation. Rather than indulging in a lifestyle in which we abuse sleep, alcohol, and games, we should strive for purpose in our lives.

As partners in Creation, we choose to further God's will toward a more unified world, or we can be distracted by humankind's many diversions. Learning to manage both is valuable to our spiritual growth. The activities in this mishnah are just examples of the many that can enhance our lives or inhibit our maturation. But these examples tell us that everything of value has its time and place, and we must reflect to discern the right balance. This keeps us involved in the world, rather than above it. "Everything has its season, and there is a time for everything under the heaven" (Ecclesiastes 3:1). In a treatise about emotional development, Rabbi Joseph B. Soloveitchik writes that human beings should embrace the totality of emotional life and live with balance, rather than in extremes:

> In the first place, the dialectical character of our existence and our total experience manifests itself in the *halakhic* principle of the totality of the emotional life. Judaism has insisted upon the integrity and wholeness of the table of emotions, leading like a spectrum from joy, sympathy, and humility (the conjunctive feelings) to anger, sadness, and anguish (the disjunctive emotions). Absolutization of one feeling at the expense of others, or the granting of unconditioned centrality to certain emotions while demoting others to a peripheral status, may have damaging complications for the religious development of the personality.[172]

Several generations after the Baal Shem Tov (the founder of Chasidism), Rabbi Nachman of Breslov (eighteenth century, Ukraine) expressed concern about the emphasis on happiness as the paramount display of religious devotion. Rabbi Nachman thought deeply about the issues facing the world and the Jewish community's response to the obstacles—physical and spiritual—that corrupt humans' ability to mirror the Divine. But he also recognized that humans are fallible, in constant need of reassurance on their journey to be good. Just as we try to balance conflicting emotions within ourselves, so too can we embrace this in our relationships. Rabbi Nachman teaches:

> The essence of *shelemut* [wholeness] is to join together two opposites. And don't be alarmed if you see a person who is in complete contrast to your mind (or your way of thinking) and you imagine that it is absolutely impossible to be at peace with that person; and also when you see two people who are indeed opposites (the one to the other); do not say that it may not be possible to make peace between them. On the contrary! The essence of the wholeness of *shelemut* is to attempt to make peace between two opposites, just as God, the Holy Blessed One, makes peace between fire and water, which are two opposites.[173]

If there is anything we need to understand to achieve alignment with the Divine, it is the notion that we are always seeking progress. If that means dedicating more time to learning, or community service, or helping those in need, then so be it. What is true is that we were never meant to be idle. Indeed, we should strive for balance and to hold onto paradox and complexity. This requires commitment, and this mishnah challenges us to distance ourselves from the dangerous perspective that life should be primarily fun. As Toni Morrison said during a commencement speech at Rutgers University in 2011, "Don't settle for happiness."[174] Joy is important, but we should live with a mission and be driven by purpose. This is what will bring happiness.

3:15

רַבִּי אֶלְעָזָר הַמּוֹדָעִי אוֹמֵר: הַמְחַלֵּל אֶת הַקָּדָשִׁים, וְהַמְבַזֶּה אֶת הַמּוֹעֲדוֹת, וְהַמַּלְבִּין פְּנֵי חֲבֵרוֹ בָּרַבִּים, וְהַמֵּפֵר בְּרִיתוֹ שֶׁל אַבְרָהָם אָבִינוּ, וְהַמְגַלֶּה פָנִים בַּתּוֹרָה, אַף עַל פִּי שֶׁיֵּשׁ בְּיָדוֹ תּוֹרָה וּמַעֲשִׂים טוֹבִים, אֵין לוֹ חֵלֶק לָעוֹלָם הַבָּא.

Rabbi Elazar the Moda'ite said: One who desecrates sacred things, who disgraces the Festivals, who humiliates their fellow in public, who nullifies the covenant of our forefather Abraham, or who perverts the Torah—though they may have Torah and good deeds, they have no share in the world-to-come.

THE CONCEPT OF SHAME is taken quite seriously in Jewish ethics. Treating another in a manner that embarrasses or degrades the person is a serious breach of ethical behavior, as well as decorum. But shame is distinct from abject humiliation. Donald C. Klein, the late social psychologist best known for his studies on the effect of humiliation on the psyche, taught that the difference between shame and humiliation is the difference between what's internal and what's external. According to Klein, "People believe they deserve their shame; they do not believe they deserve their humiliation."[175] Humiliating another leaves a slow-healing scar, because it makes public what was hidden within that person. Humiliation is the process by which one desecrates another's reputation, bringing the other to public disrepute. This loss of reputation can lead to loss of livelihood and even premature withdrawal from society (or death). Whether the humiliated person deserves it is irrelevant. The act itself is damaging to both parties.

Losing one's share in the afterlife—the world-to-come—was a standard pedagogical tool for the classical rabbis, stressing observance of the sacred laws. In this way, the *Pirkei Avot* commentators extended the even more ancient teaching that being learned and kind were not enough. Creating public harm to the religious values that Jews have venerated throughout the millennia causes irreparable damage, whether done to a human being, the tradition, the holidays, or the sacred law. One can become overconfident in one's erudition, observance, and service to others when it is not done for the pure sake of the deed; this mishnah teaches us to maintain rigor in our dealings with the Divine.

What does it mean to desecrate Judaism? Does it mean we turn our back on the commandments? Or leave the faith? Or ignore the wisdom accumulated through the ages? As we can see in this mishnah, the ancient view was yes to all. Not following the Torah to the letter was seen as an abandonment of observance, understood narrowly as the true path to living a holy, fulfilled life. Yet we know that today's Judaism is the same neither in scope nor praxis as that in the era of the Sages and prior. How do we recontextualize such stark teaching to fit the current day?

We can acknowledge that Judaism is *a humble search for truth, in which we seek the best course of action*. What this means is deliberately ambiguous. Nonetheless, we can still ponder big questions of truth when engaged in ritual practices and in the learning of Jewish textual wisdom. For example, we have guideposts for our journey—certain truths that cannot be separated from the larger corpus of Torah thought. And in fact, critiques of lower truths (empirical reality that we can observe) may actually enhance the honor of the lofty concepts pertaining to what might be called higher truth—that is, metaphysical veracity. Rabbi Kook wrote about how "religion" is not *true* religion and "Judaism" is not *true* Judaism:

> Religion is corrupted by the decline of the higher Torah, through which one gains the recognition of the greatness of God, the higher perfection that is infinite and beyond assessment. Thus our religion does not yield the noble fruit it ought to yield, it does not raise the souls from their lowly state and the numbers of those who dishonor it and desecrate it increase. However, the Jewish religion is rooted in the Infinite, which transcends every particular content of religion, and for this reason the Jewish religion may truly be considered as the ideal religion, the religion of the future, the "I shall be what I shall be" (Exodus 2:14), which is immeasurably

higher than the content of religion in the present. The ideal essence descends many levels to become the Jewish religion as a corporate religious establishment rather than the ideal essence of religion.[176]

On the topic of the duality of the realms of truth in the outer world, there is also the dichotomy found within the self. Actions have consequences, and our behavior toward others indicates how we interact with the world around us. But more so, how we look into ourselves to uproot our base nature says much about our characters. At the same time, the times we transgress our best potential is akin to the desecration of Creation, though desecration of the body and desecration of the self are two separate matters. This is not only about desecrating values, but also about the one "who humiliates their fellow in public." According to the mishnah, it may be that in the world-to-come, corrupt legislators, unscrupulous judges, and cruel prison staff could get a harsher punishment than the inmate convicted of murder. This is not moral relativism; rather, this means that people who work solely for the debasement of others—through unjust legislation, draconian punishments, or daily dehumanization—do not deserve to be rewarded for their perpetuation of prejudicial systems. A murderer does not lose his share in the world-to-come, according to the Sages, because of the possibility that he, too, was a victim of institutional humiliation. This provocative statement helps us understand that loss of eternal reward is one potential outcome of humiliating others.[177] Inflicting psychological harm is a serious matter.

This mishnah mentions the "covenant of our forefather Abraham" because of his centrality in Jewish social justice. Indeed, he was "chosen" as the global ambassador for justice, *laasot tzedakah umishpat* (Genesis 18:19). If this holy charge means something to us, we are to hold fast to our commitment to cultivate a just world.

On the flip side of the coin, honoring others is central to Jewish tradition. As it says in a moving midrash, "The Holy One said to Israel: 'My children, what do I seek from you? I seek no more than that you love one another and honor one another.'"[178] In honoring this, Judaism's highest truth, we foster continuity.

3:16

רַבִּי יִשְׁמָעֵאל אוֹמֵר: הֱוֵי קַל לָרֹאשׁ וְנוֹחַ לַתִּשְׁחֹרֶת, וֶהֱוֵי
מְקַבֵּל אֶת כָּל הָאָדָם בְּשִׂמְחָה.

Rabbi Yishmael says: Be yielding to an elder, pleasant to the
young, and receive every person with joy.

THERE IS NO RULE that determines who is "an elder" and who
is "the young." There are always those younger and older than we.
Warm-heartedness, respect, and knowing one's proper place strengthens one's moral core. This allows an individual to interact with people
of all ages and in all situations.

In Jewish thought, the *new* itself is not holy. Indeed, the new is
rendered holy only when it is an expression and outgrowth of the old
(which has moral validity in modernity). And to be sure, the *old* itself
is not holy in isolation, but only when it informs a transformative relationship with the new. This mishnah states that we are expected to
treat those older than we with a dignified respect. Concomitantly, the
Rabbis were clear that we must be pleasant to the young. It is easy to
look down upon younger generations as naïve, impulsive, or lacking
wisdom when compared to the those who are older. Rather than pro-
pose a system in which the old condescend to the young, the Rabbis
wisely explained that we must be pleasant toward everyone, no matter
their place in life. This general respect for the dignity of people of all
ages is part of the tolerant, broad, pluralistic ethos that the best of Jewish tradition sought to transmit.

When Rabbi Obadiah ben Jacob S'forno analyzes the line "Receive
every person cheerfully," he writes in his commentary on *Pirkei Avot*:

> However, do not be overbearing with them lest they be afraid to
> approach you; rather receive them with a pleasant demeanor,
> thereby drawing them close to the service of God, as we are told
> regarding Hillel, who wrapped himself in his tallit and sat in front
> of the one who inquired and said, "Ask, my son, ask" (BT *Shab-*
> *bat* 31a). Through this behavior, he brought proselytes under the

wings of the Divine Presence and "turned many away from iniquity" (Malachi 2:6).

Yet, this ideal is hard to make tangible in the real world, where we struggle for meaningful intergenerational communication in an era when modes of connection vary more than in the past. Those who have experienced the full spectrum of growing and aging and are less hurried in their actions can, at times, possess intractable views of the world that cannot be changed. Thus, it can be easy to get frustrated with members of the older generations who may seemingly act as societal barriers to progress. "Yielding" to them does not mean that the youthful must slow their collective pace, but it does mean they must include senior voices in their broader discourse and honor their dignity and wisdom, even when it appears out-of-date.

So, what does life experience mean when it comes to engendering interpersonal growth? Carl Jung observed that "act one of a young man's life is the story of his setting out to conquer the world. . . . Act two is the story of the young man realizing that the world is not about to be conquered by the likes of him."[179] Acts one and two temper each other, working in unison to create the fulfilling life.

The Rabbis are clear that we should receive everyone warmly, but they instruct us to customize our approach. They promote an egalitarian, universalistic ethos to human interaction, but also guide us to address the particulars of each encounter. We should be friendly and inviting, while exercising caution with those we've not met before. We must cultivate the emotional intelligence for differing encounters, which is part of moral and ethical development.

It is not only an ethical commitment that we should be gentle and kind toward others, it is also a theological aspiration. If we believe Judaism should flourish for millennia to come, then it must be joyful. Too many have walked away from Jewish life because it lacked joy, having found it serious and disciplined but without a pleasant and uplifting spirit. Similarly, the most successful social-change movements are not dry and angry. They have soulful music and spirited community. At their best, they are like Judaism at its best: "The ways of the Torah are pleasant, and all its pathways are peace" (Proverbs 3:17).

3:17

רַבִּי עֲקִיבָא אוֹמֵר: שְׂחוֹק וְקַלּוּת רֹאשׁ מַרְגִּילִין אֶת הָאָדָם
לְעֶרְוָה. מָסֹרֶת סְיָג לַתּוֹרָה, מַעְשְׂרוֹת סְיָג לָעֹשֶׁר, נְדָרִים
סְיָג לַפְּרִישׁוּת, סְיָג לַחָכְמָה שְׁתִיקָה.

Rabbi Akiva said: Mockery and levity accustom a person to
impropriety. The tradition is a protective fence around the
Torah; tithes are a protective fence for wealth; vows are a
protective fence for abstinence; a protective fence for wisdom
is silence.

A PSYCHOLOGICAL STUDY showed that if parents do not set up a fence
in a backyard, then children will play only in a small area of the yard.[180]
On the other hand, if a fence encompasses the span of the backyard,
children will play in the entire backyard. What does this study tell us?
Structure can provide the security for free creativity and growth.

Likewise, if an object is cherished, human nature is to protect it from
harm. While this applies to physical objects, it is relevant to spiritual
entities, as well. One approach to keep our sacred objects safe is to lock
them away from others. Or they can be displayed publicly, proudly,
shared with all; different situations call for different responses. In this
mishnah, the Rabbis teach that certain religious matters require strin-
gencies to keep them from violation.

At other times, we must remove threats to attaining what's valuable.
Striving for wisdom means turning off distracting, internal chatter.
Ethical development is not achieved in a vacuum, but its progress can
be impeded by such distraction. Wisdom itself is a precious jewel, se-
cured within the vaults of our minds, and we must protect it from the
intrusion of wanton insubstantiality—and nourish it through difficult
training and unquenchable thirst. This process is like using Talmud to
guard the integrity of Torah tradition, as is the mental dexterity of Rabbinic law protecting the complexity of biblical law.

We should not develop our minds in isolation. Rather, wisdom must
be procured from life itself. No one can tell us where we ought to put

up our own "fences." We must learn the boundaries that we need. An alcoholic needs a different boundary in relation to a bar than others do. A married person needs different boundaries regarding intimacy than does an uncoupled person. One who knows oneself to be quick to anger or impulsive behavior must set custom boundaries.

The pursuit of truth in human affairs is an accrual of historical best practices and sagacity. Consider Princeton University philosopher Susan Neiman's analysis of associate Supreme Court justice Benjamin Cardozo:[181]

> Cardozo wrote that . . . "courts have gone about their business for centuries": Logic, and history, and custom, and utility and the accepted standards of right conduct are the forces which singly or in combination shape the progress of the law. . . . If you ask how he is to know when one interest outweighs another, I can only answer that he must get his knowledge just as the legislator gets it, from experience and study and reflection; in brief, from life itself.[182]

We must truly open our eyes and minds if we wish to make accurate moral judgments. In general, the objectives we strive for in our lives are reactions to how we see the broader world. Throughout life, as we gain a greater grasp of various issues, they become more complex and more ambiguous. In response, we tend to build fences in our mind to separate what we love from what we abhor. It is crucial to be reflective and precise because there can be significant worldly implications from our intellectual conclusions. Activists know, however, that they can't stand for every cause, and they can't only lead from ideals. Indeed, idealism must be restrained with pragmatism, and being stretched too thin must be restrained by discipline.

We dare not, however, restrain our passion in our holy attempts to render adequate moral judgments. Justine Wise Polier, an outspoken activist and the first woman justice in New York said, "Passionate concern may lead to errors of judgment, but the lack of passion in the face of human wrong leads to spiritual bankruptcy."[183]

We will make mistakes and, in the process, set new boundaries for ourselves. Doing so requires discipline, tenacity, and courage. Eleanor Roosevelt taught that everything we strive to do should scare us.[184]

Courage is a muscle that needs to be worked. In this mishnah, Rabbi Akiva says that fences can protect the soul, and we have to filter out those moments that distract from our higher spiritual calling. We must have the courage of our convictions to make sense of the world. Courage is not always about going outward but sometimes about going inward, not always about acting boldly but often about learning restraint. Finding balance is how we protect our souls during their limited time on this earth.

3:18

הוּא הָיָה אוֹמֵר: חָבִיב אָדָם, שֶׁנִּבְרָא בְצֶלֶם. חִבָּה יְתֵרָה:
נוֹדַעַת לוֹ שֶׁנִּבְרָא בְצֶלֶם, שֶׁנֶּאֱמַר: כִּי בְּצֶלֶם אֱלֹהִים עָשָׂה
אֶת־הָאָדָם (בראשית ט:ו). חֲבִיבִין יִשְׂרָאֵל, שֶׁנִּקְרְאוּ בָנִים
לַמָּקוֹם. חִבָּה יְתֵרָה: נוֹדַעַת לָהֶם שֶׁנִּקְרְאוּ בָנִים לַמָּקוֹם,
שֶׁנֶּאֱמַר: בָּנִים אַתֶּם לַיָי אֱלֹהֵיכֶם (דברים יד:א). חֲבִיבִין יִשְׂרָאֵל,
שֶׁנִּתַּן לָהֶם כְּלִי שֶׁבּוֹ נִבְרָא הָעוֹלָם. חִבָּה יְתֵרָה: נוֹדַעַת
לָהֶם שֶׁנִּתַּן לָהֶם כְּלִי שֶׁבּוֹ נִבְרָא הָעוֹלָם, שֶׁנֶּאֱמַר: כִּי לֶקַח
טוֹב נָתַתִּי לָכֶם, תּוֹרָתִי אַל־תַּעֲזֹבוּ (משלי ד:ב).

He used to say: Beloved is the human for the human was
created in the image of God; it is indicative of a greater love
that it was made known to people that we were created in the
image of God, as it is said: "For human beings were made in
the image of God" (Genesis 9:6). Beloved are the people Israel,
for they are described as children of the Omnipresent; it is
indicative of even greater love that it was made known to them
that they are described as children of the Omnipresent, as it is
said: "You are children of the Eternal your God" (Deuteronomy
14:1). Beloved are the people Israel, for a gift by which the
world was created [i.e., the Torah] was given to them; it is
indicative of even greater love that it was made known to them
that they were given a gift by which the world was created, as it
is said: "For I have given you a good teaching; do not forsake
My Torah" (Proverbs 4:2).

HOW IS IT that we are made in the image of God? Through our capacity for speech? Cognition? Morality? Free will? Is it our physical appearance? We can find each of these positions advocated by different Jewish
commentators. What matters most is not how humans differ from
animals or angels, but that we understand the inherent dignity of every
human being. If we subscribe to this theology, then what moral claim
does it make upon us every day, in every human encounter?

Pirkei Avot 3:18 delves into the relationship between the terrestrial (humanity) and the heavenly (God and related celestial beings). That humanity is an image of the supernal is an extraordinary philosophical equation. It is remarkable that we, finite beings, are even allowed to exist in the same realm as the Eternal Divine, let alone reflect the Eternal's image. Like a mighty river with branching tributaries, God is the place from which all love stems and where an individual becomes imbued with spiritual energies beyond concrete thought. Here, we realize our role in the universe. We are unable to supplant the bonds that attach every person to another, nor are we able to deny that God has a particular love within creation, much as a parent loves each of their children differently.

"And the man became a living being" (Genesis 2:7). Rabbi Y'hudah says, "These words teach us that God initially provided the [first] human with a tail like an animal, but then removed it for the sake of human dignity."[185] While we are to honor animal sentience and work to protect the welfare of all creatures, God wanted us to know that while we are a part of the animal kingdom, we transcend it. To complement this thought, Rabbi Y'hoshua ben Levi says, "When a person walks on the highway, a company of angels go first, announcing, 'Make way for the image of the Holy One.'"[186] His comment suggests that it is not only that we are unique and loved, but also that we are heralded by angels as beings cut from a holy cloth.

Jean-Paul Sartre comments that "existence precedes essence." Today, this stance is generally assumed. It is possible to change virtually anything about ourselves—where we live, our ideology, our careers, our spouse, our faith, our sexuality. We are not predetermined. Instead, we embody the aspects of our lives we want the world to see. But the Torah teaches that there is one thing that can never change: Every person possesses a soul. Every one of us is created in the image of God. We will always have that inner light that shines and gives us infinite value. Here, the Torah departs from existentialism, declaring that the essence of humanity is eternal and unchangeable, preceding existence.

However, there are political implications to such a belief. Rabbi Jonathan Sacks explains:

> Power allows us to rule over others without their consent. As the
> Greek historian Thucydides put it: "The strong do what they wish
> and the weak suffer what they must" (Thucydides, 5:89). Judaism
> is a sustained critique of power. That is the conclusion I have
> reached after a lifetime of studying our sacred texts. It is about
> how a nation can be formed on the basis of shared commitment
> and collective responsibility. It is about how to construct a society
> that [honors] the human person as the image and likeness of God.
> It is about vision, never fully realized, but never abandoned, of a
> world based on justice and compassion, in which "they will neither
> harm nor destroy on all My holy mountain, for the earth will be
> filled with the knowledge of the Lord as the waters cover the sea"
> (Isaiah 11:9).[187]

The political implications of seeing every human being as equal are
enormous. In the ancient world, the Code of Hammurabi viewed the
killing of a slave as a monetary crime.[188] The Torah rejected that approach. According to the Torah, the killing of a slave was the murder
of a human, rather than mere destruction of property. It was a capital
crime.

People often make the mistake of believing that because of our
shared "image," we *are* God or that God sanctions all that we do. The
kabbalists were comfortable with a sort of reciprocity—as much as we
are created in the image of God, so too do we create God in our image.[189]
Such a theology, however, brings with it the risk of arrogance. As Anne
Lamott, a political activist and author, writes, "You can safely assume
you've created God in your own image when it turns out that God hates
all the same people as you do."[190]

Twentieth-century psychologists interpreted our understanding of
God through atheism—God is merely wish fulfillment. The kabbalists
agreed that we construct God in our own image but that such an understanding of God is true, precisely because it is our human projection.
That projection comes from our own image of God-place, and thus the
projection itself, with all its relativity and subjectivity, is itself necessarily true. It can't be stressed enough the value of having important truths
reinforced. Humans need to hear things over and over to understand
their reality. Though your spouse, children, and friends know of your

love for them, continue to tell them so. God, in acts of intimate love, tells us we are special and ensures we know we're special. How? When we remind ourselves each day that there is a task for us to fulfill, an accomplishment that has yet to be achieved within us or in the outside world, we become enabled to take something that seems impossible and render it tangible.

3:19

הַכֹּל צָפוּי וְהָרְשׁוּת נְתוּנָה, וּבְטוֹב הָעוֹלָם נִדּוֹן, וְהַכֹּל לְפִי
רֹב הַמַּעֲשֶׂה.

Everything is foreseen, yet the freedom of choice is given. The world is judged with goodness, and everything depends on the majority of one's actions.

ONE OF THE OLDEST existential questions that have vexed the minds of rational beings is the dialectic between free will and fate. Is humanity bound by a supernal force that dictates every action, or is the consciousness of the human mind the ultimate captain of moral decisions? It is a query that philosophers and theologians dedicate their lives to unraveling. The ancient Jewish Sages, too, pondered this.

In a turn toward age-old theological questions, this mishnah touches two divine characteristics: omniscience, the supposed all-knowing force, and benevolence, the force of pure and inherent good. One characteristic might contradict the other or counter a normative interpretation of the Divine.

So, two distinct problems are addressed in this passage. First, if God is all-knowing, how are humans truly free? The mishnah says that though God knows what humans will choose, humans are nevertheless free to make individual decisions. Jewish tradition is adamant about this spiritual paradox: humans are absolutely free, and God knows in advance what we will choose.

Second, God-as-judge and God-as-protector are in tension here; here, justice and mercy are presented as a dual ends of the spectrum, though there is more substance present here on second glance. If God is a judge of truth and justice, how can God also be merciful, compassionate, and all-loving? Here, too, this paradox is true: God is both the God of truth and justice and the God of mercy, compassion, and love. That such paradoxes are unlikely to be satisfactorily resolved may be beside the point. The questions themselves are to drive us to strive toward the impossible peak of unambiguous truth about the ways of

God and the universe. Our goal is to acquire as much knowledge, and as much hope, as we can and then to apply the values we discover to our ethical selves. When we speak of all people of the world "serving God," we may, in a universalistic sense, mean that we're all striving toward moral goodness, to emulate moral perfection.

We have an ethical imperative not just to realize our freedom but to expand it and actualize it. Abraham was told to depart from "your land, your birthplace, your father's house" (Genesis 12:1)—that is, to liberate himself from the various pressures to conform. Each of us must be prepared to depart from our upbringing, break from conformity, and depart from the familiar. Warren Bennis, a twentieth-century thinker on leadership, writes, "By the time we reach puberty, the world has reached us and shaped us to greater extent than we realize. Our family, friends, and society in general have told us—by word and example—how to be. But people begin to become leaders at that moment when they decide for themselves how to be."[191] Embracing our freedom is an ethical imperative that requires us to regularly rethink all of our commitments.

Our negative emotions constitute another form of enslavement. Holding resentment is like holding on to a hot coal; waiting to throw it at your enemy, you burn yourself. Negative emotions, like hatred or bigotry, can be crippling. Our spiritual work, all the more imperative for activists who are often responding to forces of evil, tyranny, injustice, and oppression, is to transform those negative emotions to positive ends, while harnessing the energy and releasing the negativity.

Rabbi Jonathan Sacks explains how freedom, as construct and as lived ideal, is not enough to sustain society. Indeed, we also need responsibility:

> But don't think *chofesh* [freedom] alone can sustain a free society. When everyone is free to do what they like, the result is anarchy, not freedom. A free society requires *cheirut*, the positive freedom that only comes when people internalize the habits of self-restraint—so that my freedom is not bought at the expense of yours, nor yours at the cost of mine.[192]

Revelation, both Sinaitic and historical, did not bind us to stagnation; rather, it gave us freedom. Immanuel Kant challenged this point, arguing that if revelation were reality, it would be calamitous for man's created freedom.[193] One loses free will and the capacity for reason when encountering divine truth. Emmanuel Levinas explained why revelation was needed for freedom: "The teaching, which the Torah is, cannot come to the human being as a result of a choice. That which must be received in order to make freedom of choice possible cannot have been chosen, unless after the fact."[194] When we received revelation, our freedom was suspended in order that we could be free.

The knowledge that we are free, while also realizing that God knows what we will choose, should inspire humility. This sense of humility doesn't have to be paralyzing, nor should it impede us on our spiritual journeys. Rather, this is an empowering humility, which inspires courage. Our freedom is a gift to be actualized. In this mishnah, right after we are reminded that we are free, we are told that God will judge us compassionately. God will be gentle with us because we will strive to do our best with our freedom.

3:20

הוּא הָיָה אוֹמֵר: הַכֹּל נָתוּן בָּעֵרָבוֹן, וּמְצוּדָה פְּרוּסָה עַל כָּל
הַחַיִּים. הֶחָנוּת פְּתוּחָה, וְהַחֶנְוָנִי מַקִּיף, וְהַפִּנְקֶס פְּתוּחָה,
וְהַיָּד כּוֹתֶבֶת, וְכָל הָרוֹצֶה לִלְווֹת יָבֹא וְיִלְוֶה, וְהַגַּבָּאִים
מַחֲזִירִים תָּדִיר בְּכָל יוֹם, וְנִפְרָעִין מִן הָאָדָם מִדַּעְתּוֹ וְשֶׁלֹּא
מִדַּעְתּוֹ, וְיֵשׁ לָהֶם עַל מַה שֶׁיִּסְמְכוּ, וְהַדִּין דִּין אֱמֶת, וְהַכֹּל
מְתֻקָּן לַסְּעוּדָה.

He used to say: Everything is given on collateral and a net is
spread over all the living. The shop is open; the Merchant
extends credit; the ledger is open; the hand writes; and
whoever wishes to borrow, let him come and borrow. The
collectors make their rounds constantly, every day, and collect
payment from the person whether they realize it or not. They
have proof to rely upon; the judgment is a truthful judgment;
and everything is prepared for the banquet.

As people created in the divine image, we are forever bound in the
debt of Creation: the unique act in which God fashioned an expansive
universe that continues to inspire awe and reverence. God could have
ceased at the creation of beasts, but did not, and instead added from the
divine essence to the mixture that brought people to life. We are only
on this earth because God willed it into existence. The mishnah's parable is striking in its simplicity and spiritual depth. Through using credit
collectors and debtors as symbols, the passage conjures an expansive
metaphor about the Divine-human relationship.

For such a relationship to be considered on equal terms, gratitude to
the Divine should be foremost in our every waking thought; we are extended credit to pursue our own dreams, wants, and spiritual desires.

Yes, we are granted freedom and opportunity, but with the caveat
that we use our time, energy, resources, and freedom morally. We are
given only 86,400 seconds every day to actualize our obligations to the
world; we are accountable for each one. Life is a gift, but our souls are

merely on loan from the empyrean vault. We repay the loan by giving our best into this world. Our spiritual gratitude translates into moral responsibility. But this understanding of one's gift and one's debt can lead to isolationism: It is on *me* to repay *my* debt, so I should go at this alone.

Here, let us consider the story of Nachshon ben Aminadav, one of the bravest individuals in the Midrash. When the Israelites left bondage in Egypt, they were chased by the Pharaoh's troop to the shores of the Red Sea. Facing doom from either direction, Moses calls upon the Divine to provide an open path. As the Midrash teaches, it was Nachshon who stepped forward rather than Moses or Aaron.[195] By his simple action of walking forward into the sea, and his complete faith, the sea bifurcated into a path to the Promised Land and the Israelites' redemption.

But leadership does not have to be in the model of a courageous solitary man taking a stand against the inconceivable. Indeed, Rabbi Patricia Karlin-Newmann, of Stanford University, offers a pointed feminist critique of Nachson's actions:

> In *Midrash T'hillim* 114:8, Nachshon reputedly pelts his brothers with stones to assure his place of primacy. The daredevil confidence of this Nachshon contrasts sharply with another vision of this moment (*M'chilta, B'shalach* 5). Huddled together, a terrified crowd looks behind at the Egyptians and forward toward water. As they yell, "I don't want to go into the sea!" Nachshon jumps up in fear; losing his footing, he falls into the waves. Overcome with terror, he cites Psalms, "Save me, O God, for the waters have reached my neck" (Psalm 69:2). Here, Nachshon—a fearful, drowning man—cries for God's help. The midrash alternately envisions Nachshon as hapless victim, brash show-off, or eager leader.[196]

If we were to see but one model for social change, we would not be strategic enough to bring about real change. This is a utilitarian argument for equality and also for egalitarianism in religion. Not every injustice requires street protest. As the late psychologist and academic Abraham Maslow writes, when one only has a hammer, it is tempting "to treat everything as if it were a nail."[197] Indeed, to repay our debt, we must exercise leadership in our unique way, which does not mean that the only strategy is to jump out to the front of the pack. Leadership must often be collaborative. Greatness is about finding our unique contribution, as the Rev. Dr. Martin Luther King Jr. said: "Everybody can be great because anybody can serve."[198]

The late scholar of leadership philosophy and American history James MacGregor Burns distinguished between transactional and transformational leaders. Transactional leaders work on issues. Transformational leaders work with people and their vision as well.

> Transforming leadership is elevating. It is moral, but not moralistic. Leaders engage with followers, but from a higher level of morality; in the enmeshing of goals and values both leaders and followers are raised to more principled levels of judgement.[199]

We often celebrate the leaders up front. But there is a reason that Moses isn't in the Haggadah: it is not about the individual, but about the whole community coming together. Gandhi is celebrated as a hero of India's independence from the United Kingdom, and a quote attributed to him states, "A small body of determined spirits fired by an unquenchable faith in their mission can alter the course of history."[200] He knew that nothing would have been accomplished through his deeds alone. He needed a small group first and then a massive movement.

There are both times and places when one must act alone, such as when no one else is acting; but more often, change comes because of leading together. Cultural anthropologist Margaret Mead is attributed as saying, "Never doubt that a small group of thoughtful, committed citizens can change the world. Indeed, it is the only thing that ever has."[201]

We are only afforded so much time on this earth. How we expend our spiritual capital is one of the most important parts of life. All we can hope for is that, by exertion of will and cultivation of character, we are prudent and judicious with our limited resources.

3:21

רַבִּי אֶלְעָזָר בֶּן עֲזַרְיָה אוֹמֵר: אִם אֵין תּוֹרָה אֵין דֶּרֶךְ אֶרֶץ,
אִם אֵין דֶּרֶךְ אֶרֶץ אֵין תּוֹרָה. אִם אֵין חָכְמָה אֵין יִרְאָה, אִם
אֵין יִרְאָה אֵין חָכְמָה. אִם אֵין דַּעַת אֵין בִּינָה, אִם אֵין בִּינָה
אֵין דַּעַת. אִם אֵין קֶמַח אֵין תּוֹרָה, אִם אֵין תּוֹרָה אֵין קֶמַח.

Rabbi Elazar ben Azaryah says: If there is no Torah, there
is no worldly occupation; if there is no worldly occupation,
there is no Torah. If there is no wisdom, there is no fear of
God; if there is no fear of God, there is no wisdom. If there is
no knowledge, there is no understanding; if there is no understanding, there is no knowledge. If there is no flour, there is
no Torah; if there is no Torah, there is no flour.

FOR MANY JEWS TODAY, Torah wisdom doesn't play a large role. Their
morality is not based on a study of our shared history, analysis of Judaism's values, or a conversation with our rich, millennia-old heritage.
There are also Jews whose heads are so deep in our tradition's ancient
commentaries that they fail to respond to today's moral challenges. Or
worse, they are responsive, but with neither contemporary nuance nor
perspective. This mishnah reminds us to be *in* the world, while being
beyond the world, and to work toward proper balance.

Like life itself, the Torah requires balance. Torah requires living in the
temporal world with all its inescapable vagaries. Each daily responsibility is connected with others. We must cultivate appropriate attitudes
toward working, learning, reflecting, and repeating. Obviously, there is
no food without work, but it is less obvious that there is no Torah without food. Indeed, the Torah is the sustaining nutrient of the soul—the
original "soul food."

In this passage, the Rabbis teach that sustenance, not asceticism,
is part of spiritual pursuits. Retreating from the world completely is
anathema to the development of well-rounded members of society.
We must be nourished and have healthy, positive energy to pursue our

ambitions and aspirations. When we embrace the joy of responsible consumption, allowing it to nourish our religious endeavors, the potential for growth is infinite. When our souls cry for strength, we shall forage through the fields of knowledge that is there for the taking.

Rabbi Jonathan Sacks writes about the mysterious dimensions of wisdom. Consider how he differentiates wisdom understood objectively versus wisdom that is spiritual:

> We should note that *chochmah*, wisdom, means something slightly different from Torah, which is more commonly associated with priests and prophets rather than kings. *Chochmah* includes worldly wisdom, which is human and universal rather than a special heritage of Jews and Judaism. A midrash states, "If someone says to you, 'There is wisdom among the nations of the world,' believe it. If they say, 'There is Torah among the nations of the world,' do not believe it" (*Lamentations Rabbah*, 2:13). Broadly speaking, in contemporary terms *chochmah* refers to the sciences and humanities—to whatever allows us to see the universe as the work of God and the human person as the image of God. Torah is the specific moral spiritual heritage of Israel.[202]

Maimonides teaches that one should "accept the truth wherever one finds it,"[203] which means that it is possible to find wisdom in unexpected places. Indeed, it is a codified spiritual practice to celebrate the wisdom found among gentiles, as if it is as worthy as wisdom derived from Jewish sources. The Sages teach:

> If you see a Jewish sage, say, "Praised is the One who has imparted divine wisdom to those who revere God." If you see a non-Jewish sage, say, "Praised is the One who has imparted divine wisdom to God's creatures." (BT *B'rachot* 58a)

This pluralistic view is at odds with the pernicious, fantastical modern Judeo-centrism—the idea that Jewish thought takes precedence in the affairs of society. Judaism repeatedly directs us to embrace the unique wisdom in our religious system, but also to look to be transformed by every person we encounter.

This mishnah challenges us to exist within the cosmic tensions that pull at us every day and, ultimately, to find balance in our lives. Our actions do not take place in a vacuum. With everything we do, there is constant action and reaction, push and pull, calm and force. Between these extremes of action, there is balance. There is a centeredness that is hard to describe in words. It can only be felt. May we be open to the possibilities to feel wisdom permeating our core.

(*For 3:22, see page 152.*)

3:23

רַבִּי אֶלְעָזָר חִסְמָא אוֹמֵר: קִנִּין וּפִתְחֵי נִדָּה הֵן הֵן גּוּפֵי
הֲלָכוֹת, תְּקוּפוֹת וְגִמַטְרִיָאוֹת פְּרְפְּרָאוֹת לַחָכְמָה.

Rabbi Elazar Chisma said: The laws of bird-offerings, and the
laws regarding the beginning of menstrual periods—these
are the essential laws; astronomy and mathematics are at the
periphery of wisdom.

THIS IS, for the modern reader, a strange teaching. Bird-offerings and
menstrual periods would not come to mind when noting the richness
of Jewish tradition. Nor, indeed, would astronomy and mathematics.
Yet, scholars in antiquity thought much about the purity of the body
through its functions and its relation to the progress of time.

Perhaps Rabbi Elazar Chisma, renowned during his life for his
mathematical talent, is referring to Jewish thinking on metaphysical
time (time as viewed from the eternal perspective rather than from the
earthly perspective). The menstrual cycle and bird-offerings are tied
to time and measurement, to astronomy and mathematics. Judaism
understands time as neither circular nor linear; rather, time from the
divine perspective is a human construction that provides order. It
allows for us to make sense—to the best of our limited perceptions—of
the incorporeality of space and existence. In our human system, we
have to embrace time to transcend it.

The Jewish philosophy toward time is complex. Will we ever end
poverty, hunger, and genocide? Is there hope that tomorrow will look
brighter than today? The social justice movement is guided by a messianic vision that a world that is more just and free is possible. Can we,
as Jews, embrace this promise of progress? Since the Holocaust, most
philosophers have rejected the idea that the Enlightenment was the
beginning of progress. Two thousand years earlier, the Rabbis rejected
the idea of progress, claiming that the generations are in a steady state
of decline. The Talmud refers to one generation as being of men and to
a later one as being of donkeys (BT *Shabbat* 112b). The Sages exempt no

one, even calling the great matriarch Sarah a monkey, when compared to Eve (BT *Bava Batra* 58a).

Additionally, astronomy has a moral component. The calendar, established according to the phases of the moon, sets holidays for the Jewish people to come together in hopeful prayer and celebration. Rabbi Elazar Chisma says to use this structure to guide the individual through, for example, "bird-offerings" and "menstrual periods." The former is about what the individual will offer to society, and the latter is about the individual's intimate and holy relationship with one's family within one's home. And while the topic may be uncomfortable, the way by which we interact with the body is experienced through changes in how it functions throughout our life. Indeed, for those living in ancient times, "vaginal blood had [great] significance" because "it contained the seed that united with the male seed . . . to produce a human being."[204]

While appreciating the brevity of our lives, we can reflect upon our opportunities to learn more. The Chafetz Chayim offers a scathing critique of those who value learning over acts of kindness:

> You occasionally see Jews who [in a praiseworthy way] learn Torah
> [as often as possible] and value their time [not wasting a minute].
> But if they do not set aside part of the day to do deeds of kindness,
> what a lack of intelligence![205]

This perceived generational decline is attributed not only to ignorance of divine truth—the prophetic *ruach hakodesh* (holy spirit) ceased to inspire humans upon the deaths of Haggai, Zechariah, and Malachi (BT *Sanhedrin* 11a)—but also to decline in ability: "In former generations, people made Torah their vocation and their trades their avocation, and they succeeded in both; in latter generations, when people made their trades their vocations and Torah their avocation, they did not succeed in either" (BT *B'rachot* 35b).

Although the Sages were concerned about spiritual and intellectual decline, this is not the whole story. Rabbi Abraham Isaac Kook embraced the Hegelian idea of historical progress:

> We should not immediately feel obliged to refute any idea that
> comes to contradict something in the Torah, but rather we should

build the palace of Torah above it. In so doing, we reach a more exalted level, and . . . the ideas are clarified. And thereafter, when we are not pressured by anything, we can confidently also fight on the Torah's behalf.[206]

Rabbi Kook further defends the idea of progress, suggesting that "an evolution marked by constant progress provides solid grounds for optimism."[207]

Others say that we need not long for the past. Rabbi Shlomo Almoli (thirteenth century, Spain) argues that greater access to information makes it "plausible that the knowledge and understanding of the latter generations should exceed that of the former ones."[208] The early Chasidic work *Midrash Pinchas* claims that while we are far from past sources of spiritual light (Creation, Sinai, the Temple), we stand closer to the anticipated "light of the Messiah" and are thus more illuminated.[209] As Rabbi Abraham Joshua Heschel writes in the third volume of his erudite tome *Torah Min Ha-Shamayim* (most often translated as *Heavenly Torah*), the means to a conceptual broadening of our universe involves going beyond the mundanity of our everyday lives and seeking something greater, perhaps something we can imagine only during our quiet moments of meditation. We are not meant to see only what our eyes can see. We are meant to let our soul out from time to time. Expanding on this image, Heschel writes:

> The purist tends to believe that his reason corresponds to reality and forgets that reason is to reality as a dwarf is to a giant. The visionary knows that truth is expressed only in fractions and is revealed only through the lens of metaphors and parables. Is it really possible to see what is concealed without a veil? Or to peek past our bounds without metaphors?[210]

Today, we have more access to transportation, medication, and technology than ever before. We have greater awareness of tragedy and more resources to combat injustice. Eradicating poverty is now only a matter of human will. In addition to the search for religious truth as barometer of progress and decline, we must be concerned with the general human welfare. For this reason, we must maintain hope in progress, in the possibility that we can create a more just world, where all children have access to quality education and all people have adequate food, shelter, and health care. We may have diminished access to more simple truths, but we have greater potential than ever to embrace the more complex truths and responsibilities of our interconnected universe.

Chapter 4

4:1

בֶּן זוֹמָא אוֹמֵר: אֵיזֶהוּ חָכָם? הַלָּמֵד מִכָּל אָדָם, שֶׁנֶּאֱמַר:
מִכָּל־מְלַמְּדַי הִשְׂכַּלְתִּי (תהלים קיט:צט). אֵיזֶהוּ גִבּוֹר? הַכּוֹבֵשׁ
אֶת יִצְרוֹ, שֶׁנֶּאֱמַר: טוֹב אֶרֶךְ אַפַּיִם מִגִּבּוֹר, וּמֹשֵׁל בְּרוּחוֹ
מִלֹּכֵד עִיר (משלי טז:לב). אֵיזֶהוּ עָשִׁיר? הַשָּׂמֵחַ בְּחֶלְקוֹ,
שֶׁנֶּאֱמַר: יְגִיעַ כַּפֶּיךָ כִּי תֹאכֵל, אַשְׁרֶיךָ וְטוֹב לָךְ (תהלים קכח:ב).
אַשְׁרֶיךָ בָּעוֹלָם הַזֶּה, וְטוֹב לָךְ לָעוֹלָם הַבָּא. אֵיזֶהוּ מְכֻבָּד?
הַמְכַבֵּד אֶת הַבְּרִיּוֹת, שֶׁנֶּאֱמַר: כִּי־מְכַבְּדַי אֲכַבֵּד וּבֹזַי יֵקָלּוּ
(שמואל א, ב:ל).

Ben Zoma says: Who is wise? One who learns from every
person, as it is said: "From all my teachers I grew wise" (Psalm
119:99). Who is strong? One who subdues one's base instincts,
as it is said: "One who is slow to anger is better than the
strong person, and a master of their passions is better than
a conqueror of a city" (Proverbs 16:32). Who is rich? One who is
happy with one's lot, as it is stated: "When you eat of the labor
of your hands, you are praiseworthy and all is well with you"
(Psalm 128:2). "You are praiseworthy"—in this world; "and all is
well with you"—in the world-to-come. Who is honored? One
who honors others, as it is said: "For those who honor Me, I
will honor, and those who scorn Me shall be degraded"
(I Samuel 2:30).

BEN ZOMA is teaching the ethics of relationships. That we are to strive
to learn from all people, humbly and without prejudice, is easy to understand, but arduous in practice. Human evil, baseless bigotry, and
hatred toward others are all too common. To overcome our human
faults, individually and in community, we seek strength not through
domination of others but through self-restraint. We are not to compare
our lot to others, but rather to learn contentment and curb jealousy. We
are to honor others. These are ethics of alterity, in other words, ethics

focused on considering the value of *otherness* in the stranger and what that brings out in our own perspectives.

One might expect a different response to Ben Zoma's questions: the wise one is the intellectual in the ivory tower; the strong one is the most physically capable; the rich one has the largest bank account; the honored one is the one with the most power. Instead, the noble values here are humility, spiritual introspection, and honoring the other instead of oneself.

Ben Zoma teaches that one should be grateful and *samei-ach b'chelko*, content with one's lot. Perhaps this teaching is beyond personal gratitude and about consciousness of the other. It can be translated as being joyous at someone else's gain. Imagine if we could live with such love for one another and truly celebrate one another's growth.

Rabbi Yechiel Michel of Zlotshov (eighteenth century, Ukraine) explains that we should learn from everyone: "We must learn not only from educated people but from everyone. Even from the uneducated and even from the wicked you can learn how to conduct yourself."[211]

Ben Zoma sets the stage for us to understand pluralism. While tolerance of diversity of belief is generally considered to be a post-Enlightenment phenomenon, we can see glimmers of it in Prophets:

> Come, let us go up to the mountain of the Eternal, to the Temple of the God of Jacob. God will teach us godly ways, so that we may walk in godly paths. . . . God will judge between many peoples and will settle disputes for strong nations far and wide. . . . Everyone will sit under their own vine and under their own fig tree, and no one will make them afraid, for the Eternal Almighty has spoken. All the nations may walk in the name of their gods, but we will walk in the name of the Eternal our God for ever and ever. (Micah 4:2–5)

Micah not only imagined but also advocated for a messianic era, when everyone will "walk in the name of their gods." This does not reduce the prophet's commitment to the one God, but he allows the possibility for different relationships to that one God.

This approach to the other is not mindless relativism, but respectful and empowering pluralism. Rabbi Yitz Greenberg, commenting on this mishnah, writes:

Pluralism means more than accepting or even affirming the other. It entails recognizing the blessings in the other's existence, because it balances one's own position and brings all of us closer to the ultimate goal. Even when we are right in our own position, the other who contradicts our position may be our corrective or our check against going to excess. . . . Pluralism is not relativism, for we hold on to our absolutes; however, we make room for others' as well.[212]

There is humility in this pluralism, where we acknowledge that we cannot see the full picture ourselves and we need others, even those who are different and with whom we disagree, to help us understand the fullness of the world around us. Rabbi Yitz continues:

Relativism . . . is the loss of capacity to affirm any standards. But the deepest religious response is pluralism—the recognition that there are plural absolute standards that can live and function together, even when they conflict. The deepest insight of pluralism is that dignity, truth and power function best when they are pluralized, e.g., divided and distributed, rather than centralized or absolutized. . . . The essential difference between pluralism and relativism is that pluralism is based on the principle that there still is an absolute truth. . . . Pluralism is an absolutism that has come to recognize its limitations.[213]

Often we get stuck in language, especially when there appears to be a paradox. For instance, Hindus may say they believe in many gods, which seems counter to Judaism's assertion of one God. Studying Hindu theology leads one to the understanding that Hindus subscribe to an ultimate divine source expressed in many ways, not entirely unlike Jewish monotheism.

So, too, some say they believe the Torah is not from heaven but mean something different from what might be inferred from the statement. Rabbi Abraham Isaac HaKohen Kook, the first Ashkenazi chief rabbi of Mandatory Palestine, explains this well:

There is denial that is like an affirmation of faith, and an affirmation of faith akin to denial. A person can affirm the doctrine of the Torah coming from "heaven," but with the meaning of "heaven" so strange that nothing of true faith remains. And a person can deny

Torah coming from "heaven" where the denial is based on what the person has absorbed of the meaning of "heaven" from people full of ludicrous thoughts. Such a person believes that the Torah comes from a source higher than that! Although that person may not have reached the point of truth, nonetheless this denial is to be considered akin to an affirmation of faith. "Torah from Heaven" is but an example for all affirmations of faith, regarding the relationship between their expression in language and their inner essence, the latter being the main desideratum of faith.[214]

Language's ability to convey true meaning is limited, and the words we choose to express ourselves are often simply how we have heard or used an expression before. Sometimes, what one says and what the listener understands do not match. We must acknowledge that God and truth are far more complex than any one individual, faction, or religion can grasp alone. Talking about these big questions may offend the absolutist's sensibilities, but absolutists can always use some agitation. Indeed, consider Eleanor Roosevelt's view on the folly of absolutist thinking:

A mature person is one who does not think only in absolutes, who is able to be objective even when deeply stirred emotionally, who has learned that there is both good and bad in all people and all things, and who walks humbly and deals charitably with the circumstances of life, knowing that in this world no one is all-knowing and therefore all of us need both love and charity.[215]

The challenge for conscientious people today is to slide neither into the easy temptation of blind absolutism (my truth is the only truth) or into relativism where there is no single entity called truth. Modern pluralism, based on the proto-pluralistic ethos of Ben Zoma, is an approach that enables us to maintain our own truths with complete rigor, while honoring the claims of others as not just possible but dignified. Embracing this means that one can progress with intellectual rigor, expanded human solidarity, and religious humility. May the day come soon when the prophesy of Micah is fulfilled: all people will walk together with God, singing one song, each with different understanding of the lyrics.

4:2

בֶּן עַזַּי אוֹמֵר: הֱוֵי רָץ לְמִצְוָה קַלָּה וּבוֹרֵחַ מִן הָעֲבֵרָה,
שֶׁמִּצְוָה גוֹרֶרֶת מִצְוָה וַעֲבֵרָה גוֹרֶרֶת עֲבֵרָה, שֶׁשְּׂכַר מִצְוָה
מִצְוָה וּשְׂכַר עֲבֵרָה עֲבֵרָה.

Ben Azzai said: Run to perform even a minor mitzvah, and
flee from sin; for one mitzvah leads to another mitzvah, and
one sin leads to another sin; for the consequence of a mitzvah
is a mitzvah, and the consequence of a sin is a sin.

> *No man is an island,*
> *Entire of itself. . . .*
> *Any man's death diminishes me,*
> *For I am involved in mankind.*[216]

WHAT IS ONE of the most indispensable mitzvot that we learn from
the Torah? According to the *Sefer HaChinuch*, it is the mitzvah of *p'ru
urvu*, be fruitful and multiply, which is listed as the first commandment.[217] On a halachic level, this means that procreation is an essential
mechanism of the world. But viewed more broadly, it means that humans were created in order to become agents of creation. It is possible,
however, for the mitzvah to mean even more. Rabbi Yaakov Culi had
a radical interpretation of this mitzvah. According to Rabbi Culi, *p'ru
urvu* is fulfilled not only through physical acts of procreation, but also
through *chidushei Torah*, novel Torah interpretations.[218] Torah study demands that each person bring ideas. *P'ru urvu* is a general command for
religious creativity—perpetuating what is just, good, and holy.

We're asked to be creators not just once, but daily. In the morning
prayer service, *Shacharit*, the *Yotzeir* prayer says, *m'chadeish b'chol yom
tamid maaseih v'reishit*, "God creates daily, constantly, the work of Creation." This means that we should yearn to be creative, *m'chadeish*, to
have an effect on the world.

Yet, it is difficult to break ingrained habits, especially negative ones.
The more we act in destructive and sacrilegious ways, the easier it is to

do so, to the detriment of our spiritual growth. Even more, when we engage in moral, righteous acts, they become less difficult and feasible. When we do something good, we are affecting not merely the outer world, but also our inner world, as we strengthen our moral muscles. Therefore, no mitzvah can really be considered minor. When we allow our moral muscles to atrophy out of unwillingness to perform a minor mitzvah, they will become too weak to perform major mitzvot, too. The moral muscles need regular exercise for the soul's long-term health.

We alone can exercise ourselves toward full potential. In *Mindset*, Stanford psychologist Carol Dweck distinguishes between "the fixed mindset" and "the growth mindset."[219] One stunts growth with a fixed mindset, a belief that one's capabilities are innate and unable to be adjusted. One can grow in one's achievements, however, if one embraces the growth mindset. Religious ritual is like exercise; at its best, it is the practice that strengthens our souls.

Rabbi Nachman of Breslov teaches that we should put important lessons into prayer.[220] Indeed, we can turn our Torah into song and embrace these melodious teachings throughout our day. More than a century later, Rabbi Yisrael Salanter teaches that people should engage in *hitpaalut*, in which we sing or chant phrases over and over, to learn their meaning.[221] When Rabbi Heschel said that participating in a march, especially the monumental March to Montgomery with Martin Luther King Jr., was like praying with our feet,[222] perhaps he meant that the demonstration, coupled with its chants, wrote the meaning of the protest on our hearts. The tactic of protest can be transformative when augmented by spiritual language.

Ritual can also take significant world events to a new level. What does it mean to truly observe Martin Luther King Day, or Memorial Day, or Yom HaShoah? How can we transform powerful historical commemorations into sustained systems? James MacGregor Burns explains:

> The most lasting tangible act of leadership is the creation of an institution—a nation, a social movement, a political party, a bureaucracy—that continues to exert moral leadership and foster needed social change long after the creative leaders are gone.[223]

Seeing every opportunity to perform a mitzvah is vital to our spiritual well-being. Appreciating all that is around us, however, is not something that comes naturally. Often, we retreat to our own wants and fears, our own basic desires. Consider that it was for the minor mitzvah, the little moments of kindness, that humanity was created. The late Thomas Merton, an American Catholic mystic and theologian, comments:

> A tree gives glory to God by being a tree. For in being what God means it to be it is obeying God. It "consents," so to speak, to God's creative love. It is expressing an idea which is in God and which is not distinct from the essence of God, and therefore a tree imitates God by being a tree.[224]

Why does the Torah want us to recognize creativity as the first divine virtue? This is elucidated in the principle of *halachta bidrachav*, which in Christian and academic circles is known by the Latin term *imitatio Dei*. Namely, we must strive to imitate the ways of God, not just in grand gestures at monumental times, but in all that we do.[224a] This is what it means to be human and created in the image of God. In doing so, we should be creative. *B'reishit bara Elohim et hashamayim v'et haaretz* is the first line of the Torah: "In the beginning, God created heaven and earth." *B'reishit bara Elohim*—God is a Being of creativity.

God creates, and then God sees that creating is good. If we emulate God and become agents of creativity, then we are asked to create as an ethical and spiritual necessity. The whole of humanity is a creative entity. And for us to be enveloped in the wonders of creation, we have to contemplate our roles in bringing new ideas, discoveries, and thoughts into being. This is what we mean by repeating *m'chadeish b'chol yom*, "creating every day." Consider when a writer is up late at night trying to finish an article on deadline: *m'chadeish b'chol yom*. When a parent is struggling to learn a more effective way to teach the child: *m'chadeish b'chol yom*. When a person realizes that they just don't understand the Talmudic passage after a few hours of concentration: *m'chadeish b'chol yom*. When a person gains insight into the suffering of others and tries to help: *m'chadeish b'chol yom tamid maaseih v'reishit*.

Everywhere in life, our efforts result in the creation of new behavior, new ideas, new insights. Humanity advances precisely because of our fascination with creating new experiences through the inspiration of divine acts. Indeed, creativity as the purpose of our existence is what Rabbi Joseph B. Soloveitchik called the charge of "majesty and humility"; the religious person must be humble and profoundly aware of our mortality, but also seek to live with the boldness and creativity of a king—that is, the one with the power to legislate, build roads, and commission art projects. He writes:

> The power stored up within man is exceedingly great, is all-encompassing, but all too often it slumbers within and does not bestir itself from its deep sleep. The command of creation, beating deep within the consciousness of Judaism, proclaims: Awake ye slumberers from your sleep. Realize, actualize yourselves, your own potentialities and possibilities, and go forth to meet your God. The unfolding of man's spirit that soars to the very heavens, that is the meaning of creation. . . . Action and creation are the true distinguishing marks of authentic existence.[225]

Courage is required to create. This is courage not in the absence of despair and doubt, but the capacity to move forward in spite of despair and doubt. We must conquer the fear that our creations will fail, be rejected, and be irrelevant.

This is a great challenge for each of us. Creativity can be spiritually rewarding, but it evokes fear and hope, discord and harmony, discomfort and determination, exuberance and angst. Creativity is not merely the moment of finding the solution. Rather it is the moment of finding the problem. Whenever we are focused on the problems to be addressed, we are creative.

In the moment of despair, when it seems that there are no answers left, our capacity for perseverance and creativity can kick in. Thomas Edison created thousands of prototypes of the light bulb before one worked. Leonardo da Vinci destroyed many of his own canvasses. Albert Einstein remarked, "I have not failed. I've just found ten thousand ways that won't work." Failure and confusion are necessary to the creative process.

In this way, we can also emulate God. Midrash teaches that God created multiple worlds, destroyed each one, and tried again, until this world was created. Our world emerged only after unsuccessful attempts.[226]

This world may have been the most perfect of the original ten, but it was still left unfinished. Why? It is because humans are destined to have a part in Creation. When we wake up to the realities of existence, we can participate in the creative process.

When life is understood as a series of moments of creation through speech, relationships, ideas, and love, we reimagine possibility. By being present and acting in the moment, we create new possibilities in the world. Jewish theology is a performative theology, in which the act (the mitzvah) is central to creating. Even further, Jewish theology is a transformative theology: in fulfilling mitzvot, we re-create ourselves and our world. As emulators of God in Creation, we are called upon to see problems as opportunities for creation. We don't just sit and complain about challenges; we create partnerships and solutions.

Discussing the Creation story, Nachmanides explains the difference between *b'riah*, "creating," and *y'tzirah*, "forming."[227] The Torah uses the language of *b'riah* to describe the initial creation of the world and the creation of humans. This is a creation called *yeish mei-ayin*, a creation out of no prior existence. Other creations are described by the Torah as *y'tzirah*. This is a creation called *yeish mi-yeish*, a creation from existing substance and existence. In the verse uttered during morning prayer *yotzeir or uvorei choshech* (Creator of light and Creator of darkness), light comes from other light, so it is the language of *y'tzirah* (forming), but darkness is a creation from nothingness, so it is the language of *b'riah* (creating).

Given that humans were created from nothing, we can be creative beyond anything ever imagined. Perhaps we may create something grand from nothing, *yeish mei-ayin*, just a few times in our lives, but *yeish mi-yeish*, creating from something, is regular and constant. This *y'tzirah*, the forming process, can be holy and transformative. We need not think of creation as just the grand and completely innovative. Rather, steady commitment and focus are also part of the life of daily possibility.

Rabbi Kook believed that this continual, daily process of creation was the core of spiritual life. He says that we should not only perpetuate our creative energies, but also become aware that at each moment we are engaged in a spiritual and practical creative process. He writes:

> Every fleeting moment we create, consciously and unconsciously, multitudes of creation beyond measure. If we would only condition ourselves to feel them, to bring them within the zone of clear comprehension, to introduce them within the framework of appropriate articulation, there would be revealed their glory and their splendor. Their effect would then become visible on all of life.[228]

It would easy for us to sink into daily routine. The Creation story reminds us of our potential to create. In the face of unforeseen challenges, which the Creation story certainly delves into with the fall of humanity from the Garden of Eden, we can still possess the courage to create. In building community, bringing about change in the world, and in careers, we have unique creative gifts to share. We were brought into the world specifically to offer our gift, to be partners with God in Creation. When God says, "Let us make human beings" (Genesis 1:26), it has been suggested that God is talking to humanity as a partner. God transcends nature, and we are asked to do the same: to acknowledge that what is does not necessarily have to be as it is. There is a kabbalistic notion that God works through us to create change in the world. To actualize God's creative potential, each of us must create.[229]

A quote attributed to playwright George Bernard Shaw says, "Life is not about finding yourself but about creating yourself."[230] Life may be about creating yourself, but it is also about making space for others to create themselves. Every person is full of potential. The opportunity within each major mitzvah and every minor mitzvah, and in every waking moment, is to imitate the Divine and miraculously create something new. The prophets taught that to be visionary and change the world requires significant creativity. We are called to inspire within ourselves an insatiable courage to create.

4:3

הוּא הָיָה אוֹמֵר: אַל תְּהִי בָז לְכָל אָדָם, וְאַל תְּהִי מַפְלִיג
לְכָל דָּבָר – שֶׁאֵין לְךָ אָדָם שֶׁאֵין לוֹ שָׁעָה, וְאֵין לְךָ דָּבָר
שֶׁאֵין לוֹ מָקוֹם.

He used to say: Do not be scornful of any person and do not
be disdainful of anything, for you have no person without
their hour and no thing without its place.

IN JUDAISM, everything that has or will be created is brought forth for
a unique reason. These reasons, mysterious to humans, are part of the
master plan for the universe. Though humanity might not be attuned
to the precise reasoning for creation, we are nonetheless partners in
ensuring that creation is accorded dignity.

However, humanity does not always see the dignity of other parts
of divine creation and disrespects other creatures. Often, due to tribal
instinct or partisan inclination, people refuse to see the inherent dignity in others and use differences to embarrass or attempt to gain an
advantage over another. Such behavior is unfortunately considered so
normal in society that it's not even recognized as malignant.

We must counteract this. Indeed, as taught in the Talmud, the act
of shaming God's creatures is akin to shaming God (BT *Bava M'tzia*
58b). We must see the value in every being, no matter its status. This approach should lead us to compassion for all. In violent ideologies based
on hierarchy, lower beings can be harmed and destroyed because they
are seen to possess no real value.

Consider the tales about the great kabbalist Rabbi Isaac Luria—the
Ari-zal—who refrained from killing insects in his study space.[231] The
Ari-zal would repeat the kabbalistic dictum that there isn't a creature
that exists on this earth whose purpose is meaningless.[232] It was said
that Rabbi Kook would refuse to uproot a plant or a flower or even kill
an insect.[233] To see our connection to divine compassion is to become
more godly ourselves.

How can we apply this to daily life? Consider this mishnah as a call for empathy to understand the pain of others, the struggles of others, and the miasma of their lives. It is not pleasant, but it is necessary. The Midrash says that when we experience rancor within our own hearts, from external or internal reasons, we should release the fetters of our distress to think about the plight of others:

> "The heart knows its own bitterness, even as with its joy no stranger can interfere" (Proverbs 14:10). What does this mean? That just as the heart is the first to feel distress when a person is anguished, so too it is the first to feel the joy when a person rejoices.[234]

Centuries later, the French philosopher Simone Weil wrote about the connection between God and humanity and the intangible forces that influence how people interact with each other:

> Not only does the love of God have attention for its substance; the love of our neighbor, which we know to be the same love, is made of this same substance. . . . The capacity to give one's attention to a sufferer is a very rare and difficult thing; it is almost a miracle; it is a miracle. Nearly all those who think they have this capacity do not possess it. Warmth of heart, impulsiveness, pity are not enough.[235]

So then, what should we take from such teachings? In the short term, we need to consider that everything matters, and everything is connected. While we should embrace humanity's endowed autonomy and agency, there is an absurdity to standing in proud declaration of the singular *I*. Don't we have to endure more with the self than we have to endure with others? The late American poet Adrienne Rich comments on this absurdity in "In Those Years":

> In those years, people will say, we lost track
> of the meaning of *we*, of *you*
> we found ourselves
> reduced to *I*
> and the whole thing became
> silly, ironic, terrible:
> we were trying to live a personal life and yes, that was the only life
> we could bear witness to

But the great dark birds of history screamed and plunged
into our personal weather
They were headed somewhere else but their beaks and pinions drove
along the shore, through the rags of fog
where we stood, saying *I*[236]

In a Chasidic parable about the dual nature of human existence, Rabbi Simchah Bunim of Przysucha (Poland) teaches that we should keep two pieces of paper in our pockets at all times. One piece of paper should say, "For my sake the world was created." The other should say, "I am nothing but dirt and ashes." Whenever we are overwhelmed by pride, we should read, "I am nothing but dirt and ashes." When we feel low and worthless, we should reach into the other pocket and read, "For my sake the world was created."[237] Ultimately, our relationship to creation depends on the worth we see in ourselves; loving others means loving ourselves. If we do not have self-respect, then seeing the grandeur in the universe is difficult to do.

Judaism rejects nihilism. Humanity does have a purpose, even if it is not apparent. Meaning is infused into everything we do and every encounter we pursue. Likewise, the phrase from the mishnah that we should "not be scornful of any person" includes the self. Respect for others is respect for ourselves, which is respect for God, who brought us forth and put us on earth for a reason. While comprehending all this spiritual wisdom might be beyond our capacity, embracing our individual potential to bring holiness into the world should never depart from our hearts and souls.

4:4

רַבִּי לְוִיטָס אִישׁ יַבְנֶה אוֹמֵר: מְאֹד מְאֹד הֱוֵי שְׁפַל רוּחַ,
שֶׁתִּקְוַת אֱנוֹשׁ רִמָּה.

Rabbi L'vitas, leader of Yavneh, said: Be exceedingly humble
in spirit, for the anticipated end of mortal humans is worms.

RABBI L'VITAS succinctly lays out an entire philosophical treatise in
one sentence. In fact, this mishnah is one of the most important ethical
teachings in all of Jewish thought. Humility is spiritually crucial, because it means that one can see and seek one's true self in a manner that
is attuned to the delicate nature of the universe. We work to perceive
ourselves as neither greater nor less than we are. We are all beings with
inner light and great potential for good. We are all beings who make
mistakes and use poor judgment from time to time.

True humility should not lead to passivity or disempowerment, but
to their opposite. Humility should lead us out of our comfort zone.
The arrogant play it safe to keep their reputations strong. Those who
are cruel suppress humility altogether, believing themselves above humility. The humble are focused on others, rather than the self, and are
willing to act, regardless of critique or social repercussions.

On the other hand, humility has its limits, especially for topics on
which humanity has no concrete answer. Highest of this intangible
knowledge is the incomprehension of what happens after our souls
leave the physical world; death is the binding element among all people. And it is common for humans to fear death. Freud suggested that
thanatos, the death instinct, was one of the driving forces of human life.[238]
But how do we allow this fear to guide us?

Perhaps we die at five distinct moments in time:

When one stops loving life
The irreversible cessation of the heartbeat
When one's body is lowered into the earth
The last time one's influence has any direct impact on posterity
The last time one's name is ever mentioned on earth

We try in vain to forestall each type of dying:

> To reverse the loss of love for life, one seeks pleasures that are ultimately empty of meaning.
>
> To forestall the cessation of the heart, one obsesses over the physical health of the body.
>
> To deny the return of the body to the earth, one seeks material goods rather than love.
>
> To increase one's direct impact after death, one seeks unilateral control over legacy.
>
> To extend the time that one's name will be mentioned after death, one seeks to build a reputation based on ostentation rather than humility.

Judaism offers solace and guidance to the individual contemplating death. Jewish holidays, each with its own core message, also respond to the need for answers about death.

> When one stops loving life, one must seek joy in the eternal (Simchat Torah).
>
> When contemplating the irreversible cessation of one's heart-beat, one learns to identify the true self within the soul, rather than in the body (Shavuot).
>
> When considering that the body will be lowered into the earth, one must learn to embrace material impermanence (Sukkot).
>
> In thinking about the last time one's influence has any direct impact through posterity, one must extend one's moral striv-ings humbly, courageously, and collaboratively (Passover).
>
> In considering the last time one's name is ever mentioned on earth, one must learn modesty before a Higher Power (Rosh HaShanah, Yom Kippur).

Unknowable and inevitable, death offers us myriad spiritual and moral opportunities for learning and reflection. Fear of death is nat-ural, but this anxiety can yield productive action. Considering one's own death can motivate and inspire. The sixteenth-century French philosopher Michel de Montaigne writes, "To begin depriving life of its greatest advantage over us, let us deprive death of its strangeness, let us frequent it, let us get used to it. . . . A man who has learned how to die has unlearned how to be a slave."[239] Certainly, one of the most serious aspects of religion is the way it compels humans to confront the void of death. The mystery of our ultimate fate gives us the impetus to improve our lives and the lives of others around the world.

On his deathbed, the nineteenth-century Chasidic rabbi Simchah Bunim of Przysucha relayed words of wisdom that encapsulate a life filled with learning. With his wife crying at his side, he turned toward her and urged silence. He said: "My whole life was only that I should learn to die."[240] Rabbi Simchah realized that while the corporeal fades, precious few artifacts remain. Indeed, only two things will remain after all five deaths: our eternal soul and the indirect effect of all we put into the world. Likewise, the Rabbis taught that a baby enters the world with fists clenched and a person dies with palms open, which signify that we enter wanting everything of this world, but we leave modestly, taking nothing with us.[241] As we edge closer to the precipice, we strive, carefully, wisely, and with all our might, to cultivate our eternal soul and channel positivity into the world. When we do so, we honor the words of Rabbi L'vitas and embrace his definitions of humility. In the end, all that lasts are the eternal contributions we've made. This is both frightening and empowering.

4:5

רַבִּי יוֹחָנָן בֶּן בְּרוֹקָא אוֹמֵר: כָּל הַמְחַלֵּל שֵׁם שָׁמַיִם בַּסֵּתֶר,
נִפְרָעִין מִמֶּנּוּ בַּגָּלוּי. אֶחָד שׁוֹגֵג וְאֶחָד מֵזִיד בְּחִלּוּל הַשֵּׁם.

Rabbi Yochanan ben B'roka said: Whoever desecrates God's
Name in secret, they will exact punishment from him in
public; unintentional or intentional, both are alike regarding
desecration of God's Name.

THE TALMUD'S SAGES understood *chilul HaShem*, desecration of God's
Name, as a wrong done in the public square (BT *Yoma* 86a). Any public
display that is contrary to Jewish ethics damages Judaism's entire spiritual enterprise. This is not only because the public square defines where
we interact with society, but also because such public interactions
shows one's character. Anyone can be pious while sitting in the pews.
Anyone can be kind to their friends and family. But to consistently act
justly with strangers marks the truly righteous person.

Maimonides taught that one can desecrate God's Name without
even sinning.[242] The means by which a person can commit a *chilul
HaShem* can surely be seen as subjective and can occur when one has
done nothing objectively wrong at all but has caused the public to talk
against them and view their commitments (i.e., God and the Torah) in
a more negative light. This is to say that we should do not only what is
right but what will appear in the public eye to be right. We are to distance ourselves not only from doing wrong but from the appearance of
doing wrong.

Rabbi Yitz Greenberg describes Rabbi Yochanan ben B'roka's other
concerns that—as we learn from this mishnah—have theological
implications:

> He seems to have been particularly sensitive to women's issues.
> Among his rulings are that a father is obligated to support his
> daughters and not just his sons (*Tosefta, Ketubbot* 4:8); that women
> are equally obligated in the *mitzvah* to be fruitful and multiply,
> which is not the majority view in the Talmud (BT *Yevamot* 65b); and

that one need be careful not to excessively degrade a woman in the course of the legal process of testing a woman accused of adultery (Numbers 5:1ff; *Sifrei, Naso* 41).[243]

The manner by which a society treats women demonstrates the establishment's values. While traditional communities feel they adhere to tradition by blocking women from leadership, their values are lowered in the estimation of outsiders. When it is a Jewish group perceived to be demeaning women, it is indeed a *chilul HaShem*.

Sheryl Sandberg, Facebook's chief operating officer, describes the current disparities in women's rights:

> There are still countries that deny women basic civil rights. World-wide, about 4.4 million women and girls are trapped in the sex trade. In places like Afghanistan and Sudan, girls receive little or no education, wives are treated as the property of their humans, and women who are raped are routinely cast out of their homes for disgracing their families. Some rape victims are even sent to jail for committing a "moral crime."[244]

Daily, we are presented with choices that affect the well-being of our inner selves. When the opportunity presents itself for us to act nobly, we should seize the moment and not let go. As well, there are multiple opportunities to *chilul HaShem*, and we are tested spiritually to resist these acts of desecration. In this way, one's character is formed.

There is still much to do across the spectrum of the Jewish community with regard to the inclusion of women in more active roles in clergy and scholarship. The Reform community is a leader in this regard, and there is still much for the Orthodox community to learn. Judith Plaskow presents a moving lesson on why it is vital that women to be present in all aspects of Jewish ritual life:

> When a woman stands in the pulpit and reads from the Torah that daughters can be sold as slaves (Exodus 21:7–11), she participates in a profound contradiction between the message of her presence and the content of what she learns and teaches. It is this contradiction [that] feminists must address, not simply "adding" women to a tradition that remains basically unaltered, but transforming Judaism into a religion that women as well as men have a role in shaping.[245]

Too often we succumb to our baser desires and do not act in accordance with our best selves, but this is not an irrevocable wrong. We always have another chance to improve ourselves, our communities, and the wider world. By recognizing where we need to improve ourselves, we place our souls on the path toward redemption.

4:6

רַבִּי יִשְׁמָעֵאל בְּנוֹ אוֹמֵר: הַלָּמֵד עַל מְנָת לְלַמֵּד, מַסְפִּיקִין
בְּיָדוֹ לִלְמֹד וּלְלַמֵּד; וְהַלָּמֵד עַל מְנָת לַעֲשׂוֹת, מַסְפִּיקִין
בְּיָדוֹ לִלְמֹד וּלְלַמֵּד לִשְׁמֹר וְלַעֲשׂוֹת.

Rabbi Yishmael, his son, said: One who studies [Torah] in
order to teach is given the means to study and to teach; and
one who studies in order to practice is given the means to
study and to teach, to observe and to practice.

EACH OF US must hold ourselves accountable, not through an external
guard, but via an internal guard. This ensures that we are not merely
speaking wisdom, but *living* wisdom. The Rabbis taught that people
should be *tocho k'boro*—the same on the outside and inside. The Ark
built by the Hebrews wandering in the desert was based on this model,
adorned with gold both outside and inside (BT *Yoma* 72b). This was
such a serious matter to the Rabbis that Rabban Gamliel decreed that
those whose insides did not have symmetry to their outsides were not
permitted to enter the *beit midrash*, the study hall; and he set a guard to
keep them out (BT *B'rachot* 28a).

Living Jewishly does not require that the individual fill every waking
moment with ritual, though this is one possible reading of this mishnah. To the contrary, the Rabbis teach that the first question asked at
the gates of heaven is about one's ethical behavior in matters of business (BT *Shabbat* 31a). Many of us have mistakenly been taught that
being religious means being rigorous about observance of ritual. While
striving to fulfill the rituals is a beautiful process, Jewish ethics are far
more central to Jewish life. According to most Jewish philosophers,
ethics are the end, with ritual the means. Maimonides teaches, "The
purpose of the laws of the Torah is to bring mercy, loving-kindness, and
peace upon the world."[246]

Similarly, being Jewish is less about one's ancestry and more about
one's character. The Sages explain, "The [Jewish] nation is distinguished by three characteristics; they are merciful, they are modest [or

bashful], and they perform acts of loving-kindness" (BT *Y'vamot* 79a). This notion is not a philosophical commitment nor is it a political ideology. Rather, it is a lasting commitment to observe and practice one's ethical and spiritual commitments.

While Judaism possesses a rigorous intellectual component, the religion is also misunderstood if treated primarily as academic. Many parents have hoped to ensure continuity by teaching their children only why Judaism matters. But for Jewish life to survive and moreover to thrive, it must not only be studied and taught, but also lived. Truly lived. Through practicing the values that we study, it is more likely that Judaism's wisdom becomes ingrained in our consciousness and in our souls. Through perseverance, vigilance, and practice, the potential of Judaism's transformative ideas can be realized in the world.

4:7

רַבִּי צָדוֹק אוֹמֵר: אַל תַּעֲשֵׂם עֲטָרָה לְהִתְגַּדֶּל בָּהֶם וְלֹא
קַרְדֹּם לֹאכַל מֵהֶן. וְכָךְ הָיָה הִלֵּל אוֹמֵר: וּדְאִשְׁתַּמַּשׁ בְּתָגָא
חֲלַף. הָא כָּל הַנֶּאוֹת מִדִּבְרֵי תוֹרָה נוֹטֵל חַיָּיו מִן הָעוֹלָם.

Rabbi Tzadok said: Do not make the [words of Torah] a crown
for self-glorification, nor an implement for one's livelihood.
So too Hillel used to say: One who exploits the crown [of
Torah for personal benefit] shall fade away. Thus whoever
derives personal benefit from the words of Torah removes
themselves from this world.

RABBI TZADOK was noted for fasting to stave off the destruction of
Jerusalem and the Jewish people. In 70 CE, when the Romans finally
razed the Temple, Rabbi Tzadok was so sick from self-deprivation that
he almost perished in the siege. Rabban Yochanan ben Zakkai asked of
the Roman commander and soon-to-be-emperor Vespasian that Rabbi
Tzadok receive medical care (BT *Gittin* 56a–b).

Today, fasting is thought of as a powerful tactic of civil disobedience
and spiritual resistance. Throughout the twentieth century, for example, the hunger strike has been used by Mohandas Gandhi (India),
Benazir Bhutto (Pakistan), and Aung Suu Kyi (Myanmar/Burma) to
protest religious warfare and the suppression of civil liberties in their
respective nations. In the United States, the labor and civil rights activist Cesar Chavez utilized hunger strikes as part of his organizing strategy to promote Latino farmworker rights. Decades before Chavez,
Alice Paul and her militant suffragist colleagues in the National Woman's Party engaged in a hunger strike after being jailed in 1917–18, as
part of their effort to obtain the vote for women.

Rabbi Tzadok, who exemplified the value of fasting as protest, also
modeled humility. While all major religions stress humility, we find
many religious people who are arrogant. In their own minds, they hold
the absolute truth, and their sense of piety makes them feel superior.
The Torah has no problem with people enjoying religious life, but the

Torah should not be used as a tool to prop up one's ego and gain social capital.

When Rabbi Hillel says in this mishnah, "One who exploits the crown shall fade away," he is warning us against using the binding utility of religion as a means to consolidate power. Yet, history has shown repeatedly that humanity is not always capable of heeding this teaching, and many of history's most heinous crimes were committed in the name of one religion or another. We must, then, use Hillel's dictum as a bulwark against crimes committed in the name of religion, whether that religion be Judaism or another. Moderating our own egos—as individuals and as members of a religious group—when encountering others will help us to cultivate an ethical center. This is not an easy task, yet it is a significant obligation.

Speaking on political leadership, Israel's first prime minister, David Ben-Gurion, said:

> You must fix your priorities. You must educate your party, and must educate the wider public. You must have confidence in your people—often greater than they have in themselves, for the true political leader knows instinctively the measure of man's capacities and can rouse him to exert them in times of crisis. . . . You must always be conscious of the element of timing, and this demands a constant awareness of what is going on around you—in your region if you are a local leader, in your country and in the world if you are a national leader. And since the world never stops for a moment, and the pattern of power changes its elements like the movement of a kaleidoscope, you must constantly reassess chosen policies towards the achievement of your aims. A political leader must spend a lot of time thinking. And he must spend a lot of time educating the public, and educating them anew.[247]

Ben-Gurion's model of leadership is about believing not in oneself but in others. Asked several times to serve as prime minister before he finally agreed, Ben-Gurion ran from power, rather than climb atop others to win political office. Further, while some simply rely upon ideology or pragmatism, Ben-Gurion advocated that we continually question and reshape our thinking.

Being reflective is part of humble leadership, which requires that one continue to feel tension about one's moral choices. In the 1970s, Chinese leader Zhou Enlai, when asked about the impact of the French Revolution, reportedly replied, "Too soon to say."[248] Indeed, it takes decades, sometimes centuries, to understand the true scope of revolutionary phenomena. In today's social media age, where everyone wants immediate and definitive response to new events, it can be difficult to exercise our patience. As part of humble leadership, the Torah teaches us to act, while continuing to reflect and revise our thinking.

4:8

רַבִּי יוֹסֵי אוֹמֵר: כָּל הַמְכַבֵּד אֶת הַתּוֹרָה – גּוּפוֹ מְכֻבָּד עַל
הַבְּרִיּוֹת. וְכָל הַמְחַלֵּל אֶת הַתּוֹרָה – גּוּפוֹ מְחֻלָּל עַל הַבְּרִיּוֹת.

Rabbi Yosei said: Whoever honors the Torah is honored by
people; and whoever disgraces the Torah is disgraced by
people.

THE TORAH'S central characteristic is human ethics. So, if we spend
time refining our relationships with others, then we will be honored by
honoring Torah. On the other hand, if our reasons for learning are less
than ideal, or even nefarious, then it is as if we have disgraced humanity's *raison d'être*. If we make ourselves noble and refined, and commit our
life to honoring people and God, then inevitably others will respect us.

In the previous mishnah, we learned that we should not seek
material gain, power, or status from Torah study and observance.
This gives context to the mishnah above, which is a window into the
minds of the Sages. From their perspective, the Torah is sacrosanct,
immutable. Using the Torah as a means of benefit should not be a
motive, although it may be a motive interwoven with more righteous
motives, such as charity and performing good deeds for the betterment
of the community.

Yet, at the same time, the motivation to do good work does not mean
we have to always be recognized for it. To be sure, our priority should
be, not to be honored, but to perform the honoring. Consider this Talmudic passage:

> A blind man came to town and Rabbi Eliezer ensured he sat in the
> most prominent place and then sat next to him [in a less promi-
> nent place]. The community assumed this blind visitor was a very
> important person since the prominent sage showed him such
> honor. Everyone started paying special honor to the blind man,
> and so he humbly inquired why he, as a poor blind man, merited
> such care. When he learned that it was because of the attention that
> Rabbi Eliezer had publicly shown him, he blessed him: "You have

shown compassion to one who is seen but who does not see. May the One who sees and is not seen receive your prayers and shower compassion on you." (JT *Pei-ah* 8:9)

The beginning of honor is our choice of words, especially in how we speak with one another. Benjamin Franklin wrote about how his speech might affect others:

> I made it a rule to forbear all direct contradiction to the sentiments of others, and all positive assertion of my own. I even forbade myself . . . the use of every word or expression in the language that imported a fixed opinion, such as *certainly, undoubtedly*, etc., and I adopted instead of them, *I conceive, I apprehend*, or *I imagine* a thing to be so and so.[249]

If we are to be honored, we are to honor other people. Being a person of valor is the essence of what it means to "honor the Torah." We are to run to support the vulnerable wherever we encounter them, and consider their honor as dear as our own. Indeed, the Talmud teaches that the Second Temple in Jerusalem was destroyed because of *sinat chinam*, baseless hatred (BT *Yoma* 9b), or the inability to honor others.

4:9

רַבִּי יִשְׁמָעֵאל בְּנוֹ אוֹמֵר: הַחוֹשֵׂךְ עַצְמוֹ מִן הַדִּין – פּוֹרֵק
מִמֶּנּוּ אֵיבָה וְגָזֵל וּשְׁבוּעַת שָׁוְא. וְהַגַּס לִבּוֹ בְּהוֹרָאָה –
שׁוֹטֶה רָשָׁע וְגַס רוּחַ.

Rabbi Yishmael, his son, said: One who withdraws from
judgment removes from oneself hatred, robbery, and [the
responsibility for] an unnecessary oath. And one who is too
self-confident in handing down legal decisions is a fool,
wicked, and arrogant of spirit.

BEING IN A POSITION of substantial authority requires, paradoxically,
enormous humility and restraint. It is all too easy for a leader, drunk
with power, to abuse the mantle of leadership. In this mishnah the Rabbis teach that a person should not seek a position of authority. When
one has authority, one should not try to increase it. In typical group
dynamics, when one is on top, others will attempt to knock one down.
Disparity in positional authority often leads to hatred and pettiness, at
the expense of group cohesion. When power struggles take over, the
fortunes of a society plummet.

The Rabbis are opposed not to power and public leadership, but to
their abuse. If we are to seek positions of community leadership, the
Rabbis implore us to exert influence through relationship building,
transparency, collaboration, and education.

Like Rabbi Yishmael ben Rabbi Yosei in this mishnah, other rabbis
also stressed the priority of peace over truth:

> The school of Rabbi Yishmael [ben Elisha] taught in a baraita:
> "Great is peace, for even the Holy One of Blessing alters [words]
> for its sake. Originally, it is written, "[Sarah said: After I have
> withered and become old, shall I again have delicate skin and give
> birth?!] And my husband is old!" but in the end [when God quotes
> Sarah's words to Abraham] it is written, "And I [Sarah] am old"
> (Genesis 18:12–13). (BT Y'vamot 65b)

For the sake of peace, God softened Sarah's words, rather than maintaining what was cruel (though accurate). This Talmudic teaching is not just about God softening Sarah's words for the sake of peace, but it is also about marriage. In a committed loving relationship, we can become so comfortable that we always speak the flat truth: "This food is lousy," or "I don't like that outfit." But here, of all places, we should seek warmth of feeling. *Sh'lom bayit*—peace in the home—is noted repeatedly in Jewish literature,[250] even given as the reason for lighting Shabbat candles on Friday night.

But there is also a biblical commandment to offer rebuke (*toch'chah*): "You shall not hate your kinfolk in your heart. Reprove your kin but incur no guilt on their account" (Leviticus 19:17). The verse teaches that we offer reproof for two reasons: (1) so that our resentments do not lead to hate, and (2) so that wrongs are not carried out for which we would be responsible. Rather than speaking *lashon hara* (speaking negatively about another) and *r'chilut* (spreading gossip), we should confront the individual directly. If we are to care about the moral and spiritual welfare of others, then we should give feedback when we see others going astray.

Yet we need not be judges of every person and reviewers of every product. Cultivating humility means that we step back and not pass judgment where it is neither needed nor helpful. Consider this in the workplace. At the office, we consistently offer positive reinforcement and constructive feedback to others to improve the quality of our collective effort. From a Jewish perspective, we are concerned not only with the effectiveness of our work, but also with the ethics of the workplace. In addition to personal accountability, all Jewish workers have a sacred duty to be a moral presence.

According to one position, the commandment of rebuke applies only when we think the other will be receptive to hearing the reproof. If not, it is considered counterproductive. "Just as there is a mitzvah for a person to say words of rebuke that will be accepted, so too there is a mitzvah for a person not to say words of rebuke that will not be accepted" (BT *Y'vamot* 65b.) It is a mitzvah only if one presumes that the other has the integrity and emotional intelligence to truly see their own blind spot and correct the wrong. The goal with rebuke, according to this position, is not just to express righteous indignation, but to create change and stop a wrong or abuse occurring before our eyes.

Rabbi Zeira dissents from this. He teaches that one should offer rebuke whether or not it is likely to be accepted (BT *Shabbat* 55a). We cannot stand by while others do wrong in our midst. Regardless of whether our voice will be heard, we cannot act as though we are indifferent. Rabbi Abraham Joshua Heschel teaches this point powerfully. In an interview Rabbi Heschel gave shortly before he passed away, he said, "We are a generation that has lost its capacity for outrage. We must continue to remind ourselves that in a free society all are involved in what some are doing. Some are guilty, all are responsible."[251] Thus, we must express outrage at wrongs. The Rabbis teach, "Everyone who can protest a wrong in one's midst and does not is responsible for those people. For the people of one's city, one is responsible for the people of the city. For the whole world, one is responsible for the whole world" (BT *Y'vamot* 54b). By not speaking, our moral integrity is in jeopardy. The Rabbis teach *sh'tikah k'hodaah*: when we stay silent we are considered to be in agreement. According to this position, we don't need to correct the wrong, but we cannot stand idly by either.

The obligation to give *toch'chah* is not simple. The Rabbis teach that no one is spiritually evolved enough to offer rebuke properly, because few are self-aware and humble; concomitantly, few are humble enough to accept rebuke properly.[252] Therefore, *Sefer Chasidim* suggests that we can give rebuke only to the ones whom we love, especially if there is a belief that the words will be heeded.[253] We must check our motives carefully before challenging another's conduct.

Of course, any feedback should be given gently, in private, at the right time, and in the appropriate environment. Most importantly, we should be sure not to shame another when challenging her or him, and this is a difficult skill to learn. Some acts require whistle-blowing when they reach a level of harm or illegality. Other acts require strong rebuke or constructive feedback.

Rebuke plays a key role in the workplace, because it ensures we have moral influence on coworkers and establish clear ethical standards. We cannot live in a world in which wrongs are ignored, nor can we work in environments in which there is indifference toward the welfare of others. Abuse must be addressed.

We cannot do this alone; we should create an open work culture in which feedback is acceptable and encouraged when boundaries are crossed. We must learn the art and ethics of critique, so that we can build a stronger society committed to truth, human dignity, and transparency. We can start by checking our own practices, taking on our own self-accounting, and inviting others to approach us when we transgress.

4:10

הוּא הָיָה אוֹמֵר: אַל תְּהִי דָן יְחִידִי, שֶׁאֵין דָּן יְחִידִי אֶלָּא
אֶחָד. וְאַל תּאֹמַר קַבְּלוּ דַעְתִּי, שֶׁהֵן רַשָּׁאִין וְלֹא אָתָּה.

He used to say: Do not act as judge alone, for no one judges
alone except One; and do not say, "Accept my view," for they
[others] are permitted [to say it], but not you.

IN THE COURSE of ethical lives, we should follow the principle of
halachta bidrachav, and emulate the ways of God (see above at 4:2,
page 195). But this mishnah teaches that such an approach has limits.
In the largest conception of Judaic thought, God should judge alone;
how dare we even consider doing so? We embrace the fallibility of our
judgment and the imperfection of our truths. We often need a group to
make such weighty decisions together to compensate for our individual
blind spots. We should model this approach of seeking counsel in our
family life, our work life, and in our religious life.

In all we do, we must be cautious in how we address others. We don't
merely say to others, not even to our children, "Accept my view, because
all others are incorrect." Rather, we speak humbly and gently. If we are
persuasive in our arguments and admirable in demeanor and behavior,
we will be given the good fortune to lead. But followers should not be
coerced to accede to authority, no matter the circumstances. Otherwise,
careless despotism could take over. We have to be vigilant to keep those
who merely crave power over others from becoming leaders. Consider
what Maimonides suggests for those of us who are striving for virtue:

> If a person is scrupulous in his conduct, gentle in his conversation,
> pleasant towards his fellow creatures, affable in manner when
> receiving them, not responding when affronted, but showing
> courtesy to all, even to those who treat him with disdain . . . such
> a person has sanctified God—and about him Scripture says, "You
> are My servant, Israel, in whom I will be glorified" (Isaiah 49:3).[254]

Engaging in gentle and compassionate language will not only ensure
we treat others respectfully but also influence our own character. It

requires work. We shouldn't believe that the laws and ethics we hold dear will survive simply out of human reverence. Everything that has been created by humans can be destroyed by humans. Institutions we revere are vulnerable to destruction without dedication to their preservation. Upholding standards for interpersonal conduct is at the foundation of preserving society's ideas and cornerstone institutions. The early twentieth-century American judge Learned Hand pondered the limits and possibilities of freedom of conscience in the modern world:

> I often wonder whether we do not rest our hopes too much upon constitutions, upon laws and upon courts. These are false hopes; believe me, these are false hopes. Liberty lies in the hearts of men and women; when it dies there, no constitution, no law, no court can save it; no constitution, no law, no court can even do much to help it.[255]

To have a life suffused with humility requires finding mentors to help guide one's decisions; this task can be difficult. Making solitary decisions or taking action based on gut instinct without considering the consequences leads to isolation, arrogance, and narcissism. How many historical figures have done just this, much to the detriment (and sometimes calamity) of themselves and others?

Each of us is responsible for our individual moral decisions. But as nascent or established leaders, our ethical deliberations require careful consideration of consequences and critique from trusted others. No one is an oracle; no one can know every possible outcome to a problem; no leader can thrive alone. Others' opinions strengthen one's own knowledge, allowing one to proceed on a path of discovery. It is important, as one develops the skills for leadership, to seek experts who can offer wise counsel.

4:11

רַבִּי יוֹנָתָן אוֹמֵר: כָּל הַמְקַיֵּם אֶת הַתּוֹרָה מֵעֹנִי – סוֹפוֹ
לְקַיְּמָהּ מֵעֹשֶׁר. וְכָל הַמְבַטֵּל אֶת הַתּוֹרָה מֵעֹשֶׁר – סוֹפוֹ
לְבַטְּלָהּ מֵעֹנִי.

Rabbi Yonatan said: Whoever fulfills the Torah despite poverty will ultimately fulfill it in wealth; but whoever neglects the
Torah because of wealth will ultimately neglect it in poverty.

OBJECTIVELY, WEALTH can provide comfort, stability, status, and
influence. But Rabbi Yonatan should be understood as speaking not
about material affluence, but about spiritual wealth and spiritual poverty. We know that this world doesn't operate so that everything evens
out over the course of time: the evil may gain wealth, while the righteous languish in squalor. This mishnah explores the equilibrium between unseen capital and the resources that nourish the soul as it exists
in the temporal realm, rather than in the soul's natural habitat of the
spiritual world.

It is possible for a person to perceive oneself as poor or rich, regardless of socioeconomic status. One can have little to get by and feel rich
compared to those who have less. One can be in the top 1 percent but
feel poor in contrast to even wealthier friends. So, if one perceives oneself as poor and commits to Torah, rather than striving to fulfill every
desire, this will shift this self-perception. This person will come to
understand oneself as wealthy, both materially and spiritually. On the
other hand, one who feels satiated by wealth and dismisses spiritual
and intellectual pursuits will only come to feel deficient, ending up feeling as though in a state of deep poverty, even when that is not the case.

Such a feeling is innate within everyone. Scottish Enlightenment
philosopher David Hume writes, "A propensity to hope and joy is real
riches: One to fear and sorrow, real poverty."[256] No matter how inade-
quate we may feel our financial state, what we do to bring joy and justice
to the world truly represents our currency and worth.

Some have argued that our subjective state of mind can predict objective results. In his work *The Wealth and Poverty of Nations: Why Some Are So Rich and Some So Poor*, late Harvard economic historian David Landes explores systemic mechanisms underlying nations' economic success or poverty. After a lengthy exploration of the progression and regression of cultures throughout history, Professor Landes concludes:

> In this world, the optimists have it, not because they are always right, but because they are positive. Even when wrong, they are positive, and that is the way of achievement, correction, improvement, and success. Educated, eyes-open optimism pays; pessimism can only offer the empty consolation of being right.[257]

In the end, material wealth will mean nothing. Money is merely a number on a bank statement, and it will be forgotten in the millennia to come. Only our actions can stand the test of time, so we should forge ahead with lives that have value beyond our wealth. Taking time to study and live by the wisdom of Torah and modeling ethics and kindness in the world will do much more than acquiring wealth for its own sake. It is possible to become a billionaire but still experience spiritual poverty that can never be displaced.

4:12

רַבִּי מֵאִיר אוֹמֵר: הֱוֵי מַעֵט עֵסֶק וַעֲסֹק בַּתּוֹרָה, וֶהֱוֵי
שְׁפַל רוּחַ בִּפְנֵי כָל אָדָם. וְאִם בָּטַלְתָּ מִן הַתּוֹרָה, יֶשׁ לְךָ
בְטֵלִים הַרְבֵּה כְּנֶגְדֶּךָ. וְאִם עָמַלְתָּ בַּתּוֹרָה, יֶשׁ לוֹ שָׂכָר
הַרְבֵּה לִתֶּן לָךְ.

Rabbi Meir said: Reduce your business activities and engage in
Torah. Be of humble spirit before every person. If you should
neglect Torah, you will come upon many excuses to neglect it;
but if you labor in Torah, God has ample reward to give you.

OF THE INNUMERABLE innovations the Torah has brought to humankind, perhaps its subtlest is that all adults are encouraged to work. And
so, we work. Men and women toiling to provide for their families is the
norm throughout the world, in contract to the Edenic ideal of realizing
God's splendor in leisure and comfort. Yet, to be fully functional beings,
we know that work should not overtake us. While we must support our
families, contribute to society's advancement, and support communal
needs, we are not to become so concerned with career advancement
or financial growth that we neglect personal and spiritual growth and
commitment to Jewish learning.

The idea that life is holy means that we can't just collapse at home
after a day's work. We owe it to our families, communities, and ourselves to have energy remaining for other pursuits and for reflection.
French philosopher Albert Camus of the existential school writes, "It
takes time to live. Like any work of art, life needs to be thought about."[258]
When we work ourselves to death, we deny ourselves the ability to see
the beauty of life.

Still, some are obliged to work harder than others. Hours and stress
from desk jobs may add up, but they don't compare to the physical
exertion of landscape, construction, caregiving, or food service jobs.
Therefore, we must strive to lessen the burdens of those who can find
no relief. One Rabbinic commentator suggests that Moses was the

chosen leader for the Jewish people because he helped others when they had burdens too large to manage alone:

> "And when he [Moses] went out to look upon his brethren, he saw their burdens" (Exodus 2:11). How did he feel when he looked upon them? As he looked at their burden, he wept, saying, "Woe is me for your servitude. Would that I could die for you!" Since no work is more strenuous than that of handling clay, Moses used to shoulder the burden and help each worker.[259]

As we consider our roles in work and assisting others, we should emulate Moses. He tried to ensure that people could pursue deeper purpose beyond work and that they would not be crushed by heavy burdens. Our prophetic mission, then, might be to seek out those whose work is invisible—the people who labor in the shadows, in a kind of modern-day servitude—and lessen their burdens.

Certainly, we should ensure that people who work have their needs met. Not everyone is given opportunities to enter the corporate world or the professions. But everyone, from the agricultural laborer, to store clerk, to maintenance staff person, has the same inherent dignity. Those with political and social power may try to use their positions to harm or exploit those with less economic power, and we must guard against such danger.

To support working people, we should ensure that people in multiple industries can organize to protect their own interests. Consider this legal ruling by Rabbi Ben-Zion Meir Chai Uziel, the first Sephardic chief rabbi of Israel:

> The law allows [for the existence of unions] in order that individual workers not be left on their own, to the point that they hire themselves out for a low wage in order to satisfy their hunger and that of their family with a bit of bread and water and with a dark and dingy home; in order that the workers may protect themselves, the law gives them the legal right to organize, and to establish stipulations that benefit the members of their profession regarding the fair distribution of work among the workers, and to achieve fair treatment and a wage appropriate for the work and sufficient to sustain their household at the standard of living as the other residents

of their city. . . . All of these things can be fulfilled only through a workers' union. Therefore, the Torah gave the Jewish people the full and legal right to organize these, even though it is possible that [such unions] will result in a financial loss for the employers.[260]

Rabbeinu Yonah, a medieval Spanish sage, teaches that if one hires a male worker who is unable to make ends meet, then one should allow him to live as if they are natural members of the home: "If you want to hire laborers and you find that they are poor, they should be [regarded as] poor members of your household; and do not degrade them, for you were commanded to have a respectful manner with them and to pay their wages."[261]

Once we achieve a work-play-learn balance, we should be humble. It is too easy to look down on others who seem to chase pleasure, or to scorn those who advance professionally (even when they did so from hard work). But when we sacrifice for the benefit of others who are vulnerable and ignored by society, we are pious. Indeed, this is what it means to be religious: to be concerned about the burdens of others and to seek social justice. We should continue to grow, while remaining humble before all people: both those who are great and those who are not yet great.

4:13

רַבִּי אֱלִיעֶזֶר בֶּן יַעֲקֹב אוֹמֵר: הָעוֹשֶׂה מִצְוָה אַחַת – קָנָה לוֹ
פְּרַקְלִיט אֶחָד. וְהָעוֹבֵר עֲבֵרָה אַחַת – קָנָה לוֹ קַטֵּגוֹר אֶחָד.
תְּשׁוּבָה וּמַעֲשִׂים טוֹבִים כִּתְרִיס בִּפְנֵי הַפֻּרְעָנוּת.

Rabbi Eliezer ben Yaakov said: One who fulfills even a single
mitzvah has gained a single advocate; and one who commits
even a single transgression has gained a single accuser. Repentance and good deeds are like a shield against retribution.

THERE ARE MULTIPLE SOURCES for the inner voices that we turn to
in our lives. We call upon our early childhood influences, genes, moral
intuition, memories of formative experiences, and creative and intellectual constructions to form our core. There is no precise metric to
gauge how such influences affect us; it varies between people. But each
of us trusts these internal voices to tell us what's just and what's iniquitous. It can be challenging to hear our inner voices and to discern from
their cacophony how to act.

When we commit to the (sometimes painful) process of *t'shuvah*,
a process of growth and repentance, we shield ourselves from slip-
ping into spiritual oblivion. Such a process is difficult, but there is
an advantage to making ourselves vulnerable. By pursuing *t'shuvah*,
we strengthen the internal advocate—what we might call our conscience—that urges us to become who we need to be. In this mishnah,
Rabbi Eliezer ben Yaakov describes *derech eretz*, the right way to act in
the world. Our spiritual journeys entwine heavenly ideals and worldly
necessities. Navigating this constant barrage of ethical choices affects
our growth as conscientious human beings. Such a path is not easy. Yet,
learning what to avoid and when ensures that our ethical standard is
hard to break, a "shield against retribution" in the world-to-come.

This mishnah could be interpreted as metaphorical rumination between those heavenly defenders and prosecutors who appear on our
day of judgment. We need to have a process to manage the internal
voices that speak up, and when we perform good deeds, we strengthen

the internal voice that encourages us to advocate for others. That voice is like a moral booster.

We always have the opportunity to learn how to interpret the events around us. After surviving the Holocaust, Viktor Frankl taught that our lives are determined not by what happens to us, but by how we respond to what happens to us; we are self-determining creatures.[262] How we interpret events and respond constitutes our being. Will this crisis lead me to despair or strengthen my resolve? Will this challenge lead me to cynicism or courage? When serving as leaders, we not only define our own reality but also we help depict the world for others. Max De Pree, a businessman and thinker who wrote about the practice of leadership, states, "The first responsibility of a leader is to define reality."[263] Others, especially in times of sorrow, often seek hope by imagining a brighter tomorrow. Such hope is essential to moral perseverance.

Often, we can feel trapped and in need of a way out of our thought patterns. The philosopher Ludwig Wittgenstein once said that he viewed his intellectual pursuits as showing "the fly the way out of the fly-bottle."[264] For too many of us today, we bang our heads against the wall and expend energy flying in circles with nowhere to land. Sometimes we need to pause, examine, and fly out of the hole. But we can also be like fish, unaware that we're swimming in water; our phenomenological reality can be too fundamental for us to even be aware of it. It takes an elevated consciousness to see what we are and where we are, and to look at and listen to the world around us.

When we err, as is the human inclination, we risk amplifying the negative voice inside that says, "Life doesn't really matter. People don't matter. Nothing really matters. Do whatever feels good and easy." Heeding this voice—the surging, dark impulse—is surely the easier path. But following this path should never be an option; it leads to inner destruction. Where we should find the strength to resist these inner urges is in our latent ability to overcome these inclinations. Every person has this capacity in-built, though it is not always apparent. When we combat what causes us to transgress our holy purpose, we inch further toward being moral beings.

4:14

רַבִּי יוֹחָנָן הַסַּנְדְּלָר אוֹמֵר: כָּל כְּנֵסְיָה שֶׁהִיא לְשֵׁם שָׁמַיִם –
סוֹפָהּ לְהִתְקַיֵּם. וְשֶׁאֵינָהּ לְשֵׁם שָׁמַיִם – אֵין סוֹפָהּ לְהִתְקַיֵּם.

Rabbi Yochanan the Shoemaker said: Every assembly that is
dedicated to the sake of heaven will have an enduring effect,
but one that is not for the sake of heaven will not have an
enduring effect.

OUR LIVES ARE SHORT. Within a few brief generations after our death,
it's likely that we will have been entirely forgotten. Our small efforts in
this world will have dissipated, and those who knew us will be left with
only snippets of memories. As individuals, our efforts are so small as
to seem almost meaningless from the perspective of eternity. However,
when we attach our efforts, our values, and our identities to the heavens, to divinity, we merge our individuality with the supernal. We go
beyond the boundaries of normal time and space and join something
that is without rational explanation. This is not easy to understand,
and such an understanding can chafe against modern, rational ways of
thinking. Yet, by thinking outside of the normal purview of everyday
experiences, we learn that we are more than individuals in a seemingly
unplotted life. We are, instead, active participants in an experiment
known as the entirety of Creation. At the same time, it is inevitable
that we all, from the richest monarch to the lowliest pauper, will have
to answer big questions when our time has come. And this overarching
schema for our lives should give us pause and also give us exhilaration.
We have so much to accomplish in our lifetimes. Where do we muster
the will to actualize our tasks?

Yet, we are also faced with the synchronous quandary of clinging to
the eternality of a divine being. How are we to place our corporeal bodies into the hands (so to speak) of something greater than we will ever
know? Throughout history, emperors, pharaohs, and dictators have
claimed divine right to justify their lust for power and relevance, but
it was always their own downfall. Rather than promote humility, they

chose megalomania. To cling to the ways of the Divine means that one should follow the most compassionate routes. Many groups come together not to generate light, but to generate heat. We must avoid these groups, because they are not for "the sake of heaven," but for their own self-preservation; they will not endure. Rather, we should find groups that pursue truth, justice, and peace.

Peace—*shalom*—does not mean the mere absence of conflict. It means that distinct individuals and groups should be connected in a compassionate and healthy manner; it's a normative paradigm. Indeed, one of God's infinite names is *Shalom* because it is peace that sustains *all* of Creation's beautiful complexity.

Indeed, pursuing peace doesn't mean finding peace with enemies, but cultivating healthy disagreement between trusted partners. This mutual discomfort, painful in the moment, is necessary for the long-term cultivation of mutual respect. Rabbi Nachman of Breslov, who was a broad thinker on the relationships that bind people, taught about the value of generative disagreement:

> Understand that a disagreement is a kind of creation of the world. For the essence of the creation of the world was that it required an empty space, since without it, everything would be in the infinite presence of God and there wouldn't be any places for the creation of the world. So God pulled the light back to the sides and the empty space was created and in it God created everything—days and measures—using speech. . . . This is similar to disagreement. If the Sages were united, there would be no place for the creation of the world, which happens only through the disagreements between them. They move away from each other, each one pulling back toward a different side.[265]

Through social agitation and constructive disruption, we move society forward. The constant push and pull between groups with like-minded objectives, but differing strategies to achieve them, can create benefit. To achieve benefit, though, requires both good motives and partners with good intentions. This is where the enduring effects of our inner selves become known. We have to be comfortable with who we are and who we hope to be. Whether we're remembered for who we are depends on the lives we lead today, but being obsessed with our legacy is counterproductive to the work that needs to be done now.

Anticipating how our lives will affect others is how we ensure our efforts will be meaningful and our legacy enduring. Our holy mandate is to refocus our attention from the micro to the macro, toward God, the Creator and Sustainer of all life in the universe. It is in this way the soul endures, that our memories are kept lit through the eons. When we dedicate our lives to something more than what we are, we allow ourselves a taste of eternity.

4:15

רַבִּי אֶלְעָזָר בֶּן שַׁמּוּעַ אוֹמֵר: יְהִי כְבוֹד תַּלְמִידָךְ חָבִיב עָלֶיךָ
כִּכְבוֹד חֲבֵרָךְ, וּכְבוֹד חֲבֵרָךְ כְּמוֹרָא רַבָּךְ, וּמוֹרָא רַבָּךְ
כְּמוֹרָא שָׁמָיִם.

Rabbi Elazar ben Shamua said: Let the honor of your student
be as dear to you as the honor of your colleague; the honor
of your colleague as the reverence for your teacher; and the
reverence for your teacher as the reverence of heaven.

THE CLASSICAL WAY of understanding a teacher-student relationship
was as a one-way power dynamic. A student shows respect to a teacher,
but a teacher only molds and disciplines. Today, we understand how
important it is to build the self-esteem of students and honor their dignity. Yet the Rabbis, in their wisdom and understanding of the mystical
element of Torah, understood these concepts long ago.

This mishnah shows such progressive thinking about the student-
teacher dyad. Teachers are among the most powerful members of
society, for they wield the tremendous weight of wisdom accumulated
throughout the millennia. That's what makes this passage so striking;
it turns the usual understanding of the teacher-student relationship on
its head.

All relationships in which one learns matter. One must revere
both colleagues and teachers. According to Jewish tradition, Rabbi
Meir honored his teacher Rabbi Elisha ben Avuyah (known as Acher,
"Other"), even after Acher was no longer lauded by his own peers (BT
Chagigah 15b). Even when others abandoned Acher, Rabbi Meir still
recognized the dynamism of his teaching and the effort he'd expended
developing Rabbi Meir's young mind. Despite other circumstances,
Rabbi Meir remembered the lasting brilliance of his teacher and the
times they shared. This connection was beyond a mere transactional
relationship; it was recognition that teachers are guides to the world.
This merits respecting.

Respecting colleagues can be more challenging, because envy can accompany competition. But consider competition among the schools of Talmudic thought and their continued mutual respect, despite intense, temperamental disagreement:

> The school of Shammai and the school of Hillel continually disagreed. What one forbade, the other permitted. Despite this, members of the school of Shammai did not refrain from marrying members of Hillelite families, and Hillelites did not refrain from marrying members of Shammaite families. This teaches us that even though they differed, they showed love and friendship toward one another, putting in practice the injunction "Love truth, but also peace" (Zechariah 8:19). (BT *Y'vamot* 14b)

Rabbi Yisrael Salanter, one of the progenitors of the modern Musar movement, teaches that people have to see intellectual disagreements not as questions of whose thinking is superior, but as discourse between those with differing personality and distinct temperament:

> In the ability to recognize evidence, all humans are equal, if they only have the intelligence to understand the evidence. But in the weight they give to the evidence, human beings differ from one another greatly. . . . And it was precisely over the weight to give arguments that the houses of Shammai and of Hillel differed. . . . Let us not wonder at the source, the cause of the spectacle of the scholars of the houses of Shammai and Hillel agreeing each with his own society—what does society have to do with it? For the reason for their dispute was the difference of their temperaments, which cannot be completely separated from reason . . . and this is the explanation of what the Rabbis said (*Eiruvin* 13b): "These and those are the words of the Living God," because (as we have said) there is no such thing as a contradiction between the different powers of the soul.[266]

The awe-inspiring aspect about learning is that one is never too late to engage in its foundational magnificence. One may think that one has nothing to contribute as a teacher, but sometimes there comes an epiphany where one reorients one's worldview to become a facilitator for curious minds. Not everyone takes that route, but all have the potential. Consider Rabbi Akiva, who deliberately transformed his simple life of being illiterate and unlearned to becoming one of the greatest teachers found within Jewish history. Rabbi Akiva's is not meant as a paradigm for all, but an illustration of what happens when one is determined never to stay satisfied with one's current condition. As it is written about him:

> Do you know how Rabbi Akiva got started as a great teacher? Until the age of forty, he had no formal schooling. Then one day, standing by a spring, he asked a companion, "Who hollowed out this stone?" His friend responded, "Akiva, haven't you read in the Torah that 'water wears away stone' (Job 14:19)? It was worn away by water from the spring falling on it constantly, day after day." Akiva thought to himself, "Is my mind harder than this stone? I will go and study Torah." So he went and studied until he learned the entire Torah.[267]

Respecting others is not only about their dignity, but also a means to respecting ourselves and our own potential. In becoming someone who values others' wisdom, we can see our own potential that is begging for actualization.

4:16

רַבִּי יְהוּדָה אוֹמֵר: הֱוֵי זָהִיר בְּתַלְמוּד, שֶׁשִּׁגְגַת תַּלְמוּד
עוֹלָה זָדוֹן.

Rabbi Y'hudah said: Be meticulous in study, for a careless
misinterpretation is considered tantamount to willful
transgression.

Truth matters.

We must guard the sacred truths of the universe. At times, human
dignity, even human life, is at stake. When it comes to our interpretations of truth, we should be cautious and, as Rabbi Y'hudah states in
this mishnah, meticulous. We must ensure that there is consistency in
how we understand faith, culture, and history. Being careless in study is
akin to being willfully ignorant. If we prepare ourselves in advance and
live committed to intellectual rigor, then we must go beneath the surface to engage, thinking critically about the issues that have mattered
throughout time. We will never fully understand everything, but it is
better to have knowledge than to be willfully ignorant of what led to the
present.

John Locke, writing to a friend in 1703, eloquently commented on
the necessity of truth: "To love truth for truth's sake is the principal
part of human perfection in this world, and the seed-plot of all other
virtues."[268] Sadly, there are some who not only engage in "careless misinterpretation," but also reject truth. Perhaps the worst example of
rejecting truth in recent decades has been Holocaust denial.

For years, Emory University professor Deborah Lipstadt battled the
libel charge against her by Holocaust denier David Irving.[269] This story
causes us to ask how anyone could deny something like the Holocaust,
which was so thoroughly documented with such enormous evidence.
But this story also makes us wonder about the contemporary struggle
to defend objective reality in a culture that seems wary, even disdainful,
of facts and truth. This troubling development is related to the prolifer-
ation of news sources, many of which represent micro-constituencies.

Whose truth are we to accept, when any such source is deemed partial and viewed skeptically?

As part of the defense of free speech, there must be accountability for the dissemination of untruth; free speech allows a person to speak truth as one sees it but does not allow one to propagate lies. Individuals who claim the truth can be categorized into three types:

> *Absolutists* (the lowest level) feel that they hold the one valid truth and thus dismiss analysis.
>
> *Multiplists* are relativists who believe everything is equally true, thus rejecting inquiry and analysis.
>
> *Evaluativists* (the highest level) understand the relativity of truth but feel there are truths more accurate than others. They invest in inquiry and research to get as close to the truth as possible.

In the postmodern era, non-truth has the lamented ability to be labeled truth. Thus, we must stress the importance of seeking and finding objective truth. From the perspective of Jewish tradition, pursuing truth is a virtue. The great Sages teach elsewhere in the Talmud, "The seal of the Holy One is truth" (BT *Shabbat* 55a; *Yoma* 69b; *Sanhedrin* 64a). The prophetic commitment to truth was so high that both Jeremiah and Daniel stopped referring to God as "great" in their prayers. Though they believed it, they did not see God acting in such a way, and so they could not call God "great" at that time because God hates lies (BT *Yoma* 69b).

Maimonides discusses the legal weight of speaking truth:

> A person is forbidden to act in a smooth-tongued and seductive manner. One must not speak [outwardly] one way and think otherwise in their heart. Rather, one's inner self should be like one's outer self. What one feels in one's heart should be the same as the words on one's lips. . . . It is forbidden to utter even a single word of deception or fraud. Rather [one should have] only truthful speech, a proper spirit, and a heart pure from all deceit and trickery.[270]

We are morally obligated to seek out the undiluted facts and to challenge anyone who disputes the most basic of elements of reality for short-term gain. When the stability of a functioning society is at stake, we must be vigilant and proactive. It is a task with prophetic dimensions, but surely one that we should be ready to accept.

Facts cannot be felt. They cannot be imbibed from some ethereal place on high. As President John Adams noted many times, "Facts are stubborn things."[271] Even when we'd rather hear news that conforms comfortably to our worldview, it is myopic for us to accept the veracity of any pronouncements without ensuring that they are, first and foremost, factually correct. In a society veering toward multiple points of view, even when the facts prove indisputable (e.g., climate change, the unemployment rate), we should avoid "careless misinterpretation" of the world. At every moment, we should analyze whether a statement that emanates from the lowest bureaucrat to the president of the United States belongs to the realm of truth. Instead of shaking our heads in outrage or exasperation whenever we hear untruth, we should recommit to truth and gathering evidence to disprove lies.

Because truth always matters.

4:17

רַבִּי שִׁמְעוֹן אוֹמֵר: שְׁלֹשָׁה כְתָרִים הֵם: כֶּתֶר תּוֹרָה וְכֶתֶר
כְּהֻנָּה וְכֶתֶר מַלְכוּת. וְכֶתֶר שֵׁם טוֹב עוֹלֶה עַל גַּבֵּיהֶן.

Rabbi Shimon said: There are three crowns: the crown of
Torah, the crown of priesthood, and crown of kingship; but
the crown of a good name surpasses them all.

IF ONE STANDS for anything at all, it is impossible to maintain a perfectly "good name." It can seem as though at every juncture in our lives,
people wait to libel us or stand against us when we want to do something that we feel is right but goes against the norm. Inevitably, when
we take a stand, we must expect fierce resistance from others. Eleanor
Roosevelt remarked, "Do what you feel in your heart to be right—for
you'll be criticized anyway."[272] We cannot lead merely to acquire a good
name, because our choices will always draw both supporters and de-
tractors. Rather, we seek to live with integrity, so that even those who
disagree with us can say that we were honest.

The three crowns that Rabbi Shimon describes in this mishnah are
our inheritance from Creation and the subsequent passing of ritual and
spiritual laws through the millennia; these three crowns represent how
Judaism is to orient itself through history to create a perfect world. In
Jewish thought, the Torah, the priesthood, and a righteous monarchy
intertwine to create a just society. These are internal spiritual elements,
which, when brought together, help to produce an externally perfect
world.

The "three crowns" here can also be contrasted with what was developed in the eighteenth century by Montesquieu in his masterwork of
legal thought *The Spirit of Laws*. In Montesquieu's rendering, "Law in
general is human reason, inasmuch as it governs all the inhabitants of
the earth." It was this thought (among others) that became fundamental to the American Constitution as "the separation of powers" and jus-
tified the need for independent judiciaries to check the ruminations of
those entrusted to draft and enact legislation.[273] It is crucial that there

are multiple roles within institutions of power and that they serve as checks and balances upon one another.

The crown of a good name, however, is earned for oneself. How we go about doing this is not complicated, according to the Sages. Indeed, the Rabbis teach that we should consider ourselves as having three names:

> Every time a person increases their good deeds, they earn themselves a new name. There are three names by which a person is called: one that their parents call them, one that people call them, and one that they earn for themselves. The last is the best one of all.[274]

But a righteous person will be too busy to be preoccupied with reputation; a truly religious person is thus engaged:

> How do we find our Parent in heaven? We find God by doing good deeds and studying Torah. How does the Holy One find us? God finds us through love, harmony, reverence, companionship, truth, peace, humility, modesty, more study, less commerce, service to the wise, discussions with students, decency, a no that is really a no and a yes that is really a yes.[275]

Likewise, the three crowns exist not to be served, but as gifts to serve the human journey. They are tools that enhance our life journeys, nourish our souls, and provide stability during times of great upheaval. The Torah itself is not something to merely obey and serve. On the contrary, every letter, every verse, and every idea is meant only to improve the human condition. As it says in the Midrash, "The commandments were given only in order to refine humanity."[276]

One who fails may think it impossible to recover one's good name. But such failures enable human greatness and triumph over adversity. The Talmud says:

> In a place where the repentant stand, the completely righteous may not stand. That is to say, penitents stand on a higher rung than those who have never sinned, because they had to make a great effort to subdue their evil impulses. (BT *B'rachot* 34b)

Repairing one's good name is simpler now than it was for the ancients, because now one can move, switch careers, and truly remake oneself. But the goal should not be to run and hide from one's past, but to own it, incorporate it into oneself, and transcend. Life comprises intellectual pursuits, spiritual commitments, and societal concerns—referred to in classical Judaism as Torah, priesthood, and kingship. It is easy to get stuck in one of them—academic goals without meditation, prayer without study, activism without intellectual practice. These commitments come to define us, but they do not have to limit us. Through our deeds, our potential is boundless; and should we live in ways attuned to the spiritual ethos of everlasting divinity, our "good name" will be remembered.

4:18

רַבִּי נְהוֹרַאי אוֹמֵר: הֱוֵי גוֹלֶה לִמְקוֹם תּוֹרָה, וְאַל תּאמַר
שֶׁהִיא תָבוֹא אַחֲרַי, שֶׁחֲבֵרֶיךָ יְקַיְמוּהָ בְיָדֶךָ. וְאֶל־בִּינָתְךָ
אַל־תִּשָּׁעֵן (משלי ג:ה).

Rabbi N'horai said: Exile yourself to a place of Torah—and
do not say, "It will come after me"—for it is your colleagues
who cause it to remain with you; "and do not rely on your own
understanding" (Proverbs 3:5).

IN ONE OF the earliest passages of the Jewish scriptural canon, God declares that "it is not good [for people] to be alone" (Genesis 2:18). This
line has contributed to endless interpretation about human nature and
the human quest to cultivate meaningful relationships. As we noted in
the commentary on 1:6, humans have struggled with physical, emotional, and spiritual isolation from the beginning of their existence.

We need family, we need friends, we need colleagues, and we need
community for support and guidance. It is certainly possible to think
that Jewish life might be akin to other spiritual traditions in which isolation and quiet reflection are among the most desirable states. Rabbi
N'horai presents to the contrary in this mishnah: People are not meant
to be cut off from one another. The purpose of growing—individually
and collectively—is to learn and become ethical beings. For too long,
the Jewish people wandered in isolation, seldom fully welcomed by
neighbors. Turning inward gave us resilience, but it was not enough.
Looking to the future, we will continue to build learning communities that resist the temptation to retreat into intellectual "exile" and
self-proposed isolation.

There are factors that make it more difficult today to find companionship. The transience of modern existence—living away from
family, working longer hours, weaker social bonds exacerbated by the
substitution of social media for physical presence, and a consumer
society that approaches relationships as transactional—aggravates this
isolation. Nonetheless, researchers at the University of North Carolina

found that the number and quality of a person's social connections have a direct correlation on long-term health. Older adults who feel socially isolated are more than twice as likely to develop high blood pressure. A healthy social life is as important as diet and exercise.[277] Rabbi Abraham Isaac Kook articulates how Judaism values partnership and friendship, writing about finding companions within community, even when people disagree:

> Part of the characteristic of Torah is that it recognizes the need for a social life with friendships, which bring to the world a good life within society. This is particularly rewarding when one's social group consists of good and scholarly people. Separation from other people and extreme asceticism, which is the approach of a significant portion of those people who, of their own, have sought closeness to *HaShem*, is a foreign idea to the Torah. For that reason, if one wants to acquire knowledge of Torah, he will succeed specifically by joining together with a group of learners, which shows the gains of avoiding isolation.[278]

As we read earlier in *Pirkei Avot*, the Rabbis advise us to "acquire for yourself a friend" (refer back to the commentary on mishnah 1:6). Such a task is possibly even more important than learning from teachers: "I have learned much from my teachers, but from my friends more than my teachers" (BT *Taanit* 7a).

Amid our bombardment by the likes, snaps, hashtags, and pins of social media, finding meaningful personal relationships is of consequence to the modern condition. A simple click is no replacement for tangible bonds. Thus, for spiritual and physical health, we should resist the current trend toward social isolation and instead embrace friendship. As with anything worthwhile, investing in friendship requires discipline. Acquiring friends and allies not only nurtures the soul, but also is indispensable for the continuing progression of humanity.

4:19

רַבִּי יַנַּאי אוֹמֵר: אֵין בְּיָדֵינוּ לֹא מִשַּׁלְוַת הָרְשָׁעִים, וְאַף לֹא
מִיִּסּוּרֵי הַצַּדִּיקִים.

Rabbi Yannai said: It is not in our power to explain either the
tranquility of the wicked or the suffering of the righteous.

THEODICY, the theological problem of the existence of evil in the
world, is introduced in this mishnah. Why do the good suffer and the
wicked prosper? Rabbi Joseph B. Soloveitchik argues that rather than
try to answer this question, we should respond to suffering.[279] The
question itself is so challenging that we risk allowing it to impede our
ability to help where we can.

When Rabbi Yannai says, "It is not in our power," he means that we
don't have the intellectual capability to understand the fullness of the
divine plan for Creation. How can a temporal being understand the
everlasting and intangible? At the same time, the subtext of Rabbi Yannai's teaching here is that humanity's real power is the ability to allevi-
ate problems. We can address human suffering by alleviating pain and
inequity in societies and bringing about peace. These are ideal goals,
though far from fully manifested today, which should speedily come to
fruition if we will them into existence.

The Rabbis explain that the greatest struggle against evil happens
within the individual. We all contain within us a good inclination, *yetzer
tov*, and an evil inclination, *yetzer hara*, in continual tension with one
another. We try to ensure that *yetzer tov* prevails, but doing so is not so
simple. Early in the Torah, we learn that we are not a *tabula rasa*: "The
human mind inclines to evil from youth onward" (Genesis 8:21). The
counter-sentiment, "My God, the soul You have given me is pure," in
the beginning of the morning prayer service, charges us to see our inner
light. It is reassurance that our goodness prevails if we allow it to guide
our days.

But just because we attempt to infuse goodness into our days does not
mean that darkness is entirely banished. Every day, there are multiple

ways darkness can invade our souls and deceive us into committing acts of moral turpitude. Or is this idea anathema to Judaic ontology, which says that all creation is good? Rabbi Isaiah Horowitz, a sixteenth-century mystic, describes the necessary dialectical relationship between good and evil:

> I have explained at length that "evil" is distilled from "good," that it has been created only for the sake of the good. Without "evil," there could not have been such a concept as "good." God arranged that people should fear God; this is why the advantage of light is something that is due to the potential power of darkness.[280]

Even if we sometimes feel helpless standing before the unbearable evils of the world, we are not helpless to address the evil within. Rabbi Yisrael Salanter explains:

> Do not say that what God has made cannot be altered—and that because God (the Blessed One) has planted within me an evil force, I cannot hope to uproot it. This is not so, for the powers of a human being may be subdued, and even transformed. . . . Humanity has the power to subdue its own evil nature . . . and to change its nature toward the good, through exercise and practice.[281]

What should we do when we discover evil within ourselves? Should we banish the evil inclination? Should we suppress and ignore it, to let it fester? Or should we find a way to let it into the world? In his discussion of a passage from 4:1 (above, page 189), the founder of Chasidism, Rabbi Israel Baal Shem Tov, teaches:

> Who is the hero who controls his evil impulse? . . . Let us take an example from the ways of the world. A person is in a room guarding a valuable possession; on hearing a thief approach, he raises a shout and the thief runs away. However, another person in the same situation will prepare chains beforehand; on hearing the thief approach, he will pounce on the thief and take him prisoner. The same can be said about tzaddikim. Some of them do not allow any questionable thought to enter their heart or mind, while there are those who take that questionable or evil thought and subjugate it in their worship of God. Thus, when answering the question

"Who is the hero . . . ?" we should really consider those who are able to capture their *yetzer hara* and use it in the service of God.[282]

Paradoxically, in our work to repair the world, we bring the evil within us—our shadow sides—into service. About the verse "You shall love the Eternal your God with all your heart [*b'chol l'vav'cha*], with all your soul [*b'chol nafsh'cha*], and with all your might [*b'chol m'odecha*]" (Deuteronomy 6:5), the Sages say:

> "With all your heart" means with both your inclinations, with the good inclination and the evil inclination; "with all your soul" means even if God takes your life; and "with all your might" means with all your money. (Mishnah *B'rachot* 9:5)

We can bring light only if we lead from light; but to do so, we must be aware of the darkness within. Eckhart Tolle, a German-Canadian thinker on spirituality, writes about the reasons why people shouldn't necessarily seek to destroy evil in our midst:

> In certain cases, you may need to protect yourself or someone else from being harmed by another, but beware of making it your mission to "eradicate evil," as you are likely to turn into the very thing you are fighting against. Fighting unconsciousness will draw you into unconsciousness yourself. Unconsciousness, dysfunctional egoic behavior, can never be defeated by attacking it. Even if you defeat your opponent, the unconsciousness will simply have moved into you, or the opponent reappears in a new disguise. Whatever you fight, you strengthen, and what you resist persists.[283]

The Talmud advises, "If you happen to meet the *yetzer hara*, you should drag him to the study house. If the *yetzer hara* is stone, then he will melt; if he is iron, he will shatter" (BT *Sukkah* 52b). Rabbi Adin Steinsaltz, one of the world's most influential contemporary Talmudists, says that we should never let down our guard:

> Rabbi Simcha Bunim of Peshisha is said to have suggested that a man should always imagine that his head is on the execution block, the evil inclination standing over him with a large axe, ready to decapitate him. One of his disciples asked, "What happens if a man does not imagine this?" Rabbi Simcha Bunim answered that this

would be a sure sign that the evil inclination has already cut off his head. If a person no longer feels any anguish and lives in tranquility and peace, then he must have already been decapitated, and that is why he has a good life, full of peace and tranquility.[284]

Rabbi Steinsaltz explains not only that our souls are in a battle between good and evil but that every person's soul has unique traits:

> *Shaar HaGilgulim*, a kabbalistic work, identifies two different types of souls and elaborates on them: souls that possess the nature of Abel and souls that possess the nature of Cain. This is not a division between good souls and evil souls, for this source attributes the nature of Cain to the souls of many great Torah leaders. Rather, the division is one of character. The souls with the nature of Abel are milder and more pleasant, whereas those with the nature of Cain are stronger and more creative.[285]

Understanding our soul type helps when the tension between urges emerges. As one kabbalistic teacher remarks, "Know yourself and you will know God."[286] Rabbi Avi Weiss shares an insight from his teacher on looking beyond the surface for the essence of a person:

> Rabbi Soloveitchik adds that every time the Talmud records an individual who speaks of doing something wrong, the third person singular is used—*hahu gavra*, "that person"—as if the individual had been overtaken by an outer evil force. When the individual recalls having acted righteously, however, the first person singular—*ana*—is used, as righteousness is one's true essence.[287]

Rabbi Soloveitchik's thinking cautions us against dismissing another person as evil. Rather, all people have multiple influences, and one sometimes loses the battle against overwhelming internal and external forces. There is moral accountability, but there is also mercy.

We must work on ourselves while continuing to protest injustice and oppression wherever we see it. God has entrusted us to be stewards of this planet and live as people of conscience committed to love and justice. We need partners to help us see what we cannot about ourselves. Simone Weil, the twentieth-century Christian mystic and philosopher, observes:

> We experience good only by doing it. We experience evil only by refusing to allow ourselves to do it, or if we do it, by repenting of it. When we do evil we do not know it, because evil flies from the light.[288]

When one is full of hatred, one layers darkness around one's inner godliness and is unable to see the holy light in other people. The sole mission of the darkened soul becomes to reduce the bright godliness of others and from the world. We must continue to add godly light to the world whenever we are able. One way is to ensure that individuals (and groups) don't end up in that abyss of darkness, rage, and terror. Restraining darkness is not enough. We must ensure that light somehow penetrates everywhere. And when we are confronted with horror, we must ensure we are more in touch with our inner light than ever.

4:20

רַבִּי מַתְיָה בֶן חָרָשׁ אוֹמֵר: הֱוֵי מַקְדִּים לִשְׁלוֹם כָּל אָדָם.
וֶהֱוֵי זָנָב לָאֲרָיוֹת, וְאַל תְּהִי רֹאשׁ לַשֻּׁעָלִים.

Rabbi Matyah ben Charash said: Initiate a greeting to every
person; and be a tail to lions rather than a head to foxes.

THIS PASSAGE is simple but profound: one not only should be friendly
with others, but also should initiate greeting. While on its face this task
might sound easy, many factors complicate such engagement, such as
encountering those we do not like, strangers, or sometimes even those
we would normally choose not to engage. It's particularly difficult to
greet an enemy, for example.

Causing another person to be humiliated in public is a serious sin,
as well having been a primary reason for the destruction of the Temple
and the expulsion of the Jewish people from their homeland, according to the Rabbis. We are challenged to suppress aversion and reach out
to others. It doesn't have to be based in friendship, but merely in the
shared connection between humans. Indeed, being a positive presence
for others requires interpersonal skill. When they first meet in Genesis
47:7–10, one would expect Jacob, the theologian, and Pharaoh, the political leader, to discuss something profound, like the meaning of life or
the famine. Instead, Pharaoh asks Jacob, "How old are you?" (Genesis
47:8), a question that seems more typical for children on a playground
than for two figures of such importance. Why begin a charged conversation with what seems an insignificant question?

Rabbi Yaakov Tzvi Mecklenburg, also known as the K'tav V'Kabbalah (nineteenth century, Germany), suggests that there are two ways
we must speak. First, we use language to communicate specific ideas,
hopes, prayers, and teachings. Second, we use language to connect us
to another; the substance and content of the conversation are secondary to its ability for us to relate to another person. In his commentary
on Genesis 47:7–8, Rabbi Mecklenburg refers to the nature of the dialogue between these two giants as *d'varim shel mah b'kach*; this phrase

can loosely be translated as "small talk." He was satisfied with the ordinary social discourse shared between Jacob and Pharaoh. They were making small talk, and that too is virtuous. We don't always have to seek the profound and complex in every conversation and relationship.

In general, Jewish law and values teach that we should limit our speech to what has moral and spiritual significance. Our significant relationships should not be built around conversations about the weather, sports scores, or celebrity gossip, but rather around deeper reflections, feelings, and insights. Rabbi Mecklenburg teaches, however, that some speech should prioritize connecting over content.

We can see this phenomenon in prayer as well. Sometimes, the goal of praying is to convey the right words and specific messages. Other times, the goal is connection between a person and God, and the specific words are less important.

Later on in *Pirkei Avot* (mishnah 6:6), it is taught that there are forty-eight tools to acquire Torah. One is *miut sichah*, limiting idle conversation. If we limit mundane conversation, the Rabbis teach, we will become closer to Torah. It is possible that *miut* shouldn't be translated as telling us to limit, but rather that the only type of conversation we should engage in is *miut sichah*, or small talk. This talk is healthy and generative. Connecting with others and having human interaction help us grow, and small talk can be an important means to that end.

Small talk is how we make others feel comfortable with us. We don't only approach others with big issues; we also value them enough to discuss the trivial things. Businesspeople have long known that small talk aids marketing. Effective small talk aids one's popularity, because people respond to those who give them attention. A series of 2010 scholarly studies revealed that small talk can boost cognitive ability, especially executive functions.[289] Thus, success can often depend on one's ability to connect to another. Nowhere is this more evident in the modern conception than in the case of the presidential election of 1932.

According to the late economic historian John Kenneth Galbraith, in the late 1920s Herbert Hoover was regarded as a hands-on businessman who, among other things, had run the successful American food relief program during and after World War I, saving millions in

Belgium, Russia, and elsewhere in Europe from starvation. These humanitarian acts established his reputation as an efficient organizer and helped secure his election to the presidency in 1928. Less than a year into his administration, on October 25, 1929, the stock market began fluctuating wildly. President Hoover issued a statement asserting that the American economy was "on a sound and prosperous basis."[290] After a few dry statements about construction and wages, he concluded with a reference to wheat bushel production, adding that this would "result in a very low carryover at the end of the harvest year." This feeble bureaucratic message, with its uncaring tone and complete disconnect from what was causing a panic, did not resonate with the American people; four days later the stock market crashed, signaling the start of the Great Depression. Hoover's inability to manage an impending crisis or communicate an effective strategy to combat the ensuing economic slump that morphed into the Great Depression led to a dramatic plunge in his popularity, as well as in the confidence of the American people in their government, their country, and themselves.

In contrast, Hoover's successor, President Franklin D. Roosevelt, was a man of enormous personal charisma, who made those interacting with him feel like he truly cared for them and was concerned with their plight. He possessed, for example, an amazing ability to remember the names of people he had met only once. When asked how, he claimed that he saw their names on their foreheads. However, a more likely explanation is that he developed a method of remembering people through nicknames; thus, one adviser was "Harry the Hat" Hopkins; even the infamous Soviet leader was "Uncle Joe" Stalin (though he was not called that to his face). Roosevelt knew how to engage and connect with people, on both large and small scales—an important criterion for a leader.

Immediately upon taking office, President Roosevelt needed to restore a sense of security and hope to the banking system, as well in the hearts of so many Americans. He seized upon the method of a direct radio appeal to reach the American people. His "fireside chats" approximated a personal conversation, in which the president referred to his radio audience as "you" and in which the talk revolved around basic explanations of problems. They were simple and casual and made the audience—the American people—feel at ease. Most importantly, they were successful: after his fireside chat on the banking crisis shortly after his inauguration on March 12, 1933, circumstances began to turn around immediately. Americans quickly began making far more deposits instead of withdrawals from banks, and the American banking system was saved. President Roosevelt held only eight of these fireside chats during his first term, yet they had an enormous influence on the American public and undoubtedly contributed much to his unprecedented four successful presidential campaigns. The American people regarded President Roosevelt as a person who cared about them and their well-being. The social skill of making small talk was necessary to help rescue a nation and its people in the midst of an unprecedented crisis. Yet, what seemed like a modern revolution in communication technology can be detected centuries earlier through Talmudic discourse.

(Indeed, as we explored in mishnah 2:9, Talmudic commentary tells us that nobody ever initiated a greeting to Rabban Yochanan ben Zakkai, because he was always first to greet others [BT *B'rachot* 17a].)

Consider opportunities for small talk that deepen interpersonal relationships:

> AMONG FAMILY: Ideology and meaning can be constructed at the elaborate Shabbat table and while doing laundry or dishes. The Rabbis taught the importance of small talk between spouses before reuniting in intimate ways, offering a chance for gentle and simple reconnection.
>
> AT WORK: Building relationships at work so often happens between meetings, in the hallway or break room. We rarely get to choose our colleagues, so getting to know them builds rapport and leads to positive outcomes.
>
> AT SYNAGOGUE during *Oneg Shabbat* or *Kiddush*: An inclusive community welcomes individuals not only when they enter the building initially, but also when the food and drink are laid out. Are elbows thrown? Is one offered a seat? Is this a place

for pleasant small talk and warm connection, or merely a time
for mindless consumption?

WHEN MEETING SOMEONE who is experiencing homelessness:
Whether or not one chooses to give money, food, or other *tze-dakah* to a person in need, interacting with our fellows who
find themselves made vulnerable is a holy opportunity for a
smile and small talk. Speak with individuals who may be on
the street, and you validate their inherent human dignity in
that brief, friendly greeting. You see them and acknowledge
their equal humanity.

It is not only while trying to change the world that social activists engage in small talk. It is also necessary to do so in intimate and everyday
relationships, along with sacred communal relationships; Buber, as we
have read, calls these "I-Thou" encounters. While our intellectual conversations about our grand ideals are crucial to our self-definition, the
earnest, connective conversations we have in the hallways and streets
can be just as important in defining us as individuals and in community.

4:21

רַבִּי יַעֲקֹב אוֹמֵר: הָעוֹלָם הַזֶּה דּוֹמֶה לַפְּרוֹזְדוֹר לִפְנֵי הָעוֹלָם הַבָּא. הַתְקֵן עַצְמְךָ בַּפְּרוֹזְדוֹר, כְּדֵי שֶׁתִּכָּנֵס לַטְּרַקְלִין.

Rabbi Yaakov said: This world is like a lobby before the world-to-come; prepare yourself in the lobby so that you may enter the banquet hall.

ONE CAN HARDLY WAIT to get to the fancy reception, but before one can enter, there is a wait. The wait can be frustrating, testing the limits of one's patience. But then, you're allowed in, greeted with loving arms and warm light. In this mishnah, Rabbi Yaakov suggests that we have one opportunity to do mitzvot and beautify our souls. This will shape eternal destiny. Whether we fully embrace this theological model, we should be inspired by its urgency.

One Jewish concept among many about the afterlife is that worldly existence is mere preparation for the soul's eternal experience. A lifetime's accumulated experiences constitute only the guide to something greater in an unknowable, intangible realm. We are to live our lives with spiritual purpose and moral rigor. Although we are often caught in the mundane, we should dedicate ourselves to good deeds and charitable endeavors whenever possible.

Consider the following Talmudic passage, which describes with breathtaking brevity the effects of our actions:

> In the world-to-come, there is neither eating nor drinking nor begetting children, neither bargaining nor jealousy nor hatred nor strife. All that the righteous do is sit with their crowns on their heads and enjoy the radiance of the Divine Presence. (BT *B'rachot* 17a)

For some, it would be an overwhelming and incomprehensible task to enjoy divine radiance (for what does such radiance entail?). For others, however, the notion of basking in the splendor of the Divine is the very definition of utopia. How might we understand a middle ground? Each of us can daily choose how to cultivate utopia: Am I a person of ideas, values, or vision? Or am I just excited about the next meal? There is no definitive answer, but pondering such existential questions can lead us toward deeper understanding of both the individual inner world and eternity.

Another, more subversive, way of understanding "the world-to-come" is by seeing it as this very world that we are yet to build. Our current world is broken, desperately in need of repair. We are to "prepare" ourselves, this mishnah teaches, to be people who help bring about "the world-to-come" for future generations, a world devoid of racism, hatred, xenophobia, and war.

In our daily living, our task is to leave the world shining more brightly than how we found it. The precise dimensions of how we are to accomplish this lofty goal are up to us to discern. This human enterprise is not about personal salvation, but collective redemption. How we join with our communities and with other communities for the common purpose of making the world more whole is our way of exercising our human potential. Finding a place in the everlasting bliss of paradise is incentive to be kind, but it shouldn't be our only goal. Instead, standing in the lobby to paradise, standing in this world, should be incentive enough to do kindnesses and create a more just and equitable society.

4:22

הוּא הָיָה אוֹמֵר: יָפָה שָׁעָה אַחַת בִּתְשׁוּבָה וּמַעֲשִׂים טוֹבִים
בָּעוֹלָם הַזֶּה מִכָּל חַיֵּי הָעוֹלָם הַבָּא. וְיָפָה שָׁעָה אַחַת שֶׁל
קֹרַת רוּחַ בָּעוֹלָם הַבָּא מִכָּל חַיֵּי הָעוֹלָם הַזֶּה.

He used to say: Better one hour of repentance and good deeds
in this world than the entire life of the world-to-come; and
better one hour of spiritual bliss in the world-to-come than
the entire life of this world.

CULTIVATING A SERIOUS spiritual presence in this world is tremen-
dously difficult. Doing so, however, can have ripple effects for generations to come. And hopefully, by dedicating time to growing in wisdom,
we will be able to influence those around us, our descendants, and our
eternal souls. Though we can never fully comprehend the world-to-
come, we should strive to do our best to make this world beyond our
world reflect what we would want to see while living in eternal splendor. To do so, we have to overcome the superficiality of modern living
and strive for more substantial interactions with friends, neighbors,
and strangers.

One of the greatest challenges for the modern person is to resist the
desires for instant gratification. At every moment, we are bombarded
with advertisements for some new technological device, or flashy car,
or cheap hamburger. But these are meaningless fads that pass in a moment. Creating something of lasting value—our inner selves—is what
matters, while navigating through the many arduous moments of life.
We can transcend the current moment and tap into our more noble
values.

The Torah itself states that a living God repents and performs *t'shuvah*. According to Rashi's interpretation of Deuteronomy 30:3 ("Then
the Eternal your God will restore your fortunes and take you back in
love. [God] will bring you together again from all the peoples where
the Eternal your God has scattered you"), an evolving *Shechinah* (Divine
Presence) goes into exile and returns with us from exile, *uva l'Tzion*

go-eil ("[God] will come as a redeemer to Zion"; Isaiah 59:20), only when we restore the Divine Presence to the lower world and heal our relationship with God. Additionally, on countless occasions, the Midrash suggests that God changes positions, feels regret, learns from humanity, and even destroys previous worlds that proved to be mistakes.[291] When this mishnah says "better one hour of repentance," we ask: "Are we alone in our attempts to change and grow?" If the Talmud repeatedly suggests that God actually engages in *t'shuvah* (BT *M'gilah* 29a), can this radical suggestion that God grows, evolves, adapts with the times, and experiences redemption pass as authentic Jewish theology?

It is possible that many of these stories are not meant to be read literally when there is a deeper spiritual truth at hand. Rabbi Bachya ibn Pakuda, an eleventh-century, neo-Platonic mystic, argues that the "duties of the heart" are on a separate plane from rational, physical reality. Certain truths can be understood only on an emotional and spiritual level. One is to "know God" with all one's heart.[292]

Such *t'shuvah* is not a response to divine sin, as that would not be coherent with traditional understandings of God. Rather, it is in search of an evolved completeness, a wholeness that expands from 10/10 to 100/100 to infinite/infinite. God is the aggregate of power and good in the universe. This aggregate can grow, but God is always the total.

T'shuvah is a divine process before it becomes a human imperative. The twentieth-century Jewish theologian Rabbi Eliezer Berkovits (1908–1992) suggests that using moral attributes to describe God is not a sign of anthropomorphism. Instead, attributes such as compassion, love, and justice are divine before they are human.[293] To be sure, God is absolutely free, and free will is the constitutive means to all *t'shuvah*. In repentance, divine energy reinvigorates the world through the emanation of divine blessing—*shefa*—and divine self-revelation emerges in every moment and being. In this *t'shuvah*, the divine essence, *atzmut*, remains constant, but God's relationship to Creation evolves, as certain divine dimensions are affected by human action and moved toward synthesis and unity. It is only with this necessary human partnership that God's expansion and healing are brought into the world.

Rabbi Kook explains that the Divine is experienced through flashes of clarity, not unlike the swiftness of a lightning bolt descending upon the earth. In this way, Rabbi Kook describes not only a human phenomenological encounter, but aspects about reality itself. He writes:

> Imagine living in a pitch-black world where the only source of light is that which is emitted by an occasional bolt of lightning. It would be impossible to truly identify one's surroundings in such a dark world. Even if the lightning occurs repeatedly, the lack of constant illumination makes this form of light inadequate. If, however, the lightning is extremely frequent—like a strobe light set to flash at a fast frequency—its illumination is transformed into a source of constant light.[294]

Such illumination is akin to humanity's relationship with the spiritual world. God is intimately connected with humankind and hears and responds to our broken selves, our *pizur hanefesh* (scattered spiritual state). Thus, monotheism is not a static entity. Rather, its essence is inherently dynamic, its divine manifestations continually expressed and renewed. Reality is not immutable physical substance, but an evolving experience.

Some reject the possibility of God's changeability, because it implies fallibility. However, change is not synonymous with failure. To state that God is incapable of expanding, growing, and adapting would be to limit divine omnipotence. Perfection is not static or stale; perfection is a state of growth, in which possibility continues to move toward actualization. One sphere of actualization is the Sabbath, when God's presence is made manifest in the world.

According to the Chabad concept of God dwelling in the earthly realm (known as *dirah batachtonin*), this manifest closeness enables connectivity between physical and spiritual reality. God contains the universe but is more than the universe. If the world evolves, then God evolves, because God is in relationship to a progressing universe and is affected by humans, even while immutable divine virtues remain. Indeed, God's presence expands into the world when humans do holy acts, achieving higher unity, *yichudah ilaah*, and lower unity, *yichudah taata*—unity in the spiritual realm and unity in the earthly domain. Thus, one test for theological truth is if the soul is transformed when the truth is embraced. Another test is whether it speaks to global injustice, because tradition teaches that *tikkun olam* is a Divine-human partnership. In a world where billions of people live in poverty, and where every day suffering is seemingly allowed to flourish, we can relate only to an immanent God who cries and suffers alongside Creation—*imo anochi b'tzarah* (Psalms 91:15), "God is with me in my suffering"—and who continues to experiment with the right balance of bestowed determinism and human freedom. Divine brokenness accompanies the journey of human brokenness; together we heal.

If the capacity to do *t'shuvah* is the pinnacle of the human condition, then repentance is a process in which we emulate God, *halachta bidrachav* (see above at 4:2, page 195). If the commandment to imitate the righteous ways of God were not to include self-improvement, this mitzvah to emulate the Divine would be lacking in its transformational potential, because theology would be divorced from human actualization. God is an ideal for us only if we can actually emulate divine behavior. This image of God as one who grows, cries, and seeks liberation and unification should motivate us to look deeper into our internal lives. Knowing that such a being, God, responds to the woes of the world, how should we react?

It is this understanding of God that should inspire us to realign the human-Divine paradigm. One reason that "God" is rarely mentioned in Jewish social justice circles is because contemporary religious culture often retreats into abstractions, rather than embracing theological models that are spiritually and personally transformative. How many more Jews will we turn away from Judaism with irrelevant theology because it conforms to some medieval notion of logic?

Rabbi Zev Wolf of Zhitomir (eighteenth century, Ukraine) explains that we cannot reach God's unity until we recover our own. Traditionally, the Hebrew month of Elul (the month leading up to Rosh HaShanah and Yom Kippur) is not just a time to engage in self-help, but also a time to look to the heavens, to emulate dynamic growth and work to heal a fractured world.

Such inner spiritual building inevitably leads to doubts and questions: How should we connect with a God who cries and evolves? If

God is in captivity and exile with us and is redeemed along with us, then there can be a real relationship. If God suffers along with all the oppressed victims of injustice, then our liberations are bound up with one another, and our experiences of immanence and alienation are intertwined. Rabbi Kook teaches that we are responsible for expanding, beautifying, and celebrating God's presence in this world. We achieve this by seeking human healing and ensuring the progress of the human enterprise of creating a just and holy world. We cannot abandon the possibility of human and societal progress so easily. God's actions serve as a reminder and motivation that a better future for the oppressed is on the horizon, waiting only for our actions and our implementation of divine healing in this universe.

4:23

רַבִּי שִׁמְעוֹן בֶּן אֶלְעָזָר אוֹמֵר: אַל תְּרַצֶּה אֶת חֲבֵרְךָ בִּשְׁעַת
כַּעְסוֹ, וְאַל תְּנַחֲמֶנּוּ בְּשָׁעָה שֶׁמֵּתוֹ מֻטָּל לְפָנָיו, וְאַל תִּשְׁאַל
לוֹ בִּשְׁעַת נִדְרוֹ, וְאַל תִּשְׁתַּדֵּל לִרְאוֹתוֹ בִּשְׁעַת קַלְקָלָתוֹ.

Rabbi Shimon ben Elazar says: Do not appease your fellow in
the time of their anger; do not console them while their dead
lies before them; do not question them about their vow at the
time they make it; and do not attempt to see them at the time
of their degradation.

IN THIS MISHNAH, Rabbi Shimon talks about emotional intelligence.
The biblical sage *Kohelet*, Ecclesiastes, says that there is a time for everything under heaven (Ecclesiastes 3:1); we must be deeply aware and
sensitive to that timing. When someone is angry, lamenting, inspired,
or ashamed, it is important to give the person distance to experience
these feelings. Even the most rational person can devolve into irra-
tionality during an emotional episode; one cannot think clearly with
normal reason when in these emotional states. Rabbi Samson Raphael
Hirsch writes, "Do not go out of your way to visit someone who suffered
something unpleasant if you know that they would rather remain alone
and unseen in their distress."

This passage also teaches that we should not rush to identify with
another who is suffering. We are to understand that the person's pain
is unique, and healing can only begin on that person's terms, not on
ours. More broadly, the Jewish people have been ravaged by tragedy for
millennia, and only now do we see the beginnings of a national healing.

A centuries-long debate has argued where ethics are grounded. Immanuel Kant grounded ethics in reason, but David Hume grounded
ethics in emotions such as sympathy, empathy, and compassion. Today,
neuro-imaging may offer a new way to resolve this issue. Brain scans
reveal that when participants are engaged in moral reasoning, there
is significant activation in areas that govern emotional processing (a
circuit running from the frontal lobes to the limbic system).[295] These

findings support the argument of New York University professor and researcher Martin L. Hoffman, a clinical psychologist who observes that the roots of human morality are located in empathy.[296] Thus, people learn to follow certain moral principles when they can put themselves in another's place. These findings also bolster the ideas of educational reformer John Dewey, who taught that lessons are best learned not when students are taught abstractly, but through real-life events that foster emotional intelligence.[297]

If we know that emotional development is a key part of moral development, then why is Jewish education so cognitively based? We teach for text mastery, intellectual reasoning skills, and memorization (all important), but often leave aside cultivation of empathy, understanding of shame, actualization of mercy, and control of anger.

Teaching prayer, Torah, and ritual should embrace a pedagogical approach that leads to both emotional and cognitive development. Giving of oneself to others is necessary to internalize altruism. Rather than leaving students to a brief and menial *chesed* project (sometimes referred to as mitzvah projects), we must ensure the right emotional experience. Since most of our emotional lives are subconscious, we should engage students in deliberate conversations to process feelings before, during, and after activities like *chesed* projects. We must ensure that when we partake in these projects, we aren't merely engaging in task completion, but furthering compassion, empathy, and other emotional strengths.

Rabbi Kook stresses the importance of emotions in education. He makes the case that intellect is deficient without emotion and that neglecting emotional cultivation is dangerous:

> Humanity cannot live with intellect alone, nor with emotion alone; intellect and emotion must forever be joined together. If we wish to burst beyond our own level, we will lose our ability to feel; and our flaws and deficiencies will be myriad despite the strength of our intellect. And needless to say, if we sink into unmitigated emotion, we will fall to the depths of foolishness, which leads to all [kinds of] weakness and sin. Only the quality of equilibrium, which balances intellect with emotion, can deliver humanity completely.[298]

While all emotions must be tended in moral development, choices matter. In his lecture "Morals and Education," the late British psychoanalyst Donald Winnicott says that religious systems can harm development by emphasizing sin and shame, rather than love and trust. Education of the emotions must be deliberate. When we cultivate compassion, we promote good citizenship. When we give space to reflect upon anger, we teach self-control. When we start conversations about fear and shame, we foster humility and self-awareness. When we talk about personal suffering and loss, we inculcate empathy and care. When students are asked to cultivate moral imagination, the most complex emotions can be actualized.

As Ecclesiastes teaches, there is "a time to weep and a time to laugh / A time to wail and a time to dance" (Ecclesiastes 3:4). To live fully, we must embrace it all. In "A Theory of Emotions," Rabbi Joseph B. Soloveitchik argues for the totality of emotional experience in religious life:

> Judaism has insisted upon the integrity and wholeness of the table of emotions, leading like a spectrum from joy, sympathy and humility (the conjunctive feelings) to anger, sadness and anguish (the disjunctive emotions). Absolutization of one feeling at the expense of others, or the granting of unconditioned centrality to certain emotions while denoting others to a peripheral status, may have damaging complications for the religious development of the personality. [299]

Modern neuroscience shows that many of the moral decisions that we make bypass the prefrontal cortex—the rational brain—creating instinctive patterns of behavior.[300] Therefore, parents and teachers need to educate children holistically, to foster their ethics. These are not mere thought experiments. The Greeks used drama to teach emotions, while Jews use real-life experience. We must expose our children to the real world, including poverty, suffering, and struggle, to foster the emotions of sympathy, empathy, compassion, and love. Through this we can fully serve the world, *b'chol l'vav'cha*—with all of our heart—to be better humans and be better with our relationship with God.

4:24

שְׁמוּאֵל הַקָּטָן אוֹמֵר: בִּנְפֹל אוֹיִבְךָ אַל־תִּשְׂמָח, וּבִכָּשְׁלוֹ
אַל־יָגֵל לִבֶּךָ, פֶּן־יִרְאֶה יְיָ וְרַע בְּעֵינָיו, וְהֵשִׁיב מֵעָלָיו אַפּוֹ
(משלי כד:יז-יח).

Sh'muel HaKatan says: "When an enemy falls, be not glad;
and when one stumbles, let your heart not be joyous. Lest
God see and be displeased—and turn divine wrath away from
[your enemy]" (Proverbs 24:17–18).

THERE IS SO MUCH to digest in this passage, one of the most perplexing in all of *Pirkei Avot*. First, Sh'muel HaKatan does not add his own
commentary, but merely quotes Proverbs. Second, Sh'muel HaKatan
is the author of the nineteenth blessing in the *Amidah*, the last-added
prayer asking God to strike down heretics; this rabbi, who takes a
strong stand against those who diverge from the tradition, also teaches
that we should never rejoice at the downfall of our enemies (BT *B'rachot*
28b–29a).

An earlier passage in Proverbs says that it is natural to celebrate
the destruction of evil: "When it goes well with the righteous, the city
rejoices; and when the wicked perish, there is jubilation" (Proverbs
11:10). Furthermore, it is written in Psalms, "You who love the Eternal,
hate evil! God preserves the souls of the pious; God saves them from
the hand of the wicked" (97:10).

But the Rabbis teach that we drop wine from the Passover seder cup
to mourn the loss of life when the Egyptians drowned in the sea.[301] The
Israelites were saved, yet they did not rejoice. This astounding Rabbinic teaching reflects, "In that hour, the ministering angels wished
to utter the song [of praise] before the Holy One of Blessing, but God
rebuked them, saying: My handiwork [the Egyptians] is drowning in
the sea; would you sing a song before me!" (BT *Sanhedrin* 39b). In addition to heeding the divine rebuke and not rejoicing at the downfall of
our oppressors, we also learn from the Torah that we should assist our
enemies (Exodus 23:5). The Rabbis of the Talmud teach that if we see

both a friend who needs help and an enemy who needs help, we should help the enemy first, to overcome our evil inclination (BT *Bava M'tzia* 32b). The commentary *Avot D'Rabbi Natan* (A 23:1) even teaches that a hero is someone who can turn his enemy into a friend.

In the anecdote recounted above (2:7, page 82), B'ruriah, the most influential female Talmudic sage, tells her husband, Rabbi Meir, that we should pray not for the end of sinners, but for the end of sin. Rabbi Meir prays for them to repent, and they do (BT *B'rachot* 10a). Additionally, Rabbi Meir Simcha of Divinsk (nineteenth century, Lithuania) teaches, "There is no festival or holiday in Israel celebrating the downfall of enemies."[302] While it undoubtedly appears that holidays historically did include the celebration of the downfall of enemies (such as in the Purim story), Rabbi Meir Simcha seems to be teaching that today we should interpret those texts differently and certainly not celebrate it ourselves.

While it is difficult to resist ordinary human emotion, when we control fury and instead develop our innate potential for kindness—inner and outer—we emulate the Divine. People are meant to hold two truths simultaneously: that human beings can unleash both kindness and wrath. It is for us to cultivate the former and wrestle with the latter. We should strive to suppress the evil inclination that is always attempting to permeate our everyday existence, and to attune to the good inclination: the divine part of ourselves. And even though it is difficult, we should learn to hold love for the enemy even when it seems humanly impossible. This world, the world of the holy triumphing over mundane cruelty, is based on miracles. We should embrace these miracles whenever we can.

אות

4:25

אֱלִישָׁע בֶּן אֲבוּיָה אוֹמֵר: הַלָּמֵד יֶלֶד – לְמָה הוּא דּוֹמֶה?
לִדְיוֹ כְתוּבָה עַל נְיָר חָדָשׁ. וְהַלָּמֵד זָקֵן – לְמָה הוּא דּוֹמֶה?
לִדְיוֹ כְתוּבָה עַל נְיָר מָחוּק.

Elisha ben Avuyah said: One who studies [Torah] as a child, to
what can they be likened? To ink written on fresh paper. And
one who studies [Torah] as an older person, to what can they
be likened? To ink written on smudged paper.

THERE IS SOMETHING BEAUTIFUL about erasure marks. Smudged
paper is an indication of reflection and refinement, of ideas blossom-
ing, blotted out, and engaged anew. But, while it is important that
every child have access to "ink" and "fresh paper," this is not universally
true: worldwide, children are regularly denied the basic human right of
education. This lack leads to countless social and economic problems.
Education is a priority in the Torah, and thus should be in our world.

In this mishnah, Elisha ben Avuyah is speaking of himself, viewing
his mind and soul like "smudged paper." He was incorrect. Elisha ben
Avuyah came to be called Acher (Other) because he left Jewish tradition. He believed he was beyond *t'shuvah* (repentance) and his life no
longer redeemable.[303] His misrepresentation of Torah's ideals cost him
community; Torah teaches that anyone can return to become one's best
and true self.

In fact, this mishnah teaches that there are two ways to learn. One
writer uses a pen, not an eraser. She writes with confidence exactly what
comes to mind. No smudges appear on her paper, but it is an imperfect
first draft. Another writer uses pencil and erases and edits. There are a
lot of smudges due to numerous corrections. Her writing is more noble
because it has been refined.

In the Torah portion *Vayeilech*, we are given the description of the ritual of *hakheil* (from the verb "assemble"), to take place every seven years,
during which the king would come to the public sphere to educate the
people (Deuteronomy 31:10–12). "Gather the people—men, women,

children, and the strangers in your communities—that they may hear and so learn" (31:12). This is the Torah's model for inclusive education. Abraham ibn Ezra writes in his commentary that this public learning takes place at the beginning of the Sabbatical year, when field work is forbidden. This ensures that everyone is able to take a break from work to grow intellectually.

The Torah teaches that to offer education fairly, we should periodically rethink labor and economic systems. As a general matter, education benefits all of society, and an increase in education reduces the potential for poverty, increases prosperity, promotes children's health, improves sexual health, reduces teen pregnancy, and promotes civil rights and democratic attitudes. Thus, to confirm the teaching of the Torah, improving education is one of the most effective ways to create a more just world.

UNESCO documented the worldwide effort toward its goal to achieve universal literacy by 2015. The number of primary-school-age children who do not attend school was reduced from 105 million in 1990 to 61 million. However, progress has halted in the past decade. Today, more than half of unschooled children in the world live in sub-Saharan Africa, where war prevents 28 million from attending school. Speaking before a class of primary school students in Dili, the capital of East Timor, former secretary-general of the United Nations Ban Ki-moon described the benefits of education: "Education promotes equality. Learning lifts people out of poverty. Life skills can even prevent disease and save lives, and whole economies can prosper. That is how we build productive societies—one lesson at a time."[304] His statement echoes the broad precepts inherent in the Torah.

Yet, this disparity in access to education should also be a call to action. Jewish law mandates not only that we teach, but also that we appoint teachers everywhere. The *Shulchan Aruch* says:

> Every community is required to appoint teachers; a city without a teacher should be put under a ban until the inhabitants thereof appoint one. If they persist in not appointing a teacher, the city should be destroyed, for the world exists only through the breath of schoolchildren.[305]

Perhaps we might return to the Sabbatical year to remind ourselves to invest in education, if we wish to move nations out of poverty. At the present time, only 2 percent of humanitarian aid goes to education.[306] The Talmud teaches that "Jerusalem was destroyed only because they neglected [the education of] schoolchildren." Even further, "Schoolchildren may not be made to neglect [their studies] even for the building of the Temple" (BT *Shabbat* 119b). We must heed this message before yet another generation is lost to ignorance, prejudice, and war.

We are obliged to take the Jewish injunction to educate children to its next level. Maimonides teaches, "It is commanded on each and every wise person to teach every student, even though they are not their children, since the students that one teaches are called one's children."[307] Saving one child results in saving many more than one. The Talmud teaches that "one who teaches a child Torah is considered to have taught that child and that child's children and grandchildren, to the end of the generations" (BT *Kiddushin* 30a).

There are ways to improve education. Regarding places where armed conflict has disrupted the educational system, UNESCO and the EFA Global Monitoring Report note policies that work, such as a shift from humanitarian aid to multiyear investments, and pooled resources to reduce bureaucracy and help the transition to government-run programs. If donor nations converted mere days of military spending to education aid, billions of dollars could be redirected toward a long-term vision of every child receiving a quality education.[308]

In the twenty-first century, immediate rewards are typically prioritized over long-term gains. In the United States, we need to work for education reform to ensure smaller class sizes, school accountability, better teacher training and incentives, and higher academic standards. We need to prioritize funding for education, and we cannot delay. We cannot expect struggling villages and nations to address this challenge alone. The Torah commands us to pursue justice, as well as educate the next generation. As Jews who hold the value of education so highly, we must be at the forefront of the policies that alter global education opportunities for the better. As a people, we must be the paper that supports the fresh ink.

4:26

רַבִּי יוֹסֵי בַּר יְהוּדָה, אִישׁ כְּפַר הַבַּבְלִי, אוֹמֵר: הַלָּמֵד מִן
הַקְּטַנִּים – לְמַה הוּא דוֹמֶה? לְאוֹכֵל עֲנָבִים קֵהוֹת וְשׁוֹתֶה
יַיִן מִגִּתּוֹ. וְהַלָּמֵד מִן הַזְּקֵנִים – לְמַה הוּא דוֹמֶה? לְאוֹכֵל
עֲנָבִים בְּשֵׁלוֹת וְשׁוֹתֶה יַיִן יָשָׁן.

Rabbi Yosei bar Y'hudah of K'far HaBavli says: One who
learns Torah from the young, to what can that person be
likened? To one who eats unripe grapes or drinks wine from
its fermentation vat. But one who learns Torah from the old,
to what can that person be likened? To one who eats ripe
grapes or drinks aged wine.

THIS MISHNAH says again that the wisdom of the aged is to be deeply
valued. This wisdom is not a guaranteed product of age or even of experience. One can retreat to the past, becoming scarred, negative, and
cynical with age, but this passage focuses on the positive experiences
that accrue during a lifetime. In this way, the metaphor of grapes and
wine—the former squeezed and fermenting into the latter—is a paradigm for how the Rabbis saw the natural world. Everyone has the
potential to become something finer than at the start. The processes
that transform the humble grape into holy wine are similar to those
that transform the unlearned student into the noble master. Between
the two poles of experience, growth is encouraged, change is encouraged, and even life itself is encouraged.

To be sure, one can become less wise with age, susceptible to suspi-
cions and superstitions. Therefore, the act of ensuring that we don't
succumb to the false prejudices of the world is what allows us to develop
into moral, spiritual beings. With more experiences and more time to
process and grow, we increase the likelihood of having cultivated some
significant wisdom. And ultimately, that is the purpose of this teaching.
Going out into the world without perspective is akin to squandering
our ability to cultivate the ethics we need to thrive as productive human
beings.

A mitzvah from the Torah says to honor the elderly (Leviticus 19:32). Rashi, on this verse, writes that this mitzvah applies not only to wise elders, but also equally to ignorant ones. The Rabbis suggest that although many elderly people may have forgotten much of their wisdom in their later years, this does not diminish their value: "Be mindful of the elderly who have forgotten their teaching for reasons that are not their fault, as it is said that the tablets and the broken tablets rested [together] in the ark" (BT *B'rachot* 8b; see Deuteronomy 10:1–2).

Maimonides states that it is an incontrovertible law to honor the elderly, even if we do not consider them wise:

> We should stand before an old man of exceedingly advanced age, even if he is not a sage. Even a sage who is young is obligated to stand before a sage of exceedingly advanced age. Nevertheless, he need not rise to his full height, and need only show some token of respect.[309]

The Torah suggests that one can assume that the elderly hold certain types of wisdom. Deuteronomy 32:7 reads, "Remember the days of old, / Consider the years of ages past; / Ask your parent, who will inform you, / Your elders, who will tell you." The Book of Job is more explicit: "With age comes wisdom, and length of days brings understanding" (12:12). The Rabbis believed that the elderly had wisdom from which we all could learn (BT *Kiddushin* 32b).

We should consider from whom we are attaining our wisdom, as well as how we balance our perspectives. In addition to learning from the aged, the Rabbis are clear that we must engage and support the elderly. *B'reishit Rabbah, Parashat Tol'dot*, says, "We learn that everyone who welcomes in an elderly person, it is as if one has welcomed in the Divine Presence." Some explain that this is due to the wisdom and dignity of the elderly. Others explain that it is due to their challenges: "Rabbi Yochanan would stand before the elderly Arameans and say, 'How many troubles and experiences have passed over them'" (BT *Kiddushin* 33a). Wise or not, this is a vulnerable population that is to be cared for and with respect.

Sadly, today, too many of the elderly in our communities are neglected. Shocking statistics reveal some of the economic challenges that seniors face:

> From 2011 to 2012, the rate of extreme poverty rose by a statistically significant amount among those 65 and older, meaning that a growing number of them were living at or below 50 percent of the poverty line. In 2012, this was $11,011 a year for an older person living alone.[310]

In many cities, monthly rent alone exceeds income, even for those above the poverty line. It appeared that in 2006 (before the recession) fewer than one in ten of the elderly lived in poverty.[311] However, more than 22 percent lived below the 150 percent poverty level ($13,000 per year). Then, health-care costs are not factored into poverty statistics. Taking these costs into consideration, an adjusted 2006 poverty rate for the elderly would be about 32 percent. Many elderly people have suffered from long-term unemployment, debts, insufficient savings, and inadequate social security support—all exacerbated by increasing costs of living and uncertain changes to health-care access.

Furthermore, there are serious health risks that seniors face as they age, such as falls, responsible for thousands of serious injuries, disability, and deaths each year.[312] The combination of decreased bone mineral density and lessening vision leads to an increasing tendency for falls that may result in bone fracture, with hip fractures especially dreaded, as they lead to disability and the necessity for institutional care. Increased urgency for urination (often caused by diuretics and prescription medications) can also lead to falls, as the elderly rush to get to a bathroom before they have an accident. Other health risks such as presbyopia (the inability to see near objects) and visual problems such as macular degeneration or diabetic retinopathy make seeing and avoiding obstacles increasingly difficult. The inability to reach one's feet (the feet are especially vulnerable to infection, and those with diabetes may be at risk of losing their feet if an infection is unattended) is also a serious problem, and something as simple as trimming one's toenails becomes virtually impossible or fraught with the risk of cuts and infections.

Unfortunately, the growing elderly population faces yet another threat: abuse and neglect. As people live longer, the quality of life does not necessarily increase with the years. Alzheimer's disease, dementia, Parkinson's, and other disabling conditions often prevent the elderly from taking care of themselves; and caregivers—either family members or underpaid eldercare workers—are often put under tremendous strain as their relatives/patients deal with the symptoms of their respective conditions. At times, the result of the caregivers' frustration, attitude/demeanor, and workload leads to abuse (physical beatings, sexual assault) or neglect (allowing bedridden patients to develop bedsores by not turning them over periodically, not giving them medication in a timely fashion, failing to clean their urine and excrement). While these instances are hard to quantify, government sources estimate that hundreds of thousands of the elderly suffer from abuse or neglect annually. It is no wonder that many elderly people diligently try to avoid going to an "old age" home.

We can do our part to help the elderly by ensuring that home therapists visit to ensure that risks for falls are minimized (by removing throw rugs and excessive furniture, for example), that doctors regularly visit and check on seniors, and that seniors who are bedridden are regularly bathed and turned so that they do not develop bedsores. In addition, we should all take care of available services. For example, the Program of All-inclusive Care for the Elderly (PACE) provides qualifying Medicare and Medicaid patients guaranteed services. PACE supplies primary, hospital, home, and adult day care, with nursing, meals, transportation, and social services, provided by an interdisciplinary team of medical providers, therapists, and home and personal care attendants.

We can further help by ensuring that Social Security is bolstered and not weakened as an "entitlement." After all, employees pay all their working lives into the fund, so they are merely receiving what they have rightfully earned. In June 2013 alone, the Social Security Administration paid thirty-seven million retired workers an average monthly benefit of $1,269. This amount is clearly inadequate to pay for rent, food, health care, and other expenses. Since more than half of all American workers have no private pension plan, more than a third have no retirement savings, and by 2033 there will be more than seventy-seven million elderly people, our need to provide resources for the elderly will become even more critical. The Jewish community has a particularly elderly community, and there are significant poverty challenges among many, especially elderly Holocaust survivors in the United States and in the former Soviet Union.

Strong communal programs can offer continued learning opportunities for seniors and build cross-generational community. And there are countless ways to honor seniors beyond the merely symbolic. We can all find more ways to help, hands-on, and advocate for their needs in society. Rebbe Nachman of Breslov wrote that one can "gauge a country's prosperity by its treatment of its elders."[313] To fulfill this mitzvah, and ensure our society's prosperity, we should honor our elders at every opportunity.

4:27

רַבִּי מֵאִיר אוֹמֵר: אַל תִּסְתַּכֵּל בַּקַּנְקַן, אֶלָּא בַּמֶּה שֶׁיֵּשׁ בּוֹ.
יֵשׁ קַנְקַן חָדָשׁ מָלֵא יָשָׁן, וְיָשָׁן שֶׁאֲפִלּוּ חָדָשׁ אֵין בּוֹ.

Rabbi Meir says:[313a] Do not look at the vessel, but what is in it;
there is a new vessel filled with old wine, and an old vessel that
does not even contain new wine.

THIS MISHNAH continues the theme of the last two *mishnayot*: youth
without guidance from older generations is a waste of potential. Here,
Rabbi Meir is still in dialogue with his teacher, Rabbi Elisha ben
Avuyah. Rabbi Meir, now a wise spiritual leader, was disappointed that
his teacher Elisha (Acher) did not return to studying Torah and Jewish
philosophy. Rabbi Meir experienced inner agony as he tried to con-
vince Acher, with whom he had been so intimate, to return to the ways
of a Jewish life. This mishnah is a powerful Jewish literary and spiritual
example: Rabbi Meir lamented that Acher would never take another
look at his inner world and return to the task for which his soul was
sent to earth. In some ways, Acher, or "Other," is called this precisely
because he turned away from his mission.

What do the vessels in this mishnah really symbolize? Why would
Rabbi Meir be cryptic, rather than straightforward, with his thoughts?
This metaphor is about giving our souls over to our higher purpose.
"Submission" is not a celebrated word among spiritual or social pro-
gressives, and for good reason. Submission to an external authority
is not the way we think to shake up societal order. But, internally, we
might consider acts of submission in which we give ourselves over to
our Creator, who made us for a unique purpose. Rabbi Abraham Isaac
Kook explains:

> Submission to God, which is something natural to every creature,
> to every being in which individuality reveals itself . . . does not en-
> tail sorrow and oppression, but rather, pleasure and uprightness,
> sovereignty, and inner courage crowned with total beauty. . . . [This
> is achieved] through contraction of the soul before its Creator.[314]

This mishnah also deals with the legacy of the human soul (what is in the vessel). A good portion of Jewish thought on the soul is found in the Kabbalah, but we see some interesting analogues to Jewish thought in gentile culture. Plato said that humans have three souls: the appetitive, spirited, and intellectual.[315] In Judaism, these are *nefesh*, *ruach*, and *n'shamah*. In Platonic thought, as in Judaism, all three matter. How we show up within ourselves determines how we show up outside of ourselves. If we are not fulfilled inside, we won't be fulfilled on the outside. Likewise, there is a midrash about the soul's continuous need to grow and evolve:

> "And the soul is not sated" (Ecclesiastes 6:7). This is analogous to a provincial who married a princess. Even though he brings her everything in the world, he does not satisfy her. Why? Because she is a princess. Similarly, even if a person brings his soul all the delicacies of the world, they are nothing to her [i.e. she is not satisfied]. Why? Because she comes from Above.[316]

So then, what is the ethical lesson in this mishnah? When we neglect our purpose, we neglect the reason we have been temporarily placed in this world. It is our obligation to overcome disappointment and pride and to achieve what we can in the limited time we're allowed. Just as Rabbi Meir taught not to be unfairly judgmental of ourselves (or, at least, our superficial outer selves), so too is he teaching here not to miss opportunities to engage with others' true selves. If we see others only in a transactional way (what can they give to me?), we miss potential for connection and meaningful relationship. Further, from a social change perspective, someone may be our opposition in one campaign but an ally in another. We should not simply label others as inside or outside our camp, but allow ourselves to see them more deeply.

4:28

רַבִּי אֱלִיעֶזֶר הַקַּפָּר אוֹמֵר: הַקִּנְאָה וְהַתַּאֲוָה וְהַכָּבוֹד
מוֹצִיאִין אֶת הָאָדָם מִן הָעוֹלָם.

Rabbi Eliezer HaKappar says: Jealousy, lust, and glory remove
a person from the world.

Rabbi Eliezer HaKappar's teaching in this mishnah is as grand in
scope as it is austere in phrasing. In just a brief sentence, Rabbi HaKappar says that to be truly present in this world means to ground oneself
in one's own situation. We should feel gratitude for what we have, yearn
for what we can productively become, and seek tools for spiritual contentment and ethical development.

When one wants what another has, one is no longer present in one's
own situation. Instead, one has veered off into envy in yearning for
another's property or status. Similarly, lust is yearning for another person's body. Wishing for glory is yearning for recognition. But yearning
and lust are not positive virtues in the Torah. All too often, we project
our yearnings onto others, and when we see them achieve where we fail,
we feel envy. Being covetous is a moral failing to which all are vulnerable. Rather than removing ourselves from the world, we must be present in it. Doing so demonstrates progression from weak-willed souls to
resolute, determined human beings.

The contemporary practice of mindfulness is generally thought of as
a spiritual or psychological exercise, in which one notices one's breathing, posture, random thoughts, or deliberation in action. Yet mindfulness also has a moral component to it: if we don't address certain
moral vices, we cannot be present in the world—we are removed from
the world; distractions can conquer us.

In the modern technological era, we find it increasingly difficult to
concentrate for long periods of time on one task. Between text messages, phone, e-mail, and social media, we repeatedly respond to com-
munications from all directions. Our brains continually adjust to these
technologies. University of California (Irvine) professor Gloria Mark

has found that in the workplace, the average employee gets around eleven minutes of focus before being interrupted. It then takes around twenty-five minutes to return focus to the original task.[316a]

Such distraction has been a long-term trend, and there are many suspected culprits. Some believe that television, with commercials interrupting programming every eight minutes or so, lessened the attention span of baby boomers. Later, popular music videos, where the camera angles change every few seconds, were blamed for a generation of teenagers who had difficulty concentrating. Now, social media are blamed for brief attention spans. In 1858, when Abraham Lincoln debated Stephen Douglas for a seat in the Illinois Senate, Lincoln's opening statement alone comprised more than 8,750 words. Prior to the 1960 presidential election, Kennedy and Nixon gave opening statements that were each seven minutes long—far shorter than Lincoln's of a century before, but far longer than what we hear today.

Carnegie Mellon University's Alessandro Acquisti and Eyal Peer showed that those who are interrupted are not only slower to complete a task, but also make 20 percent more mistakes than those who are interrupted less frequently;[316b] that's the difference between a B student (80%) and a C student (76%). From health care to driving a car, distraction can lead to fatal mistakes.

In *The Gay Science* (1882), Friedrich Nietzsche explains the importance of intellectually interacting with the world and the value of focusing and immersing oneself on all life learning beyond books:

> We do not belong to those who have ideas only among books, when stimulated by books. It is our habit to think outdoors—walking, leaping, climbing, dancing, preferably on lonely mountains or near the sea where even the trails become thoughtful. Our first questions about the value of a book, of a human being, or a musical composition are: Can they walk? Even more, can they dance?[317]

We miss so much when distracted by banalities. In January 2007, the *Washington Post* conducted an experiment near a subway platform during the morning rush. Renowned professional violinist Joshua Bell played his Stradivarius for forty-five minutes wearing blue jeans and a baseball cap. Bell played several pieces, including a portion of a Bach partita, rewarding the listener who stayed for any period of time. More than a thousand people passed him without noticing; only seven people stayed for at least one minute. One recognized Bell from a concert he had given previously at the Library of Congress.[317a]

Are we so distracted that we cannot pause for genius? Are we so tied to our devices that we cannot hear music? Do we tune out beauty if it is instantly recognizable, or because our hearing is blocked by our own earbuds? We can speculate on the reasons, but it does not bode well for our society if people are so self-absorbed that they ignore the rest of the world. Can we remake the world if we do not even notice it? There are benefits to cultivating the new art of hyper-multitasking, as well as times and places to heed distractions. However, to be effective, we need focus. Even further, to be spiritually attuned, we need times of wholeness without being fractured by interruption. Nachmanides argued that we miss some of the most significant revelations in our lives because we have not prepared our hearts.[318]

Of course, we don't have to get rid of technology, or reduce its value. We do not need to practice techno-abstinence. But we must learn techno-moderation, to reduce external stimuli to awaken our internal worlds.

To be spiritually alive, we must emotionally prepare for periods of concentration, or we risk missing gems below the surface. We have to be aware of the feelings that shrink our potential in the world—jealousy, lust, and glory—and focus instead on those sensibilities that bring light into the world. Shunning the negative and embracing the positive—hearing the beauty of the musician in the subway station—equalizes us, engages us, and allows to look beyond the mundane.

4:29

הוּא הָיָה אוֹמֵר: הַיִּלוֹדִים לָמוּת, וְהַמֵּתִים לִחְיוֹת, וְהַחַיִּים
לִדּוֹן – לֵידַע לְהוֹדִיעַ וּלְהִוָּדַע שֶׁהוּא אֵל, הוּא הַיּוֹצֵר, הוּא
הַבּוֹרֵא, הוּא הַמֵּבִין, הוּא הַדַּיָּן, הוּא עֵד, הוּא בַּעַל דִּין,
וְהוּא עָתִיד לָדוֹן. בָּרוּךְ הוּא, שֶׁאֵין לְפָנָיו לֹא עַוְלָה וְלֹא
שִׁכְחָה, וְלֹא מַשּׂוֹא פָנִים וְלֹא מִקַּח שֹׁחַד, שֶׁהַכֹּל שֶׁלּוֹ. וְדַע
שֶׁהַכֹּל לְפִי הַחֶשְׁבּוֹן. וְאַל יַבְטִיחֲךָ יִצְרְךָ שֶׁבַּשְׁאוֹל בֵּית
מָנוֹס – שֶׁעַל כָּרְחֲךָ אַתָּה נוֹצָר, וְעַל כָּרְחֲךָ אַתָּה נוֹלָד, וְעַל
כָּרְחֲךָ אַתָּה חַי, וְעַל כָּרְחֲךָ אַתָּה מֵת, וְעַל כָּרְחֲךָ אַתָּה
עָתִיד לִתֵּן דִּין וְחֶשְׁבּוֹן לִפְנֵי מֶלֶךְ מַלְכֵי הַמְּלָכִים, הַקָּדוֹשׁ
בָּרוּךְ הוּא.

He used to say: The newborn will die; the dead will live
[again]; the living will be judged—in order that they know,
teach, and become aware that the Eternal is God, the Eternal
is the Fashioner, the Eternal is the Creator, the Eternal is
the Discerner, and the Eternal is the Judge, the Eternal is
Witness, the Eternal is the Plaintiff, and the Eternal will
judge. Blessed is God, before whom there is no inequity, no
forgetfulness, no favoritism, and no acceptance of bribery, for
everything is God's. Know that everything is according to the
reckoning. And let not your evil inclination promise you that
the grave will be an escape—for against your will you were
created; against your will you were born; against your will you
live; against your will you die, and against your will you are
destined to give an account before the Ruler of Emperors, the
Holy One of Blessing.

A FUNDAMENTAL TENET of Jewish faith is that the universe will ultimately become just. Now, we ought to be able to look at the world and
see its chaos, injustice, and brokenness. But that is not all we should
see. We need to understand that God has stepped back from the world

(*tzimtzum*), in order to increase our free will and ability to partner to repair this world. Yet, our collective enterprise to repair the brokenness inevitably falls short. We cultivate faith that through the infinity of time, all will work out in the best manner, in ways that we cannot comprehend.

We have trouble feeling loved because we don't feel seen; we don't feel heard. Rabbi Yehuda Amital, *rosh yeshivah* of Yeshivat Har Etzion and a former member of the Knesset, taught:

> Every generation has its own cry, sometimes open, sometimes hidden; sometimes the baby itself doesn't know that it's crying, and hence we have to try to be attentive to the hidden cries as well.[319]

In the world today, there are countless invisible people with hidden cries. They are victims of deep injustices and violent oppression. They are the boys who wash dishes at restaurants and the men who wash cars. They are the girls who make hotel beds and the women who serve in homes. They are the slaves confined by our penal code and others objectified as sex workers. They are the homeless, spending their days in the shadow of our contempt and their nights in our parks of denial. Theirs are the open cries reverberating within our souls and the loud cries of the streets. Theirs are the subterranean cries of those yearning for support and comfort.

Jewish spirituality urges us to see beyond the physical and sanctify the unseen. This is what Rabbi Amital means: We should hear the hidden cries from people who are separated from everyday life, who are not allowed to function on the same level as those who walk past them in the street or do not see them working in the stockroom of a fancy restaurant. These are the refugees whose plights are hidden through veiled eyelids, the homeless man who sleeps on a bed of cardboard and garbage, and the immigrant who spends her early mornings and late evenings traveling between jobs that exploit her willingness to support her family. These are the invisible people. These are the voices crying out for us to hear. Cultivating the ability to listen and respond is the central goal of the Jewish ethical demands for equity and justice.

Isn't it also true that a person who lacks the basics often wishes to remain unseen, for fear of capitulating to dependence? Deep shame is felt when one is at the lowest, without even the means to make even slight inroads into self-improvement. This brings anger, too, which along with shame hinders one's ability to seek help. A bitter cycle. When Nelson Mandela became the first democratically elected president of South Africa, he said, "As we are liberated from our own fear, our presence automatically liberates others." Let's take this admonition to heart. We need the courage to see and make seen the victims of injustice among us.

Rabbi Dov Baer ben Avraham, a Chasidic master known as the Maggid of Mezritch (eighteenth century, Poland/Lithuania), speaks powerfully of *yeish mei-ayin*, "creation out of nothing." He teaches that helping those who lurk in the shadows is akin to something coming into existence that previously did not exist, providing light to something that previously was unseen, comparing this to the creation of the universe itself.

Jewish law demands not only that we see, but that we be seen—*yireh*, *yeira-eh*—in Jerusalem during festivals (BT *Chagigah* 2a). This law is not a relic. It is moral training for our eyes and our hearts; we are to be open and see those who are unseen. Connecting and supporting the unseen is not distraction from tradition, but tradition's actualization. Greater than lending money or giving *tzedakah* to a poor individual, the Rabbis tell us, is providing partnership (BT *Shabbat* 63a). Seeing all people as equal goes far toward treating them with respect and dignity. We cannot discount those who are different.

Fortunately, people can help make visible those whom society deems invisible. We accomplish this by letting the vulnerable seek the succor they need. We offer unconditional love and hope without judging status. Only hope and love can bring solace. Every time we encounter people who dwell in the shadows, those who are ignored due to their situation, their appearance, or circumstance, we must transcend our fears and prejudices to lend a hand. Some of the most terrifying times in our lives will be those when we feel as though we barely exist, when we don't feel acknowledged by the world, let alone appreciated or loved. These times remind us to recommit to help others who feel hopeless.

Let's remember the stranger who lurks in the periphery. Let us be his friend, her family, and their advocates. We live in a precarious time. Demagoguery and political expediency have cleaved our nation into haves and have-nots. Public assistance, so vilified when it has supported struggling families and individuals, flows plentifully into the pockets of those who have sought to swindle our society, usually through fraud or gaming the system to line up tax breaks into undeserving pockets. For too long, policies injurious to the vulnerable have proliferated, leaving us less empathetic. Our purpose is to rectify this. With love toward all of Creation, we must open our ears to the voiceless and our eyes to the invisible.

Chapter 5

5:1

בַּעֲשָׂרָה מַאֲמָרוֹת נִבְרָא הָעוֹלָם, וּמַה תַּלְמוּד? וַהֲלֹא
בְּמַאֲמָר אֶחָד הָיָה יָכוֹל לְהִבָּרְאוֹת? אֶלָּא לְהִפָּרַע מִן
הָרְשָׁעִים, שֶׁמְּאַבְּדִין אֶת הָעוֹלָם שֶׁנִּבְרָא בַּעֲשָׂרָה מַאֲמָרוֹת,
וְלִתֵּן שָׂכָר טוֹב לַצַּדִּיקִים, שֶׁמְּקַיְּמִין אֶת הָעוֹלָם שֶׁנִּבְרָא
בַּעֲשָׂרָה מַאֲמָרוֹת.

With ten utterances the world was created. What does this
teach us? Indeed, could it not have been created with one
utterance? This was to exact punishment from the wicked who
destroy the world that was created with ten utterances, and
to bestow goodly reward upon the righteous who sustain the
world that was created by ten utterances.

WHAT IS THE NATURE of our speech? Is it a direct result of our physical mind or our spiritual self? Does what we say define who we are?
These questions are present as we begin the fifth chapter of *Pirkei Avot*.
This mishnah departs from the worldly questions discussed in the last
several *mishnayot* and prepares us to think about how speech, as an em-
ulation of the Divine, is the creative enterprise of humanity.

When God set out to build this world, nothing was "good" before
God deemed it so through speech. This seems a simple tautology, but
Jewish theology rejects that. The goodness of divinity permeates what
has been and what will be created, even if humanity doesn't understand
the intrinsic meaning. Throughout Jewish history, we have not merely
tried to build in isolation. Creative building is a collaborative social
experience that requires partnership, with holy speech as the support
structure. Our deeds, like our words, work in conjunction with divinity
to spur the processes of a more enlightened soul.

One way to view speech is through the lens of prayer, and a way to
view prayer is as a spiritual practice that refines the intentions that underlie our speech. Consider this passage from Rabbi Joseph B. Soloveitchik about the connection between the heart and the mouth:

> The very essence of *tefillah* [prayer] expresses itself in a romance
> rather than in disciplined action, in a great passionate yearning
> rather than a limited cold achievement, in a movement of the soul
> rather than performance of the lips, in an awareness rather than in
> action, in an inner longing rather than a tangible performance, in
> silence rather than in loud speech.[320]

Similarly, Rabbi Schneur Zalman of Liadi (eighteenth century, Bela-
rus), a Chasidic master whose corpus of thought centers around spiritual joy, teaches:

> Every divine soul possesses three garments. They are the thought,
> speech, and action of the mitzvot of the Torah. For when persons
> fulfill . . . the commandments, their souls are clothed with the . . .
> mitzvot of the Torah.[321]

Rabbi Adin Steinsaltz notes that speech is only a single aspect of
the person, and its consequences are deeper than simple conveyance:
"Speech is the garment of thought, expressing the thought even as
it veils its deeper dimensions."[322] A generation earlier, Rabbi Kook
reflected that a person on a progressively spiritual path comes increasingly to see the importance of speech:

> As the soul is elevated, we become acutely aware of the tremen-
> dous power that lies in our faculty of speech. We recognize clearly
> the tremendous significance of each utterance; the value of our
> prayers and blessings, the value of our Torah study and of all of our
> discourse. We learn to perceive the overall impact of speech. We
> sense the change and great stirring of the world that comes about
> through speech.[323]

Now, there is a crucial difference between religious piety and social
freedom. While in our personal ethics we should be vigilant to speak
with precision, we should be sure to allow the freedom of speech for
others. Consider how Harvard Law School professor Alan Dershowitz,
who has been at the forefront defending the First Amendment and the
consecrated value of freedom of speech, articulates this point:

> The virtue of a [legal] code is that it leaves no room for "common
> law crimes" of a broad discretion. The vice of a code is that it is often

under-inclusive—it excludes conduct (or, in this case, speech) that is novel or that was not considered by the codifiers. In the area of freedom of expression, that virtue trumps its vice: It is better to have rules regulating speech that are under-inclusive than to have rules that are over-inclusive. . . . Moreover, if a violent reaction to speech is deemed to justify censorship, then the threat to commit violence overpowers "the victims" of provocative speech to serve as censors. It thus incentivizes and encourages violent reactions to bad speech. (It may also encourage, perhaps unconsciously, some victims to exaggerate the outrage they feel, because the law rewards such exaggerated feelings with the power of censorship.) This "violence veto" should not be encouraged by the law. Hard as it may be to arrest the good "victims" rather than the bad provok-ers, the First Amendment requires that the government side with the "bad" speakers, rather than the "good" violence-threateners.[324]

Ultimately, what is the value of speech to promoting holiness in the world? When God began the process of creating the world, there was no intent to bring forth a finished product. Rather, Creation would be ongoing, and humanity would emulate this generative approach to endeavors great and small. There are no vistas that can't be scaled without ingenuity. As we participate in lifesaving and life-enhancing holy work, it is as if we have saved the world. We must understand how important our own speech is and the effect it has on others. At the same time, in fostering a pluralistic society, we must be sure to allow freedom for different types of expression, even that with which we vehemently disagree.

When we participate in any activities that have a physically or spir-itually destructive component, it is as if we have destroyed the world. Our moral challenge, then, is not only to guard what we say, but also to watch how we speak. What thoughts occupy our mind as we open our lips? What ideas do we want to contribute positively to the world? It all begins with mere words but ends with eternal deeds.

5:2

עֲשָׂרָה דוֹרוֹת מֵאָדָם וְעַד נֹחַ, לְהוֹדִיעַ כַּמָּה אֶרֶךְ אַפַּיִם
לְפָנָיו – שֶׁכָּל הַדּוֹרוֹת הָיוּ מַכְעִיסִין וּבָאִין, עַד שֶׁהֵבִיא
עֲלֵיהֶם אֶת מֵי הַמַּבּוּל.

There were ten generations from Adam to Noah—to show the
degree of God's patience; for all those generations angered
God increasingly, until God brought upon them the waters of
the flood.

5:3

עֲשָׂרָה דוֹרוֹת מִנֹּחַ וְעַד אַבְרָהָם, לְהוֹדִיעַ כַּמָּה אֶרֶךְ אַפַּיִם
לְפָנָיו – שֶׁכָּל הַדּוֹרוֹת הָיוּ מַכְעִיסִין וּבָאִין, עַד שֶׁבָּא
אַבְרָהָם אָבִינוּ וְקִבֵּל שְׂכַר כֻּלָּם.

There were ten generations from Noah to Abraham—to
show the degree of God's patience; for all those generations
angered God increasingly, until our forefather Abraham came
and received the reward of them all.

THE MIDRASH TEACHES that humanity is to emulate God's mercy,
not God's judgment.[325] We can't flood the world, but we can emulate
the patience shown toward the generations who angered God. How
trivial are the moments that trigger impatience: waiting at a red light; a
line in the grocery store. God invested so much in Creation, only to be
disappointed by human inability to cherish our sacred responsibility. If
God's patience was possible then, why do we have so little now, when
confronted by such small frustrations?

These *mishnayot* ruminate on genealogical progression, and each
contains a powerful message. Though each is brief, they echo a theme
found elsewhere in *Pirkei Avot*: the transmission of wisdom through
the generations. Judaism is not static. While rituals only incrementally
change and fundamental principles are left rather intact, Judaism's vi-
brancy is in how people breathe life into these traditions.

Such intellectual and spiritual vigor applies to our grander endeavors in this life. While we are all susceptible to bouts of jealousy, melancholy, anger, and avarice, we are not less capable of charity, faith, altruism and love. God imbued in humans the capacity to bring great light into the world—as well as darkness.

It would be unfair to counsel those burdened with injustice to have patience, but we must set realistic goals. The Rev. Dr. Martin Luther King Jr. speaks of this tension at the end of "Letter from Birmingham Jail":

> If I have said anything in this letter that is an understatement of the truth and is indicative of an unreasonable impatience, I beg you to forgive me. If I have said anything in this letter that is an overstatement of the truth and is indicative of my having a patience that makes me patient with anything less than brotherhood, I beg God to forgive me.

It is challenging to sit with ambiguity and in tension. The poet Rainer Maria Rilke says:

> Be patient toward all that is unresolved in your heart.... Try to love the questions themselves.... Do not now seek the answers, which cannot be given because you would not be able to live them—and the point is to live everything. *Live the question now.* Perhaps you will then gradually, without noticing it, live among some distant day into the answers.[326]

Indeed, we must feel the urgency to lead and respond where necessary. Where we came from is not as important as where we want to be. We must emulate God and cultivate the patience necessary to be reflective, merciful, and kind. Our obligation, as thoughtful people dedicated to enhancing light, is to know when we stray from the righteous path toward iniquity. Knowing that we are not perfect, but constantly evolving—intellectually and spiritually—is part of becoming better people.

5:4

עֲשָׂרָה נִסְיוֹנוֹת נִתְנַסָּה אַבְרָהָם אָבִינוּ וְעָמַד בְּכֻלָּם,
לְהוֹדִיעַ כַּמָּה חִבָּתוֹ שֶׁל אַבְרָהָם אָבִינוּ.

Our forefather Abraham was tested with ten trials, and he
withstood them all—to show the degree of our forefather
Abraham's love for God.

ETHICAL TESTS and trials are a recurring theme in *Pirkei Avot* and the
Torah. Such tests are meant to measure spiritual fidelity, and of course,
those tested do not always realize perfect results. Abraham was repeatedly tested and shown to be imperfect. Still, his faith and character
were such that he is the spiritual father and role model for three of the
world's religions.

All is never lost. This mishnah teaches that perseverance and hope
are built into our spiritual DNA. Abraham was tested with many challenges: exile from his childhood home, physical threats to himself and
his wife, the startling command to kill his son—he remained faithful
throughout. We learn from Abraham's travails and resilience that all
of us face challenges in our lives. Some may knock us down, but our
character is tested by our ability to rebound, to remain hope-filled and
without cynicism. It is too easy to develop negativity and distrust, especially after experiencing life's overwhelming challenges. Faith should
remind us that at any moment, there are more acts of loving-kindness
than acts of hate. At any moment, there are strangers holding the hands
of those passing from this world, teachers exhibiting extreme patience
for children slow at learning, individuals giving their time and empathy
to those in need.

Trials are everywhere, continually. The Torah says, "Remember the
long way that the Eternal your God has made you travel in the wilderness these past forty years, in order to test you by hardships" (Deuteronomy 8:2). We learn from this that God had the Children of Israel
wander in the wilderness for forty years not as divine punishment, but
as a test.

To become resilient, we must not dismiss our failings or our scars, but carry this brokenness with us. As noted at 4:26, the Rabbis teach that both the broken tablets and the whole tablets were kept in the Holy Ark (BT *B'rachot* 8b). We bring both our perfections and our imperfections with us, our strengths and our weaknesses. We carry them together in our consciousness. The Exodus from Egypt placed an entire nation (men, women, and children alike) in transience, confusion, and misery for decades as a test. Today, too, the Jewish people are being pushed and tested, with questions about how our communal identity will look within the next century or two. How will we meet challenges, given such great blessings? How will we interact with the nation-state of Israel? How much of the Jewish experience will our grandchildren hold? That God continues to test us as individuals and as a nation must be more than *s'char v'onesh* (reward and punishment), more than God merely keeping score or flexing God's power.

God's deeds are not random, even when humanity cannot understand the reasoning behind such actions. Judaism's belief in a benevolent and personal God precludes the possibility of random tests. The theodicy in the Book of Job challenges students old and young alike. Surely, the wager between God and *HaSatan* (the Prosecutor) wasn't agreed to in vain.

God's tests teach about people's capacity for compassion and spiritual depth. Nachmanides argued that the *Akeidah*, the Binding of Isaac, was this kind of test for Abraham, who accepted the profound moral challenge to sacrifice his own son and prevailed over hardship.[327] Maimonides and Rabbi David Kimchi—known as Radak (twelfth century, Provence)—argue that the *Akeidah* was not to test Abraham, but to teach future adherents that Abraham's faith and perseverance set the gold standard for the rest of us.[328] Rabbi Kook went even further, saying that Abraham was tested to prove to the pagan religions that monotheism can match the religious passion of pagan worship through inward sacrifice, without the need for the barbarism of human sacrifice.[329]

Rabbi Zadok HaKohen Rabinowitz, known as Rav Tzadok of Lublin (nineteenth century, Poland), teaches that just as a person needs to believe in God, so too does one need to believe in oneself.[330] These days, many of us struggle less with why we are tested by God and more with how we can overcome obstacles and live a happier, more meaningful, more successful life. Do we believe in our own capacity to overcome in the face of adversity?

Talmudic commentary beautifully posits that the Torah is the seasoning for the *yetzer hara*, or evil inclination. Rabbi Dov Baer ben Avraham—the Maggid of Mezritch—observes that since the *yetzer hara* is the main dish and the Torah is the seasoning, we must serve God with the full ecstasy of the *yetzer hara*.[331] The purpose is not to destroy or subdue the *yetzer hara*, but rather to spice it, thereby channeling its energy toward good. This means that when we experience struggle, we should use all the temptations that appear before us and channel that energy toward the good, rather than dismiss the temptation. The Midrash explains that without the *yetzer hara*, there would be no business or procreation; we need desire for self-advancement to further societal goals.[332]

Rabbi Nachman of Breslov, in his radical way, suggests that God is the test itself.[333] God is hidden within the test, just as God was hidden in the Burning Bush. He proposed a spiritual meditation in which we don't see God as the one placing an obstacle before us, but rather see the face of God within the challenge itself. This is an opportunity to disrupt the spiritual danger and fear within challenges—and see a loving God in their midst.

When we see every challenge as a test (from God, from our boss, of our will), we risk falling into binaries, in which the only possible result is success or failure. Rabbi Meir Leibush ben Yehiel Michel Wisser, a nineteenth-century Russian sage known as the Malbim, suggests that God asks of us what is beyond the limits of human nature.[334] Because what's asked is beyond our normal capabilities, the possibilities are limitless. We see this theology in post-Holocaust thought as well. Viktor Frankl, in *Man's Search of Meaning*, contends that survival in the concentration camps was usually not about physical strength, wealth, political connections, or religiosity, but about the ability to construct meaning, the ability to make sense of the immense challenge placed before them. We are ultimately driven by a search for meaning.[335]

For the Jewish community, there are options for the future other than just *moshiach* (messianic redemption) or *galut* (exile). As individuals, there are options other than success or failure. Deepest learning and self-revelation come from encountering each obstacle, regardless of success. By seeing the face of God in each test, we not only grow religiously, but also learn to persevere, as we rechannel our desires productively.

Mother Teresa was one of the most significant makers of religious change of our time because she upended the role of the nun in Catholic social action; instead of a person who primarily studies and prays in the seminary, Mother Teresa modeled the nun as one who serves the needy in the streets. There is a story about Mother Teresa (possibly anecdotal, but still relevant) that deeply touches my heart. One day while in India, Mother Teresa heard the crying of an old sick woman lying in a dumpster. This woman would not pass away because she said she was so resentful of her sons who had neglected her and left her to die alone in the dumpster. Mother Teresa looked the old woman in the eyes and demanded that she forgive them. The woman took her last deep breath, forgave her sons, and passed away. This woman located and removed the obstacle that stood between herself and her ability to let go. What are the emotional and spiritual obstacles in our lives that we must remove so that we start to live?

5:5

עֲשָׂרָה נִסִּים נַעֲשׂוּ לַאֲבוֹתֵינוּ בְמִצְרַיִם וַעֲשָׂרָה עַל הַיָּם.
עֶשֶׂר מַכּוֹת הֵבִיא הַקָּדוֹשׁ בָּרוּךְ הוּא עַל הַמִּצְרִיִּים
בְּמִצְרַיִם וְעֶשֶׂר עַל הַיָּם.

Ten miracles were performed for our ancestors in Egypt and
ten at the Sea. Ten plagues did the Holy One of Blessing bring
upon the Egyptians in Egypt and ten at the Sea.

WHAT IS THE UTILITY of a miracle? Is a miracle meant solely to show
off the power of God over the natural world, or is there a deeper pedagogical mechanism at play? Should we step back to ponder whether
miracles are necessary for understanding our inner selves and our position in the universe? If miracles are sometimes necessary, but not ideal
for the conception of a world that operates according to nature, what
about the agency of revelation? It seems that in the long arc of Jewish
history, revelation was a divine compromise. Nature as divinely created
should be sufficient without later divine intervention.

This mishnah connects the miracles to the plagues. This is the complexity of divine intervention—with every positive intervention, there
may be a loss as well. While the Israelites were liberated, the Egyptians
were plagued. Divine miracles are a paradox—the loss of free will is
coupled with human responsibility. We should not rely on miracles, but
believing that miracles have changed the world for the better propels us
through the difficulties of existence.

Nonetheless, we strive for the faith that interventions are unnecessary, that the order of the world that God put in place is fundamentally
good. We come to understand, through studying the ancient texts as
well as coming to know the sparks that reside within us, that when
interventions do occur, they should be accomplished for the benefit of
the world.

From the opening book of the Torah onward, it seems God is continually disappointed with humanity—which, though imbued with heavenly spark, can never live up to divine expectations. From the expulsion

from Eden, to Cain's murder of Abel, the failings of the generation of
the Flood, and the necessary dispersion at Babel, humans fail repeatedly. Relying upon reason, conscience, and intuition should have been
enough to guarantee human goodness, but God foresaw the need for
intervention to reinforce human morality.

Revelation: this was a dangerous task. A mandate inevitably leads
to rebellion, as is seen from the first recorded human error (eating the
fruit from the Tree of Knowledge). So, God compromises by revealing
to humans what they should already know but need assistance internalizing. Thus, the Torah becomes the blueprint for human moral and
spiritual potential.

But then again, the Sages of the Talmud say explicitly that the Torah
reinforces what people could have learned from intuition and experience: "If we had not received the Torah, we would have learned modesty from watching a cat, honesty from the ant, and fidelity from the
dove" (BT *Eiruvin* 100b). There were, of course, the chosen few who
understood the holy and true path before the rest of humanity. In the
Abrahamic traditions, we call these learned few the Patriarchs. The
Rabbis teach that the Patriarchs already knew the Torah on their own,
without revelation: "Abraham our Father fulfilled the entire Torah before it was given, even the laws of the Sabbath food preparation on a
festival" (BT *Yoma* 28b).

Centuries later, Rabbi Levi Yitzchak of Berditchev—known as the
K'dushat Levi (eighteenth-century, Ukraine—explains that the Patriarchs knew the Torah intimately through their limbs: "248 positive
commandments of the Torah parallel our 248 spiritual limbs; the
Torah's 365 prohibitions are parallel to our 365 spiritual sinews."[336] It is
through the corporeality of the body—mind and experience—that we
have the capacity to learn the contents of the Torah without external
revelation.

Medieval Jewish philosophers, such as Maimonides[337] and Saadyah
Gaon,[338] say that the dual entities of reason and revelation do not
contradict each other. Humans were not properly reaching the moral
level God expected they would through reason, and so divine mercy
provided an adapted plan: thunderbolts, lightning, and the direct word

of God. Here, Rabbi Levi Yitzchak of Berditchev teaches that God is "clothed" at Sinai and "unclothed" at the miracles of the Red Sea; revelation is more about deep intellectual and spiritual comprehension of values than about divine connection.[339]

To demonstrate how human failure leads to revelation-as-concession, Rabbi Obadiah ben Jacob S'forno argues that the laws of kashrut were given because of the sin of the Golden Calf.[340] These stipulations weren't part of the original plan, but were revealed later to reconcile the Divine-human relationship after another colossal human failure. Furthermore, according to S'forno, it was not the initial goal for revelation to happen for one people in particular. God had attempted to form more universal covenants through Noah and Abraham, but these did not work to sustain moral commitment as intended.[341] Thus, according to the traditional understanding of the act, God narrowed this particular revelation to one people. And as can be discerned, this act is not ideal for the God of all creation. All people should have access to this revelation, but Jewish history argues that it wasn't possible. Only some would desire such a covenant.

Only moments after revelation, there was confusion and disagreement; truth was fragmented. Thus, while we always have access to certain forms of higher truth, revelation is imperfectly understood by the human mind. Although the messages and laws of God were conveyed from the eminence of a perfect Transmitter, the limits of the human being were ever present in the experiment of action by way of revelation. And though the human spirit can be pliant toward God's will, the mind does not always bend toward it. Therefore, we are left with tension between the revelation of the past and the truth of contemporary spiritual life. The Chasidic masters conveyed that sparks of light and truth, however fragmented and garbled, are still found everywhere for those seeking to find them.

A religious person may be committed both to the revelation at Sinai and to the God-given truth within. For the word of God to be living, it must be alive in us—through our minds and our souls. We now live with a more complicated and less ideal world, because we can embrace both revelation and reason. In a post-Holocaust world, and a world in which falsehoods are treated as fact, we can never again silence common moral intuition and human conscience out of obedience to authority. To be religious means having the courage to align oneself to walk in the ways of God—with thoughts constantly turned toward charity, justice, and kindness—all the while moving past human authority that blocks our intellectual and spiritual responsibilities.

Rabbi Kook teaches that to silence our conscience is to destroy our fear of heaven, a fear that is crucial for an involved life of spiritual development and religious richness.[342] These inherent God-given capacities—namely, reason, intuition, and conscience—are not given their proper weight with respect to inner growth. Instead, too often, the majority of religious time is allocated simply toward obeying historical revelation ("tradition"). But perhaps this need not be our primary task. Indeed, our priority must be this innate divine revelation—to guard and cultivate the holiness of our inner world.

5:6

עֲשָׂרָה נִסְיוֹנוֹת נִסּוּ אֲבוֹתֵינוּ אֶת הַמָּקוֹם בַּמִּדְבָּר, שֶׁנֶּאֱמַר:
וַיְנַסּוּ אֹתִי זֶה עֶשֶׂר פְּעָמִים, וְלֹא שָׁמְעוּ בְּקוֹלִי (במדבר יד:כב).

With ten trials did our ancestors test the Omnipresent in the wilderness as it is said: "They have tested Me these ten times and did not heed My voice."

SOMETIMES PEOPLE seem to test God from laziness or lust, but at other times, the test is out of human virtue. Theodicy, or explaining the apparent lack of divine presence during adversity, has long stymied both theologians and laypeople. In the Bible, there are many instances of seemingly senseless cruelty and abandonment: Cain murdering Abel; Hagar and Ishmael left to die in the desert; Pharaoh enslaving entire generations of Hebrews; the tribulations of Job.

Where was God during the Holocaust? Where was God to liberate the ghettos and stop the pogroms? Where was God when I needed the presence of the Divine in my life? With the pervasiveness of injustice and oppression in the world, what should our response to God's silence and inaction be? Most importantly, how can there be a benevolent, omnipotent God while so much suffering exists in the world—suffering that's like a wound upon all of humanity?

It has been reported that after emerging from a near-death experience, virtually everyone pledges to live differently—with more joy, more focus, and more appreciation. Usually within months, pledges are broken, and people return to old routines.[343] So too, the Israelites sang songs of liberation after crossing the sea, marking the end of four centuries of horrible slavery. Immediately after freedom was granted, at their greatest triumph against despotism and forced submission, they began complaining and testing the patience of God. God might well have wondered if these were the right people to liberate and move toward Sinai and the Promised Land.[344] God tells Moses that God is going to destroy all the Israelites and start over again with Moses (Exodus 32:10–12). After all, why not? If one people is going to be "chosen," then why not ensure you indeed have the right group that is fully committed?

These questions speak to the deeper notion of how the immortal, eternal Divine interacts with the delicate reality of human existence. Surely, that which proclaims itself a protector of all should keep all from harm. The late biblical scholar Yochanan Muffs of the Jewish Theological Seminary writes:

> Biblical religion does not seem to require the man of faith to repress his doubts in silent resignation. Abraham, Jeremiah, and Job, all men who question God's ways, are hardly numbered among the wicked. There is even some evidence that God demands such criticism, at least from His prophets (cf. Ezekiel 22:3).[345]

The mainstream approach teaches that God is perfect, humans are imperfect, and protesting God's actions is ignorant, immoral, and childish. The alternative view holds that protesting against God is not futile but deeply religious and moral. Some strands of Rabbinic thought not only allow, but also celebrate human confrontation with God. God seems to embrace this view, too. In countless challenges, protests, and confrontations with God in the Torah, God rarely critiques or punishes the challenger. We have much to learn from the journeys, even the follies, of our ancestors. Our challenge is to hold onto gratitude and, in moments of chaos and tension—like the Israelites in the wilderness—draw upon faith to be our best.

There is a place in Judaism for those who struggle with faith and wonder about God's role during adversity. How are we to relate to an imperfect world or our imperfect relationship to the Divine? We can recognize that none of us is born perfect. Every breath is but another opportunity, another chance, to improve our existence in this world.

5:7

עֲשָׂרָה נִסִּים נַעֲשׂוּ בְּבֵית הַמִּקְדָּשׁ: לֹא הִפִּילָה אִשָּׁה מֵרֵיחַ
בְּשַׂר הַקֹּדֶשׁ. וְלֹא הִסְרִיחַ בְּשַׂר הַקֹּדֶשׁ מֵעוֹלָם. וְלֹא נִרְאָה
זְבוּב בְּבֵית הַמִּטְבְּחַיִם. וְלֹא אֵרַע קֶרִי לְכֹהֵן גָּדוֹל בְּיוֹם
הַכִּפּוּרִים. וְלֹא כִבּוּ גְשָׁמִים אֵשׁ שֶׁל עֲצֵי הַמַּעֲרָכָה. וְלֹא
נָצְחָה הָרוּחַ אֶת עַמּוּד הֶעָשָׁן. וְלֹא נִמְצָא פְסוּל בָּעֹמֶר וּבִשְׁתֵּי
הַלֶּחֶם וּבְלֶחֶם הַפָּנִים. עוֹמְדִים צְפוּפִים וּמִשְׁתַּחֲוִים רְוָחִים.
וְלֹא הִזִּיק נָחָשׁ וְעַקְרָב בִּירוּשָׁלַיִם מֵעוֹלָם. וְלֹא אָמַר אָדָם
לַחֲבֵרוֹ צַר לִי הַמָּקוֹם שֶׁאָלִין בִּירוּשָׁלָיִם.

Ten miracles were performed in the Holy Temple: No woman
miscarried because of the aroma of the sacrifices; the sacrifices never became putrid; no fly was seen in the place where
the sacrifices were prepared; no seminal emission occurred
to the High Priest on Yom Kippur; the rains did not extin-
guish the fire on the altar-pyre; the wind did not disperse the
vertical column of smoke from the altar; no disqualification
was found in the Omer, or in the Two Loaves, or in the Show-
bread; the people stood crowded together, yet prostrated
themselves in ample space; neither serpent nor scorpion ever
caused injury in Jerusalem; nor did any person say to their
fellow, "The space is insufficient for me to stay overnight in
Jerusalem."

A MIRACLE is an occurrence that defies the natural world. Mighty rivers can be bent at a whim; the sun will remain in the sky for days at a
time; the cosmos is expanded and contracted instantly. Real time and
space can be transmuted through a miracle. When the Divine chooses
to employ such a tactic in the physical world, there is no turning away
from the power and grandeur. But, as we can discern from this mishnah, as time progressed, God's deployment of miracles diminished.

At first, miracles were performed for the Jewish people out in
the open—the plagues, the parting of the Red Sea, the revelation at

Sinai—all witnessed by countless numbers. No one present could deny that something singular had occurred. But as history progressed, miracles became more local and particular in scope.

The progression from slavery to sovereignty dulled the power of miracles. During the Temple era, miracles became limited to the Temple. The Rabbis teach that miracles ceased altogether during the post-Temple era. As God pulls divine intervention away from the world, human responsibility and agency increase. This contraction provides us with a challenge and hope. It's not as if miracles have vanished from our experience. Rather, it is that they will resume once humanity is willing to live in peace and cultivate the soul as its object of interest.

According to Jewish rationalist philosophers, God stepped away from the world and put nature in place. Miracles are built into nature. But according to Jewish mystics, every moment requires God's engagement and intervention. Indeed, every moment is miraculous. Nachmanides explains the metaphysical structure of everyday miracles:

> Via the great public miracles, we admit to the existence of the hidden miracles [of nature], which are the very foundation of the entire Torah. For we have no share in the Torah of our teacher Moses, until we believe that all our affairs and events are miracles, and are not based upon so-called natural law. That is true for the individual as well as for the group—that is, if any of us performs a mitzvah, our reward will facilitate our success [in life], and if we violate a mitzvah, our punishment will cut us off [from life]; all of a human's being and activity is governed by divine decree.[346]

Viewed through the long arc of history, we see that Judaism itself is a miracle. After expulsions, inquisitions, pogroms, and genocides, it is extraordinary that the Jewish people have survived. But more than that, the Jewish people have thrived and had an impact on the world. Judaism brings together the notions of particularism and universalism within a singular faith. Rabbi Jonathan Sacks writes, "Judaism is about the miracle of unity that creates diversity."[347] The contraction and expansion of the potential for miracles starts with us. It ends with us. It is our obligation to ensure that miracles return to the world to assist us in the uplift of a world that begs for light.

5:8

עֲשָׂרָה דְבָרִים נִבְרְאוּ בֵּין הַשְּׁמָשׁוֹת: פִּי הָאָרֶץ, וּפִי הַבְּאֵר,
וּפִי הָאָתוֹן, וְהַקֶּשֶׁת, וְהַמָּן, וְהַמַּטֶּה, וְהַשָּׁמִיר, וְהַכְּתָב,
וְהַמִּכְתָּב, וְהַלֻּחוֹת. וְיֵשׁ אוֹמְרִים: אַף הַמַּזִּיקִין, וּקְבוּרָתוֹ
שֶׁל מֹשֶׁה, וְאֵילוֹ שֶׁל אַבְרָהָם אָבִינוּ. וְיֵשׁ אוֹמְרִים: אַף צְבָת
בִּצְבָת עֲשׂוּיָה.

Ten things were created at twilight [on the eve of the first
Shabbat]: the mouth of the earth; the mouth of the well; the
mouth of the donkey; the rainbow (which was Noah's sign
that there would be no future floods); the manna; the staff;
the *shamir* worm; the script; the inscription; and the tablets.
Some say also destructive spirits, Moses's grave, and the ram
of our forefather Abraham. And some say also tongs that are
made from tongs.

EACH OF US should be challenged to embrace a Sabbath, when we refrain from work, employing others, and the pressures of consumerism.
From Friday night until the following Saturday evening, work ceases.
For many, relinquishing technology can be a particular challenge of
creating a Shabbat practice. But the reward is sweet. Turning off technology frees up precious time to talk with family and friends, read and
learn, pray and meditate, as well as to build commitment to one another
and reflect upon our lives. Shabbat is a time to develop our intellectual
and spiritual creativity. We focus on cultivating positivity and shutting
out toxicity. Those who don't already observe the Sabbath in the most
traditional ways could learn from others who have embraced some alternative model of Shabbat that embraces new modes of mindful rest
and unplugging.

We are in an age of constant demands on our time and attention. As
the insatiable demand for more consumer goods delivered at a quicker
pace becomes normalized, workers experience more oppression, animals are more readily abused, the environment is harmed, and leisure

time is diminished. All contribute to unhealthy people and a sick society. This is where the Sabbath comes in. The Sabbath acts as the great adjuster to both temporal and intangible time.

This mishnah reflects on this concept. Six days of labor represent human potential, what we create with our God-given faculties. Shabbat, paradoxically, is the zenith of actualization. Each of these phenomena said to have been created in this mishnah represents the complex intersection between potential and actualization, fate and destiny, the unpredictable and the inevitable. These phenomena go beyond the myopia of thinking about the self. They force us to expand our consciousness, which in turn allows people to reflect and think about the broad issues facing the world today. These attributes of Shabbat should give us focus and the drive to turn dreams into reality. What does this mean? Consider these examples about the elucidating power of Shabbat:

> The Sabbath is about animal welfare: one may not work one's animals one day a week. We are learning about how we must prioritize, as Jewish law does, the reduction of pain of all sentient creatures.
> The Sabbath is about environmental justice: one may not work the land one day a week. We are learning about how we must prioritize, as Jewish ethics does, the reversal of governmental and corporate policies that are destroying our planet.
> The Sabbath is about taking care of one's inner being: one must refrain from working oneself one day a week, in order to recharge for the next six.

Today, many people do not consider the biblical prescription of the Sabbath in their efforts to move society forward in a meaningful way. Others believe the Sabbath to be solely a religious imperative, but one doesn't have to be religious to embrace the Sabbath's principles. A day to shut off digital and worldly distractions is a gift, but it is also an ethical enterprise sorely needed right now. Michael Walzer, professor emeritus at the Institute of Advanced Study at Princeton, writes, "Sabbath rest is more egalitarian than vacation because it can't be purchased: it is the one thing that money can't buy. It is enjoined for everyone, enjoyed by everyone."[348]

In his 1951 book *The Sabbath*, Rabbi Abraham Joshua Heschel writes:

> To set apart one day a week for freedom, a day on which we would not use the instruments which have been so easily turned into weapons of destruction, a day for being with ourselves, a day of detachment from the vulgar, of independence of external obligations, a day on which we stop worshipping the idols of technical civilization, a day on which we use no money. . . . Is there any institution that holds out a greater hope for man's progress than the Sabbath?[349]

So then, what are the benefits of observing a Sabbath in a mostly secular society? At its core, the Sabbath is about protecting the rights of workers. Employers may not mandate work seven days a week due to the Sabbath. Laws banning work—and related activities—on the Sabbath are nearly as old as the English colonies in America. Puritan settlers in the Massachusetts and the Virginia colonies passed laws as early as the 1620s outlawing commercial activities on the Sabbath, followed by other colonies as they joined the nascent American territory. In the early nineteenth century, Calvinist New Yorkers literally put chains across their streets to prevent business and travel on the Sabbath.[350]

As religious restrictions declined, worker exploitation could proliferate. After years of hard-fought struggle, the Fair Labor Standards Act of 1938 established a minimum wage, overtime pay, and maximum hours for most full-time workers, although it did not specifically ban work on the Sabbath.[351] Some states, such as New York, mandate that employers must give their employees "twenty-four consecutive hours of rest in any calendar week."[352] Laws banning work on the Sabbath became popular again by the 1960s, when thirty-four states had blue laws; today, only one county (Bergen County, New Jersey) has such a statute.

Such laws are recent and still evolving, but they signal that something is needed among the tumult of contemporary life. Thousands of years ago, the Sages taught that one day a week we may not work our worker, our animal, our land, or even ourselves. Though they could not have foreseen how people live today, they recognized that both labor and rest are vital to the creation of inner fortitude.

Today, the Sabbath means the possibility for inner development and certainly development of the ethical self. How so? By setting aside one day to focus on the inner self, we gain clarity about both our inner world and the outer world. Not having to worry about the externalities that plague society means we can dedicate precious time to what is important for our souls to grow.

Dedicating a single day in the week to refrain from activity will not solve all the problems found in society. It may, however, give everyone a deserved respite from the incessant stresses of the world. Including a regular day of pause and reflection, perhaps, will affect our outlook during the other six days of our busy, productive, and spiritual week.

5:9

שִׁבְעָה דְבָרִים בַּגֹּלֶם, וְשִׁבְעָה בֶחָכָם: הֶחָכָם אֵינוֹ מְדַבֵּר
בִּפְנֵי מִי שֶׁהוּא גָדוֹל מִמֶּנּוּ בְּחָכְמָה, וְאֵינוֹ נִכְנָס לְתוֹךְ
דִּבְרֵי חֲבֵרוֹ, וְאֵינוֹ נִבְהָל לְהָשִׁיב, שׁוֹאֵל כָּעִנְיָן וּמֵשִׁיב
כַּהֲלָכָה, וְאוֹמֵר עַל רִאשׁוֹן רִאשׁוֹן וְעַל אַחֲרוֹן אַחֲרוֹן,
וְעַל מַה שֶׁלֹּא שָׁמַע אוֹמֵר לֹא שָׁמַעְתִּי, וּמוֹדֶה עַל הָאֱמֶת.
וְחִלּוּפֵיהֶן בַּגֹּלֶם.

Seven traits characterize an uncultivated person and seven a
learned person. Those who are learned do not begin speaking
before one who is greater than them in wisdom; they do not
interrupt the words of their fellow; they do not answer impet-
uously; they question with relevance to the subject and reply
accurately; they discuss first things first and last things last;
about something they have not heard they say, "I have not
heard"; and they acknowledge the truth. And the reverse of
these characterize an uncultivated person.

TODAY, PEOPLE OFTEN SEEK quick spiritual highs to spark intensity
of emotion. The Torah teaches that this is folly. The path of righteousness requires spiritual commitment, and it means avoiding thrills for
their own sake.

This mishnah focuses on verbal transmission. What one says needs
to be communicated humbly and accurately, clearly thought out, and
brought before others in a structured and clear manner. Merely expressing oneself is not enough; doing so in a way that will work for the
receiver is important to the dissemination of truth, as well.

Becoming a cultivated person requires knowing one's potential.
Those with a nuanced sense of spiritual introspection and self-awareness know that there are multiple dimensions to their inner world.
When we invest in inner exploration, we can discover worlds within
worlds. The many spiritual dimensions of humans are awe-inspiring
and warrant serious contemplation.

The Rabbis point out that there are four distinct Hebrew terms that represent the totality of the human being: *adam*, *ish*, *gever*, and *enosh* (BT *Shabbat* 54b). Each word means "person," but each connotes singular distinct spiritual dimensions. For example, *adam* is the most elevated, as a person is created in the image of God. The mystical side of this equation is fascinating. Kabbalah advises that each of these four aspects of the human being also represents a different level of soul—in descending order: *adam* is *chayah*; *gever* is *n'shamah*; *enosh* is *ruach*; and *ish* is *nefesh*. There is also a damager, *maaveh*, in Talmudic thought. Rabbi Joseph B. Soloveitchik taught that a *maaveh* is a human damager—one who is alienated from the spiritual self (BT *Bava Kama* 3b). Though this terminology can be complex, the underlying idea is that each human being is composed of several spiritual dimensions working in tandem to create the best person one can be.

It is our task to see the spiritual complexity in other people and humbly serve others. In the process, we will flourish in our own spiritual and religious complexity. We must embrace different human characteristics, recognize our spiritual dimensions, and seek spiritual transformation through service, good deeds, and learning. And one part of spiritual reflection is to acknowledge our place within space and time. In mishnah 3:1, Akavya ben Mahalalel says, "Know where you came from, to where you are going, and before whom you will give justification and reckoning . . . —before the Ruler of Emperors, the Holy One of Blessing." We are judged on who we are in the moment and how our decisions have the ability to have an effect on even the most seemingly inconsequential aspects of our lives.

But another aspect of spiritual reflection focuses on the eternal. One must attempt to access the eternal levels of the soul within the self to spiritually progress. To discover one's inner spiritual world, one must learn from others and support others in their spiritual journeys. Rabbi Yisrael Salanter teaches that another's physical needs are one's own spiritual needs. When we take care of others as *adam*, as *ish*, as *enosh*, as *gever*—even when others are liable to become *maaveh*—we develop important spiritual depth in ourselves.

A cultivated person is one who is intentional in relationships as well as in communication. Conveying large ideas is a trait of a learned person, but so is the ability to step back and listen to those who have more experience in the world. Researchers in the fields of psychology, following on the work of Albert Mehrabian, professor emeritus of psychology at the University of California, Los Angeles, have found that most of human communication in everyday contexts is nonverbal.[353] Thus, we should be exacting with words, but also with the full communicative experience. We should search for spiritual transformation and follow the teachings of the heart of Judaism; with practice and discipline, one can access inner worlds and transformative inner light.

5:10

שִׁבְעָה מִינֵי פֻּרְעָנִיּוֹת בָּאִין לָעוֹלָם עַל שִׁבְעָה גוּפֵי עֲבֵרוֹת:
מִקְצָתָן מְעַשְּׂרִין וּמִקְצָתָן אֵינָן מְעַשְּׂרִין, רָעָב שֶׁל בַּצֹּרֶת בָּא
– מִקְצָתָן רְעֵבִים וּמִקְצָתָן שְׂבֵעִים. גָּמְרוּ שֶׁלֹּא לְעַשֵּׂר, רָעָב
שֶׁל מְהוּמָה וְשֶׁל בַּצֹּרֶת בָּא. וְשֶׁלֹּא לִטּוֹל אֶת הַחַלָּה, רָעָב
שֶׁל כְּלָיָה בָּא.

Seven kinds of punishment come to the world for seven kinds
of transgressions: if some people tithe and others do not,
a famine caused by lack of rain ensues, some go hungry and
others are satisfied; if all decided not to tithe, general famine
caused by both armed bands and drought ensures; and [if they
also decided] not to separate the challah, a famine caused by
destructive drought ensues;

5:11

דֶּבֶר בָּא לָעוֹלָם עַל מִיתוֹת הָאֲמוּרוֹת בַּתּוֹרָה שֶׁלֹּא נִמְסְרוּ
לְבֵית דִּין, וְעַל פֵּרוֹת שְׁבִיעִית. חֶרֶב בָּאָה לָעוֹלָם עַל עִנּוּי
הַדִּין, וְעַל עִוּוּת הַדִּין, וְעַל הַמּוֹרִים בַּתּוֹרָה שֶׁלֹּא כַהֲלָכָה.
חַיָּה רָעָה בָּאָה לָעוֹלָם עַל שְׁבוּעַת שָׁוְא, וְעַל חִלּוּל הַשֵּׁם.
גָּלוּת בָּאָה לָעוֹלָם עַל עֲבוֹדָה זָרָה, וְעַל גִּלּוּי עֲרָיוֹת, וְעַל
שְׁפִיכוּת דָּמִים, וְעַל הַשְׁמֵט הָאָרֶץ.

pestilence comes to the world for the death penalties prescribed by the Torah that were not carried out by the court,
and for illegally using the fruits of the Sabbatical year; the
sword of war comes to the world for the delay of justice, for the
perversion of justice and for interpreting the Torah decision
in opposition to the law; wild beasts come upon the world for
vain oaths and for desecration of God's Name; exile comes to
the world for idolatry, for immorality, for bloodshed, and for
working the earth during the Sabbatical year.

5:12

בְּאַרְבָּעָה פְּרָקִים הַדֶּבֶר מִרְבֶּה: בָּרְבִיעִית, וּבַשְּׁבִיעִית,
וּבְמוֹצָאֵי שְׁבִיעִית, וּבְמוֹצָאֵי הֶחָג שֶׁבְּכָל שָׁנָה. בָּרְבִיעִית –
מִפְּנֵי מַעְשַׂר עָנִי שֶׁבַּשְּׁלִישִׁית. בַּשְּׁבִיעִית – מִפְּנֵי מַעְשַׂר
עָנִי שֶׁבַּשִּׁשִּׁית. בְּמוֹצָאֵי שְׁבִיעִית – מִפְּנֵי פֵּרוֹת שְׁבִיעִית.
בְּמוֹצָאֵי הֶחָג שֶׁבְּכָל שָׁנָה וְשָׁנָה – מִפְּנֵי גֶזֶל מַתְּנוֹת עֲנִיִּים.

At four periods [of the seven-year Sabbatical cycle] pestilence
increases—in the fourth year, in the seventh year, in the year
following the Sabbatical year, and annually following the
Sukkot festival. In the fourth year, for [neglecting] the tithe
of the poor in the third; in the seventh year, for [neglecting]
the tithe of the poor in the sixth; in the year following the
Sabbatical year, for [violating the laws of] the Sabbatical
produce; annually, at the conclusion of the festival of Sukkot,
for robbing the poor of their gifts.

HISTORICALLY, the relationship between God and Creation has been
understood as one of divine intervention. Nowadays, however, we
understand the effect of human behavior on all Creation. As humanity becomes more interconnected, the behavior of someone in New
Guinea can affect someone living in New York, although we don't
necessarily know how. Despite some uncertainty about the effects of
human behavior, the Rabbis teach in these *mishnayot* that people do
indeed feel the moral consequences of their behavior.

Nonetheless, the implicit consequences are clear: All of modern
humanity shares responsibility for itself, although countless people,
blinded by their own tribalism, would reject this idea. Indeed, we are
largely responsible for our fate. While it is not helpful to suggest that
another's suffering is punishment for sin, it may be helpful to view
one's own suffering as an opportunity for growth.

Yet, for all the sin in the world, no one is forced to commit it. The fact
that sin is committed anyway calls up an eternal theological question:
Is humanity prohibited from going against the norms laid out in the

Torah, or is the Divine allowing humanity to do so? Sages throughout Jewish history have grappled with humanity's complex relationship with the heavens. Rabbi Nachman of Breslov says that such intellectual and spiritual contradictions are "conundrums without answers" or "conundrums from the void."[354]

These "conundrums" continue to fascinate religious thinkers due to their complex consequences. Centuries after Rabbi Nachman, the late neo-Chasidic rabbi Shimon Gershon Rosenberg—known as Rav Shagar (twentieth century, Israel)—writes about the dichotomy between divine omnipotence and human free will:

> This constriction (*tzimtzum*), which made way for the void (*chalal hapanui*), will be comprehensible only in the Messianic Age, as one must note that it comprises two diametrically opposed aspects. The *chalal hapanui* came about through the constriction, for God withdrew divinity from there, so to speak, and no divinity remains there, so to speak. Were that not the case, it would not be a void, everything would be infinitude (*ein sof*), and there would be no space in which to create the cosmos. But the truth is that there is nevertheless divinity there, too, for indeed nothing can exist without God's vitality. That is why the void will remain utterly inscrutable until the Messianic Age.[355]

If humanity is granted existence, then we must heed the limitations of the human-imbued faculties with which we operate in the world. To comprehend the significance of choice, we must understand how moral errors transgress the ethical norms of humanity. Rav Shagar continues:

> According to Rabbi Nachman, *tzimtzum* is a paradox: On the one hand, in order for the world to exist, the Holy One of Blessing must withdraw from the cosmos. On the other, it is impossible for anything to exist without God. Conceptions of God's infinitude and unity, to the effect that "God's Presence fills all the earth" (Isaiah 6:3), imply that nothing exists outside of God, and, consequently, that there can be no existence devoid of divine vitality. In any event, the reality of the *chalal hapanui* [the void] is at the root of all the metaphysical contradictions that cannot be resolved in a rational manner.[356]

Yet, what happens when we do not follow the Torah by the letter? What does it mean to not fulfill every commandment? Are we doomed to eternal punishment for not following every commandment to the letter? Will we be denied a spot in the world-to-come? Such eschatological considerations may be intellectually significant, but perhaps not so important to our daily lives. We are meant to overcome the pettiness and myopia that impede our regular lives, and it's a virtue to work toward a world in which there is no more violence. If the Jewish tradition models anything, it is that humanity can repent collectively and individually for sins. We must open our hearts and make the world less hospitable to hatred. This is how we will triumph in bringing heavenly ideals to earth.

While we wish to see a more just world, we see value in teaching that there will be punishment for those who pervert justice. We're also skeptical, because we don't see the world operate in a completely just manner. Sometimes, no matter how much we pray for peace, we see only violence and war on the news. And when we don't see the wicked punished consistently, we curse the abdication of divine justice. Despite having to live in the tension between free will and divine omniscience, we still must bring about that world we wish to see—in which the righteous prosper and the plans of the wicked are foiled with vigor and spiritual resolve.

5:13

אַרְבַּע מִדּוֹת בָּאָדָם: הָאוֹמֵר שֶׁלִּי שֶׁלִּי וְשֶׁלְּךָ שֶׁלָּךְ – זוֹ מִדָּה
בֵּינוֹנִית, וְיֵשׁ אוֹמְרִים זוֹ מִדַּת סְדוֹם. שֶׁלִּי שֶׁלָּךְ וְשֶׁלְּךָ שֶׁלִּי –
עַם הָאָרֶץ. שֶׁלִּי שֶׁלָּךְ וְשֶׁלְּךָ שֶׁלָּךְ – חָסִיד. שֶׁלָּךְ שֶׁלִּי וְשֶׁלִּי
שֶׁלִּי – רָשָׁע.

There are four character types among people: (a) One who
says, "My property is mine and yours is yours," is an average
character type, but some say this is characteristic of Sodom;
(b) "Mine is yours and yours is mine" is an unlearned person;
(c) "Mine is yours and yours is yours" is scrupulously pious;
(d) "Yours is mine and mine is mine," is wicked.

IN THE TORAH portion *B'har*, in Leviticus, God says to the Children of
Israel: "The land must not be sold beyond reclaim, for the land is Mine;
you are but strangers resident with Me" (25:23). This phrase is a shift in
how humans interact with their surroundings: This earth, perhaps the
entirety of the universe, is not our property. We own nothing. All is on
loan from the Creator, and we should be generous with what we have
on loan from God.

Altruism runs deep in religious philosophy. Within Christianity,
altruism usually means that human beings are to selflessly sacrifice
comfort and well-being to give to others. This emerges from a theology in which the Christian redeemer (divinity in human form) gave the
ultimate sacrifice and thus serves as a model for humanity. Consider
Mother Teresa, who left her country, had no family, and served the
poor in the streets of a foreign land. Within Judaism, giving to others
is an imperative, but there is generally more acknowledgment of self-
interest and the complexity of motives while doing so.

The Torah eschews modern theories of economics. Jewish philosophy no more condemns capitalism than it defends socialism. These are
human-developed theories and modes of society. Ownership is a de-
fensible right granted from God, sacred in its own way, but temporary.

Rather, Judaism's spiritual emphasis is not on accumulating, but on giving. We claim that it is mine first, and then that it is yours. Sharing and giving away wealth are righteous actions.

The Hebrew word for sacrifice is *korban*, which comes from *karav*—to draw close. In sacrifice, our goal is to become closer to the other or Other: "Give readily and have no regrets when you do so" (Deuteronomy 15:10). Our motives are not purely altruistic, not purely self-sacrificial; there is no virtue in feeling bad after giving. This is reflected in other thought traditions as well. Aristotle argues that something would be wrong if we felt bad when we gave.[357] Rather, the virtuous person has one's emotions and actions in harmony, feels good when doing good, and bad when doing bad.

In the Talmud, the Rabbis comment that one should "give tithes in order that you shall be enriched" (BT *Taanit* 9a). Gaining as others gain is more sustainable. In one of the earliest commentaries on *Pirkei Avot*, Rabban Yochanan ben Zakkai argues that we seek atonement through acts of kindness.[358] Our motive may be to fulfill the psychological need for purity and remove guilt, but we help others in the process.

Rabbi Moshe Cordovero (sixteenth century, Safed, Ottoman Palestine) says, "All souls are united, and each soul contains a part of all others."[359] His student, Rabbi Eliyahu de Vidas (sixteenth century, Hebron, Ottoman Palestine), elaborates:

> Even though your body's material substance separates you from your friend, the *nefesh*-soul of both of you is a spiritual entity, and the tendency of the spirit is to make you cleave to your friend with unbroken unity. When your *nefesh*-soul becomes aroused to love a friend, your friend's *nefesh*-soul will be equally aroused to love you in return—until both of your souls are bound to form one single entity.[360]

Andrew Carnegie demonstrated this in his giving. When workers launched a strike for better pay and lower hours in 1892 at his Homestead steel plant, Carnegie backed a brutal crackdown that included crushing the union and deaths. Later in his life, Carnegie expressed regret, publicly changed his outlook, and became one of the greatest champions for philanthropy in the United States. By the time he died in

1919, he had donated a vast amount of his fortune to charity, including the construction of twenty-five hundred public libraries and universities around the United States.

Today, far more people know about Carnegie Hall than about the Homestead strike. We need not judge others who give, neither the millionaires nor those who give on any level: "A human being sees what is visible, but God sees into the heart" (I Samuel 16:7).[361]

Mark Zuckerberg and his wife, Dr. Priscilla Chan, are an example of extraordinary philanthropists today. In their early thirties, already they have donated hundreds of millions to health care and education, including $100 million to the public school system in Newark, New Jersey. In 2015, Zuckerberg pledged to donate 99 percent of his Facebook stock (valued then at about $45 billion) to charity over the course of his lifetime.[362]

Zuckerberg's giving pledge is part of a growing trend in the realm of the ultra-wealthy. Like others who have joined the giving pledge, including Bill and Melinda Gates and Warren Buffett, Zuckerberg is not going to sell his stock immediately and donate the cash. Rather, all of these billionaires will donate up to 50 percent of their adjusted gross income by donating the stock itself when it reaches a certain value. This maximizes the deduction while avoiding other taxes. Meanwhile, charities that are given these stocks can then sell them without the need to pay an additional capital gains tax on the contribution. Over the next several years, for example, Zuckerberg will donate no more than $1 billion annually; with this substantial amount, many will benefit. The fact that a philanthropist will receive tax benefits should be no grounds for critique; any incentive to give should be used if it helps others. Of these, only Zuckerberg is Jewish, but the philanthropy of all accommodates their self-interest while being altruistic.

Those of us without access to wealth can still be philanthropic, by giving time, compassion, talent, reusable goods, and money. It matters that we foster a culture of giving, especially a culture that builds a healthy and just society that helps those in need. While every person possesses distinct needs and aspirations—human and religious— we should seek to fulfill the personal need to give back to the world.

Even when not driven by a pure altruism, we are motivated by self-actualization, the wish for a meaningful life, or religious fervor. Imagine if we viewed the world in such a fashion: investing in ourselves by investing in others. Ultimately, the sparks of our souls all return to the same bonfire. We are all different, but we are also one. We are loved by others because we show them love. We live in a community that is joyous and meaningful because we invest in it.

Even without access to tremendous wealth, we can still do tremendous good for others. The perfect should not be allowed to become the enemy of the good. Recognition is not to be the primary motive, but it is fine if it accompanies one's giving. We are more concerned with helping others than perfect purity in motives. And we are better people for it.

5:14

אַרְבַּע מִדּוֹת בַּדֵּעוֹת: נוֹחַ לִכְעוֹס וְנוֹחַ לִרְצוֹת – יָצָא
הֶפְסֵדוֹ בִשְׂכָרוֹ. קָשֶׁה לִכְעוֹס וְקָשֶׁה לִרְצוֹת – יָצָא שְׂכָרוֹ
בְּהֶפְסֵדוֹ. קָשֶׁה לִכְעוֹס וְנוֹחַ לִרְצוֹת – חָסִיד. נוֹחַ לִכְעוֹס
וְקָשֶׁה לִרְצוֹת – רָשָׁע.

There are four types of temperament: (a) One who is angered
easily and pacified easily, their loss is offset by their gain; (b)
one who is hard to anger and hard to pacify, their gain is offset
by their loss; (c) one who is hard to anger and easy to pacify
is pious; (d) one who is easily angered and hard to pacify is
wicked.

THE TALMUD TEACHES, "A person is recognizable through three
things: their pocket, their cup, and their anger" (BT *Eiruvin* 65a). How
we spend, how we drink, and how we show anger exhibit our uninhib-
ited essence. "Anyone who is angry—if they are wise, their wisdom flees
from them. If they are a prophet—their prophecy flees from them" (BT
P'sachim 66b). We achieve and maintain wisdom when we learn steady
self-control. When anger steers us, we not only lose the best part of ourselves, but also we neglect the wisdom imbued in us by God. "One who
is angry does not consider even the Divine Presence important" (BT
N'darim 22b).

Controlling one's anger and cultivating godliness are connected.
Rabbi Yerucham Levovitz (nineteenth/early twentieth century, Poland), an ethicist and leader of the Mir Yeshiva,[363] teaches about the
connection between humility and anger:

> If a person wants to discern his or her level of humility, look at how
> you behave when someone speaks ill of you and insults you. If you
> become angry, know that you are arrogant, because the humble
> person does not become angry. Even though anger and arrogance
> are two separate *midot*, anger is impossible without arrogance. One
> who comes to anger often is because he or she is more arrogant.[364]

Wishing that one were born with a disposition toward tranquility is insufficient. Learning *musar* and reducing the propensity to mindless anger is far better. Strengthening one's ability to be pacified when stressed or angered is so difficult, but allowing anger to take control is a disservice to all that we have to achieve in this life. There is so much at stake: our human relationships and our relationship to God. Without these, we are purposeless, destined to become poor in our spiritual wealth. Building one's personal sense of fulfillment, patience, and virtue will go a long way to bringing the world together.

Anger is universally considered a vice. We are asked to emulate the Divine, who is *erech apayim*, "slow to anger" (Exodus 34:6; Numbers 14:18). The Rabbis refer to anger as a form of idolatry, in which one worships oneself. Thus, the Rabbis teach that one must be slow to anger and easy to appease. Rabbi Nachman of Breslov teaches, "There is no peace in the world because there is too much anger. You can make peace only with joy."[365] The Rabbis teach, "One who sees an idol that has not been destroyed pronounces the blessing, 'Blessed is God who is slow to anger.'"[366] This suggests that God should be angry at how much unchallenged evil remains in the world, yet God has allowed humanity to be the ambassadors of truth and the defenders of justice. We emulate this divine patience, frustrated at an unredeemed world, while still feeling urgency.

A classic midrash teaches that God is patient not only with the just. Pointing to the biblical idiom that refers to God as forbearing—*erech apayim* (e.g., Exodus 34:6)—Rabbi Yochanan notes that it employs a more marked dual form (*apayim*) rather than the simpler singular form (*af*). Playing on this mundane grammatical feature, he explains that it actually alludes to a double application of divine patience: "God delays anger with the righteous and delays anger with the wicked" (JT *Taanit* 2:1; BT *Eiruvin* 22a). We, too, are to refrain from expressing anger.

Expressing anger, however, can be useful. Maimonides taught that one should not let anger be self-consuming, but one can pretend to be angry to educate young children who are doing wrong.[367]

While not a sustainable form of emotional energy, anger can catalyze people toward a goal. Anger can be useful for social justice activists, for example. Princeton University's Jeff Stout, a religious ethics scholar, writes in his book *Blessed Are the Organized*:

> Anger is one of the most important traits they [organizers] look for in potential leaders. Someone who professes love of justice, but is not angered by its violation, is unlikely to stay with the struggle for justice through thick and thin, to display the passion that will motivate others to join in, or to have enough courage to stand up to the powers that be.[368]

Daily, we must respond quickly to social problems and injustice, but without allowing anger to dominate one's psyche or persona. Sustained anger takes up extraordinary energy, and as activists we must preserve our energy, to ensure we are effective. The Chasidic rabbis instruct us not to subdue our anger, for that leads to lost potential. Rather, we should channel our anger into healthy emotions that increase constructive action. Mohandas Gandhi observed that "anger controlled can be transmuted into a power that can move the world." Professor Stout describes "just anger," which

> stands midway between despairing rage and liberal squeamishness about the vehement passions. A politics of just anger aims to restore the spirit of democracy to democratic culture, a spirit disposed to become angry at the right things in the right way and use this passion to motivate the level of political involvement essential to striving for significant social change.[369]

In general within Stout's epistemology, too often the powerful insist that victims remain passive; and then those leaders view the righteous anger of the oppressed as a violation of an elite code of decorum. The proper role of social organizers, Stout notes, is to oppose this code and disrupt the normative deceptive calm of oppression.[370]

Our anger shows us that we care about just treatment. If we did not think of ourselves as bound together, then we would not be angered by the unjust behavior of some. To feel anger is to feel the importance of our relationships and all they demand. Stout writes, "Accordingly, the individual who rarely experiences anger in response to injustices . . . [shows] slavishness and apathy. A central task of a leader . . . is to help others transform themselves from slavish or apathetic victims into people who behave and feel as citizens do."[371] Relatedly, Albert Camus, French existentialist and member of the French Resistance, writes, "I rebel—therefore we exist."[372]

Regarding understanding our reaction to others and how it affects our inner self, Rabbi Joseph B. Soloveitchik writes:

> Of course, love is a great and noble emotion, fostering the social spirit and elevating man, but not always is the loving person capable of meeting the challenge of harsh realities. In certain situations, a disjunctive emotion, such as anger or indignation, may become the motivating force for noble and valuable action.[373]

The greatest Jewish philosophers of the last century recognized this truth: controlled and righteous anger, in defense of the weak and exploited and other noble causes, is no vice.

In "Prayer for Peace," Rabbi Abraham Joshua Heschel writes:

> O Lord, we confess our sins, we are ashamed of the inadequacy of our anguish, of how faint and slight is our mercy. We are a generation that has lost its capacity for outrage. We must continue to remind ourselves that in a free society all are involved in what some are doing. Some are guilty, all are responsible.[374]

We must be outraged, as our prophets once were, when we encounter oppression and injustice. This is what it means to be alive and to be Jewish. Anger is unhealthy, but also human. We should dismiss rage (*cheimah*) when it comes from self-righteousness. However, when anger (*af*) is experienced in response to another's pain, we should harness the emotion so as to respond to a greater calling.

5:15

אַרְבַּע מִדּוֹת בַּלְמֵדִים: מְמַהֵר לִשְׁמוֹעַ וּמְמַהֵר לְאַבֵּד – יָצָא
שְׂכָרוֹ בְהֶפְסֵדוֹ. קָשֶׁה לִשְׁמוֹעַ וְקָשֶׁה לְאַבֵּד – יָצָא הֶפְסֵדוֹ
בִשְׂכָרוֹ. מְמַהֵר לִשְׁמוֹעַ וְקָשֶׁה לְאַבֵּד – חָכָם. קָשֶׁה לִשְׁמוֹעַ
וּמְמַהֵר לְאַבֵּד – זֶה חֵלֶק רַע.

There are four types of learners: (a) One who grasps quickly
and forgets quickly, their gain is offset by their loss; (b) one
who grasps slowly and forgets slowly, their loss is offset by
their gain; (c) one who grasps quickly and forgets slowly, is
wise; (d) one who grasps slowly and forgets quickly, this is a
bad portion.

WHAT IS THE PURPOSE of learning? Is the transmission of knowledge
from one generation to the next a deep philosophical exercise? Is it a
bureaucratic activity meant to reinforce a top-down understanding of
history? Learning is many things at once: personal improvement, developing discipline, and learning to discern reality from fiction. There
are many opinions about what constitutes the model student, but
learning requires analytical skill and training the memory. Learning
requires that students and teachers see life anew, with openness, but
that we also return to restudy what's familiar to strengthen our values.

Enlightenment thinker Jean-Jacques Rousseau writes in *The Social
Contract*, "Man is born free; and everywhere he is in chains."[375] He says
that *l'homme sauvage*—natural humanity, the species in its freest and
least inhibited state—was replaced by *l'homme civilisé*—enlightened and
civilized humanity, which is concerned with ethics and morality. Over
time, as humanity became more self-aware and controlled, we also became alienated from our natural selves and became stuck in a web of
complex social conventions and conformist behavioral patterns. This
has harmed human-human and human-Divine relationships. In addition, societal demands and distractions have become so great that it has
become more difficult to do the work that we are here in the world to

do—to actualize our unique gifts to bring light into the world wherever possible. We need to question the best allocation of our time. Should we spend an hour on social media or volunteer at a food bank? Do we take in a movie with friends or advocate for the rights of the vulnerable? While our obligations don't have to be zero sum in nature, we should always be aware that we aren't meant to be idle, especially in times of societal tumult. We have to act and be active. That is our obligation during troubled times.

But if our society is guided by comfortable, conflict-averse decision-making, how can we engage in the hard work to improve society? How can we even discover our own personal cause? We can view this process on both the physical and spiritual planes. Physically, we have unique talents and passions. Spiritually, we have unique callings toward our actualization.

There are divergent views on how to arrive at our true natures. In *Emile*, Rousseau says that the individual can discover the authentic self only when educated in isolation from society; he also notes that such a person would be miserable.[376] For the Jewish people, by contrast, the education process is about community and fostering lasting partnerships (*chevruta*). We must all do what we can to discover ourselves, while remaining immersed in society. Yet, the question becomes, can we ever recover our original, authentic nature? In his novel *Ah, But Your Land Is Beautiful*, the late Alan Paton, a South African author and critic of apartheid, writes, "When I go up there, which is my intention, the Big Judge will say to me, 'Where are your wounds?' And if say I haven't any, he will say, 'Was there nothing to fight for?'"[377]

We each have to answer this question. Each year, prior to Passover, many Jews search and remove errant pieces of *chameitz* (leavened foods) from our homes. But why do we perform the ritual of removing the *chameitz* from our homes *only*? Rabbi Yisrael of Vizhnitz, a nineteenth-century Chasidic master, was said to have been walking with a friend on the way to search for the *chameitz*. At some point in the journey, Rabbi Yisrael stopped and opened his cloak. Uncovering his chest, he said, "You know that the real *chameitz* is the *chameitz* in the heart—check me here!"

By checking the *chameitz* of the heart, we search for the spiritual blocks we have accumulated that blind us from our true nature and highest potential. We must break through pride to reach that deeper place. The first-century philosopher Philo asked what we can learn from the nature of *chameitz*. He answered that as leaven is banned because it is "puffed up," so we must guard against the self-righteousness that puffs us up with false pride.[378] Pride and complacency—these are the qualities we seek to remove from our character. This is the lesson of *chameitz*, Passover, and the civilized world.

Modernity led to the caging of the soul and some part of human potential. We cannot go back in time, but we must still find avenues to deepen insight, discovery, and freedom. To assist us properly on our path, we must seek the greatest wisdom in the world, which means that we should find teachers who understand and guide us. By finding the right balance of righteousness and wisdom, we grow intellectually into ourselves and develop love of learning and humanity, equally.

5:16

אַרְבַּע מִדּוֹת בְּנוֹתְנֵי צְדָקָה: רוֹצֶה שֶׁיִּתֵּן וְלֹא יִתְּנוּ
אֲחֵרִים – עֵינוֹ רָעָה בְּשֶׁל אֲחֵרִים. יִתְּנוּ אֲחֵרִים וְהוּא
לֹא יִתֵּן – עֵינוֹ רָעָה בְּשֶׁלּוֹ. יִתֵּן וְיִתְּנוּ אֲחֵרִים – חָסִיד.
לֹא יִתֵּן וְלֹא יִתְּנוּ אֲחֵרִים – רָשָׁע.

There are four types of donors to charity: (a) Those who
want to give but do not want others to give—they begrudge
what belongs to others; (b) those who want others to give but
themselves do not want to give—they begrudge what belongs
to themselves; (c) those who want to give and for others to
give—they are pious; (d) those who do not want to give and do
not want others to give—they are wicked.

DONATING TO CHARITY is most effective when, beyond helping the
recipient, the donation also inspires others to give. There is tremendous virtue to anonymous giving. But when we contribute to society in
a meaningful way, we also work to build a culture in which significant
giving is the norm.

The nineteenth-century Galician Chasidic rabbi Chayim Halberstam—known as the Sanzer Rav—was so committed to helping the
poor that he would not rest each day until every last penny he owned
was distributed to those in need. During Sukkot, he would try to give
even more, so that the poor did not have to spend the holiday worrying
about the post-festival bills. As he sat in his unadorned sukkah, he said
that while others outfitted their sukkot expensively, his sukkah was or-
namented with *tzedakah*. When it was suggested to him that not every
beggar was honest, the Sanzer Rav said:

> Do you know the difference between you and me? I'm willing to
> give to a thousand poor people, even if 999 are dishonest, just
> to help the one who really needs the help. You are willing to turn
> down 999 valid requests just to protect yourself from the one who
> is taking advantage of you.[379]

The Sanzer Rav was so serious about not shaming an individual who may be in need that he challenged his own son. There is a story about a struggling individual who came to the Rav for assistance in buying a tallit for his future son-in-law. Just as the Rav was about to buy the new tallit for him, the Rav's son interjected, "How can you tell this lie? I saw you just yesterday buying a tallit!" The poor man quickly fled in humiliation. The Rav, startled, reprimanded his son, suggesting that the man may have needed something else for the wedding, like a wedding dress, which he was embarrassed to request, so he asked for a tallit instead. The son, realizing what he had done, asked the poor man for his forgiveness. The poor man returned to the Rav and asked whether to forgive the son. The Rav said that he should forgive him, but only on the condition that the Rav's son pay for the wedding.[380]

This idea also raises challenging questions about how we prioritize Jewish virtues for our children. Our children worry about a big test, social pressures, and making a team. We certainly don't want our children to be anxious or afraid, but how can we prioritize virtues more heavily so that it becomes even more important to help others than to succeed socially?

We must teach our children to honor the dignity and trust the honesty of those who approach us with their needs.

At the same time, we should be considerate of different personality types, to encourage all to give. In *Switch: How to Change Things When Change Is Hard*, Chip and Dan Heath examine why some college students donated to a canned-food drive and others did not. The researchers divided students into two groups: the students most likely to donate ("saints") and those least likely to contribute ("jerks"). They asked whether the solicitation approach could affect the likelihood that jerks would contribute. Some saints and some jerks received a general solicitation letter for the food drive the following week. Others received a detailed letter, with a specific request, location, and suggested time/date. Of those who received the general solicitation, 8 percent of the saints gave, and none of the jerks gave. When sent a letter with specifics, 42 percent of the saints donated, as did 25 percent of the jerks as well. The authors of *Switch* explain, "If you're hungry and need a can of food, you're three times better-off relying on a jerk with a map than on a budding young saint without one."[381]

Asking others to give is not calling on them to sacrifice, but rather inviting them toward self-actualization. Indeed, we are defined not by what we have, but by what we give. This mishnah, the Sanzer Rav, and *Switch* remind us that by devoting ourselves to giving, educating children to give, and inspiring others to give, we become the change we want to see in the world. Ensuring that the next generation has reason to contribute is foundational to Jewish wisdom. May this wisdom never cease.

5:17

אַרְבַּע מִדּוֹת בְּהוֹלְכֵי לְבֵית הַמִּדְרָשׁ: הוֹלֵךְ וְאֵינוֹ עוֹשֶׂה –
שְׂכַר הֲלִיכָה בְּיָדוֹ. עוֹשֶׂה וְאֵינוֹ הוֹלֵךְ – שְׂכַר מַעֲשֶׂה בְּיָדוֹ.
הוֹלֵךְ וְעוֹשֶׂה – חָסִיד. לֹא הוֹלֵךְ וְלֹא עוֹשֶׂה – רָשָׁע.

There are four types among those who go to the house of
study: (a) One who goes but does not study has the reward for
going; (b) one who studies (at home) but does not attend (the
house of study) has the reward for accomplishment; (c) one
who goes and studies is pious; (d) one who does not go and
does not study is wicked.

THERE ARE THREE LEVELS of *tikkun* (repair): *tikkun atzmi* (repair
of the self), *tikkun kahal* (repair of the community), and *tikkun olam*
(repair of the world). Religious life without all three is, at best, lacking
in spiritual effectiveness and, at worst, lacking in Jewish authenticity.
We must listen and be guided by the moral compass that God has
placed within us.

This mishnah continues the theme of four types of people. Here,
the Rabbis explore the importance of attendance. In a time of live-
streaming, video recording, podcasts, and instant communication, it is
often easier to remain at home, rather than join with others in learning.
Technology can make the Torah more accessible, but virtual learning
should not substitute for learning with others face-to-face, which also
promotes safe communities, challenging intellectual dialogue, and
spiritual connection.

Engagement with others in the real world, especially about moral
issues, supersedes virtual connection. Meeting our spiritual needs and
doing meaningful work requires breaking away from the computer and
phone and their addicting, endless stream of information, entertainment, and communication. As well, we need to invest time in Jewish
texts and explore the wisdom within ourselves to grow our spirituality.

The medieval philosopher Y'hudah HaLevi proposes that religious practices and virtues are distinct from natural or intellectual ones. He says that intellectual law, which all humans can comprehend without revelation, precedes even divine law and cannot be neglected in religious life. But human beings are fickle and are prone to disregard rules even when they have been laid out in a clear manner. So it has always been, even for the Jewish people. For HaLevi, following revelation, but not natural morality, is rebellious and a failure to fulfill one's collective responsibilities:

> When Israel's rebelliousness got to the point that they disregarded [even] the intellectual and governmental laws—which are [as] indispensable for [the existence of] every group as certain natural things are indispensable for every individual, like eating and drinking, moving and resting, and sleeping and being awake—but nevertheless held fast to the [various] acts of worship pertaining to the sacrifices and other divine commandments, which are based on hearing [i.e., revelation alone], [God] became satisfied with less from them.[382]

To be sure, human reasoning may pale in comparison to the moral understanding that one can glean from revelation, but HaLevi believed in the primacy of the intellectual law: "For the divine law can be fulfilled completely only after perfect adherence to the governmental and intellectual law has been achieved."[383] HaLevi ends with his highest religious imperative: "What does God require of you but to do justice, to love kindness, and to walk humbly with your God?" (Micah 6:8). Commitment to Jewish tradition and law demands a sophisticated moral compass.

HaLevi was not the first to connect Jewish religion and natural morality; the Talmud had him beat by hundreds of years. Remember the words we've previously read from Rabbi Yochanan: "If we had not received the Torah, we would have learned modesty from watching a cat, honesty from the ant, and fidelity from the dove" (BT *Eiruvin* 100b). Earlier, the Torah tells us that God called all Creation good (Genesis 1:31). Yet, even more than the rest of the flora and fauna crafted from the mind of the Divine, humans are singularly *good* because of their given capacity for conscience, reason, and empathy.

Perhaps the greatest modern proponent of natural morality was Rabbi Abraham Isaac Kook, who writes:

> Morality, in its natural state, with all its profound splendor and might, must be fixed in the soul, so that it may serve as a substratum for the great effects emanating from the strength of Torah.... Every element of Torah must be preceded by *derech eretz* [natural ethical behavior].[384]

In an extreme example of this principle, the late Rabbi Yehuda Amital suggests that if starving and left with the choice between meat forbidden by the Torah or a human corpse (forbidden only by the Rabbis), one must eat the former, due to the primacy of natural law.

Rabbi Avraham Yeshaya Karelitz, the Chazon Ish, explains the distinction between *r'tzon haTorah* (the will of the Torah) and *r'tzon HaShem* (God's will). There are clear ethical mandates (*r'tzon HaShem*) that cannot be found in biblical verses. The medieval rabbis, for example, proposed eleven different biblical verses to use as proof for the prohibition against *tzaar baalei chayim* (harming animals). They knew that it had to be *r'tzon HaShem* even if it was not explicitly *r'tzon haTorah*. Our natural morality allows us to understand *r'tzon HaShem* merely through living.

But for these concepts to work, we need to understand the spheres in which they operate. For that, we need to intellectually assimilate the dimensions of Judaic religiosity. Religiosity has two dimensions: spiritual introspection and engagement with the world. We look into our sacred texts, rituals, community, and social problems; but we must also look into ourselves, cultivate spirituality, nurture our own reason and faith, and find our authentic Jewish calling. Now, Jews must learn how to connect the outer religious life with the inner religious life more closely. We can do the disorderly work of the world only if we have done the messy work inside ourselves. This requires a respect for our natural morality; this is the potential placed in us at Creation and that we continue to nurture.

When, as Jews, we do not cultivate our internal moral compass and intertwine our universalistic nature (natural morality) with our particularistic nature (Torah and Jewish consciousness), we risk losing ourselves and our unique moral potential.

Y'hudah HaLevi reminds us of our natural morality and compels us to engage in the internal spiritual and moral work to change ourselves, the Jewish community, and the world. This requires learning, reflection, meditation, prayer, and teamwork. Clergy and educators who prioritize ritual observance over social responsibility not only misrepresent the Torah, they put the moral relevance of Jews in question. They abdicate Judaism's moral mission. Our tradition and the tools God imbued within every last living soul call on us to be exemplary moral beings—toward ourselves and all humanity.

5:18

אַרְבַּע מִדּוֹת בְּיוֹשְׁבֵי לִפְנֵי חֲכָמִים: סְפוֹג וּמַשְׁפֵּךְ מְשַׁמֶּרֶת
וְנָפָה. סְפוֹג – שֶׁהוּא סוֹפֵג אֶת הַכֹּל. מַשְׁפֵּךְ–שֶׁמַּכְנִיס בְּזוֹ
וּמוֹצִיא בְזוֹ. מְשַׁמֶּרֶת – שֶׁמּוֹצִיאָה אֶת הַיַּיִן וְקוֹלֶטֶת אֶת
הַשְּׁמָרִים. וְנָפָה – שֶׁמּוֹצִיאָה אֶת הַקֶּמַח וְקוֹלֶטֶת אֶת
הַסֹּלֶת.

There are four types [of students] that sit before the sages—
a sponge, a funnel, a strainer, and a sieve: a sponge, which
absorbs everything; a funnel, which lets in from one end and
lets out from the other; a strainer, which lets the wine flow
through and retains the sediment; and a sieve, which allows
the flour dust to pass through and retains the fine flour.

WE MUST BE AWARE not to become so absorbed in our studies that we
neglect performing righteous deeds. Education is not a competition to
determine who is the smartest, but a continuous process. Likewise, to
be Jewishly literate is to be active and responsive to social issues. The
Torah supports us meeting our obligations in the world, while still empowering us to pause and reflect; we come to learn balance between action and thinking. To absorb these juxtaposing virtues, we must learn
Torah in a manner that empowers our conscience and moral intuition.
It is radical, then, that the Rabbis taught that we should not absorb
every teaching we come across. We should attend to the basic moral
principles in each teaching; we shouldn't take all information *prima
facie*. In our religious education, we have to be selective, as well; one can
learn Torah the incorrect way. The Torah, if used incorrectly, can create
extremist, destructive, and zealous personalities.[385]

The Talmud says about Rabbi Meir, "He found a pomegranate, ate
the fruit within it, and threw away the peel" (BT *Chagigah* 15b). On our
own, we're not always so discerning, so we rely on people and systems
to hold us accountable. Ever hit the snooze button even though you had
been certain the night before that you needed to be awake early? Ever

have an extra piece of cake even though you had been certain an hour earlier that it would be the wrong choice? Little actions like these make us wonder why we trust ourselves to make decisions without knowing every outcome in advance. David DeSteno, director of the Social Emotions Group at Northeastern University, writes:

> Misplaced trust typically occurs because of two cognitive glitches. The first . . . is that our predictions for how much we'll want something in the future are often swayed by how we're feeling right now. In one of their experiments, participants' expectations of what they'd like to eat for breakfast tomorrow were principally influenced by how hungry they were today. This tendency to give too much weight to extraneous momentary feelings poses a big problem when it comes to gauging the trustworthiness of future-you. The second glitch is that your mind tends to discount the value of future rewards, meaning that as the time between you and a potential reward shrinks, your desire for it grows.[386]

Combine the two—immersion in the present and discounting the future—and humans can make some really poor choices. Perhaps one shouldn't trust oneself when the alarm clock sounds, but should instead have faith in the previous evening's decision to set the alarm.

Jewish tradition offers two ways to address accountability: (1) imperative—feeling a sense of moral and spiritual obligation to find the time to commit to the principles that have been enshrined in Jewish tradition throughout history; and (2) community—surrounding yourself with others who have the same commitments. On issues with which we struggle, we cannot depend on trusting ourselves. Rather, we must have faith in a rule, or trust a valued person to help us make the appropriate decision; and we learn when to let personal preference give way to others' guidance.

What type of student do we want to be? Each day, we experience moments that affect our attitudes and consciousness. A primary function of religion is to help us live in the present, while also having a view to the bigger, divine picture.

5:19

כָּל אַהֲבָה שֶׁהִיא תְלוּיָה בְדָבָר – בָּטֵל דָּבָר וּבְטֵלָה אַהֲבָה.
וְשֶׁאֵינָהּ תְּלוּיָה בְדָבָר – אֵינָהּ בְּטֵלָה לְעוֹלָם. אֵיזוֹ הִיא
אַהֲבָה שֶׁהִיא תְלוּיָה בְדָבָר? זוֹ אַהֲבַת אַמְנוֹן וְתָמָר.
וְשֶׁאֵינָהּ תְּלוּיָה בְדָבָר? זוֹ אַהֲבַת דָּוִד וִיהוֹנָתָן.

Any love that depends on a specific cause, when that cause is
gone, the love is gone; but if it does not depend on a specific
cause, it will never cease. What sort of love depended upon
a specific cause? The love of Amnon for Tamar. And what
did not depend upon a specific cause? The love of David and
Jonathan.

LOVE IS NOT fairy-tale romance, but full dedication to another being.
To love another means that we wish to give ourselves to another. We
give without expecting return, precisely because we love them. We're
motivated by the relationship to develop into our best selves. When we
love, we offer empathy, comfort, and support to others, motivated by
their needs, rather than by our own.

In Jewish tradition, love is more action than emotion. Writing in the
1960s, Rabbi Joseph B. Soloveitchik explains:

> The Bible spoke of the commandment to love one's neighbor
> (Leviticus 19:18). However, in Talmudic literature, emphasis was
> placed not only upon sentiment, but upon action, which is moti-
> vated by sentiment. The *Choshen Mishpat*, the Jewish code of civil
> law, analyzes not human emotions but actual human relations.
> The problem of *Choshen Mishpat* is not what one feels toward the
> other, but how he acts toward him.[387]

Rabbi Jonathan Sacks, the former chief rabbi of the United Kingdom,
explains that deeds of loving-kindness shift one's inner being toward
godliness and covenant building. He notes that *chesed*, usually translated as "kindness," may also be translated as "love." This is love expressed through deed, in a covenant of holiness. Here is mutual respect

for the integrity and freedom of the other through acts of *chesed*, which have a deep emotional component:

> [*Chesed*] exists only in virtue of emotion, empathy, and sympathy, feeling-with and feeling-for. We act with kindness because we know what it feels like to be in need of kindness. . . . Societies are only human and humanizing when they are a community of communities built on face-to-face encounters—covenantal relationships.[388]

The late French philosopher Emmanuel Levinas writes that the image of a "face" is a key to what makes us human. Sacks interprets Levinas thus: "Society is faceless; *Chesed* is a relationship of face to face. The Pentateuch repeatedly emphasizes that we cannot see God face to face. It follows that we can only see God in the face of another."[389]

Of course, if possible, we ought to strive to see the face of another even within our own families—though depending on individual family situations, this process may be more complex. In a story about the Kapishnitzer Rebbe, a prominent New York businessman was asked to see the rebbe about an opportunity to give charity. He stressed that he would go to the rebbe in Brooklyn, but the rebbe chose to go to the man's office, for he had an important message.

When the Kapishnitzer Rebbe arrived, the man put his phone on hold and left his customers waiting while he invited the rebbe into his office. There, the rebbe detailed the dire financial situation of a family with many children. The breadwinner of the family had lost his job and was in poor health, and only immediate action would stave off ruin. The businessman offered $1,000 but wondered why the rebbe had to deliver the message in person. The story concludes, "Pen poised above his checkbook, the man asked, 'For whom is the check?' The Rebbe stared at the floor for a few long moments, then answered, 'For your brother.'"[390]

Love, of course, does not have to take the form either of money or of physical interaction. Rabbi Yaakov Yisrael Kanievsky, the Steipler Rav (twentieth century, Israel [born in Poland]), endured poverty and harassment by Russian authorities because of his Jewish observance. Yet, despite his hardships, Rabbi Kanievsky was a scholar renowned for his combination of wisdom and common sense and was widely sought for advice. A young man once complained to the Steipler Rav, "I don't know which way to turn. My home is in constant chaos. I come home every Friday afternoon before Shabbat and the dishes are still in the sink, there are diapers everywhere, and the floor is not even swept. My wife is just not getting things done. I can't live like this anymore." The Steipler Rav looked at the young man with incredulity and said, "You don't know where to turn? I'll tell you. Turn to the nearest closet and take out a broom. Has it occurred to you that you can help?!"[391]

Accepting another for who one is, rather than what one might become or once was, guides us toward understanding the divine dimensions of love. Popular culture has altered the meaning of love into something akin to ephemeral amusement. When we love only one aspect of a person—their intellect, their power, or their physical appearance—we do not love. We are infatuated by that person, attracted to an element that overwhelms the heart, but subtracts from the analytical part of our mind; we act on base instinct alone. To love another means to love the full person, regardless of wealth, appearance, job, or faults. To love is to accept the fullness of the other's being. Love is not tangential to Judaism, but fundamental: the love of God, the love of a spouse, the love between parent and child, the love of our people, and the love for all people. Love is more than mere emotion, for it is expressed through deeds, particularly acts of genuine loving-kindness.

5:20

כָּל מַחֲלֹקֶת שֶׁהִיא לְשֵׁם שָׁמַיִם – סוֹפָהּ לְהִתְקַיֵּם. וְשֶׁאֵינָהּ
לְשֵׁם שָׁמַיִם – אֵין סוֹפָהּ לְהִתְקַיֵּם. אֵיזוֹ הִיא מַחֲלֹקֶת
שֶׁהִיא לְשֵׁם שָׁמַיִם? זוֹ מַחֲלֹקֶת שַׁמַּי וְהִלֵּל. וְשֶׁאֵינָהּ
לְשֵׁם שָׁמַיִם? זוֹ מַחֲלֹקֶת קֹרַח עֲדָתוֹ.

Any dispute that is for the sake of heaven will endure; but one
that is not for the sake of heaven will not endure. What sort
of dispute was for the sake of heaven? The dispute between
Shammai and Hillel. And which was not for the sake of
heaven? The dispute of Korach and his company.

IT IS EASY to fall into the trap of arguing in order to be right and inflate
one's ego, but such a pattern will detract from intellectual nourishment.
Every argument will become an opportunity for arrogance, rather than
to understand another's ideas. This was the downfall of Korach, the
most significant figure to challenge the leadership of Moses during
the wanderings in the wilderness. Korach thought that if he fomented
argument within leadership, he could topple Moses and himself lead
the Hebrews to the Holy Land. Korach paid dearly for this mistake (see
Numbers 16:31–32). The Rabbis teach that respectful argument must
be attached to proper motives and righteous integrity. Arguing "for the
sake of heaven" means that the argument is beyond one's own ego; the
argument is to perpetuate good.

Developing skills requires that we learn to adapt. Remain ideolog-
ically isolated, and one's ideas will never be challenged and one will
never learn to argue. Remain intellectually engaged, and one's thinking will adapt and one's skills in argument improve as new information
emerges. Why does Noah send the dove to find dry land, and why does
the Torah devote multiple verses to this incident (Genesis 8:6–12)?
Noah must wait until the ark reaches dry land, regardless of what the
dove finds. But it is human nature to seek knowledge, even if one cannot change the course of affairs.

At the heart of the Talmudic process, and of all pedagogy in Judaism, is *machloket*, "dispute"—the term that is featured in our mishnah. What it refers to is not merely intellectual exercise, but a reminder of the importance of multiple opinions in determining truth. One should remain humble, even uncertain, about one's own position, learn to engage respectfully with others, and maintain a dialectical approach that embraces nuance and complexity.

> Rabbi Abba stated in the name of Sh'muel: For three years, there was a dispute between Beit Shammai and Beit Hillel, the former asserting, "The halachah is in agreement with our views," and the latter contending, "The halachah is in agreement with our views." Then a *bat kol* [voice of God] issued, announcing, "[The utterances of] both are the words of the living God, but the halachah is in agreement with the rulings of Beit Hillel." Since, however, both are the words of the living God, what was it that entitled Beit Hillel to have the halachah fixed in agreement with their rulings? Because they were kindly and modest, they studied their own rulings and those of Beit Shammai, and were even so [humble] as to mention the actions of Beit Shammai before theirs. (BT *Eiruvin* 13b)

Without humility, one risks standing on the wrong side of history, which is filled with examples of both leaders who humbly adapted and of those whose villainy was in intransigence. When Joseph warned that Pharaoh's dreams foretold famine following abundance, surplus grain was stored for the lean years (Genesis 41:25–31). Joseph could have become complacent, because Egypt was used to plenty, but instead he anticipated scarcity and adapted. In contrast, the last king of Babylon, Belshazzar, ignored the "writing on the wall" (Daniel 5:25–28). In his ignorance and intransigence, Belshazzar celebrated what he thought would be a long, secure reign, even while battalions of Persians and foreign invaders were at the gate, eager to overthrow him and conquer Babylon.

We dare not retreat in fear when we encounter challenges; and when we argue for what is right, we should do so knowing that our words are heard by the divine ear. While knowing that the world is not just black-and-white, and we must weather the storm of opposition if our ideals are to remain holy. Considering the contrary argument, one gains knowledge, but one finds opportunity for dissent when dissent is just. According to Rabbi Elyse D. Frishman, "When we listen to Torah, we are listening to God's voice. But this is not necessarily what God speaks; it reflects what we hear. Dialogue between two people grows not from what is said but from what is heard."[392]

To prepare for changed reality (personally and collectively), we should look outside of the "ark" to embrace the eventualities of the new world. It is our spiritual vocation. How will contemporary leadership answer the challenge of climate change, for example? The response of some is that we must simply stop talking about it, as if the immediate and growing calamity will therefore just disappear.

But who will win the argument—the Josephs and Daniels of our age? Or the Belshazzars and Pharaohs? The choice is ours.

5:21

כָּל הַמְזַכֶּה אֶת הָרַבִּים – אֵין חֵטְא בָּא עַל יָדוֹ, וְכָל
הַמַחֲטִיא אֶת הָרַבִּים – אֵין מַסְפִּיקִין בְּיָדוֹ לַעֲשׂוֹת
תְּשׁוּבָה. מֹשֶׁה זָכָה וְזִכָּה אֶת הָרַבִּים, וּזְכוּת הָרַבִּים
תְּלוּיָה בּוֹ, שֶׁנֶּאֱמַר: צִדְקַת יְיָ עָשָׂה, וּמִשְׁפָּטָיו עִם־יִשְׂרָאֵל
(דברים לג:כא). יָרָבְעָם בֶּן נְבָט חָטָא וְהֶחֱטִיא אֶת הָרַבִּים,
וְחֵטְא הָרַבִּים תָּלוּי בּוֹ, שֶׁנֶּאֱמַר: עַל־חַטֹּאת יָרָבְעָם אֲשֶׁר
חָטָא וַאֲשֶׁר הֶחֱטִיא אֶת־יִשְׂרָאֵל (מלכים א, טו:ל).

Whoever influences the masses to become meritorious shall
not be the cause of sin; but one who influences the masses to
sin will not be given the means to repent. Moses was meritorious and influenced the masses to be meritorious, so the merit
of the masses was to his credit, as it is said: "He executed the
Eternal's judgments and God's decisions for Israel" (Deuteronomy 33:21). Jeroboam ben Nebat sinned and caused the masses
to sin, so the sin of the masses was charged against him, as it is
said: "For the sins of Jeroboam that he committed and that he
caused Israel to commit" (I Kings 15:30).

WHY DID THE RABBIS place so much faith in those who seek the mantle of leadership? Don't extraordinary people routinely fail to live up
to their potential? Why did the Rabbis believe that certain people are
capable of such heroism?

Is Judaism primarily individualistic, in which every adherent is
accountable primarily to oneself? Or, is Judaism collectivist, in which
what benefits all is paramount? To answer, consider the very real tension
today between the needs of the many and individual liberty—a tension
experience by all people, as well as by Jews. Reconciling this tension into
cooperation is beyond philosophical imperative; it is a call to action.
But how do we make the leap from experiencing tension to acting on
our discomfort? There is no easy answer, but one of the most productive means by which to engender change is to take on the mantle of

leadership in whichever form is most meaningful. Not everyone has the skills or desire to form organizations, lead new missions, and take action. On the other hand, others find that when pushed, taking on a leadership role complements their skill set well and is quite meaningful. Wherever we are needed, we can find the correct skills that correspond with our individual personalities and idiosyncrasies. Thus, when there is a vacuum for meaningful leadership, all one needs is the temerity to lead.

Indeed, becoming a leader and bringing warmth to a cold world is perhaps one of the greatest roles we can inhabit as people of conscience. Consider Noah. The Chasidic masters refer to him as a *tzaddik im peltz*, a "righteous person with a fur coat." Rather than lighting a fire to keep others warm, Noah put on a coat metaphorically; he saved himself in the ark. But our task, the Rabbis teach, is to account for the needs of others in our own lives. We gain merit through constructive deeds that allow the world to progress justly.

Even though the role of a leader is usually to inspire and model attributes of goodwill and strength, this mishnah does not say that a leader will never sin. Rather, it says that leadership will not be penalized when the people sin. Leaders cannot be expected to win over every heart and mind, nor should they be held accountable for all of the behaviors (virtuous or malicious) of their followers.

Ideally, Judaism and religion in general do not just exist in private life, but influence collective, public affairs. Our spiritual journey is not measured merely through personal piety, but by how we elevate and influence others. Do we bring others closer to God, or do we push them away? Why wait, when we can act? Do we help others strengthen their moral convictions, or do we undermine them?

According to the Book of Esther, Haman told Ahasuerus that the Jewish people were scattered and dispersed (*m'fuzar umforad*). He stressed their vulnerability, claiming that they lacked unity (*achdut*), collective responsibility, and shared purpose (3:8). But Haman failed. The Jews of Persia united to defeat Haman's bigotry; and each year at Purim, we recommit to preserving and strengthening our cherished people, even in the midst of internal fragmentation and enmity.

While Jews are commanded to show compassion to all human beings, *ahavat hab'riyot*, we also have the mitzvah to love fellow Jews, *ahavat Yisrael*, and take responsibility for fellow Jews, *arvut*. This principle primarily means to help others do mitzvot[393] and to prevent others from doing wrong, *aveirot*:

> Regarding all sins in the Torah, persons are punished for what they did; yet here [regarding an oath taken in vain], they are punished for what they did and for what the whole world did. . . . And regarding all the sins in the Torah, this is not so? But surely it is written "They shall stumble over one another" (Leviticus 26:37)—each person because of the sin of the other. This teaches that *all of Israel are responsible one for the other!* That is [only in situations] where they could have objected but failed to do so. (BT *Sh'vuot* 39a–b)

Rabbi Aharon Lichtenstein says that when Jews returned to the Land of Israel and achieved sovereignty, *arvut* increased.[394] This raises interesting questions about our era. To continue growing spiritually, we must journey beyond the familiar. The first step is to create pluralistic communities, in which all Jews can learn from one another, while honoring diversity. The second step is to repair community and the world together. Further, we are to cultivate love for one another and often even stand up for others whom we know to be good, when they are attacked, even when they may not be the best that they can be. We build trust and community when we stand up for others struggling in what can often be a competitive, and even ruthless, culture. Even if we do not agree with each other on anything, the shared destiny of the Jewish people rests on the wisdom we have cultivated for millennia.

On the other hand, when Jewish individuals are held accountable for their wrongs, so is the collective community:

> Any householder who can prevent his household [from sinning], but does not, is seized for [the sins of] his household; [if he can prevent] his townspeople, he is seized for [the sins of] his townspeople; if the whole world, he is seized for [the sins of] the whole world. (BT *Shabbat* 54b)

Not only do we need to help one another, we need to learn from one another, foster relationships, and act in solidarity. All Jews are needed in the spiritual adventure of learning Torah, whether in the study halls or on the streets. As we know, the Sages teach that a wise individual is someone who can learn from anyone (see *Pirkei Avot* 4:1).

Rabbi Y'hudah HaLevi explains that all Jews are like instruments in an orchestra.[395] To make an orchestra, you can't have only a lone trumpet, a hidden bassoon, or careless timpani. You need powerful brass, emphatic woodwinds, and active percussion. You need soul. You need heart. You need vision. Similarly, the kabbalists say that each Jew represents a single letter of Torah. If one letter is missing on a Torah scroll, the entire scroll becomes void; so it is with the Jewish people. And Rabbi Yoel Sirkis—also known as the Bach, who lived in the seventeenth century—teaches that the traditional daily prayer that God "give us our share of Your Torah" (*v'tein chelkeinu b'Toratecha*) presupposes that every individual has a special portion that only he or she can reveal.[396] Each individual is crucial to the collective.

At the heart of Judaism is the knowledge that we all have a unique mission in the world. We weren't placed on this earth merely to survive or even to thrive. We are here to perpetuate holiness in all its manifold forms. Each of us must be activists, in our own unique ways. It is not Jewishly acceptable to say it is not one's personality to push back against injustice, in one way or another. We should always be aware that Jewish internal fragmentation can be used as evidence of Jewish vulnerability by those who wish to exploit our people. We may waver between embracing diversity and striving for unity, but we must be unequivocal about our commitment to a culture of respect, inclusion, and collaboration.

5:22

כָּל מִי שֶׁיֵּשׁ בּוֹ שְׁלשָׁה דְבָרִים הַלָּלוּ, תַּלְמִידוֹ שֶׁל אַבְרָהָם
אָבִינוּ, וּשְׁלשָׁה דְבָרִים אֲחֵרִים, תַּלְמִידוֹ שֶׁל בִּלְעָם: עַיִן
טוֹבָה, וְרוּחַ נְמוּכָה, וְנֶפֶשׁ שְׁפָלָה – תַּלְמִידוֹ שֶׁל אַבְרָהָם
אָבִינוּ. עַיִן רָעָה, וְרוּחַ גְּבוֹהָה, וְנֶפֶשׁ רְחָבָה – תַּלְמִידוֹ שֶׁל
בִּלְעָם. מַה בֵּין תַּלְמִידָיו שֶׁל אַבְרָהָם אָבִינוּ לְתַלְמִידָיו
שֶׁל בִּלְעָם? תַּלְמִידָיו שֶׁל אַבְרָהָם אָבִינוּ יוֹרְשִׁין לְגַן עֵדֶן,
שֶׁנֶּאֱמַר: לְהַנְחִיל אֹהֲבַי יֵשׁ, וְאֹצְרֹתֵיהֶם אֲמַלֵּא (משלי ח:כא).
אֲבָל תַּלְמִידָיו שֶׁל בִּלְעָם יוֹרְשִׁין גֵּיהִנָּם וְיוֹרְדִין לִבְאֵר
שַׁחַת, שֶׁנֶּאֱמַר: וְאַתָּה אֱלֹהִים תּוֹרִדֵם לִבְאֵר שַׁחַת, אַנְשֵׁי
דָמִים וּמִרְמָה לֹא־יֶחֱצוּ יְמֵיהֶם. וַאֲנִי אֶבְטַח־בָּךְ (תהלים נה:כד).

Whoever has the following three traits is a disciple of our forefather Abraham; and [whoever has] three different traits is a disciple of Balaam. One who has a good eye, a humble spirit, and a meek soul is a disciple of our forefather Abraham. One who has an evil eye, an arrogant spirit, and a greedy soul is a disciple of Balaam. How are disciples of our forefather Abraham different from disciples of Balaam? Disciples of our forefather Abraham inherit *Gan Eden* (paradise), as is said: "To cause those who love Me to inherit an everlasting possession [the world-to-come], and I will fill their storehouses [in this world]" (Proverbs 8:21). But disciples of Balaam inherit *Geihinam* (hell) and descend into the well of destruction, as is said: "And You, O God, shall lower them into the well of destruction; men of bloodshed and deceit shall not live out half their days. But as for me, I will trust in You" (Psalm 55:24).

OF ALL THE PEOPLES in the world, the Jewish people is called upon to be a positive role model and global leader for justice. This burden is complicated by history's unrelenting bigotry toward Jews. But this divine calling began with Abraham, and we answer it still. While Abraham's virtues allowed him to act with seeming ease, it is a more challenging task for his spiritual progeny. Although Abraham erred, his growth remains the hallmark of his greatness. He continued to seek ways to increase holiness and justice in the world.

All face adversity in life; some adversity impedes our functioning. Rabbi Menachem Mendel of Kotzk (late eighteenth/mid-nineteenth century, Poland) explains that Abraham's most difficult moment was coming off the mountain after the Binding of Isaac.[397] This incident was so traumatic that Abraham never recovered, though he overcame countless earlier tests. Prior to this final trauma, Abraham spent his life seeking to perpetuate blessings into the world. In contrast, the messenger Balaam tried to bring only curses into the world. Whether to curse or bless the world is a regular choice: Will I embrace my power? Will I bring hope or despair to the world, offer destruction or salvation, invoke blessing or curse? To be a descendant of Abraham, there can be only one option.

Once we understand our emotions, we can transform our inner world. The Chasidic sages thought deeply about how human beings can develop courage within the soul. All of us, no matter our background, have felt negativity well up inside us. Sometimes it is dormant, ready to explode at a moment's notice. Or perhaps it's in the open, clouding us in defeatism or depravity. The Chasidic masters teach that, generally, we ought to channel internal negative energy toward the good, and channel fear and despair toward holiness.[398] When we are not aware or in control of our inner negativity, we can oppress others and, thus, alienate God from human connection. Through redemptive acts of love and justice we bring God's presence into the world; we construct the spiritual universe on the moral playing field. To bring such redemption, we must gain awareness and control of our spiritual and psychological challenges.

In *Fire in the Soul*, spiritual psychologist Joan Borysenko describes three categories of courage that develop when encountering challenges in life:

Willful courage: cultivating the will to function in spite of fear.

Psychological courage: willing to become more honest, to face old pain, and to become one's true self.

Spiritual courage: learning to transform moments of fear into states of love and joy; seeking the sacred within the mundane and difficult aspects of life.[399]

We often look toward external comforts to allay our fears. Rabbi Kook teaches that this is dangerous and that we should instead turn toward developing inner perfection.[400] The Rabbis want us to face the primary human fear, death, head-on (see mishnah 3:1). To be honest about our fears, we should understand that they trigger uncomfortable emotional responses; we must hold them carefully, rather than be held by them.

Many people try to distract themselves from their concerns. Embracing emotional paradox is an authentic path, in which we make ourselves vulnerable to the full emotional intensity of extremes before resigning to sustained tension.

Many look to change their location when things aren't right. We often assume one's location determines one's mental state. On vacation, one is happy; at work, one is unhappy; at home, one is rested. But a change of location does little to change one's mental state. The Talmudic teaching "Change your location, change your luck" (BT *Rosh HaShanah* 16b) was intended to spur us to alter our outlook, acknowledging that it is within our power to create a change in our outlook and options. Shift the inner world, and the outer world shifts, too.

The Rev. Dr. Martin Luther King Jr. transformed his inner world, making his fears sources for vision and joy. The night before his assassination, Dr. King said:

> Well, I don't know what will happen now. We've got some difficult days ahead. But it doesn't matter with me now. Because I've been to the mountaintop. . . . And I've looked over. And I've seen the promised land. . . . I'm not fearing any man. Mine eyes have seen the glory of the coming of the Lord.[401]

The philosopher Kahlil Gibran called pain "the bitter pill of the inner physician," a wake-up call from a tough world that "breaks the shell of our understanding."[402] Revelations emerge when we break the shells hiding our true selves. We can wake up to new dimensions of joy. While this mishnah presents a stark choice, we shouldn't let the negative forces of the universe wash over us. Every day is a new calling, a new beginning to go back into the world, to face its unceasing desire to return to wholeness.

5:23

יְהוּדָה בֶן תֵּימָא אוֹמֵר: הֱוֵי עַז כַּנָּמֵר, וְקַל כַּנֶּשֶׁר, וְרָץ כַּצְּבִי,
וְגִבּוֹר כָּאֲרִי, לַעֲשׂוֹת רְצוֹן אָבִיךָ שֶׁבַּשָּׁמָיִם.

Y'hudah ben Teima said: Be bold as a leopard, light as an
eagle, swift as a deer, and strong as a lion, to carry out the will
of your Parent in heaven.

AMONG OUR HIGHEST PRIORITIES should be contributing to social
change. Jews have been at the vanguard of many modern social change
movements, even when we have also experienced marginalization
from mainstream society and within the movements themselves. We
have used our religious understanding and historical narrative of oppression, beginning with the enslavement of the Hebrews in Egypt, but
the most significant inspiration for our advocacy has been Jewish social
values, passed on through generations, that emphasize the unique role
Jews must play among the world's nations.

That this mishnah opens with a series of animal similes shows both
how simple and how profound it is. Animals are not merely instrumental to human pursuits, but reflect how we struggle through this complex world. Consider this story of how we might learn from animals:

> After the Maggid's death [in 1722], his disciples came together and
> talked about the things he had done. When it was Rabbi Schneur
> Zalman's turn, he asked them, "Do you know why your master
> went to the pond every day at dawn and stayed there for a while be-
> fore coming home again?" They did not know why. Rabbi Zalman
> continued, "He was learning the song with which the frogs praise
> God. It takes a very long time to learn that song."[403]

Be Bold as a Leopard

Jewish thought emphasizes linear history, associated with empowered
destiny. Compared to a model of cyclical history, a culture of fate in
which one is powerless to affect the swings of change, we work toward
progress, bolstered by the past. We embrace the responsibility that

accompanies free will, along with core values. But, we are a stubborn people, which is why, the Rabbis suggest, we were chosen to receive the Torah: "A *Tanna* taught in the name of Rabbi Meir: Why was the Torah given to Israel? Because they are insolent" (BT *Beitzah* 25b). That strength of will must be harnessed to support our families and communities, but also to serve as a "light unto the nations" (Isaiah 42:6; 49:6). Rabbi Jonathan Sacks writes:

> The concept of a covenantal bond between God and man is revolutionary and has no parallel in any other system of thought. For the ancients, man was at the mercy of impersonal forces that had to be placated. For Christianity, he is corrupt, tainted by an original sin that only the saving grace of God can remove. In Islam, man is called to absolute submission to God's will. In secular humanism, man is alone in a universe blind to his hopes and deaf to his prayers. Each of these is a coherent vision, and each has its adherents. But only in Judaism do we encounter the proposition that, despite their utter disparity, God and man come together as "partners in the work of creation." I know of no other vision that confers on mankind so great a dignity and responsibility.[404]

While Jews take pride in the uniqueness of Judaism, the tradition emphasizes the importance of global solidarity. When it comes to saving lives, for instance, Jewish law does not differentiate between Jews and gentiles. For Nachmanides, *tzedakah* (charity) has limits, but *pikuach nefesh* (saving lives) does not:

> We are commanded to save the life of non-Jews and to save them from harm, that if one was drowning in a river or if a stone fell upon one, then *we must use all of our strength* and be burdened with the rescue; and that if one was [deathly] ill, we must engage a healer.[405]

Found throughout Jewish thought are distinct meta-values geared toward justice: *chesed, mishpat*, and *tzedek*. *Chesed*, "kindness" or "love," is taking care of those around us through little acts of altruistic empathy. *Mishpat* is concerned with righting wrongs, reciprocity, equality, security, and social order. *Tzedakah*, meaning social and/or economic justice, is about the systemic imperative to construct and maintain a sustainable, just society that provides for the vulnerable.

Such values should motivate us to think deeply about our roles in staving off social wrongs and perpetuating kindness; in all that we do, working toward a more perfected world should be foremost. We should be motivated by the broader Jewish ethos to live *halachta bidrachav*, following the merciful ways of God (see above at 4:2, page 195). The important lesson to be derived, however, is not to operate in our own spheres, but to act as a larger community. Judaism emphasizes that each one of us has a unique role to play in leading change. It is tragic when people disregard their contributions, because everyone, no matter their place in the world, has something meaningful to offer.

Consider these five models to bring the world back together:

1. *Education* is how we understand complex situations, develop spiritual practice, learn leadership skills, and build knowledge that guides change. *Pirkei Avot* shows how the relationship between teachers and pupils elucidates the path of moral empowerment.

2. *Social entrepreneurship* creates sustainable enterprises that add value to society and contribute to the welfare of communities. It leverages novel ideas and cross-sector collaboration, especially between human services and businesses, to address present and future needs.

3. *Protest* brings immediate attention to crises but is best used as part of a larger, organized campaign for change. Agitators use radical and often creative methods to raise awareness and provoke public outrage. Protests have been the catalyst for reform along a broad spectrum of racial and gender inequalities.

4. *Advocacy* calls on the powerful—government officials, corporate leaders, business leaders—to implement top-down change. President Theodore Roosevelt's Square Deal launched the modern conservation movement by protecting much federal land from development, and President Lyndon B. Johnson's Great Society passed anti-poverty and healthcare legislation. Advocates—those hitting the streets and doing their part in the civic process—are often individuals

with recognized influence, who work on behalf of constituent groups to press lawmakers for real, positive societal changes.

5. *Community organizing* is complementary to advocacy; it is a bottom-up method to build power among the many to achieve common objectives by demanding change. Organizing requires patience, skill, focus, and commitment. It has been most successful in organized labor, farmworker rights, immigrant rights, and, of course, civil rights in the United States.

How, then, do we become responsible for one another? The Hebrew term for responsibility, *acharayut*, possibly has as its root *acher*, "other." To be responsible means to respond to the other, often born in a moment when no one else is present to assist. Hillel says, "In a place where there are no leaders [those of moral courage taking responsibility], strive to be a leader" (see *Pirkei Avot* 2:6). Each of us must ask: how does my particular position make me uniquely capable and responsible? Our answers will be influenced by proximity (who needs me in my town), relationships (who needs me among those I love), and severity (what crises or disasters require immediate action).

Be Light as an Eagle

Each of us must discover our unique passion. Many still respond to the most pressing global issues of our age with apathy; there is a shortage of passionate, visionary justice-seekers to lead us. We need radically inspired activism and community service. We need enflamed souls, who will pour their love, tears, sweat, and resources into immediate and systemic change. Maimonides helps us understand that we are obliged to be radically excessive in our healing of the world when we follow the path of Jewish piety. We must not only invigorate our general commitments to altruism, human rights, and activism, but also find our unique passions and then pursue them through service to the world. The *Sh'ma* commands us to serve (via love of God) with all our resources, *uvchol m'odecha*. Maimonides explained the virtues of excess in ethical pursuits:

The *chasid* [pious man] is the wise man who has inclined somewhat to an extreme in his ethical attributes . . . and his deeds are greater than his wisdom. Therefore he is called a *chasid*, in the sense of excess, because full commitment in a matter is called *chesed* [loving-kindness].[406]

We cannot evaluate our social justice options by utilizing formulaic conventions or religious dogma. Rather, we should follow conscience and reason to make life better for others and join with similar communities of other faiths that strive to improve the world. We must create open discourse so that our identities and lives can inspire responsibility; this is how we become enthusiastic and committed to our work. When we choose projects that feel right and speak to our souls, we ensure a sustainable commitment through deeper investment. When our souls are enflamed with passion for the causes we choose, we are moved to the kind of excessive devotion praised by Jewish tradition.

In order to serve those who cry out to us, we must find the unique power that enables each of us to make a difference. Nachmanides said that when circumstance puts someone in a position of influence, one is obligated to use that power to save others.[407] Rabbi Joseph Caro, best known as the author of the *Shulchan Aruch*, held that one must "expose oneself to possible danger [*safeik sakanah*] to save a human life."[408] Indeed, Rabbi Shlomo Zalman Auerbach (twentieth century, Israel) argues:

> In relation to the obligation to pay the costs of saving the life of a sick person who is in danger of dying: From the straightforward reading of [BT] *Sanhedrin* 73a we see that one is obligated to do everything to save him, and if not, one transgresses the negative commandment: Do not stand idly by the blood of your neighbor.[409]

Be Swift as a Deer

We are constrained by time, money, location, and relationships; tragically, we cannot help everyone. Given these limitations, what methods are appropriate to make the world a more just, safe, moral, and holy place? Whose needs should be a priority? When considering who needs help, it's easy to feel overwhelmed.

Emphasize methods of social action that make the greatest change, while furthering a flexible approach in order to make use of diverse talents. Some people are philanthropists, others are community organizers or advocates, and others are social workers or clergy. All must join to build a powerful base, while adhering to the principle *Chanoch lanaar al pi darko*, "Educate based on the path of the particular student" (Proverbs 22:6).

After identifying core values and concerns, we must learn to use our spheres of influence and skills effectively. If we are connected to power or wealth or have particular expertise, these should be taken into account. In addition to an assessment of our advantages and capabilities, we must understand the environment. We may be placed in an urgent situation and must act without delay:

> [In the name of Nachum Ish Gam Zu]: A poor man came and stood before me on the road, and said to me, "My teacher, sustain me [give me something to eat]!" I responded to him, "Wait until I unload some food from the donkey." I did not have a chance to unload the donkey before his soul departed [he died of hunger]. I went and fell on my face [fell into depression based on my insensitivity at having not prevented this man's death at the chance I was given]. (BT *Taanit* 21a)

We are all confronted with these opportunities. But sometimes, even decisions made with the best intentions don't achieve the desired effect. Peter Singer, a professor of bioethics at Princeton University, firmly rooted in the school of moral consequentialism, suggests that the superior path is a life of asceticism, in which one donates everything beyond one's basic needs to those who struggle to survive on a day-to-day basis.[410] A moral consequentialist is not merely interested in the cultivation of virtue or in preserving rights. The consequences of any individual act can be greater than intelligence can acknowledge. Thus, all moral deliberation must acknowledge this. The question is not whether it is right to do X at this moment, but how doing X might affect all parties in the future.

However, donating the majority of one's personal income, as Singer advocates, should not be done at the expense of creating change in other necessary ways. For example, a business owner may, in fact, be able to generate greater change by reforming the company's labor or environmental practices than by donating money.

Though we can best contribute in areas where we have the most passion and potential for influence, still, we cannot do so alone. We must work in partnership with our community, the people most affected by the problem, and experts. Coming face-to-face with others is a necessary element of working for social change. Even with limited resources, we should maintain personal relationships with those we seek to help, in order to understand their needs on their terms.

Yet, there is room for self-interest. Rabbi Joseph B. Soloveitchik writes:

> What one is longing for is his own self-fulfillment, which he believes he will find in his union with the other person. The emotion leaves its inner abode in order to find not the "you" but the "I.".... It only indicates that, because of self-interest, the person is committed to a state of mind which, regardless of one's self-centeredness, promotes goodwill and unites people.[411]

Self-interest, concomitant with a desire to spread good, is acceptable. Additionally, as we support each other, we are obligated to challenge each other respectfully. The Rabbis expected that we would hold others in our sacred communities accountable for our collective responsibility.[412]

Be Strong as a Lion

Of course, Jewish ethics is not only about avoiding wrong. We are mandated to repair the world (*tikkun olam*) from brokenness. We must go beyond our capacities to reach for the stars. This requires strength of mind, as well as our heart's purest convictions. We are asked to partner with others to help each other meet the potential for moral leadership. Encouraging growth for those in our communities by setting positive examples is a vital part of the Jewish moral enterprise and of creating a vibrant, just society. *Talmud Torah*, "the study of Torah," is a central responsibility for all Jews, no matter denomination or affiliation; yet, addressing communal needs has equal weight in our tradition.[413] Jewish education demands intellectual rigor, while also committing us to justice, charity, service, and interpersonal ethics. The Rabbis explain that one should not be content and comfortable when others suffer. Rather, they argue, "At a time when the community is steeped in distress, a person should not say, 'I will go to my house and eat and drink, and peace be upon you, my soul'" (BT *Taanit* 11a).

To make the greatest possible contribution to the world, each of us must take a *cheshbon hanefesh*, "self-accounting," of our influence and calling. When we address issues we are passionate about and contribute where we have the greatest potential, we ensure maximum sustainability and impact. To be sure, there are traditional minimum prescriptions for *tzedakah*, core responsibilities to family and community, and hierarchies of Jewish values. Rabbi Moshe Sofer (late eighteenth/early nineteenth century, Slovakia), however, maintains that any great need overrides the traditional hierarchy of priorities.[414] Rabbi Yechiel Michel Epstein, known as the Aruch HaShulchan, is even more explicit:

> There is something about this that is very difficult for me because if we understand these words literally—that some groups take priority over others—that implies that there is no requirement to give to groups lower on the hierarchy. And it is well known that every wealthy person has many poor relatives (and all the more so every poor person), so it will happen that a poor person without any rich relatives will die of hunger. And how could this possibly be? So it seems clear to me that the correct interpretation is that everyone, whether rich or poor, must also give to poor people who are not relatives.[415]

The strong among us are those who combine the best of intellect and soul to solve the complexity of the world's problems. We should use our strength not to be the best athletes, nor should we use our power to defeat others; we should treat this enterprise seriously. Rather, the best use of our strength is to fulfill the tasks that life presents us, live rigorously by our values, and connect with our Creator. For each of us to realize our full potential in the project of repairing the world, we must measure the efficacy of our work. We must be bold, light, swift, and strong . . . and adaptable. As a global Jewish community, we can reach new heights to create concrete change that brings peace and dignity to all human beings.

5:24

הוּא הָיָה אוֹמֵר: עַז פָּנִים לְגֵיהִנָּם, וּבֹשֶׁת פָּנִים לְגַן עֵדֶן.
יְהִי רָצוֹן מִלְפָנֶיךָ, יְיָ אֱלֹהֵינוּ וֵאלֹהֵ אֲבוֹתֵנוּ, שֶׁתִּבְנֶה עִירְךָ
בְיָמֵינוּ, וְתִתֵּן חֶלְקֵנוּ בְּתוֹרָתֶךָ.

He used to say: The brazen goes to *Geihinam* (hell), but the
shamefaced goes to the Garden of Eden. (May it be Your
will, God, our God and the God of our forefathers, that You
rebuild Your city in our days, and grant us our share in Your
Torah.)

BEING SHAMEFACED, *boshet panim*, can be understood as being humble or bashful. Humility can also signify the collective shaming of
the Jewish people through history. This mishnah can thus be read as
addressing character development, or as a condemnation of antisem-
itism. God stands with the oppressed, those who are shamed, and not
with the oppressor. The prayer included is neither addendum nor commentary, but aspiration. It places centuries of baseless hatred toward
Jews into perspective: This oppression will not have been for naught.
We shall have a homeland, sovereignty, and connection with the Creator. Central to this prayer is Judaism's focus on keeping Creation and
revelation burning brightly while we focus on redemption.

When we talk about the Edenic vision of the world, we are concerned
with the sources of divine light. Jewish tradition proposes that there
are three sources of light that shine on the world:

> The light of Creation—*Or B'reishit*
> The light of revelation—*Or Sinai*
> The light of redemption—*Or Mashiach*

We take the light of *Or B'reishit* and *Or Sinai*, which pull us back into
history, but use them to propel us forward to *Or Mashiach*—redeemed
soul, redeemed Torah, redeemed society, and even a redeemed God. For
many Jews, modernity runs counter to our religion's very survival, but
to be modern means to situate ourselves in the future, at the forefront

of social change and paradigm shifts, guided by the Torah and fueled by *Or Mashiach*, the light of redemption.

In the fifth century BCE, Protagoras led the philosophical transition from a focus on the universe toward a focus on human values. This shift in understanding set the intellectual stage for Socrates and Plato to explore questions of virtue, justice, and human experience. The Rabbis were on the same page but spoke in the language of law and narrative rather than philosophy. Traditionally, Jewish thinkers embraced *y'ridat hadorot*,[416] the idea that humanity has been in decline since the revelation at Sinai and rendered impotent in our spiritual pursuits. Perhaps there is value in understanding one's individual insignificance when compared to the history of all humanity. Indeed, since the Enlightenment, society has elevated the individual, perhaps going so far as to neglect the collective good; and today we should meaningfully interweave the two—focus on the cosmos, universe, world, nation, or society from the perspective of the individual and focus on the greatness of past contributions in addition to current progress.

The power that accompanies light can cause us to misperceive our own greatness. Such hubris stands in direct contrast to the humility that we must cultivate. Consider this (extreme) verse:

> It has been taught: "God is angered every day" (Psalm 7:12). . . . [And when is God angry?] A baraita was taught in the name of Rabbi Meir, "When the sun shines [in the morning] and all the kings of the East and West place their crowns on their heads and bow to the sun, the Holy One of Blessing [God] immediately becomes angry." (BT *B'rachot* 7a)

In Carl Stern's 1972 interview with Rabbi Abraham Joshua Heschel on the NBC program *The Eternal Light*, Rabbi Heschel said:

> Let them [young people] remember that there is a meaning beyond absurdity. Let them be sure that every little deed counts, that every word has power, and that we can, everyone, do our share to redeem the world in spite of all absurdities and all the frustrations and all disappointments. And above all, remember that the meaning of life is to build a life as if it were a work of art. You're not a machine. And you are young. Start working on this great work of art called your own existence.[417]

Focusing on redemption stirs within us the realization that our every little action is significant. Everything we do affects something else. One of the great tragedies of the human condition is that millions of people live honest and earnest lives, filled with love and dedicated to the service of others, but pass from the world never fully appreciating their own greatness and holiness, because they neither fit society's definition of hero, nor sought accolades.

Our unique gifts are made all the more powerful when they become illuminated through the infinite potential brought by divine light. The prerequisite for this divine illumination is understanding its source, which is the presence of God within the structure of the universe. Divine light is more than a physical object. Indeed, this light is suffused with possibilities of eternity. Achieving such understanding means striving with all our might to learn. Religion, if primarily situated in the past, can birth complacency, stagnation, and an exclusionary spirit, which enable the practitioner to retreat from modernity into the ghetto. The Rev. Dr. Martin Luther King Jr. taught, "The ultimate measure of a man is not where he stands in moments of comfort and convenience, but where he stands at times of challenge and controversy."[418] Supreme Court justice Oliver Wendell Holmes once admonished a young colleague, "It is required [that you] share the passion and action of [your] time at the peril of being judged not to have ever lived."[419] We must leave our comfort zone to engage in our present time and strive for a better future.

Let us take to heart the understanding that we were endowed with *Or B'reishit*, blessed with *Or Sinai*, and that it is now our duty to seek *Or Mashiach* through the spiritual cultivation of inner light. All of us are blessed with ideas, gifts, skills, and feelings to improve the world. Each person can contribute in a way that no one else can.

To cultivate the divine light in our lives is to embrace our identity as a people blessed with incredible tradition and to utilize the knowledge, spiritual revelation, and ethical obligations that come from our past to make the world we inhabit more holy and just, not only for ourselves, but for all forms of life. This is our duty, our path toward everlasting *Or Mashiach*.

5:25

הוּא הָיָה אוֹמֵר: בֶּן חָמֵשׁ לַמִּקְרָא, בֶּן עֶשֶׂר לַמִּשְׁנָה,
בֶּן שְׁלֹשׁ עֶשְׂרֵה לַמִּצְוֹת, בֶּן חֲמֵשׁ עֶשְׂרֵה לַתַּלְמוּד,
בֶּן שְׁמוֹנֶה עֶשְׂרֵה לַחֻפָּה, בֶּן עֶשְׂרִים לִרְדוֹף, בֶּן שְׁלֹשִׁים לַכֹּחַ,
בֶּן אַרְבָּעִים לַבִּינָה, בֶּן חֲמִשִׁים לָעֵצָה, בֶּן שִׁשִּׁים לַזִּקְנָה,
בֶּן שִׁבְעִים לַשֵׂיבָה, בֶּן שְׁמוֹנִים לַגְּבוּרָה, בֶּן תִּשְׁעִים לָשׁוּחַ,
בֶּן מֵאָה כְּאִלּוּ מֵת וְעָבַר וּבָטַל מִן הָעוֹלָם.

He used to say: A five-year-old begins Scripture; a ten-year-old begins Mishnah; a thirteen-year-old becomes obliged to observe the commandments; a fifteen-year-old begins the study of Talmud; an eighteen-year-old goes to the marriage canopy; a twenty-year-old begins pursuit [of a career]; a thirty-year-old attains full strength; a forty-year-old attains understanding; a fifty-year-old can offer counsel; a sixty-year-old attains seniority; a seventy-year-old attains a ripe old age; an eighty-year-old shows strength; a ninety-year-old becomes stooped over; a hundred-year-old is as if they are dead, passed away and ceased from the world.

RABBI LEVI YITZCHAK of Berditchev, the K'dushat Levi, teaches that there are two types of wonder a person can experience in his or her life: *yirat p'nimit* and *yirat chitzonit*, internal and external awe.[420] At about the same time in history, Immanuel Kant writes, "Two things fill me with wonder: the starry sky above me and the moral law within me."[421] Though these two individuals were worlds apart, both thought deeply about cultivating rich inner lives. It is well within our ability to simultaneously cultivate a deep spiritual relationship with the world and a profound inner spiritual center that lasts throughout our too-short lives.

This mishnah teaches about the relationship between learning and aging. First, we are not to view aging as something negative. Rather, as an individual advances in years, one gains wisdom, and one's participation in society becomes more valuable.

The last two stages of life should give youth a sense of urgency, as well as feelings of humility: each young person will one day, if they are fortunate, become old and frailer. Read this passage prescriptively, and it says that spiritual life is a process of exercising one's morality, rather than one's muscles. The young are to protect the old, and the old are to nurture the young. This cycle fortifies the relationships between the generations, creating a sustainable bridge of knowledge and enlightenment. Thus, the goal in life is not to hit conformist milestones, but to be alive—that is, to develop the inner life. When we are wearing a headset, we can easily forget that everyone else's reality isn't enriched by the music that we hear. A vibrant religious life can be like wearing those headphones. One sees and feels spiritual realities through ritual and prayer that others may not be experiencing. That music, when authentic, continues to play at work, home, anywhere.

All people have their unique subjective abilities to perceive deep spiritual truths. Rabbi Yaakov Tzvi Mecklenburg writes:

> The truth is that the people of Israel were not all equal in their spiritual level. And they did not see or perceive the same kind of revelation at Sinai. Rather, each one was able to receive this revelational experience only in accordance with the spiritual condition of [their] soul. Every Jew saw something, but what they experienced was directly proportional to the preparation they had put into it. Those who were less prepared experienced only a minimal level of revelation at Sinai. And the one who prepared more received more. And this is the meaning of a "consuming fire." The perception of God's greatness is exactly the same as the way fire takes holds of various objects. There are items that are by nature combustible and when you touch them with a flame they produce an enormous fire. But, there are other items that when you put a flame to them remain immune and nothing will happen to them. Just like nature has made certain materials receptive to fire, so it is with the Sinai revelation.[422]

Those who are on fire, who keep their focus on the mission and their eyes on the prize, resemble angels on earth. In the Jacob's ladder story, the angels were "going up and coming down" the ladder (Genesis 28:12). The ancient Rabbis point out that the order seems wrong: angels should descend first and only then ascend back to the heavens.

Rabbi Lawrence Kushner offers an elegant explication of this thought based upon the midrash in *B'reishit Rabbah* (68:12):

> But there is another, even more obvious interpretation. The angels did not reside in heaven at all. They lived on earth. They were ordinary human beings. And, like ordinary human beings, they shuttled back and forth between heaven and earth. The trick is to remember, after you descend, what you understood when you were high on the ladder.[423]

If we are connected to heaven and we are connected to earth, then people should be committed to ideals that call for creating pragmatic change: Sit in light and sit in darkness. Be aflame and rekindle. Ascend and descend. If we wish to cultivate ourselves to live and lead in the physical world, then we must look inside ourselves for the spark of spirituality, developing our inner point, the *n'kudat p'nimit*.

Rabbi Jonathan Sacks offers insight into the traditional Jewish psyche: "Jews were always a tiny people, yet our ancestors survived by believing that eternity is found in the simple lives of ordinary human beings. They found God in homes, families and relationships."[424] As Rabbi Sacks writes, the Jewish religion proposes that tuning in to our souls can connect us to a miraculous existence. It is a shame that anyone waits until retirement or until they are less busy. By then, perhaps, the ability to live fully might be drained. Living fully cannot be put on hold. The mind and soul are instruments that must be played to keep the music alive.

Meditation and prayer are but two ways to light our souls on fire. To be meaningful, prayer needs to emanate from one's being, rather than just be rote recitation of liturgy. Bachya ibn Pakuda observes, "Prayer without *kavanah* [spiritual focus] is like a body without a soul."[425] Similarly, Maimonides teaches, "True *kavanah* means freedom from all extraneous thought and complete awareness of the self within the greater presence of the Divine."[426] And in her moving verse, American poet Mary Oliver writes in "Praying" about the delicate nature that prayers have on the psyche and the soul:

> It doesn't have to be
> the blue iris, it could be

weeds in a vacant lot, or a few
small stones; just
pay attention, then patch

a few words together and don't try
to make them elaborate, this isn't
a contest but the doorway

into thanks, and a silence in which
another voice may speak.[427]

Prayer is perpetual struggle, and we must work to instill in ourselves its imperfect yearning. We cannot lapse into rhythmic routine, but must approach prayer with wonder aimed at its incorporeal beauty. Writing in 1949, the physicist Max Planck explains how wonder, a wonder that is not too far off from the awe that prayer should engender, fuels scientific inquiry:

> The feeling of wonderment is the source and inexhaustible fountainhead of the desire for knowledge. It drives the child irresistibly on to solve the mystery, and if in his attempt he encounters a causal relationship, he will not tire of repeating the same experiment ten times—a hundred times—in order to taste the thrill of discovery over and over again. The reason why the adult no longer wonders is not because he has solved the riddle of life, but because he has grown accustomed to the laws governing this world picture. But the problem of why these particular laws, and no others, hold, remains for him just as amazing and inexplicable as for the child. He who does not comprehend this situation, misconstrues its profound significance, and he who has reached the stage where he no longer wonders about anything, merely demonstrates that he has lost the art of reflective reasoning.[428]

Just as Planck explains how age and routine make us lose our sense of wonder for science, the same applies with prayer and meditation. We simply grow accustomed to the process, words, and actions. As Planck discerned, however, wonder and amazement can still abound. We just "misconstrue its profound significance."

We must always seek to keep the ideals of our religion, prayers, and vocations alive, regardless of the challenge of growing accustomed to our practices. Contemporary philosopher Susan Neiman writes that keeping ideals alive can seem a losing battle, an unattainable goal that causes great distress, but that human dignity requires love for ideals:

> Keeping ideals alive is much harder than dismissing them, for it guarantees a lifetime of dissatisfaction. Ideals are like horizons—goals toward which you can move but never actually attain. Human dignity requires the love of ideals for their own sake, but nothing guarantees that the love will be requited. You might fail to reach your object, all your life long.[429]

In religion, we don't only engage in private spirituality; we also engage in synergistic striving—in collective covenant. While taking part in religious traditions and practices with community, we affect each other deeply and come to grow together. Theodore White, a political journalist, describes how a piece of metal and a block of gold, when held together, will exchange molecules through a process our eyes cannot see, akin to the way people share parts of themselves with others:

> When people are pressed close, they act the same way. Part of you enters them, part of them enters you. It is humbling and frightening to think that every person you've hated, or feared, or ran away from, or even loved is now a part of you. It is humbling and exacting to know that by our merely being together over the years, throughout close proximity, something happens within us that even science cannot describe.[430]

One by-product of communal interaction and support is inspiration for deeper thinking and creativity. Yet, even in solitude, a human is creative, endowed with independent thinking and ingenuity. From the beginning of time, humans have always had creative potential, even in isolation. Rabbi Yosei, one of the Sages, describes how Adam used his creativity to breed mules:

> Two things entered the thoughts [of God] to be created on Erev Shabbat but were not created until the departure of Shabbat. At the departure of Shabbat, God placed in Adam understanding reflective of the divine model. And [as a result] Adam brought two stones and ground them together, and flame shot out from them.

He brought two animals [a horse and a donkey] and crossbred them, and a mule issued from them. (BT *P'sachim* 54a)

Rabbi Yosei's teaching addresses the question of how people function within societies and learn. For centuries, philosophers and laymen have compared learning collectively with learning independently. John Locke argues that one should be educated within the norms of community,[431] whereas Jean-Jacques Rousseau argues that, theoretically, one should be isolated, because each individual has unique developmental and educational needs, according to each individual's unique nature; Rousseau makes the point that one must be oneself.[432]

The Kotzker Rebbe teaches that one of the most spiritually poisonous types of religious life is to engage in activity because someone else does it or because it is one's routine.[433] On the other hand, as Jews, we understand both the power of community and routine. One of the greatest rewards we can ever give to others is to light their spiritual fire and inspire them to fulfill their life purpose. In each encounter, we have the choice and power to lower others or to raise them up. We rise in solidarity when we help others rise.

We, the Jewish people, have upheld our ideals for thousands of years, enduring hateful and murderous persecution because of our steadfast refusal to turn from them. Our devotion to idealism sets us apart, and we must never shy from it. Instead, we must wear it as a badge of honor and imbue our actions with it. In all we do, we must strive to be fully engaged, ever mindful of the meaning of our actions, and cognizant of the power we have to lift our brothers and sisters to new heights. Each moment provides this holy opportunity, and we must not forsake the moment. Through learning, leading, and prayer, we have incredible opportunities to reach new levels within ourselves and embrace the light that burns inside. We must cultivate that light to live meaningfully. There is no need to wait until we have more time, more money, fewer responsibilities; as Rabbi Jonathan Sacks suggests, all we must do is turn our souls on, and we will connect to the marvelous. It should be our prayer that we live each day with open hearts, open minds, and open souls, ever aware of others. And ourselves.

5:26

בֶּן בַּג בַּג אוֹמֵר: הֲפָךְ־בָּהּ וְהַפֶּךְ בָּהּ, דְּכֹלָּא בַהּ. וּבַהּ תֶּחֱזֵי,
וְסִיב וּבְלֵה בַהּ, וּמִנַּהּ לָא תְזוּעַ – שֶׁאֵין לָךְ מִדָּה טוֹבָה
מִמֶּנָּה. בֶּן הֵא הֵא אוֹמֵר: לְפֻם צַעֲרָא אַגְרָא.

Ben Bag Bag says: Delve in it [the Torah] and continue to delve
in it, for everything is in it; look deeply in it; grow old and
gray over it, and do not stir from it, for you can have no better
portion than it. Ben Hei Hei says: The reward is in proportion
to the exertion.

IN SOME EDITIONS of *Pirkei Avot* (including this one), the fifth chapter concludes with this warm and direct teaching. Go, Ben Bag Bag and
Ben Hei Hei say, and learn the Torah in all its forms. After multiple
mishnayot that present litanies about the many forms people take in the
world, this mishnah points to what's fundamental about Jewish learning. All a person has to do is study the Torah and grow in one's wisdom.
This is the key to a healthy intellectual life. But, of course, our Jewish
texts are not easy. They require work. We have become familiar with
the tactics of bigots, who distort our religious texts to advance their hatred, although most people in our pluralistic society reject such tactics.
If there is a guiding principle to Jewish epistemology, it is that Torah
is an expansive exercise of the mind. The whole of Torah is dedicated
to the radical notion that human beings are better than their physical
selves, that we have the inherent ability to develop our potential and
make it real in the world. We take the mundane aspects of life—food,
sleep, sex—and elevate them. We take our physical matter and transform it into something inexpressible.

Through the Torah, we can find the basis for all matters in life; we can
find our relationship to everything divine and everything corporeal. To
actualize the ideal of the living Torah, *Torat chayim*, we must remove all
limitations from it; it must speak to all aspects of our life and elevate
our existence at all moments. As Ben Hei Hei implies in this mishnah,

it takes hard work to maintain this type of consciousness, and we will only experience the gains if we invest through this holy process.

How might we respond to a skeptic who points to the morally troubling verse "When . . . the Eternal your God delivers them to you and you defeat them, you must doom them to destruction: grant them no terms and give them no quarter" (Deuteronomy 7:1–2)? Or, consider the many admonitions in the Torah to be kind to strangers and to remember that we were once strangers in the land of Egypt (Exodus 22:20). How do we reconcile this command: "In the towns of the latter peoples, however, which the Eternal your God is giving you as a heritage, you shall not let a soul remain alive. No, you must proscribe them—the Hittites and the Amorites, the Canaanites and the Perizzites, the Hivites and the Jebusites—as the Eternal your God has commanded you" (Deuteronomy 20:16–17)? Or this: "Samuel said to Saul, 'I am the one the Eternal sent to anoint you king over God's people Israel. Therefore, listen to the Eternal's command! . . . Now go, attack Amalek, and proscribe all that belongs to him. Spare no one, but kill alike men and women, infants and sucklings, oxen and sheep, camels, and asses!'" (I Samuel 15:1–3)?[433a]

Four philosophical approaches assist in understanding troubling biblical and Jewish texts. The *divine command morality argument* says that because God is the source and determiner of all morality, there is no contradiction between morality and God's commands. Only the divine mind can understand the grand moral picture. Thus, moral reasoning and authority are only the products of God and nothing else. The underlying logical problem in this argument is that humans must abandon God's greatest gifts: moral conscience, reason, and autonomy.

Second is the *subservience argument* proposed by nineteenth-century philosopher Søren Kierkegaard: if there is a contradiction between religion and morality, it is only because God has the power to suspend morality.[434] Humans must abandon our conscience in a heroic sacrifice to the divine command, which transcends all. This Binding of Isaac–type mentality creates a religious personality that is unquestioningly subservient. The problem here is that one must consciously act against one's own moral intuition, and that is spiritually and socially dangerous. The quintessential heretical argument says that when morality contradicts the religious command, we must choose morality over religious duty. This individual may be moral but is not generally deemed religious.

The *casuistic argument* says that humanity needs both human morality and divine command and that all contradictions can be resolved. Through moral reasoning, we understand and embrace the divine command. We will never be compelled to obey anything we view as immoral if we cultivate our intellectual and spiritual faculties to understand how religion and morality are reconciled.

The fourth approach, the *presupposed compatibility argument*, is perhaps the most compelling and demanding for the modern religious person. In working every day to understand our texts, our world, and our hearts and souls, we can best achieve our Jewish mission. The tenth-century rabbi Saadyah Gaon explained that if one finds a contradiction between tradition and reason, then one has made a mistake, because the two are compatible to the alert mind.[435] To correct this mistake, relearn the text, analyzing it over and over, until reason is consistent with tradition. Read charitably, we should never heed the human faculty for moral reasoning alone. The text is merely the starting point for a greater journey.

Rabbi Kook summarizes this later point:

> It is forbidden for religious behavior to compromise a personal, natural, moral sensibility. If it does, our fear of heaven is no longer pure. An indication of its purity is that our nature and moral sense becomes more exalted as a consequence of religious inspiration. But if these opposites occur, then the moral character of the individual or group is dismissed by religious observance, and we have certainly been mistaken in our faith.[436]

The best purpose for studying our sacred texts is not to fixate on troublesome passages or justify the behavior of another era, but to become motivated to act in the true spirit of *tikkun olam*. When we read Abraham's powerful plea, "Must not the Judge of all the earth do justly?" (Genesis 18:25), we are given the privilege to challenge all axiomatic dogmas and work toward the comprehensive truth of the universe. We should bear in mind that Abraham came from Ur in

Mesopotamia, in modern-day Iraq. This region has for millennia been plagued by absolutist god-kings, who waged brutal war on one another. Even when codes of law were created, they often only reinforced the extreme powers of the monarch. We should be grateful that we emerged from this land as a people of faith, law, and morality, while acknowledging that we have not always measured up to our ideals.

Chapter 6

6:1

רַבִּי מֵאִיר אוֹמֵר: כָּל הָעוֹסֵק בַּתּוֹרָה לִשְׁמָהּ זוֹכֶה לִדְבָרִים
הַרְבֵּה. וְלֹא עוֹד, אֶלָּא שֶׁכָּל הָעוֹלָם כֻּלּוֹ כְּדַי הוּא לוֹ. נִקְרָא
רֵעַ, אָהוּב, אוֹהֵב אֶת הַמָּקוֹם, אוֹהֵב אֶת הַבְּרִיּוֹת, מְשַׂמֵּחַ
אֶת הַמָּקוֹם, מְשַׂמֵּחַ אֶת הַבְּרִיּוֹת. וּמַלְבַּשְׁתּוֹ עֲנָוָה וְיִרְאָה.
וּמַכְשַׁרְתּוֹ לִהְיוֹת צַדִּיק וְחָסִיד, יָשָׁר, וְנֶאֱמָן. וּמְרַחַקְתּוֹ מִן
הַחֵטְא. וּמְקָרַבְתּוֹ לִידֵי זְכוּת. וְנֶהֱנִין מִמֶּנּוּ עֵצָה וְתוּשִׁיָּה,
בִּינָה וּגְבוּרָה, שֶׁנֶּאֱמַר: לִי־עֵצָה וְתוּשִׁיָּה, אֲנִי בִינָה, לִי
גְבוּרָה (משלי ח:יד). וְנוֹתֶנֶת לוֹ מַלְכוּת וּמֶמְשָׁלָה וְחִקּוּר דִּין.
וּמְגַלִּין לוֹ רָזֵי תוֹרָה, וְנַעֲשֶׂה כְּמַעְיָן שֶׁאֵינוֹ פוֹסֵק, וּכְנָהָר
שֶׁמִּתְגַּבֵּר וְהוֹלֵךְ. וֶהֱוֵי צָנוּעַ וְאֶרֶךְ רוּחַ, וּמוֹחֵל עַל עֶלְבּוֹנוֹ.
וּמְגַדַּלְתּוֹ וּמְרוֹמַמְתּוֹ עַל כָּל הַמַּעֲשִׂים.

Rabbi Meir said: Those who engage in Torah study for its
own sake merit many things; furthermore, [the creation of]
the entire world is worthwhile for their sake alone. They are
called, "Friend, Beloved." They love the Omnipresent, love
God's creatures, gladden the Omnipresent, and gladden God's
creatures. [The Torah] clothes them in humility and awe; it
makes them fit to be righteous, devout, fair, and faithful. It
moves them away from sin and draws them near to merit.
From such persons, people enjoy counsel and wisdom, understanding, and strength, as it is said: "Mine are counsel and
wisdom, I am understanding, mine is strength" (Proverbs 8:14).
[The Torah] gives such persons sovereignty and dominion
and analytical judgment; the secrets of the Torah are revealed
to them; they become like an unceasing fountain and like a
steadily strengthening river. They become modest, patient,
and forgiving of insult to themselves. [The Torah] makes them
great and exalts them above all things.

THE PROCESS of spiritual growth is intricate. Humans are delicate beings, and the more we change, the more we try to impede such change. This is inevitable; this is human nature. For most of our lives, we become accustomed to routine; we repeat actions day in and day out. Our self-perception fluctuates little while moving through life's daily banalities. But when the routine is disrupted, we learn how we'll cope with alien experiences. This begins at birth; what right-thinking person would ever want to leave the warmth and support of the womb? This first action of personhood becomes the framework for living a life in which one overcomes arduous obstacles and takes control of one's destiny.

Throughout our development—intellectual, physical, emotional—we are given opportunities to expand our minds, go into the world, and devour the manifold philosophies that explain the human condition. As we do so, knowledge grows, as does appreciation for the multiple cosmologies that guide human potential. But to master spiritual development, we have to break the internal blockages that hold us back. Intellectually, we have to challenge truths to reach higher truths, trouble inner paradigms and mental models, and attain new heights with our wits and wisdom.

We need to be receptive to the notion of being spiritually creative in all of our endeavors; it is far too much trouble to consider being spiritually destructive. Indeed, this latter consideration only contracts one's potential, limiting the scope of one's development by using the nuanced language and broad beauty of religious philosophy and using it to destroy, maim, and inflict horrors on others. At the same time, using spirituality in creative ways breaks down obsolete norms and dilates our minds to receive novel ideas and experiences. In *torah lishmah*, learning for its own sake, we have a potential to inhabit a creativity that is also productively destructive. Is there a way to harmonize these seemingly contradictory views? Rabbi Kook explains:

> There is a holiness that builds and a holiness that destroys. The benefits of the holiness that builds are visible, while the benefits of the holiness that destroy are hidden, because it destroys in order to build what is nobler than what has been built already.

One who understands the secret of the holiness that destroys can mend many souls, and one's capacity for mending is in accordance with one's understanding. From the holiness that destroys there emerge great warriors who bring blessing to the world. . . . One whose spirit cannot reach out to the wide horizons, one who does not search for the truth with their whole heart, cannot tolerate spiritual destruction but neither do they have any edifices they have built themselves.[437]

This is true not only for our inner world but also for all revolutions. A prior societal model has to be destroyed for a new and more advanced model to emerge. Pain and loss are involved in drastic change, whether it occurs slowly or rapidly. But we feel this in miniature throughout our lives: The interests of a child cannot be the same as those of an adult. In that gap of time, a new person emerges, invigorated from past experiences but ready to face new ones.

This is why the Israelites needed forty years wandering in the desert to transition from being slaves to being a free people. To destroy the slave mentality is no small matter. While physical fetters can be snapped within moments, it takes longer to escape the prison of negative beliefs. And this is what God asks of us each day. Each of us must retreat to the desert to reflect and transition, but then emerge into our own promised land to live with our new truths.

Incorporating the vast fount of knowledge of Torah learning into our lives is a reward rather than a burden for the Jewish people. When we reach a new understanding of divinity, human interconnectivity, and the dynamism of spiritual maturation, then we can celebrate our elevated consciousness. We may mourn that the previous relationship with God and the cosmos is now dead, never to be recovered, but we can also rejoice. The world is filled with a new light, and there is no choice but to carry on. We must destroy inner worlds in order to build new ones. When we realize the vastness of our potential, we can in turn dedicate our full selves to our Creator and the holy mission with which we have been tasked. By studying our sacred texts, we open ourselves to the possibility of receiving divine assistance should we want to let it into our hearts.

This is not an easy task, nor was it ever meant to be. Indeed, when we become people who cling to wisdom and yearn for higher truth, we can achieve so much more than ever imagined. From this intellectual pursuit, it is essential that we cultivate the right character traits (*midot*) and move toward becoming spiritually enlightened people.

6:2

אָמַר רַבִּי יְהוֹשֻׁעַ בֶּן לֵוִי: בְּכָל יוֹם וָיוֹם בַּת קוֹל יוֹצֵאת מֵהַר
חוֹרֵב וּמַכְרֶזֶת וְאוֹמֶרֶת: אוֹי לָהֶם לַבְּרִיּוֹת מֵעֶלְבּוֹנָהּ שֶׁל
תּוֹרָה – שֶׁכָּל מִי שֶׁאֵינוֹ עוֹסֵק בְּתַלְמוּד תּוֹרָה הֲרֵי זֶה
נָזוּף, שֶׁנֶּאֱמַר: נֶזֶם זָהָב בְּאַף חֲזִיר, אִשָּׁה יָפָה וְסָרַת טָעַם
(משלי יא:כב). וְאוֹמֵר: וְהַלֻּחֹת מַעֲשֵׂה אֱלֹהִים הֵמָּה, וְהַמִּכְתָּב
מִכְתַּב אֱלֹהִים הוּא, חָרוּת עַל־הַלֻּחֹת (שמות לב:טז). אַל תִּקְרִי
חָרוּת אֶלָּא חֵרוּת, שֶׁאֵין לְךָ בֶּן חוֹרִין אֶלָּא מִי שֶׁעוֹסֵק
בְּתַלְמוּד תּוֹרָה. וְכָל הָעוֹסֵק בְּתַלְמוּד תּוֹרָה הֲרֵי זֶה
מִתְעַלֶּה, שֶׁנֶּאֱמַר: וּמִמַּתָּנָה נַחֲלִיאֵל וּמִנַּחֲלִיאֵל בָּמוֹת
(במדבר כא:יט).

Rabbi Y'hoshua ben Levi said: Every single day a heavenly
voice emanates from Mount Horeb, proclaiming and saying,
"Woe to them, to the people, because of [their] insult to the
Torah!" For whoever does not occupy themselves with the
Torah is called, "Rebuked," as it is said: "Like a golden ring
in a swine's snout is a beautiful woman who turns away from
good judgment" (Proverbs 11:22). And it says: "The tablets are
God's handiwork and the script was God's script *charut*
[engraved] on the tablets (Exodus 32:16). Do not read *charut*
[engraved] but *cheirut* [freedom], for you can have no freer
person than one who engages in the study of the Torah.
And anyone who engages in the study of the Torah becomes
elevated, as it is said: "From Mattanah to Nachaliel, and from
Nachaliel to Bamot" (Numbers 21:19).

REVELATION IS THE CENTRAL, powerful moment in the Judaic religious narrative. Scores of thinkers and theologians have wrestled with
the manifold dimensions of revelation and its role in Jewish destiny. Yet
the splendor of revelation is nearly impossible for twenty-first-century
minds to grasp. We should nonetheless strive to access the experience

of our ancestors. In the Talmud, there is vigorous debate on how the Israelites responded to the revelation at Mount Sinai:

> And Rabbi Y'hoshua ben Levi said: With every single statement that emanated from the mouth of the Holy One of Blessing, the souls of the Jewish people departed [from their bodies], as it is stated: "My soul departed as God spoke" (Song of Songs 5:6). Now, since their souls departed after the first statement, how could they have received the second statement? [God] brought down the dew with which God will resurrect the dead in the future and resurrected them. (BT *Shabbat* 88b)

In this mishnah, Rabbi Y'hoshua ben Levi teaches something quite radical: "Every single day a heavenly voice emanates from Mount Horeb." Revelation continues. Indeed, revelation was never intended to be a single moment in history. Instead, it was the start of a living, reciprocal relationship, an ongoing communication. We are charged with listening to the past while concentrating on the present. When they seem to clash, listen more closely. When we listen to past and present, inward and outward, we attain our freedom. It is a liberty built upon responsibility and commitment to the noblest truths, which will set us free from our base instincts, desires, and the most fleeting ideologies of our time. Former American Jewish World Service president Ruth Messinger remarked, "Listening is a prerequisite for action. Listening is a principle for living Jewishly in a globalized world."[438] As the world is evolving fast, we must listen more and more deeply and responsively.

But there is discord:

> And Rabbi Y'hoshua ben Levi said: With every single statement that emanated from the mouth of the Holy One of Blessing, the Jewish people retreated twelve miles, and the ministering angels helped them to totter back. (BT *Shabbat* 88b)

There is a distinct paradox in this account of the Israelites approaching the Divine. The first narrative tells of love—a return to God—but the second shows fear and backing away with awe. The first is about the limits to human understanding of the truth of revelation, and the latter is about the limits to human courage.

By definition, revelation means that we learn something powerful or startling that we did not know before. With religious revelation, we do not merely walk away with new knowledge, but also with a strengthened spiritual relationship. Further, revelation is effective only if it leads to holistic transformation. We cannot live the same way after attaining this new knowledge and after this relationship has been strengthened. Our minds, hearts, and relationship to the Revealer are transformed. We are called upon to imitate the Divine and thus create our own relationships that include intimate revelation; indeed, revelation should not be limited to intellectual and religious learning.

We share concern for those we love, and we assert justice for strangers. So too, must we embrace learning with strangers and revelation with those we love. In this sacred space, we can allow ourselves to be vulnerable and embrace shared experience that will change us. Some commentators suggest that God revealed only the nearly silent *alef* of *anochi*—the first word of the Ten Commandments (Exodus 20:2).[438a] This suggests that spiritual presence is just as important as the actual content. Sometimes just an *alef* (א), spoken with all one's being, can be deeply revelatory.

When participating in religious life, we should take profoundly inspirational and transformative moments from text and tradition and assimilate them into daily life. Sinaitic revelation should become a part of daily prayer and living. The wedding canopy, the chuppah, should be carried into daily love and responsibilities. On a regular basis, celebrating the Sabbath is a consistent reminder of the sanctity and preciousness of time.

When we pray, we seek to connect to the Above. But that leads to another question about revelation: Does God pray as well?

In one Talmudic story, the Rabbis teach that God does indeed pray:

> Rabbi Yochanan said in the name of Rabbi Yosei ben Zimra: "How do we know that God prays? Because it says: 'I will bring them to My holy mountain, and make them joyful in My house of prayer [literally: house of My prayer]' (Isaiah 56:7). It does not say 'house of *their* prayer,' but 'house of *My* prayer.' This teaches that God prays. What does God pray? 'May it be My will before Me that

> My mercy will suppress My anger, and that My compassion will prevail over My [other] attributes, and that I will deal with My children with compassion, and that I may treat them beyond the strict interpretation of law.'" (BT *B'rachot* 7a)

Imagine for a moment the radical nature of this discussion. Alongside their erudition, the Rabbis show their ability to make God an immediate and perceptible presence. Their depiction of God isn't that of a divine being who fades into the background to let humanity do all of the inner work that it takes for prayer. God is an active participant in the rituals, rather than simply a distant observer of them.

Relatedly, another passage goes so far as to suggest that God even "wears" *t'fillin* during prayer (BT *B'rachot* 6a). Of course, some commentators don't take these teachings literally. After all, to whom would God pray? Further, God doesn't have to inhabit a body—as we are to understand the idea of a body—in order to don *t'fillin*. This teaching is still valuable. We learn that prayer is a sign not of weakness but of strength. It takes courage and humility to pause and reflect upon ourselves and existence. God prays and thus praises Creation and reflects upon existence. We learn that God intentionally made the world imperfect, so that humans could be partners in Creation:

> A certain philosopher asked Rabbi Hoshaya and said to him: If circumcision is so beloved [by God], why wasn't the first man created circumcised? . . . [He replied:] Everything created during the six days of Creation requires further work. For example, mustard seeds must be sweetened, legumes must be sweetened, wheat must be ground, and man must be improved.[439]

The first humans were the last of Creation, in order to show that they had no part in the initial stages:

> Our Rabbis taught: Adam was created [last of all beings] on the eve of Sabbath. And why? Lest the heretics say: The Holy One of Blessing had a partner [Adam] in God's work of Creation. Another answer is: In order that, if our minds become [too] proud, we may be reminded that the gnats preceded us in the order of Creation. Another answer is: That [Adam] might immediately enter upon the fulfillment of a commandment, the observance of the Sabbath.

> Another answer is: That he might straightway go in to the banquet.
> The matter may be compared to a king of flesh and blood who built
> palaces and furnished them, prepared a banquet, and thereafter
> brought in the guests. So too, Adam was created in a world that
> was already prepared. (BT *Sanhedrin* 38a)

Humans played no part in the initial creation of the world, but we
have a huge part in the future of the world. And for millennia, humans
have turned to prayer for our own needs, as well as for the needs of others. Recent research indicates that Jews may be less likely than many
others to pray. The Pew Research Survey released in 2013 showed that
55 percent of all Jews viewed religion as very or somewhat important
in their lives, versus 44 percent who viewed it as not too or not at all
important.[440] Compare this with 79 percent of all Americans who
viewed religion as very or somewhat important. According to the Pew
Research Center's earlier 2007 U.S. Landscape Survey, 58 percent of
Americans prayed daily, ranging from 80 percent among Black Protestants, 71 percent among Muslims, 58 percent among Catholics, 53
percent among mainline Protestants, and (last among major religions)
26 percent among Jews.[441]

The efficacy of prayer has been put to scientific trial, with mixed
results. A Mississippi study of patients concluded that direct person-
to-person prayer sessions improved depression and anxiety scores, but
did not affect cortisol levels.[442] Another study of Christian prayers for
strangers undergoing heart surgery found that there was no effect on
the outcome, regardless of whether the patient knew about the praying,
and that there was an increased rate of complications following surgery
among those who had been prayed for.[443] We don't consider prayer to
be magic. Rather, prayer can improve the person who prays, by ground-
ing us and filling us with inspiration, hope, and positive energy.

Dr. Sir Sarvepalli Radhakrishnan writes:

> Religion is not a movement stretching out to grasp something,
> external, tangible and good, and to possess it. It is a form of being,
> not having, a mode of life. Spiritual life is not a problem to be solved
> but a reality to be experienced. It is new birth into enlightenment.[444]

Religion pushes us to deeper experience. Rather than merely analyzing our existence, we must immerse ourselves in the deepest and highest form of living. Sometimes we can solve problems, but sometimes we are humbled before the challenges. President Barack Obama, channeling a Lincoln-esque oration, said, "I have been driven many times to my knees by the overwhelming conviction that I had nowhere else to go."[445]

Today, we are surrounded by personal, local, national, and global challenges. There is much work to do. Even though we are capable of much, we must humble ourselves through prayer and introspection. God can create or destroy the world in a moment, yet God is found in God's own prayer immersed in truth, hope, and love. So, too, we can achieve much, but we must pause to consider the correct path. Revelation is not merely a historical phenomenon, but a way of life. We can open our eyes and hearts to the profundity of the soul's capacity for love, amazement at the infinitude of the universe, and the beauty of loving relationships. In sacred moments, God continues to speak with us. Embracing the holy everyday revelation is a recommitment to the Sinaitic experience. Even more so, embracing spontaneous sacred moments of divine and human revelation is essential to spiritual growth and renewal. That is where revelation is truly found.

6:3

וְהַלָּמֵד מֵחֲבֵרוֹ פֶּרֶק אֶחָד, הֲלָכָה אַחַת, פָּסוּק אֶחָד, דָּבָר
אֶחָד, אוֹ אֲפִלּוּ אוֹת אַחַת – צָרִיךְ לִנְהָג בּוֹ כָּבוֹד, שֶׁכֵּן
מָצִינוּ בְּדָוִד מֶלֶךְ יִשְׂרָאֵל, שֶׁלֹּא לָמַד מֵאֲחִיתֹפֶל אֶלָּא שְׁנֵי
דְבָרִים בִּלְבַד, וּקְרָאוֹ רַבּוֹ אַלּוּפוֹ וּמְיֻדָּעוֹ, שֶׁנֶּאֱמַר: וְאַתָּה
אֱנוֹשׁ כְּעֶרְכִּי, אַלּוּפִי וּמְיֻדָּעִי (תהלים נה:יד). וַהֲלֹא דְבָרִים קַל
וָחֹמֶר: וּמַה דָּוִד מֶלֶךְ יִשְׂרָאֵל, שֶׁלֹּא לָמַד מֵאֲחִיתֹפֶל אֶלָּא
שְׁנֵי דְבָרִים בִּלְבַד, קְרָאוֹ רַבּוֹ אַלּוּפוֹ וּמְיֻדָּעוֹ, הַלָּמֵד
מֵחֲבֵרוֹ פֶּרֶק אֶחָד, הֲלָכָה אַחַת, פָּסוּק אֶחָד, דָּבָר אֶחָד,
וַאֲפִלּוּ אוֹת אַחַת – עַל אַחַת כַּמָּה וְכַמָּה שֶׁצָּרִיךְ לִנְהָג
בּוֹ כָּבוֹד. וְאֵין כָּבוֹד אֶלָּא תוֹרָה, שֶׁנֶּאֱמַר: כָּבוֹד חֲכָמִים
יִנְחָלוּ (משלי ג:לה) וּתְמִימִים יִנְחֲלוּ־טוֹב (משלי כח:י). וְאֵין טוֹב
אֶלָּא תוֹרָה, שֶׁנֶּאֱמַר: כִּי לֶקַח טוֹב נָתַתִּי לָכֶם, תּוֹרָתִי
אַל־תַּעֲזֹבוּ (משלי ד:ב).

One who learns from another a single chapter, a single
halachah, a single verse, a single Torah statement, or even a
single letter, must treat them with honor. For thus we find in
the case of David, king of Israel, who learned nothing from
Achitophel except for two things, yet called him his teacher,
his guide, his intimate, as it said: "You are a person whom I
value, my guide and my intimate" (Psalm 55:14). One can derive
from this the following: If David, king of Israel, who learned
nothing from Achitophel except for two things, called him his
teacher, his guide, his intimate—one who learns from another
a single chapter, a single halachah, a single verse, a single
statement, or even a single letter, how much more must one
treat them with honor! And honor is due only for Torah, as it
is said: "The wise shall inherit honor" (Proverbs 3:35) "and the
perfect shall inherit good" (Proverbs 28:10). And only Torah is
truly good, as it is said: "I have given you a good teaching, do
not forsake My Torah" (Proverbs 4:2).

PUT SIMPLY, the spiritual center of Judaism is learning. That learning inspires gratitude, which brings us closer to our Creator and assists us to fulfill our worldly mission. Furthermore, learning brings us joy. Feeling gratitude toward those who help us learn not only is beneficial for our spiritual development, but also ensures that we properly honor these teachers.

We can preach and teach all day long, but if we don't demonstrate our values, we cannot influence others. Transformative education happens through mentorship and a life of modeled virtue. A Talmudic tale:

> Rabbi Yochanan stood and kissed [Rabbi Elazar] on the head. Rabbi Yochanan said, "Blessed is the Eternal, the God of Israel, who gave such a son to Abraham our father; for he knows how to understand, and investigate, and expound upon the works of the Chariot [a particular mystical revelation]. There are those who preach well, yet they do not practice. There are those who practice well, but they cannot preach. You practice what you preach! Happy are you, Abraham our father, that Elazar ben Arach is your offspring!" (BT *Chagigah* 14b)

The study of Torah cannot remain confined to discussion in academic circles. Torah must be lived. The Rabbis taught the danger of merely studying Torah, while missing the soul of the tradition (see mishnah 4:6). One cannot be a true teacher without observing and practicing what one studies and teaches. This is not so easy when one is an idealistic dreamer who espouses many values.

For example, David Ben-Gurion, Israel's first prime minister, did not simply preach equality, but modeled it, too. Ben-Gurion received far too many letters to answer on his own, but when he saw one that was from three Arab men who were out of work, he made calls on their behalf to find them jobs.[446] Such behavior was neither easy nor typical in the 1950s, amid continued conflict and suspicion between the Jews and their Arab neighbors.

Responsible people treat all with the dignity they deserve. Children watch their parents closely. It is not from a dinner table lesson that the children will learn values, but by watching how their parents talk to one another, how their father speaks with the cashier, and how their mother converses with the insistent telemarketer. To teach virtue, one must model virtue. To parent with values, one must live with those values consistently, even when one thinks no one is watching. Rabbi Abraham Isaac HaKohen Kook teaches, "The pure righteous do not complain of the dark, but increase the light; they do not complain of evil, but increase justice; they do not complain of heresy, but increase faith; they do not complain of ignorance, but increase wisdom."[447]

Rabbi Kook lived up to this teaching as a tremendous force of pro-active good. We are to be sources of light and walk within that light. It is all too elementary to profess virtue, but to live with virtue is the real challenge. At the same time, it is all too easy to offer a rant complaining about the system, without taking the steps to improve the system; we must work to change the system each day to further the just and holy society we want.

Rabbi Israel Meir Kagan—known as the Chafetz Chayim, one of the foremost Jewish *musar* leaders and halachists of the late nineteenth/early twentieth century—tells a story about kindness done at great sacrifice:

> The townspeople employed a rabbi to teach their boys, but they were unable to pay him. . . . Instead, the parents took turns providing meals for him. . . . After many years, the rabbi's wife died, his children moved away and he was left alone. No longer able to teach, he was replaced by a new rabbi. . . . Only one woman felt a continued obligation to support the man who had taught her children so well. . . . For five years, until the end of the rabbi's life, she repeated her daily climb of the stairs to his small apartment to bring him his lunch.
> . . . The war quickly crushed the small Jewish community's tenuous existence. The woman, however . . . died of natural causes. Most of the townspeople were herded away to their deaths, but this woman's grandchildren . . . were led to a small apartment, where a brave gentile woman risked her life to hide them . . . [and] provided their meals. . . . Her apartment sustained several raids and searches, but her "fugitives" were never discovered.
> When they emerged from hiding, the children learned that their refuge had once belonged to a different tenant—the old rabbi their

grandmother had fed. The same stairs the gentile woman climbed, bearing their provisions, had born their grandmother upward as well, on a mission of *chesed* that, decades later, saved their lives.[448]

Living with kindness inspires others to act with kindness. It inspires the heavens to offer support on earth in miraculous ways we may never expect. Ultimately, though, "we do not rely upon miracles" to ensure a vision of a repaired world (JT *Yoma* 1:4). Instead, we can live with constant inspiration and radical giving, expecting nothing in return.

6:4

כָּךְ הִיא דַרְכָּהּ שֶׁל תּוֹרָה: פַּת בְּמֶלַח תֹּאכֵל, וּמַיִם בִּמְשׂוּרָה
תִּשְׁתֶּה, וְעַל הָאָרֶץ תִּישַׁן, וְחַיֵּי צַעַר תִּחְיֶה – וּבַתּוֹרָה אַתָּה
עָמֵל. וְאִם אַתָּה עוֹשֶׂה כֵּן, אַשְׁרֶיךָ וְטוֹב לָךְ (תהלים קכח:ב).
אַשְׁרֶיךָ – בָּעוֹלָם הַזֶּה, וְטוֹב לָךְ – לָעוֹלָם הַבָּא.

This is the way of Torah: Eat bread with salt, drink water
in small measure, sleep on the ground, live a life of depri-
vation—but toil in the Torah! If you do this, "You are
praiseworthy, and all is well with you" (Psalms 128:2). "You are
praiseworthy"—in this world; "and all is well with you"—in
the world-to-come.

THE TALMUD TEACHES that the Torah was given not to angels, but to
imperfect humans. But what distinguishes humans from angels?

Let's step back. The world-to-come promises splendors the likes of
which human beings will never witness in our lives. Though we can
dream about this ideal, it has no bearing in our day-to-day, material
world. We can imagine heaven, but we must operate in human reality.
Even so, we are responsible to shape the world to look more like the
heaven we imagine.

If we believe in human dignity, what are we willing to sacrifice for
others' dignity? If we believe every human being has infinite value, what
are we willing to do to save a life? These are not easy questions.

But how do these questions relate with respect to making our lives
more productive in the present? Judaism shuns asceticism and eschews
life apart from the world's bounty, even though the tradition favors
spiritual over material goals. Living a life of luxury does not outweigh
becoming a person of character, who is principled, seeks God, and
serves one's community. We often work so much to obtain free time,
only to waste it on worthless pursuits because we're so exhausted from
working. Rather, we need to set aside valuable time for spiritual goals.
This is how we approach the ether where the angels take their residence.

Angels hold a tenuous place in the history of Jewish theology, with many different positions taken by thinkers through the generations. Although this reference to angels might seem like a fait accompli of their existence, some Jewish philosophers did not take the idea of angels literally. Maimonides argued that textual reference to an angel was prophetic vision, rather than actual existence. The talking serpent in the Garden of Eden should be considered an allegory, and Balaam's talking donkey, a dream.[449] In Maimonidean angelology, angels have essence but no form.

Other Jewish thinkers understood angels literally and even considered them to be protectors of the righteous (BT *Chagigah* 16a). Other sources describe mitzvot (such as tzitzit) as angels that protect. A midrash states:

> A person who does one mitzvah is given one angel. One who does two mitzvot is given two angels. One who does all the mitzvot is given many angels—as it says, "God will assign angels to you" (Psalm 91:11). Who are these angels? They are the ones who guard the person against harm.[450]

It has generally been taught that angels lack free will and are merely the servants of God.[451] Other spiritual leaders teach that angels follow human behavior and are vicariously affected by our own leadership and worship. The Rabbis teach that what we do in this world is of utmost importance. The Chasidic master Rabbi Dov Baer ben Avraham, the Maggid of Mezritch, teaches, "Know that all that is above is dependent on you."[452] Rabbi Schneur Zalman of Liadi, the Alter Rebbe, teaches, "In the upper worlds, the preciousness of this world is well appreciated. The ministering angels . . . would forgo everything for one 'Amen, *y'hei sh'meih raba*' said by a Jew with full concentration!"[453]

Debate emerged about whether one can pray to an angel and if such prayer is acceptable. The kabbalists argued that one can and must pray—not to, but through, angels—to reach the highest throne. Those in the rationalist camp argued that one must not pray to anything that might even appear to be an angel, because one may only pray to God. The early Reform liturgists removed all references to angels in the prayer book. However, in the liturgical practices of the Orthodox communities, the kabbalists have mostly won this argument. One example of a familiar prayer referencing angels is the opening Friday night song, *Shalom Aleichem*:

> Peace be to you, ministering angels, messengers of the Most High, Majesty of majesties, Holy One of Blessing.

Throughout Jewish theological sources, we find that angels are given unique attributes, such as Michael, angel of mercy; Gabriel, angel of justice; Raphael, angel of healing; and Uriel, angel of illumination. It follows that when one masters a divine attribute, one has realized the angelic component of one's nature. Still, rabbis, philosophers, and text differ regarding the nature of angels and the depth of human characteristics and experiences that angels may share with us. In one source, the angel is considered a virtuous messenger of God, contrasted with the demon:

> Raba pointed out a contradiction. It is written, "I do speak with him in a dream" (Numbers 12:6), and it is written, "The dreams speak falsely" (Zechariah 10:2). There is no contradiction; in the one case it is through an angel, in the other through a demon. (BT *B'rachot* 55b)

Other sources suggest that an angel can be evil:

> It was taught: Rabbi Yosei bar Y'hudah said: Two ministering angels accompany man on the eve of the Sabbath from the synagogue to his home, one a good [angel] and one an evil [one]. And when he arrives home and finds the lamp burning, the table laid and the couch [bed] covered with a spread, the good angel exclaims, "May it be even thus on another Sabbath [too]," and the evil angel unwillingly responds, "Amen." But if not, the evil angel exclaims, "May it be even thus on another Sabbath [too]," and the good angel unwillingly responds, "Amen." (BT *Shabbat* 119b)

Furthermore, angels are generally considered outside of human experience, not subject to human temptation, and thus of a completely different nature. But one Talmudic passage explores angelic envy of humans, who can serve God through the Torah in a way that angels cannot.

When Moses ascended to the heavenly realms, the angels who served there in the Divine Presence [protested] saying, "Sovereign of the universe, what is a human being doing among us?" "He has come to receive the Torah," answered God. They responded, "How can You be giving to creatures of flesh and blood this beloved treasure, which You kept to Yourself for 974 generations before the creation of the world?" God said to Moses, "You answer them." Moses replied, "I am afraid that they will burn me with the fire of their mouths." God told him, "Hold on to My throne of glory and give them an answer."

Moses said to God, "Sovereign of the universe, what is written in the Torah that You are giving to me? 'I am the Eternal your God, who took you out of the land of Egypt.'" He then turned to the angels. "Did you go down to Egypt? Were you Pharaoh's slaves? What good is the Torah to you? What else is written there? 'You shall have no other gods besides Me!' Do you live among the gentiles who serve idols [that you must be warned against them]? What else is written there? 'Remember the Sabbath day to sanctify it!' Do you ever work that you should need a day of rest?" On hearing these words, the angels immediately admitted to the Holy One of Blessing that God was right to give the Torah to Moses. (BT *Shabbat* 88b)

While there are angels in heaven, perhaps humans can act as angels—as pure emissaries of God—on earth. When one transcends one's own self-interest and fulfills the will of God by helping another, one has transcended one's own humanity. Perhaps there are angels inside each of us—the angel who told Abraham not to sacrifice his son Isaac, the angel that Jacob wrestled, the angel who helped guide Joseph when he was lost—and when we bring our will in accord with that purest self, we actualize our holy potential.

When we struggle each day with moral choices, which internal angel will say, "May it be even thus on another Sabbath [too]"? We make the choice each day to live as angels or demons. May we choose each day to sanctify the heavens by living with compassion and empathy as we actualize our inner angelic self. This world's toil is not to punish, but to bring us closer to the eternal truth of divine goodness and justice.

6:5

אַל תְּבַקֵּשׁ גְּדֻלָּה לְעַצְמְךָ, וְאַל תַּחְמֹד כָּבוֹד. יוֹתֵר מִלִּמּוּדְךָ
עֲשֵׂה. וְאַל תִּתְאַוֶּה לְשֻׁלְחָנָם שֶׁל מְלָכִים, שֶׁשֻּׁלְחָנְךָ גָּדוֹל
מִשֻּׁלְחָנָם, וְכִתְרְךָ גָּדוֹל מִכִּתְרָם, וְנֶאֱמָן הוּא בַּעַל
מְלַאכְתְּךָ שֶׁיְּשַׁלֶּם לְךָ שְׂכַר פְּעֻלָּתֶךָ.

Do not seek greatness for yourself, and do not crave honor;
let your performance exceed your learning. Do not lust for
the table of kings, for your table is greater than theirs, and
your crown is greater than their crown; and your Employer is
trustworthy to pay you remuneration for your deeds.

THE BIBLICAL PROPHET Micah says, "What does God require of you?
But to do justice, love mercy, and walk humbly with God" (6:8). Today,
many feel as if they are missing out on the finer aspects of life that others have: *others* have more material wealth or more honors; *others* are
happier and more accomplished; *others* are simply greater. The Rabbis
remind us to acquire perspective on what is truly great and what is truly
honorable. Further, the God of justice ensures that those who missed
out or experienced injustice will indeed be paid.

In this mishnah, the Rabbis refer to God as an Employer. From the
humblest worker to the highest-paid CEO, all are under the sovereignty of the Divine. We are reminded of *halachta bidrachav*, imitation
of the Divine (see above at 4:2, page 195), and thus must emulate God
by paying proper wages and treating all with respect.

Respect for workers begins in our own Jewish institutions. At times,
religious institutions have been at the forefront of progress by showing
forceful leadership. While most Americans know the pivotal impact
of Rev. Dr. Martin Luther King Jr.'s Southern Christian Leadership
Conference on the civil rights movement, there were other religion-
inspired movements as well. Rev. Dr. Anna Howard Shaw (1847–1919),
an ordained minister with a medical degree, served as president of the
National American Woman Suffrage Association. Typical of her ora-
tory is this 1888 speech to the International Council of Women:

> Let me in the name of my Master say to the young women here today if you have a bit of truth, hold fast to that which God had given you; let no power, no injustice, no obstacle, no scorn, no opposition, let nothing extinguish the flame.[454]

Rev. Dr. Shaw said that her faith had given her strength: "Nothing bigger can come to a human being than to love a great Cause more than life itself, and to have the privilege throughout life of working for that Cause."[455]

Faith should inspire our own leadership to ensure equal dignity and respect for everyone. We must call on all who think of themselves as of a principled faith to examine how far they are willing to go to protect the desperate. How can we ensure that every church, synagogue, and mosque pays its workers a living wage? Uses union contractors? Limits animal-product intake for the sake of human health, the environment, and animal welfare? Promotes eco-friendly practices? Is fully inclusive of its members of diverse ethnicities, gender and sexual orientations, socioeconomic statuses, and abilities? In short, how do we ensure that religious institutions are robust engines that engender change and social progress? The greatest contribution that spiritual leaders and religious institutions can contribute is both the spiritual and practical framework to understand moral living. For religion to be front and center once again in social change, it must preach less and model more.

This mishnah, and all of *Pirkei Avot*, references God as the central imperative of how we chose to behave and use our time and resources. Why, though, at a typical American Jewish social justice event, does no one invoke God? When our community accepts the role of the Divine in social change and moral development, we can embrace the most powerful part of our tradition.

When the Jewish social justice movement neglects the Divine, the primary source of our sense of responsibility is denied. By neglecting the Divine, we deprive the movement of its holiness and much of its inspiration. Following are seven reasons why Jews engaging in social justice should embrace God in activism and community service.

Halachta Bidrachav (Imitatio Dei)

The Torah tells us that God is merciful and commands us to emulate God's ways (*halachta bidrachav*). The Talmud makes this connection explicit (BT *Sotah* 14a). The Rabbis explain that God is not a vengeful, power-hungry dictator, but rather a merciful, moral healer; and this is the path we must follow. We must attend carefully to the *means* of social change (our character) in addition to the *ends* (assisting the vulnerable). Further, this means that being like God requires action. Our role model is no less than the Creator of heaven and earth. The bar is set high.

Tzelem Elohim

The Mishnah teaches that to save one life is to save a world (*Sanhedrin* 4:5); humanity is created in God's image (*tzelem Elohim*) and is therefore sacred. Rabbi Abraham Isaac Kook goes so far as to argue that there is no such thing as an atheist, since God is in each one of us, and our souls long for their eternal source (*ikvei hatzon, edar hayakar*). When we embrace that each human is created in the image of God, we have the strongest model for ensuring the unshakable dignity in all.

Humility

We must remember that the position of God has already been filled. That we can in no way play the role of God should inspire humility. All too often, there can be arrogance in change makers who see themselves as heroes rather than as servants. The greatest Jewish leader, Moses, is described as "a very humble man, more do than any other human being on earth" (Numbers 12:3).

History

The Torah describes God as taking the Israelites *mibeit avadim*, "from the house of bondage," when God took the Israelites out of Egypt (Exodus 13:3). This shows that God entered history to play an active role to rescue the persecuted. God is the master liberator of the oppressed. Over time, God empowers humanity more and more to act on their own, for better or for worse.

Obligation

Social justice is neither optional nor reserved for a particular Mitzvah Day. When we act as if we are divinely commanded to heal the world each and every day, we raise the bar. Religion reminds us that we are held accountable for fulfilling and exceeding our obligations at the end of our lives. God cares that we have lived up to our end of the partnership; embracing our obligations grants us dignity.

Rabbi Abraham Joshua Heschel explains that our dignity is a result not only of any rights, but also of divine obligations:

> Our commitment is to God, and our roots are in the prophetic events of Israel. The dignity of man stands in proportion to his obligations as well as to his rights. The dignity of being a Jew is in the sense of commitment, and the meaning of Jewish history revolves around the faithfulness of Israel to the covenant.[456]

Walking with the Divine

When we struggle for justice as part of our relationship with God, we do not walk alone. When we look evil in the face to combat it with love, God stands with us. "As I walk through the valley overshadowed by death, I fear no evil, for You are with me" (Psalm 23:4). Embracing religion is not comfortable conformity, but rising to a challenge. Embracing God is not believing blindly, but empowering oneself.

God is everywhere. Rabbi Menachem Nachum of Chernobyl, the MeOr Einayim (eighteenth century, Poland/Lithuania), explains that Abraham didn't actually depart from God when he left the divine presence to greet the three visitors from the desert (see our discussion of Genesis 18 above, page 17). Rather, God was present in the ethical encounter, because "the whole earth is filled with God's glory" (Isaiah 6:3). When we remember that the Divine is present in all places and moments, we feel compelled to embrace the holiness of each moment and its ethical demands.

The Ideal

The notion of progress is rooted in the messianic vision: we envision paradigms of the perfect, like the heavenly realm, and we progress toward those ideal models by bringing them down to earth. There is a Temple located in the heavens that sits directly above the Temple on earth.[457] The same God who makes the heavens emanate with the holy sparks of kindness and wisdom also illuminates our earthly existence.

For those who take religion beyond the letters on the page or the routine of ritual, there is no room for cynical determinism. Rather, we are free and empowered to bring about real progress in the world. The kabbalists explain that the world is saturated with divinity, which longs to return to its divine source. Such return is through ritual praxis and good acts, *tikkunim*. Messianism, however, covers not only eschatological reality (messianic times) but also the process (repairing the world in each moment).

On this topic, Rabbi Jonathan Sacks writes:

> In Judaism, faith is not acceptance but protest, against the world that is, in the name of the world that is not yet but ought to be. Faith lies not in the answer but the question—and the greater the human being, the more intense the question. The Bible is not a metaphysical opium but its opposite. Its aim is not to transport the believer to a private heaven. Instead, its impassioned, sustained desire is to bring heaven down to earth. Until we have done this, there is work still to do.[458]

One can certainly be moral and effective in social justice work without embracing God, just as one can be devout without pursuing social justice. But even looking beyond social justice, embracing God offers potential to raise the bar for what we must achieve and how we must achieve it. God is the most powerful reality ever encountered and, like no other, can inspire humankind to ideal goodness and transformative justice. Relying solely on human authority is a failure to recognize the power and truth of our destiny, while acknowledging a power beyond us demands social protest, not divine submission. Together, as servants, we serve God by taking the initiative to heal the world.

6:6

גְּדוֹלָה תוֹרָה מִן הַכְּהֻנָּה וּמִן הַמַּלְכוּת, שֶׁהַמַּלְכוּת –
בִּשְׁלֹשִׁים מַעֲלוֹת, וְהַכְּהֻנָּה – בְּעֶשְׂרִים וְאַרְבַּע,
וְהַתּוֹרָה נִקְנֵית בְּאַרְבָּעִים וּשְׁמוֹנָה דְבָרִים: בְּתַלְמוּד,
בִּשְׁמִיעַת הָאֹזֶן, בַּעֲרִיכַת שְׂפָתַיִם, בְּבִינַת הַלֵּב, בְּשִׂכְלוּת
הַלֵּב, בְּאֵימָה, בְּיִרְאָה, בַּעֲנָוָה, בְּשִׂמְחָה, בְּשִׁמּוּשׁ חֲכָמִים,
בְּדִבּוּק חֲבֵרִים, בְּפִלְפּוּל הַתַּלְמִידִים, בְּיִשּׁוּב, בְּמִקְרָא,
בְּמִשְׁנָה, בְּמִעוּט שֵׁנָה, בְּמִעוּט שִׂיחָה, בְּמִעוּט תַּעֲנוּג,
בְּמִעוּט שְׂחוֹק, בְּמִעוּט דֶּרֶךְ אֶרֶץ, בְּאֶרֶךְ אַפַּיִם, בְּלֵב טוֹב,
בֶּאֱמוּנַת חֲכָמִים, וּבְקַבָּלַת הַיִּסּוּרִין, הַמַּכִּיר אֶת מְקוֹמוֹ,
וְהַשָּׂמֵחַ בְּחֶלְקוֹ, וְהָעוֹשֶׂה סְיָג לִדְבָרָיו, וְאֵינוּ מַחֲזִיק טוֹבָה
לְעַצְמוֹ, אָהוּב, אוֹהֵב אֶת הַמָּקוֹם, אוֹהֵב אֶת הַבְּרִיּוֹת,
אוֹהֵב אֶת הַצְּדָקוֹת, אוֹהֵב אֶת הַתּוֹכָחוֹת, אוֹהֵב אֶת הַמֵּי
שָׁרִים, מִתְרַחֵק מִן הַכָּבוֹד, וְלֹא מֵגִיס לִבּוֹ בְּתַלְמוּדוֹ, וְאֵינוּ
שָׂמֵחַ בְּהוֹרָאָה, נוֹשֵׂא בְעֹל עִם חֲבֵרוֹ, וּמַכְרִיעוֹ לְכַף זְכוּת,
וּמַעֲמִידוֹ עַל הָאֱמֶת, וּמַעֲמִידוֹ עַל הַשָּׁלוֹם, וּמִתְיַשֵּׁב
בְּתַלְמוּדוֹ, שׁוֹאֵל וּמֵשִׁיב שׁוֹמֵעַ וּמוֹסִיף, הַלָּמֵד עַל מְנָת
לְלַמֵּד, וְהַלָּמֵד עַל מְנָת לַעֲשׂוֹת, הַמַּחְכִּים אֶת רַבּוֹ, וְהַמְכַוֵּן
אֶת שְׁמוּעָתוֹ, וְהָאוֹמֵר דָּבָר בְּשֵׁם אוֹמְרוֹ. הָא לָמַדְתָּ שֶׁכָּל
הָאוֹמֵר דָּבָר בְּשֵׁם אוֹמְרוֹ מֵבִיא גְאֻלָּה לָעוֹלָם, שֶׁנֶּאֱמַר:
וַתֹּאמֶר אֶסְתֵּר לַמֶּלֶךְ בְּשֵׁם מָרְדֳּכָי (אסתר ב:כב).

Torah is greater than priesthood or royalty; for royalty is
acquired along with thirty prerogatives, and the priesthood
with twenty-four [gifts], but the Torah is acquired by means
of forty-eight qualities, which are: study, attentive listening,
articulate speech, intuitive understanding, discernment,
awe, reverence, modesty, joy, purity, ministering to the sages,
closeness with colleagues, sharp discussion with students,
deliberation, [knowledge of] Scripture, Mishnah, limited

business activity, limited sexual activity, limited pleasure, limited sleep, limited conversation, limited laughter, slowness to anger, a good heart, faith in the sages, acceptance of suffering, knowing one's place, being happy with one's lot, making a protective fence around one's personal matters, claiming no credit for oneself, being beloved, loving the Omnipresent, loving [God's] creatures, loving righteous ways, loving justice, loving reproof, keeping far from honor, not being arrogant with one's learning, not enjoying halachic decision-making, sharing one's fellow's yoke, judging one favorably, setting one on the truthful course, setting one on the peaceful course, thinking deliberately in one's study, asking and answering, listening and contributing to the discussion, learning in order to teach, learning in order to practice, making one's teacher wiser, pondering over what one has learned, and repeating a saying in the name of the one who said it. For you have learned this: Whoever repeats a word in the name of the one who said it brings redemption to the world, as it is said: "And Esther said to the king in the name of Mordechai" (Esther 2:22).

As we approach the end of *Pirkei Avot*, the Rabbis return to the essence of Jewish pedagogy: engaging with the timeless wisdom of the Torah. Indeed, the most beautiful aspect of Torah engagement is that it is never complete. It requires a lifetime of study, a lifetime of dedication, which foster a lifetime of character development. This mishnah lists so many "qualities" needed for spiritual growth because learning is neither mere intellectual activity, nor an automatic route to enlightened bliss. It mirrors the rest of life—sometimes tedious and grueling, always arduous. One stays true to one's purpose through the necessary engagement with one's need to grow in one's spiritual self.

Torah study and self-improvement are not just ends in themselves, but are also the means to supporting others. We prepare ourselves for moral decisions yet to be made. The late Professor Steve Covey, best known for his work *The 7 Habits of Highly Successful People*, attributed much of his thinking to a quote[459] that he believed Viktor Frankl to have written; the source of the quote has been up for dispute,[460] but its message still resonates. Indeed, this thought that the "moral moment" is the one between stimulus and response is a powerful reminder that our actions have tangible consequences on the world around us. The quote reads in part: "In that space [after a stimulus] is our power to choose our response . . . [and] in our response lies our growth and our freedom." While other animals have predictable responses to particular stimuli, humans are blessed with the capacity to pause and think before making choices, moral or immoral. Through education, experience, and knowledge, people learn to make decisions with the hope that they land on the moral side of each choice.

Self-improvement is an ongoing project. Learning Torah, supporting Israel, helping the Jewish poor, funding Jewish day schools—there seem to be endless specifically Jewish concerns. How can one justify giving time to more-universal social justice issues? Rabbi Abraham Isaac HaKohen Kook writes:

> There are some righteous individuals who are very great and powerful, who cannot limit themselves to *K'neset Yisrael* [the Jewish community] alone, and they are always concerned for the good of the entire world. . . . These *tzaddikim* [righteous people] cannot be nationalists in the external sense of the term because they cannot stand any hatred, or iniquity, or limitation of good and mercy, and they are good to all, as the attributes of the Holy One of Blessing is good to all and God's compassion is over all of God's works.[461]

There are some who will give their holy energy largely to their family, and others who will prioritize building the Jewish community and Israel with all of their might. These are wonderful and necessary endeavors. But Rabbi Kook, a pluralist attuned to the diversity and complexity of souls, teaches that there are righteous others who cannot remain parochial, but need to go beyond the Jewish community.

Too many leaders, both in Jewish social justice movements and beyond, feel marginalized from the Jewish community. Some even describe themselves as bad Jews. The opposite is true. Those dedicating themselves to supporting the poor, sick, and alienated are model Jews, even if they are not religiously devout in other ways. Abraham was chosen precisely because he was committed to *tzedakah umishpat*, pursuing justice. Lurianic Kabbalah teaches that our role in this world is to find hidden sparks, liberate them from their evil shells (*k'lipot*), and elevate them. Social justice activists who support the vulnerable do exactly this.

Rabbi Yisrael Salanter, founder of the Musar movement, teaches that there are two steps to controlling negative desire: *kibush hayetzer*, conquering and controlling one's desire, and *tikkun hayetzer*, repairing/fixing one's desire. Desire is difficult to control, so we rely on both steps in the midst of moral challenges. By contrast, Chasidic thought suggests that we channel our negative desire toward the good, without losing any of its energy or force.

Let's examine moral courage at a time when the stakes were high. Raphael Benjamin West, mayor of Nashville from 1951 to 1963, was content with the status quo in this "Athens of the South"—a city that prided itself on institutions of higher learning and classical architecture. This façade, however, masked the ugliness of Nashville's racial segregation. In early 1960, after the lunch counter sit-ins began in the South, Fisk University students began their own. Black students waited in vain to be served, while their white peers asked that their black companions be served first. At first, Mayor West was placid, milquetoast. When white gangs attacked the protestors, police arrested and jailed those being attacked. Mayor West offered separate black and white lunch counters, which was rejected by the students. Then the home of Z. Alexander Looby—a prominent black lawyer and civil rights leader—was firebombed; students led twenty-five hundred protesters in silence to the steps of City Hall. Student leader Diane Nash asked the mayor, "Do *you* feel it is wrong to discriminate against a person solely on the basis of their race or color?" Mayor West later recalled:

> I found that I had to answer it frankly and honestly—that I did not agree that it was morally right for someone not to sell them merchandise and refuse them service. . . . If I had to answer it again I would answer it in the same way again because it was a moral question and it was one a man has to answer and not a politician.[462]

Mayor West surprised everyone by replying, "I appeal to all citizens to end discrimination, to have no bigotry, no bias, no discrimination."[463] Nashville became the first city in the South to desegregate lunch counters. Diane Nash later served on a presidential commission to promote the passage of the Civil Rights Act and worked for social justice causes for decades.

Many Jews also took up the cause of civil rights with fervor. While Rabbi Abraham Joshua Heschel is usually the first name that appears in the popular conception of Jews marching with Martin Luther King, there were many other Jewish leaders and clergy putting themselves in harm's way to stand up for what was right. As just one example, Rabbi Jacob Rothschild, of The Temple in Atlanta, one of the most vibrant Reform synagogues in the South, made it well known that he was on the side of equality for all people. In response to his activism voice against bigotry, The Temple was bombed in 1958. But Rabbi Rothschild did not give in to fear and was soon back to advocating for what was right. When Martin Luther King won the Nobel Peace Prize in 1964, Rabbi Rothschild organized a banquet in his honor.[464]

Moral leadership requires quick decisions in uncertain, cacophonous, and often hostile environments. Once there is moral clarity, we must move quickly. To pursue the good, Rabbi Moshe Chayim Luzzatto teaches that we must run to seize the opportunity:

> Alacrity consists of two elements: one that relates to the period prior to the commencement of a deed, and the other that relates to the period that follows the commencement of a deed. The former means that prior to the commencement of a mitzvah a person must not delay (its performance). Rather, when its time arrives, or when the opportunity (for its fulfillment) presents itself, or when it enters our mind, we must react speedily, without delay, to seize the mitzvah and to do it. We must not procrastinate at this time, for no danger is graver than this. Every new moment can bring with it some new hindrance to the fulfillment of the good deed.[465]

One must first know the good, and then one must be ready to run with full force toward completion of the good. Many obstacles, even from well-intentioned people, are sure to arise.

Even in the midst of terrible tragedy, individuals can make moral choices. In January 2015, terrorists went on a rampage, killing innocent people who worked for the French satirical magazine *Charlie Hebdo*. An associate of these terrorists split off to find victims from among the Parisian Jews. He found them at a kosher supermarket, where people were getting last-minute items before Shabbat. Lassana Bathily, a Muslim native of Mali who immigrated to France as a teen, worked at the market. When the Islamic terrorist broke into the store and murdered four people, Bathily guided Jewish customers to refuge and survival in the store's freezer. After this incident, 420,000 people signed a successful petition for the French government to grant Bathily citizenship. Bathily said, "Yes, I helped Jews get out. We're brothers. It's not that we're Jewish or Christian or Muslim, we're all in the same boat. You help so you can get through this attack."[466]

To demonstrate *z'rizut*, "alacrity," run fast to do what's right when the opportunity presents itself. Some live their lives this way, and we should find these remarkable human beings and cling to them. Receive their light, and channel it to others. When they are attacked, stand at their side, even if it's difficult. Watch these moral models who operate with higher consciousness and consistent commitment to serving others.

When tempted to do wrong, lengthen the pause between stimulus and response, to reflect and steer closer to the moral direction. On the other hand, when presented with the opportunity to do good, shorten that pause, and simply run toward the good.

6:7

גְּדוֹלָה תוֹרָה, שֶׁהִיא נוֹתֶנֶת חַיִּים לְעֹשֶׂיהָ בָּעוֹלָם הַזֶּה
וְלָעוֹלָם הַבָּא, שֶׁנֶּאֱמַר: כִּי־חַיִּים הֵם לְמֹצְאֵיהֶם, וּלְכָל־
בְּשָׂרוֹ מַרְפֵּא (משלי ד:כב). וְאוֹמֵר: רִפְאוּת תְּהִי לְשָׁרֶּךָ וְשִׁקּוּי
לְעַצְמוֹתֶיךָ (משלי ג:ח). וְאוֹמֵר: עֵץ־חַיִּים הִיא לַמַּחֲזִיקִים בָּהּ,
וְתֹמְכֶיהָ מְאֻשָּׁר (משלי ג:יח). דְּרָכֶיהָ דַרְכֵי־נֹעַם וְכָל נְתִיבוֹתֶיהָ
שָׁלוֹם (משלי ג:יז). כִּי לְוְיַת חֵן הֵם לְרֹאשֶׁךָ, וַעֲנָקִים לְגַרְגְּרֹתֶיךָ
(משלי א:ט). תִּתֵּן לְרֹאשְׁךָ לִוְיַת־חֵן, עֲטֶרֶת תִּפְאֶרֶת תְּמַגְּנֶךָ
(משלי ד:ט). כִּי־בִי יִרְבּוּ יָמֶיךָ, וְיוֹסִיפוּ לְךָ שְׁנוֹת חַיִּים (משלי ט:יא).
אֹרֶךְ יָמִים בִּימִינָהּ, בִּשְׂמֹאלָהּ עֹשֶׁר וְכָבוֹד (משלי ג:טז). כִּי אֹרֶךְ
יָמִים וּשְׁנוֹת חַיִּים וְשָׁלוֹם יוֹסִיפוּ לָךְ (משלי ג:ב).

Great is Torah, for it confers life upon its practitioners, both
in this world and in the world-to-come, as it is said: "For they
[the teachings of the Torah] are life to those who find them,
and a healing to one's entire flesh" (Proverbs 4:22). And it says:
"It shall be healing to your body, and marrow to your bones"
(Proverbs 3:8). And it says: "It is a tree of life to those who grasp
it, and its supporters are praiseworthy" (Proverbs 3:18). "Her
ways are ways of pleasantness, and all her paths are peace"
(Proverbs 3:17). "They are a garland of grace for your head, and
necklaces for your neck" (Proverbs 1:9). "It will give to your
head a garland of grace, a crown of glory it will deliver to you"
(Proverbs 4:9). "Indeed, through me [the Torah] your days shall
be increased, and years of life shall be added to you" (Proverbs
9:11). "Lengthy days are at its right, and at its left are wealth
and honor" (Proverbs 3:16). "For lengthy days and years of life,
and peace shall they add to you" (Proverbs 3:2).

THE WORLDLY RESPONSIBILITIES of Jewish practice supersede
dogmas about the afterlife. Maimonides suggested that it would be
harmful to spend too much time thinking about that which cannot be

known, such as the messianic era and the world-to-come. Indeed, he steered us away from apocalyptic thinking.[467]

The Torah is primarily about life. It is the compass that points us toward all that is righteous and good. The Torah itself a living, breathing entity, *Torat chayim*, which guides countless people through both minutiae and grander experiences. It is intended not only as a blueprint, but also as a mechanism to perpetuate life. Its teachings inspire us to advocate for human dignity and human life. The Torah also reflects on eternal life. When we remind ourselves how insignificant is our existence, we learn that we can anticipate eternal life in which we will one day be reconnected with the source of all existence. This doesn't mean that we can neglect our obligations; rather, we are to make the brief time we have in this universe meaningful.

The Torah also deals with the end of life. Two of the possible Sukkot haftarot describe the end-of-days war of Gog and Magog. Ezekiel (38:18–39:16) and Zechariah (14:1–21) paint a complex picture of the destruction of our imperfect world, the war against evil, and the victory of God and the Jewish people in a battle for truth. Both haftarot describe a future war fought against nations oppressing Israel, in which God rises to fight against the enemies of Israel. Rashi argues that these haftarot describe the same end-of-days war, with "every man's sword against each other" (Ezekiel 38:21) and God's intervention.

Is this story meant to be understood literally or as religious metaphor? Modern thinkers have suggested that Jews experienced these wars or are in the midst of them. Elijah ben Solomon Zalman, the Vilna Gaon, said that the Gog and Magog war will take place on Hoshana Rabbah, the seventh day of Sukkot.[468] Others claimed that World Wars I and II were the wars of Gog and Magog, preparing the world for the coming of the Messiah, started by the Jewish return to Israel. Prior generations of Chasidic teachers saw the Jewish struggles with France and Russia as the wars of Gog and Magog.

Contemporary thinkers echo past rabbis, urging us to focus on contemporary crises rather than imaginary doomsday scenarios. Deepak Chopra notes that Americans should focus on the changing world, in which nations will have to curtail their indiscriminate use of natural resources, and in which both crude nationalism and religious intolerance become credible threats. He warns against those who focus on the end of the world: "reactionary forces, fueling an undercurrent of fear, promoting a fantasy of America as a perfect society where privilege is a birthright and the rest of the world exists on a plane almost beneath notice."[469]

This theme of global destruction is not new. We saw that God destroyed the world with the Flood, followed by Noah rebuilding the world. All civilization was broken again and dispersed at the Tower of Babel. After the Holocaust, the Jewish people needed to re-create a lost Jewish world. Now, we are asked again to step out of our known world and imagine a new one. If your world were destroyed, how would you rebuild it? How would you change it?

We cannot go to the woods and wonder alone. To dream, we must do it together. And we must do it with those who have been excluded from the actualization of past dreams. Toni Morrison said in a television interview, "All paradises, all utopias are designed by who is not there, by the people who are not allowed in."[470] The best dreamers of the future are often those denied the dreams of yesterday.

The stories of apocalypse that we read may tempt us to think about how the world could be destroyed, but our moral challenge is to think about how we will reconstruct the world, how we rebuild after the storms. Stories of destruction divide us with fear. Stories of construction, though, unite us with hope.

In the eighteenth century, the American revolutionary generation understood that they were building a new world. In 1948, those building the new Jewish state understood that they were creating a new world. When we parents hold our newborn child for the first time, we understand that we are holding a new world. Rashi explains that Noah's name is *Noach* because of the *nechamah*, the comfort, he brought to the world. How did he do that? He invented the plow. To build the world, start plowing. That is our work—to dream, but also just to start working.

Today, much of contemporary discourse is dominated by the details of how we are going to build. But in the midst of debate on how we structure society, we have lost sight of what we are trying to build together. That is bigger than any individual's pocketbook, discrete policy, politician, or generation. It is ultimately what we leave in this world. The project of Judaism is designed to push us away from self-interest and toward a grander vision for society, global meaning, and long-term impact. Our question should not be so much "What will the world be like after me?" but rather "How can the world be molded into its best form?" For the Jewish people, the answer always extends from Torah.

6:8

רַבִּי שִׁמְעוֹן בֶּן מְנַסְיָא אוֹמֵר מִשּׁוּם רַבִּי שִׁמְעוֹן בֶּן יוֹחַי:
הַנּוֹי, וְהַכֹּחַ, וְהָעְשֶׁר, וְהַכָּבוֹד, וְהַחָכְמָה, וְהַזִּקְנָה, וְהַשֵּׂיבָה,
וְהַבָּנִים – נָאֶה לַצַּדִּיקִים וְנָאֶה לָעוֹלָם, שֶׁנֶּאֱמַר: עֲטֶרֶת
תִּפְאֶרֶת שֵׂיבָה, בְּדֶרֶךְ צְדָקָה תִּמָּצֵא (משלי טז:לא). וְאוֹמֵר:
עֲטֶרֶת זְקֵנִים בְּנֵי בָנִים, וְתִפְאֶרֶת בָּנִים אֲבוֹתָם (משלי יז:ו).
וְאוֹמֵר: תִּפְאֶרֶת בַּחוּרִים כֹּחָם, וַהֲדַר זְקֵנִים שֵׂיבָה (משלי
כ:כט). וְאוֹמֵר: וְחָפְרָה הַלְּבָנָה וּבוֹשָׁה הַחַמָּה, כִּי־מָלַךְ יְיָ
צְבָאוֹת בְּהַר צִיּוֹן וּבִירוּשָׁלַיִם, וְנֶגֶד זְקֵנָיו כָּבוֹד (ישעיהו כד:כג).
רַבִּי שִׁמְעוֹן בֶּן מְנַסְיָא אוֹמֵר: אֵלוּ שֶׁבַע מִדּוֹת, שֶׁמָּנוּ
חֲכָמִים לַצַּדִּיקִים – כֻּלָּם נִתְקַיְּמוּ בְּרַבִּי וּבְבָנָיו.

Rabbi Shimon ben Y'hudah says in the name of Rabbi Shimon ben Yochai: Beauty, strength, wealth, honor, wisdom, old age, hoary age, and children—these befit the righteous and befit the world, as it is said: "Ripe old age is a crown of splendor, it can be found in the path of righteousness" (Proverbs 16:31). And it says: "Children's children are the crown of the aged, and the glory of the children is their father's" (Proverbs 17:6). And it says: "The splendor of young men is their strength, and glory of old men is hoary age" (Proverbs 20:29). And it says: "The moon will grow pale and the sun be shamed, when the Eternal, Master of Legions, will have reigned on Mount Zion and in Jerusalem, and honor shall be before God's elders" (Isaiah 24:23). Rabbi Shimon ben M'nasya said: These seven qualities that the Sages attributed to the righteous were all realized in Rabbi and his sons.

SCIENCE HAS FOUND that no two tears are physically alike. Every act of crying is unique, as if each emotional outpouring, unique in its own right, must be expressed distinctively. A midrash teaches that there are six kinds of tears, three beneficial and three harmful.[471] Such a statement shows that humans are predisposed to understanding the nuances of our own emotions and that even tears can be used as vehicles for growth and inner reflection.

This mishnah recognizes the uniqueness of each human as something that never existed before and never will again. Rabbi Shimon's scope dares us to think less about our physical selves and more about our spiritual well-being.

If we are engaged in passionate, creative Torah learning, then our body's age is meaningless. The physical body may get older, but the soul only grows stronger. Getting older means that one has had more of a chance to learn, grow, and internalize the timeless precepts that preceded and will succeed one's corporeal existence. When you engage with life, you are sage-ing more than aging. Most important to the Torah enterprise is that learning makes us more righteous and more engaged in the universe.

Yet, the cruel irony of learning is that the human life span is remarkably short. We require daily spiritual activities to remind us of this stubborn truth. A person who lives to eighty will take about 672,768,000 breaths, but the shofar sounds a noise only if someone blows into it. So, too, our soul prays only if we allow God to breathe through us. Tap into the divine breath that breathes through you like a divine shofar! Feel the gratitude, the intimacy.

When we encounter others, we must see beyond the surface. Rabbi Alexandri, a scholar from the amoraic era (ca. 200–500 CE), teaches, "If a common person uses a broken vessel, it is considered a disgrace. But not the Holy One of Blessing. All of God's vessels are broken. 'God is near the brokenhearted' (Psalm 34)."[472]

To achieve the highest holiness, we must gain freedom. Many consider themselves free who, from the Torah's perspective, remain enslaved. Rabbi Kook explains that there are intelligent slaves whose being is full of freedom, and there are free individuals whose being consists of the spirit of a slave.[473] The real slave is one who lives in conformity, seeking to be honored by others. The free individual experiences inner individuality and the eternal illumination of God within oneself.

The opportunities to truly see ourselves and others are right before our eyes. Therein lies our freedom and, indeed, our dignity. To emulate the Divine, we should be focused on the most powerless rather than the most powerful, the most broken rather than the most fortunate. We must witness the suffering right before our eyes. A Chasidic tale:

> The Sassover Rebbe entered a hotel, and sat beside two local peasants. As the two peasants sat at the bar and drank, they began to fall into a drunken stupor. One turned to his friend and said, "Tell me, friend, do you love me?" His colleague responded, "Of course I love you. We're drinking companions. Naturally I love you." Then the first one said to his friend, "Then tell me, friend, what causes me pain?" His colleague said, "How should I know what hurts you? I'm just your drinking buddy." He said, "If you loved me you would know what causes me pain."[474]

Opening our eyes requires readiness to cry and see others' tears. All express emotion differently; some tear up at the slightest stimulus, while others are dry-eyed amid the most trying situations. Though emotions and tears are deeply personal, they also reflect spirituality and connection to God. Let us further explore the theological significance of our tears.

Rabbi Jonathan Sacks tells of a Chasidic rebbe during the Holocaust and of the danger of divine tears:

> In the Warsaw ghetto there lived and died a great and saintly Hassidic Rebbe, Rabbi Kalonymous Shapiro. Throughout the years 1941–1943 he taught his disciples, and wrote down [their] addresses . . . in a book. Knowing he would not survive, he buried the book under the ground. It was discovered after the war. As the weeks went by, Rabbi Shapiro saw his community, his friends, his family, his children, one by one, taken to the extermination camps. And still he taught, though with greater and greater pain, until one day, he told his disciples that God Himself was weeping, and if a single tear were to escape from heaven to earth, it would destroy the world.[475]

In this anecdote, we see the preciousness of inhabiting the memory of where we are and the tears that are shed when we imbue objects with significance. Even objects that have no inherent holiness can be rendered sacred through contextual circumstance. Such a thought is also based upon a Talmudic teaching:

> What are the *z'vaot* [i.e., what does this term *z'vaot* mean]? Rabbi K'tina said, "An earthquake." Rabbi K'tina was walking along the road. When he came to the door of the house of a bone necromancer, [the earth] shuddered and quaked. He said, "Does the necromancer know how such an earthquake comes to be?" He shouted out to him, "K'tina, K'tina, why should I not know? When the Holy One of Blessing remembers God's children, who endure the misery among the nations of the world, God sheds two tears into the Great Sea, and its sound is heard from one end of the world to the other, and this is [what we perceive as] an earthquake!" (BT *B'rachot* 59a)

Not only do God's tears affect us. Rabbi Levi Yitzchak of Berditchev, the K'dushat Levi, taught that the emotions we express on earth deeply affect the heavens.[475a] God hears and feels our pain—a profound idea that we should consider during our times of agony. Our tears, pain, oppression, and anxiety reach the heavens. The Talmud teaches, "The 'meek [*tz'nuot*]' among them weep, and their tears reach the heavenly throne because the gates to accept 'those who are oppressed' and the gates to accept 'tears' are never closed" (BT *Bava M'tzia* 59b).

This Talmudic lesson from *B'rachot* teaches something extraordinary: Tears are miraculous, and the eyes behind the tears are the gateway into realms mysterious and eternal. Tears are an external divine reminder of the intensity of our inner, and hidden, worlds. These simple drops of water reveal something complex and profound about the human spiritual condition. Regardless of how we each express our emotions—readily or reluctantly—we should take time to consider the power and uniqueness of our being and self-expression.

6:9

אָמַר רַבִּי יוֹסֵי בֶּן קִסְמָא: פַּעַם אַחַת הָיִיתִי מְהַלֵּךְ בַּדֶּרֶךְ
וּפָגַע בִּי אָדָם אֶחָד, וְנָתַן לִי שָׁלוֹם וְהֶחֱזַרְתִּי לוֹ שָׁלוֹם. אָמַר
לִי: רַבִּי, מֵאֵיזֶה מָקוֹם אָתָּה? אָמַרְתִּי לוֹ: מֵעִיר גְּדוֹלָה שֶׁל
חֲכָמִים וְשֶׁל סוֹפְרִים אָנִי. אָמַר לִי: רַבִּי, רְצוֹנְךָ שֶׁתָּדוּר
עִמָּנוּ בִּמְקוֹמֵנוּ? וַאֲנִי אֶתֵּן לְךָ אֶלֶף אֲלָפִים דִּינְרֵי זָהָב
וַאֲבָנִים טוֹבוֹת וּמַרְגָּלִיּוֹת. אָמַרְתִּי לוֹ: בְּנִי, אִם אַתָּה
נוֹתֵן לִי כָּל כֶּסֶף וְזָהָב שֶׁבָּעוֹלָם, אֵינִי דָר אֶלָּא בִמְקוֹם
תוֹרָה – לְפִי שֶׁבִּשְׁעַת פְּטִירָתוֹ שֶׁל אָדָם אֵין מְלַוִּין אוֹתוֹ
לֹא כֶסֶף וְלֹא זָהָב וְלֹא אֲבָנִים טוֹבוֹת וּמַרְגָּלִיּוֹת, אֶלָּא
תוֹרָה וּמַעֲשִׂים טוֹבִים בִּלְבַד, שֶׁנֶּאֱמַר: בְּהִתְהַלֶּכְךָ תַּנְחֶה
אֹתָךְ, בְּשָׁכְבְּךָ תִּשְׁמֹר עָלֶיךָ, וַהֲקִיצוֹתָ הִיא תְשִׂיחֶךָ (משלי ו:כב).
בְּהִתְהַלֶּכְךָ תַּנְחֶה אֹתָךְ – בָּעוֹלָם הַזֶּה. בְּשָׁכְבְּךָ תִּשְׁמֹר עָלֶיךָ
– בַּקֶּבֶר. וַהֲקִיצוֹתָ הִיא תְשִׂיחֶךָ – לֶעָתִיד לָבֹא. וְכֵן בְּדָוִד הוּא
אוֹמֵר: טוֹב־לִי תוֹרַת־פִּיךָ מֵאַלְפֵי זָהָב וָכָסֶף (תהלים קיט:עב).
וְאוֹמֵר: לִי הַכֶּסֶף וְלִי הַזָּהָב, נְאֻם יְיָ צְבָאוֹת (חגי ב:ח).

Rabbi Yosei ben Kisma said: Once I was walking on the road, when a certain man met me. He greeted me and I returned his greeting. He said to me, "Rabbi, from what place are you?" I said to him, "I am from a great city of scholars and sages." He said to me, "Rabbi, would you be willing to live with us in our place? I would give you thousands upon thousands of golden dinars, precious stones, and pearls." I replied, "Even if you were to give me all the silver and gold in the world, I would dwell nowhere but in a place of Torah." For when a person departs from this world, neither silver, nor gold, nor precious stones, nor pearls escort him, but only Torah study and good deeds, as it is said: "When you walk, it shall guide you; when you lie down, it shall guard you; and when you awake, it shall speak on your behalf" (Proverbs 6:22). "When you walk, it shall guide"—in this world; "When you lie down, it shall guard you"— in the grave; "and when you awake, it shall speak on your behalf"— in the world-to-come. And so with [regard to King] David it says: "I prefer the Torah of Your mouth above thousands in gold and silver" (Psalm 119:72). And it says: "Mine is the silver, and Mine is the gold, says God, Master of Legions" (Haggai 2:8).

A PASSAGE in the Bible challenges the notion of human-divine relations. Before God decides to destroy Sodom, Abraham argues that even Sodom, for all its moral turpitude, should be spared (Genesis 18:16–32).

In this mishnah, the Rabbis remind us not to succumb to wealth for its own sake. Affluence is fleeting. Only our souls and their embedded beauty and wisdom have lasting power. To grow spiritually we need to be surrounded by competent partners. Unchecked wealth cannot purchase these partners, but it does serve to accentuate and, oftentimes, bring out the lingering darkness in ourselves. To move into the light, we have to grow to accept ourselves for who we are and who we choose to be. We have to do the best we can with what we have, to open our hearts, and to be ever mindful that the best things in life—love, growth, happiness—are for the taking should we choose to grab them and hold them tight.

Case in point: Never underestimate community and its positive influences on our lives. Neighborhoods, schools, places of worship—all matter. A truly inclusive community and society is one that goes beyond mere tolerance, to ensure that all have access to the pious, wise, and righteous. To do so, we must move beyond the naïve value of tolerance, the idea that people can despise the values of a group yet still tolerate its presence. This type of tolerance is anathema to real social change, a weak reaction by a society too timid to ask difficult questions about our relationships with one another. Instead, we must further religious pluralism and cultural inclusion.

While it was presumed that modernity would help society move beyond religious intolerance, there are still influential sectors within our culture that are not yet willing to accept diversity. Despite the terrible predicaments that face the world today, we must reverse the trend of growing intolerance. We have no real choice; if we want our country to remain the leader of the free world, we must lead the way. To start, we cannot claim to understand or value those from another religious or cultural background if we are not willing to undertake the difficult task of truly getting to know them. Avoiding these relationships will lead to misunderstanding and intolerance. As citizens of the world, we pay a terrible price when we cultivate ignorance by refusing to learn and understand the religious traditions of others. That ignorance can lead to violence. Furthermore, we must come to see the value of the religious practices of our fellow human beings. Religious pluralism enables us to hold on to our core values, which in turn allows us to see sparks of truth in another's absolute values.

When our goal is religious pluralism, we no longer line up armies, police, sanctions, and threats to prevent the Hobbesian "war of all against all."[476] Rather, we strive for understanding and appreciation of differences. Tolerance is a stepping-stone to reach this goal, but not the end itself. The end is mutual appreciation and a healthy celebration of difference, without being disingenuous.

Each of us is responsible to be open and critical of our own faith, hold extreme voices in our communities accountable, cultivate relationships with those in other faith communities, and pursue peace and understanding in all possible ways. We do so not because we're proud of our liberal attitudes, but because it has the potential to lead to palpable results. Through community dialogue and personal interaction, we must find courageous moderates and pluralists who have a positive influence, especially in more extremist and intolerant groups. Global stability and the serenity of our souls on this earth rest upon our success in this endeavor.

6:10

חֲמִשָּׁה קִנְיָנִין קָנָה הַקָּדוֹשׁ בָּרוּךְ הוּא בְּעוֹלָמוֹ, וְאֵלּוּ הֵן:
תּוֹרָה, קִנְיָן אֶחָד; שָׁמַיִם וָאָרֶץ, קִנְיָן אֶחָד; אַבְרָהָם, קִנְיָן
אֶחָד; יִשְׂרָאֵל, קִנְיָן אֶחָד; בֵּית הַמִּקְדָּשׁ, קִנְיָן אֶחָד. תּוֹרָה
קִנְיָן אֶחָד, מִנַּיִן? דִּכְתִיב: יְיָ קָנָנִי רֵאשִׁית דַּרְכּוֹ, קֶדֶם
מִפְעָלָיו מֵאָז (משלי ח:כב). שָׁמַיִם וָאָרֶץ קִנְיָן אֶחָד, מִנַּיִן?
שֶׁנֶּאֱמַר: כֹּה אָמַר יְיָ, הַשָּׁמַיִם כִּסְאִי וְהָאָרֶץ הֲדֹם רַגְלָי,
אֵי־זֶה בַיִת אֲשֶׁר תִּבְנוּ־לִי וְאֵי־זֶה מָקוֹם מְנוּחָתִי (ישעיהו
סו:א). וְאוֹמֵר: מָה־רַבּוּ מַעֲשֶׂיךָ, יְיָ, כֻּלָּם בְּחָכְמָה עָשִׂיתָ,
מָלְאָה הָאָרֶץ קִנְיָנֶךָ (תהלים קד:כד). אַבְרָהָם קִנְיָן אֶחָד, מִנַּיִן?
שֶׁנֶּאֱמַר: וַיְבָרְכֵהוּ וַיֹּאמַר, בָּרוּךְ אַבְרָם לְאֵל עֶלְיוֹן, קֹנֵה
שָׁמַיִם וָאָרֶץ (בראשית יד:יט). יִשְׂרָאֵל קִנְיָן אֶחָד, מִנַּיִן? שֶׁנֶּאֱמַר:
עַד־יַעֲבֹר עַמְּךָ, יְיָ, עַד־יַעֲבֹר עַם־זוּ קָנִיתָ (שמות טו:טז).
וְאוֹמֵר: לִקְדוֹשִׁים אֲשֶׁר־בָּאָרֶץ הֵמָּה, וְאַדִּירֵי כָּל־חֶפְצִי־בָם
(תהלים טז:ג). בֵּית הַמִּקְדָּשׁ קִנְיָן אֶחָד, מִנַּיִן? שֶׁנֶּאֱמַר: מָכוֹן
לְשִׁבְתְּךָ פָּעַלְתָּ, יְיָ מִקְדָּשׁ אֲדֹנָי כּוֹנְנוּ יָדֶיךָ (שמות טו:יז).
וְאוֹמֵר: וַיְבִיאֵם אֶל־גְּבוּל קָדְשׁוֹ, הַר־זֶה קָנְתָה יְמִינוֹ
(תהלים עח:נד).

Five possessions did the Holy One of Blessing acquire in this world, and they are: Torah, one possession; heaven and earth, one possession; Abraham, one possession; Israel, one possession; the Holy Temple, one possession. From where do we know this about the Torah? Since it is written: "God acquired me [the Torah] at the beginning of God's way, before God's works in time of yore" (Proverbs 8:22). From where do we know this about heaven and earth? Since it is written: "So says God. The heaven is My throne and the earth is My footstool; what House can you build for Me, and where is the place of My rest?" (Isaiah 66:1). And it says: "How abundant are Your works,

God—with wisdom You made them all—the earth is full of Your possessions" (Psalm 104:24). From where do we know this about Abraham? Since it is written: "And God blessed him and said: Blessed is Abram of God the Most High, who acquired heaven and earth" (Genesis 14:19). From where do we know this about the people Israel? Since it is written: "Until Your people passes through, God, until it passes through—this people You acquired" (Exodus 15:16); and it [also] says: "But for the holy ones who are in the earth and the mighty, all my desires are due to them" (Psalm 16:3). From where do we know this about the Holy Temple? Since it is written: "The place You made to dwell in, Eternal One, / The sanctuary, Eternal [God], which Your hands established" (Exodus 15:17). And it says: "And God brought them to God's sacred boundary, to this mountain that God's right hand acquired" (Psalm 78:54).

IN THIS PENULTIMATE MISHNAH, the Sages take an introspective approach to divinity. They consider the nature of God and God's role in history. God, who told Abraham to leave his ancestral home, who guided the Hebrews through the desert, who resided in the heart of the Temple, is not an apathetic being. There is no removal from the world with God, and there is no distance between any individual and the Divine. This is a God who invests in this world and even "acquires" possessions within it. By being present in people's souls, God feels the spirits of Creation and attempts to lead people on the right path.

In this mishnah, we see something metaphysically exceptional: God "acquires." God can possess things, which seems paradoxical for a being whose reign spans the width of the universe. What is going on here? Consider that so much of human experience is about producing, acquiring, and consuming and that here we learn how to follow the divine path in relation to consumption. Jewish tradition is rich with wisdom about food consumption, for example; feeding the indigent and hungry, labor practices, treatment of animals, fair trade, environmental impact, and healthful practices can all be guided by Judaism.

Consequently, the Torah represents this lingering spirituality in a physical sense. Heaven and earth—two sides of reality—represent spatial existence. Abraham is the human dimension of pursuing justice in this world; Israel, the idea of human community and covenantal relationship; the Holy Temple shows the value of service. In these, God's five possessions, all of religious life can be found. In pursuing them, God is discovered.

Chasidic thought shows a complex relationship to the material world. On the one hand, the *chasid* (individual striving for a pious life of service) should seek to transcend the material, while on the other hand, one is charged with elevating the material. Can these two approaches be reconciled, and what are the spiritual practices associated with each?

A certain type of *chasid* attempts to negate and transcend the concrete and the mundane, notably through *bitul hayeish*, in which one seeks to negate one's being. Moving from being to nothingness, one transcends physical reality and physical concerns. One achieves this state via the *derech hachasidut*, the pious asceticism of disowning materialism, through a radical clinging to God (*d'veikut*) and breaking free from materialism (*gashmiut*).

Many Chasidic thinkers understood the human to be composed of two components: *nefesh habehemit* (the animalistic soul) and *nefesh ha'Elokit* (the godly, spiritual soul). This seems to imply rejection of the unified self, in which the physical and the spiritual are integrated. One seeks to remove materialism (*hafshatat hagashmiut*) through prayer to reach the divine core of the self; transcending the mind by stripping away the barriers to God's presence—*hafshatat hamachshavah*—is also a goal. The value for this process can be called *hishtavut*, equanimity, in which all values connected to this world are seen as vain and empty. This is achieved via *histalkut*, withdrawal from physical thinking and concerns. The *chasid* denounces all ties to the physical world, which is impure, valueless, and an impediment to serving God, *avodat Elohim*.

Another type of *chasid* seeks to elevate the mundane, earthly world. This is called *avodah b'gashmiut*, which means that one serves God through the body and seeks the Divine in the physical. This is a way to illuminate the mundane and the intentions associated with it. While *d'veikut* is generally understood as transcendence of physicality, one might see *d'veikut b'otiot*, a clinging to God through the divine letters, as an engagement with the physical. Chasidic thinkers have argued that God can be seen only in a finite form, in a clothed form (*levush*), and that we need the concrete to perceive and connect to God. This is a radical shift from the common understanding of God as incorporeal.

Should one seek to actualize the soul and the soul's service by embracing materialism, or should one disown it completely? The Baal Shem Tov, the founder of Chasidism, sought to embrace and to elevate the physical world, though it seems that he lived quite ascetically. Chasidim today speak of the vanities of the material world; however, many seem to take part in fine cuisine and technology, along with the rest of Western culture.

If one dismisses physical realities as part of one's piety, how can one also care about another's pain? The Hebrew University's Rachel Elior, a professor of Jewish philosophy, writes:

> The suffering of the material world was replaced by an optimism derived from the recognition that there is more to existence than meets the eye and that shared social and spiritual responsibility can ease the confrontation with reality.[477]

This seeming tension is eased by a spiritual view of the world that includes the physical but also transcends it. By taking responsibility for our existence and others, we can access the deeper spiritual truths hidden within the physical. Elior continues the argument for the egalitarian ethos of Chasidism:

> The idea that every individual is a sanctuary for the divine essence that fills the universe with its glory accords equal value to all members of the community and all modes of worship by virtue of the radical claim that "God wants to be served in all modes. . . . God can be served in everything.[478]

Martin Buber says that "Hasidism is kabbalah that has become ethos."[479] Living piously, at its best, is about transforming every encounter into an ethical embrace. The tension between the physical and spiritual is resolved by a responsibility to the other. Elior suggests:

Hasidism linked the mystical ascent to the higher worlds with social responsibility in the material universe and saw the significance
of the physical world only in the divine animation that sustains it.
In doing so, Hasidism proposed a new relationship between the
spiritual and material. The perpetual transition from nothingness
to being is reflected in the figure of the *tzaddik* (righteous person),
who attaches himself to the higher worlds and channels spiritual
and physical abundance to his followers. Some have interpreted
this as a form of quietism (indirect activism), that by being *me-
tzamtzem* (retracting oneself from the world) God's overflowing
goodness will pour over upon other humans; this quietism must
be transformed to an activism.[480]

Avodah b'gashmiut means that we serve God through both our bodies and others' bodies. Collective service is a value; one seeking piety
must care about one's fellow. Even for those who strive to reject physicality, there is spiritual value in purifying ourselves through engaging
mindfully in the physical world and through helping others attain their
physical needs. A good person is one who performs *chesed* (love and
kindness), is righteous (*tzaddik*), and does *tzedakah* (righteous acts).
We seek spiritual existences to break away from the mundanities of
the world. Spiritual courage allows us to transcend materialism, while
also allowing us to check in on our physical needs. And in this way, we
seek to subvert physical needs with spiritual needs to flourish as human
beings.

It is our task to ignite the holy sparks within our souls and seek out
that divinity that resides within. It is there for us, hovering above our
consciousness, if only we have the temerity to reach for it. In this way,
we emulate acquiring only the positive elements of the universe, ultimately gaining a direct conduit to the supernal holiness of God.

6:11

וְכֻלָּם שֶׁבָּרָא הַקָּדוֹשׁ בָּרוּךְ הוּא בְּעוֹלָמוֹ – לֹא בְּרָאָם אֶלָּא
לִכְבוֹדוֹ, שֶׁנֶּאֱמַר: כֹּל הַנִּקְרָא בִשְׁמִי, וְלִכְבוֹדִי בְּרָאתִיו
יְצַרְתִּיו אַף־עֲשִׂיתִיו (ישעיהו מג:ז). וְאוֹמֵר: יְיָ יִמְלֹךְ לְעֹלָם
וָעֶד (שמות טו:יח).

All that the Holy One of Blessing created in this world was
created solely for God's own glory, as it is said: "All that is
called by My name, indeed, it is for My glory that I have created it, formed it, and made it" (Isaiah 43:7). And it says: "The
Eternal will reign for ever and ever" (Exodus 15:18).

HERE WE ARE, at the end of a long, meaningful journey. After six
chapters of Jewish ethics, epistemology, anecdotes, homilies, and
philosophical inquiry, the mishnah concludes with the reminder that
although focus has been placed on interpersonal relations and growth
of the inner self, Judaism is ultimately centered around God. At the end
of the mishnah, we reflect on what we have witnessed over the course
of *Pirkei Avot*. Here, collected for the ages, are the words that guided
countless people on their spiritual journeys. These words of ethics, philosophy, and love give us strength, hope, and a sense of obligation to
our fellow. Because God is completely benevolent, we should emulate
God's divine ways. All that we have read, ruminated on, and reacted to
has been about achieving the highest good. With this conclusion, we
are reminded to grow and be humble, because we are under God's loving authority.

In ritual, we prioritize the right side over the left, to signify that love
and kindness, *chesed*, outweigh strength and justice, *g'vurah*. In striving to emulate God, we cultivate both but work to ensure that *chesed*
outweighs strength. Batya Gallant explains the stages of spiritual
development:[481]

> R. Tzadok Hakohen teaches us that spiritual growth follows a pre-
> dictable sequence. Just as, physically, an infant learns to sit before

learning to stand up, or, intellectually, a child first engages in intuitive thinking before he/she can engage in concrete operational
thinking, there is also a clear developmental sequence (first *chesed*,
then *gevurah*, then *emet*) to spiritual growth.[482]

We learn kindness, and then strength and courage, and only finally do
we learn truth. This is not only a map for advancing children in their
spiritual development, but also a sequence of thought for the spiritually advanced to encounter life's challenges.

We should seek out compromise and a gentle approach, rather than
a strictly true or just approach. A midrash teaches:

> Greater is that which is said about Aaron than that which is said
> about Moses. Regarding Moses, it is said that only men wept for
> him, whereas for Aaron both the men and the women wept, be-
> cause he pursued peace and loved peace and made peace between a
> husband and his wife and between a woman and her friend.[483]

If Moses is the leader for all of humankind, then how is it that only
one gender wept for him? The contrast between Moses and Aaron
here shows human potential for compromise. If Moses modeled love
by being strict toward the people, then Aaron is the leader who walks
among the people, building and healing fractured relationships. This
is the dialectic between love and justice, in which love is the victor over
justice.

Learning the art of compromise is arduous. So much must happen
on global, national, and interpersonal fronts. But first we must consider our own egos, not letting our tribal tendencies take hold of our
better nature. We must be willing to retreat from absolutes for the sake
of peace on earth. One might think that absolutism is a sign of strength
and that one with moral clarity shouldn't budge. Judaism proposes this
counterintuitive approach arguing that compromise is the approach of
the wise:

> Rabbi Y'hoshua ben Karcha says, "It is a mitzvah to seek compro-
> mise." As it is written, "Truth and peaceful judgment should you
> judge in your gates (Zechariah 8:16)." It would seem that where
> there is judgment there is no peace, and where there is peace there

is no judgment. What is the judgment that incorporates peace? Compromise. (BT *Sanhedrin* 6b)

The Rabbis valued religious compromise. In the Talmud, Rabbi Yochanan says that Jerusalem was destroyed in the time of the Romans because the people judged only according to the Torah (BT *Bava M'tzia* 30b). The astonished counter: "What kind of judgment should they have applied—that of the sorcerers?" The reply: "What Rabbi Yochanan meant was that litigants insisted on strict enforcement of the law and were unwilling to compromise."[484]

One's character is measured not solely by one's ideals, but also by willingness to compromise for the sake of human dignity. There are, of course, values that should not be compromised. But for the sake of peace, we often compromise, even when certain of the truth. Rashi taught that doing "'the right and the good' [Deuteronomy 6:18] refers to a compromise, within the letter of the law." The Talmud teaches that God prays to control the limits of divine power that could destroy the universe with but a single thought:

> May it be My will that My mercy may suppress My anger, and that My mercy may prevail over My [other] attributes, so that I may deal with My children in the attribute of mercy and, on their behalf, stop short of the limit of strict justice. (BT *B'rachot* 7a)

If God is to pray for God's own kindness to prevail over justice, then certainly we should do the same. In all we do, we must focus on building a world imbued with compassion, healing, and peace rather, than on unswerving truth, strict judgment, and punishment. Being right is not always the same thing as doing right. *Pirkei Avot* compels us to ask ourselves: How can we take the high road today? How can we take the challenge of pursuing justice beyond the personal and into our civic and business interactions? It is our duty to work toward compromise, no matter the circumstance, so that the world will become more just, equitable, and peaceful. These questions may be difficult, but responding to them is our sacred imperative.

Conclusion

As we end our *Pirkei Avot* journey, let us take a moment to consider what we have learned. Through the course of these six chapters, the enormity of Jewish ethical philosophy has been discussed rigorously, but with surprising intimacy. While we cannot know if the Sages of the Mishnah understood that their wisdom would be studied and analyzed for millennia, the precepts here have been the foundation for Jewish moral pedagogy. *Pirkei Avot* is a bedrock of forthright principles for goodness and holiness and has centered Judaism as one of the world's foremost ethical movements.

Throughout Jewish thought, humanity's primary responsibility is to protect and prioritize the most vulnerable individuals. Rabbi Ahron Soloveichik notes that "God takes the side of the aggrieved and the victim."[485] When there is conflict, God cannot withhold support for the one suffering. The Rabbis make this point time and time again. The Talmud, supporting the verse "Justice, justice, shall you pursue" (Deuteronomy 16:20), teaches that the disadvantaged should be given preference, all else being equal. Maimonides, too, teaches that even if the disadvantaged arrive later to a gathering than other people, they should be given precedence.[486]

So, where do we look for justice? Rabbi Ahron Soloveichik writes, "A Jew should always identify with the cause of defending the aggrieved, whosoever the aggrieved may be, just as the concept of *tzedek* [justice] is to be applied uniformly to all humans regardless of race or creed."[487] The need to perform acts of charity and righteousness should be ever present in the Jewish soul. This is what it means to be Jewish: prioritize healing where there is suffering; relieve those in need; bring one's full heart into the world to help others, no matter their background, faith, or condition.

To bring our dreams of a unified world into reality, we need one another. To heal the maladies of human nature—avarice, mendacity, tribalism—we need one another. When we succumb to our natural fears of change, we cease growing. Meanwhile, what lies dormant yearns to reach full potency. It is our challenge and our obligation to transform communities that shirk engagement into communities that radiate compassion at every turn, turn strangers into friends, and transfigure mourners into healers.

In our pursuit of a lasting holiness that will rest upon this earth, we must take responsibility for pursuing the moral good in our private realm and justice in the public realm and pray for strength from the Creator. But we do not cry out to God for simplistic judgment, nor do we ask God to work alone to bring about redemption. We must raise up issues of justice into the world ourselves; we must organize on a grassroots level for change; we must take courageous responsibility for pervasive injustice in our society. Sometimes that is in line with law, and sometimes it is acting against the legal system. In either case, pursuing justice in our world today is the value that wins out.

The *Kitzur Shulchan Aruch*, a nineteenth-century work of Jewish jurisprudence by Rabbi Shlomo Ganzfried, teaches:

> It is prohibited for a person to appeal for judgment from heaven [in other words, divine retribution] against someone who has wronged them. This prohibition applies only if there is recourse to attain justice here on earth. [And if so,] anyone who cries out to heaven about someone else is punished first.[488]

While it is true that there is an ultimate Judge in the world-to-come, during this life we perform the hard work to manifest peace and justice. This is a sizable task. Throughout history, Jews often lacked access to fairness and justice; but today we live in a different era. We have religious oversight, secular courts, and effective grassroots networks; there are many ways to act on behalf of righteousness.

Sometimes, wise people make decisions that impede the moral growth of the community. In the Talmud, the Sages decreed after the destruction of the Temple that Jews should no longer marry; in the minds of the Sages, the destruction meant the end of the Jewish people.

The people ignored the decree and built families (BT *Bava Batra* 60b). When existence seems at its lowest, it takes courage and conviction to see that all is not lost.

At times, we must defy inherently unjust decrees. The Talmud relays how Miriam persuaded her father, Amram, to have children with her mother, Jocheved, despite Pharaoh's decree that Hebrew boys were to be murdered at birth. Amram insisted on no more children, to avoid the Egyptian infanticide. Miriam rebuked her father, telling him that this was even worse than Pharaoh's decree (BT *Sotah* 12a). Against an unjust tyranny, the Hebrews were determined to survive. In Henry David Thoreau's 1849 essay "Civil Disobedience," Thoreau writes that if injustice "is of such a nature that it requires you to be the agent of injustice to another, then I say, break the law."[489]

To build intentional communities properly, we must build covenants of trust and commitments to honor the deepest dignity of each individual. In a democratic society, we must open the tent wide and lead with our theology of hospitality; each of us has so much to contribute to those in our communities. Indeed, life within broader society cannot simply pertain to commerce and politics: we must show compassion to one another and foster an ethic of care. Abraham and Sarah ran from the tent to serve strangers in their camp (Genesis 18); so too must we look beyond our closest community to serve others. We journey not in isolation, but in a web of interconnected relationships.

We need one another in the deepest way. Our collective spaces cannot merely be political realms but must also be experienced personally. Those around us may not be friends, but in our fragmented society, they must be more than mere strangers. In Jewish law, we are told that it is unjust to be swayed by a person's poverty or to favor the case of the poor over the rich in a dispute. Within the court, this matters (Exodus 23:3, 6)—but does it still apply today, when the disparity between poor and rich is such that the poor often can no longer advocate for themselves?

Every individual should have the same fair opportunity to blossom into who they are meant to be; we must be committed to truth and the divine understanding of justice and love for all people. Unfortunately, this is not yet reality. Even if it were so, Judaism teaches that we must go over and above the strictures of society—*lifnim mishurat hadin*—to support those more vulnerable (BT *Bava M'tzia* 83a). Furthermore, we learn that God created and destroyed many worlds that were built upon the foundation of *din* (judgment), and then God finally created this world built upon *rachamim* (mercy).[490] Our world can't exist on pure judgment. Rather, as fallible beings working toward a goal of Divine-human reconciliation, we rely upon the grace, empathy, and kindness of both God and people.

We must be committed to the truth to be sure that the justice system is fair for all parties. Yet we should view ourselves as among the most responsible of change makers if we are to choose the path of ensuring justice for all. To give voice to the voiceless and support the unsupported is a holy role. This is Jewish activism. The Rabbis teach, "Even if a righteous person attacks a wicked person, God still sides with the victim."[491] All people deserve our love and care, but we must follow the path of God and make our allegiances clear: we stand with the destitute, oppressed, alienated, and suffering.

If we have so much to do to repair a broken world, why study *Pirkei Avot?* As demonstrated throughout this book, we can address the messy outer work of the world only if we address the messy inner work in our lives. Study, meditation, prayer, learning, debate, and spiritual journeying ensure that we remain open and evolving, and that we will challenge ourselves to achieve the unique potential within. If we truly seek to change the world, the Sages can stimulate us to do this in more nuanced and effective ways. These timeless teachings from the Rabbis are merely the start for endless discussions about our identities and values. May the teachings found within *Pirkei Avot* continue to inspire us to learn and to grow, to bring holy compassion to every facet of our lives.

And now back to chapter 1.

Notes

INTRODUCTION

1. This is not the literal meaning of the word *avah*, but a homiletical interpretation on the verse.

1a. See Abraham Ezra Millgram, *Jewish Worship* (Philadelphia: Jewish Publication Society of America, 1975), 195; Shemuel Safrai, *The Literature of the Sages*, vol. 1 (Philadelphia: Fortress Press, 1987), 274; Martin Sicker, *The Moral Maxims of the Sages of Israel: Pirkei Avot* (New York: iUniverse, 2004), 13. In many communities, studying a Jewish text before the conclusion of the Sabbath is a normal part of the day. The study of *Pirkei Avot* between Passover and Shavuot is special because the ensuing weeks are meant for Jews to reflect and ask serious ethical questions about the state of the world.

2. In translating the *mishnayot* here, for the sake of inclusivity, I have translated male language as "one" or "oneself" whenever the text is not referring specifically to a man or woman, rather than use gendered language. I've avoided and removed any gendered language for God except when quoting a passage that was originally written in English, to keep the exact wording used.

3. Irving (Yitz) Greenberg, *Sage Advice* (Jerusalem: Maggid, 2016), x.

4. Ibid., xii.

5. Senesh, besides being a poet, was a parachutist in the British army in Mandatory Palestine. During a campaign to save Hungarian Jews, she was caught at the Yugoslavian border, tortured, and executed. Her published works remain popular in Israel.

CHAPTER I

6. Emmanuel Levinas, *Totality and Infinity: An Essay on Exteriority*, trans. Alphonso Lingus (Boston: Kluwer Academic Publishers, 1991), 305.

7. Martin Buber, "Spinoza, Sabbatai Zevi, and the Baalshem," trans. Dr. Greta Hort, in *Hasidism* (New York: Philosophical Library, 2015), 96.

8. This phrase is also the title of a 2004 book by Professor Tamar Ross that cites Rav Kook's philosophy.

9. Elimelech of Lyzhensk, *Noam Elimelech*, "Commentary on *Parshat Vayeishev*."

10. See Jacob Immanuel Schochet, *Mystical Concepts in Chassidism* (New York: Kehot, 1979), 108n10; Elliot R. Wolfson, *Alef, Mem, Tau: Kabbalistic Musings on Time, Truth, and Death* (Los Angeles: University of California Press, 2006), 125; Schneur Zalman of Liadi, *Likutei Torah, Sh'lach* 37d.

11. Mira Beth Wasserman, "Holding the Waters at Bay," in *Seven Days, Many Voices*, ed. Benjamin David (New York: CCAR Press, 2017), 54.

12. Maimonides, *Mishneh Torah, Hilchot T'shuvah* 3:4.

13. *B'reishit Rabbah* 10:6.

14. See Lawrence Kohlberg, *The Philosophy of Moral Development: Moral Stages and the Idea of Justice* (New York: Harper & Row, 1981).

15. S'forno, Commentary on Exodus 4:22.

16. See Judah Goldin, *The Fathers According to Rabbi Nathan* (New Haven, CT: Yale University Press, 1990), 39.

17. Yosei ben Yoezer and Yosei ben Yochanan were known as part of the succession of *zugot* (pairs) who led their community between the second century BCE and the first century CE. They were major leaders in their time (*nasi*, or president; *av beit din*, or head of the court, respectively). Yosei ben Yoezer was later martyred by the Greeks for teaching Torah.

18. Maimonides, *Mishneh Torah, Hilchhot Yom Tov* 6:18.

19. Binyamin Lau, *The Sages*, vol. 1 (Jerusalem: Maggid, 2007), 98–99.

20. Rabbeinu Yonah Gerondi, *Sefer HaYirah*.

21. *Sichat Y'ladim: Avot* 3:14; *miut sichah: Avot* 6:6.

22. I present a heteronormative reading here, but the main point stands no matter the genders of the spouses: We are reminded to hold even our private conversations— those we hold with spouse or life partner—to high standards, rather than allowing ourselves and our partners to fall into harmful talk.

23. Jonathan Sacks and Marc D. Angel, *The Koren Pirkei Avot* (Jerusalem: Koren, 2015), 11.

24. Irving Greenberg, *Sage Advice* (Jerusalem: Maggid, 2016), 24.

25. Ibid.

26. Judith Plaskow, *Standing Again at Sinai: Judaism from a Feminist Perspective* (New York: HarperCollins, 1990), 1.

27. "A Conversation with Justice Ruth Bader Ginsburg," interview by Lynn Sherr on November 15, 2000, *The Record of the Association of the Bar of the City of New York* 56, no. 1 (winter 2001): 18; purl.org/ccar/pa-01.

28. "The Supreme Court: Excerpts from Senate Hearing on the Ginsburg Nomination," *New York Times*, July 22, 1993; purl.org/ccar/pa-02.

29. Hannah Greenebaum Solomon, Presidential address at reception given by the New York Section, National Council of Jewish Women, 1896.

30. Nadine Subailat, "NBA Teams with Sheryl Sandberg to "Lean In" for Women and Equality," *ABC News*, March 4, 2015; purl.org/ccar/pa-03.

31. Sheryl Sandberg with Nell Scovell, *Lean In* (New York: Knopf, 2013), 5.

32. Ibid., 8.

33. Anita Diamant, *The Red Tent* (New York: Picador, 1997), 2.

34. Kook, *Ein Ayah, B'rachot* 9:340–41.

35. Maimonides, *Guide for the Perplexed* 3:49.

36. Joseph B. Soloveitchik, *Family Redeemed* (Jerusalem: Ktav, 2000), 27–28.

37. S'forno, *Commentary on Pirkei Avot* 1:6.

37a. The Hebrew word *kol* can be read as "every person" or as "the entirety of a person." Thus we can discern this mishnah as saying both that we should judge *every* person favorably and that we should judge the *entirety* of a person favorably.

38. This line of thought can be attributed to Rabbi Jonathan Sacks's commentary on *Parashat Noach*, which in turn is based on the Chasidic thinking of Rabbi Menachem Mendel of Kotzk.

39. Rav Kahana teaches that the problem was that the unanimity toward conviction was not merely the final vote but the consensus from the beginning (BT *Sanhedrin* 17a). The problem was that there wasn't a fair trial from the start. Clearly, they didn't work hard enough to investigate the matter properly and seek the truth to fulfill the mandates of justice. To discourage lazy jurisprudence, the defendant simply goes free. This is a deterrent to judges who are busy and overly eager to move on to other matters.

40. See Martin Buber, "The Beginnings of Hasidism," in *Hasidism* (New York, Philosophical Library, 2015).

41. Chafetz Chayim, *Shmirat HaLashon, Shaar Haz'chirah*, chap. 17.

42. *B'reishit Rabbah* 8:5.

43. Quoted in Alan Morinis, *Every Day, Holy Day: 365 Days of Teachings and Practices from the Jewish Tradition of Mussar* (Boston: Trumpeter, 2010), 25.

44. *Vayikra Rabbah* 34:3.

45. *Tanchuma, Vayikra* 3.

46. See Viktor Frankl's influential work *Man's Search for Meaning* (Boston: Beacon Press, 1959).

47. This quote is featured prominently on Steinem's official website; purl.org /ccar/pa-04.

48. Carl Jung, *Contributions to Analytical Psychology* (New York: Harcourt, Brace & Company, 1928), 193.

49. Carl Jung, *Psychology and Alchemy* (New York: Routledge, 1953), 99.

50. Martin Buber, *Tales of the Hasidism*, vol. 2, trans. Olga Marx (New York: Schocken Books, 1948), 283.

51. Quoted in Pinchas H. Peli, *On Repentance: The Thought and Oral Discourses of Rabbi Joseph Dov Soloveitchik* (New York: Jason Aronson, 1984), 249.

52. Greenberg, *Sage Advice*, 45–46.

53. Macy Nulman, *The Encyclopedia of Jewish Prayer: The Ashkenazic and Sephardic Rites* (New York: Jason Aronson, 1993), 292, s.v. *Shaysh Zekhirot*.

54. Sacks and Angel, *The Koren Pirkei Avot*, 22.

55. Greenberg, *Sage Advice*, 50–51.

56. Howard Zinn, *You Can't Be Neutral on a Moving Train: A Personal History of Our Times* (Boston: Beacon Press, 2002), 4–5.

57. Kook, *Orot HaKodesh* 3:273.

58. Michael Fishbane, *Sacred Attunement: A Jewish Theology* (Chicago: University of Chicago Press, 2008), 13.

59. Sacks and Angel, *The Koren Pirkei Avot*, 24.

60. Quoted in Alan Morinis, *With Heart in Mind: Mussar Teachings to Transform Your Life* (Boston: Trumpeter, 2014), 92.

61. The Second Temple was destroyed in 70 CE by the Roman Empire.

62. Robert Cover, "Nomos and Narrative," *Harvard Law Review* 99 (1983): 4–68; found in Greenberg, *Sage Advice*, 58–59.

63. Greenberg, *Sage Advice*, 59.

64. Rabbi Ben-Zion Meir Chai Uziel, *Mishp'tei Uziel*, introduction; see also Peter Y. Medding (ed), *Sephardic Jewry and Mizrahi Jews*, Volume 22 (Oxford University Press: New York, 2007), 135.

65. Sacks and Angel, *The Koren Pirkei Avot*, 27.

CHAPTER 2

66. *Midrash HaNe-elam al Rut, Zohar Chadash*, 75b–c.

67. James L. Kugel, *In the Valley of the Shadow: On the Foundations of Religious Belief* (New York: Free Press, 2011), 3.

68. Moshe Chayim Luzzatto, *Path of the Just*, chap. 2.

69. See Alan Brill, "Grandeur and Humility in the Writings of R. Simhah Bunim of Przysucha," in *Hazon Nahum: Studies in Jewish Law, Thought, and History Presented to Dr. Norman Lamm on the Occasion of His Seventieth Birthday* (Jerusalem: Ktav, 1998), 447.

70. Kevin J. Haley and Daniel Fessler, Nobody's Watching? Subtle Cues Affect Generosity in an Anonymous Economic Game," *Evolution and Human Behavior* 26 (2005): 245–56; purl.org/ccar/pa-05.

71. Of course, surveillance has limits. While the "panopticon" model of a prison where all can be seen at all times may be effective, it is also inhumane. Human beings have a right to privacy.

72. See Berel (Brooklyn: Shaar Press, 2003), 54.

73. Irving (Yitz) Greenberg, *Sage Advice* (Jerusalem: Maggid, 2016), 68.

74. Ibid.

75. *Avot D'Rabbi Natan* 11.

76. *Avot D'Rabbi Natan* 11; *Mishnah K'tubot* 5:5.

77. Joseph B. Soloveitchik, *Halakhic Man* (Philadelphia: Jewish Publication Society, 1984), 101.

78. Rabbeinu Bachya, *Kad HaKemach*; Meir Tamari, *With All Your Possessions: Jewish Ethics and Economic Life* (New York: Free Press, 1987), 31.

79. Maimonides, *Mishneh Torah, Hilchot Talmud Torah* 3:10.

80. Martin Buber, *I and Thou*, trans. Ronald Gregor Smith (New York Continuum, 2004), 51; see also Justin Wintle, ed., *New Makers of Modern Culture*, vol. 1 (New York: Routledge, 2007), 222.

81. Buber, *I and Thou*, 51.

82. See Eugene B. Borowitz, *Choices in Modern Jewish Thought: A Partisan Guide* (West Orange, NJ, Behrman House, 1983), 164.

83. Meiri, Commentary on BT *Sotah* 20b.

84. Maimonides, *Mishneh Torah, Hilchot T'shuvah* 3:11.

85. Quoted in Greenberg, *Sage Advice*, 77.

86. Menachem Mendel of Kotzk, *Maggidei HaEmet*.

87. Brené Brown, *Daring Greatly: How the Courage to Be Vulnerable Transforms the Way We Live, Love, Parent, and Lead* (New York, Gotham Books, 2012), 61.

88. Maharal bases his mystical analysis upon the verse in Deuteronomy 33:2, "Lightning [also translated as 'fire'] flashing from God's right [hand, to the people of Israel]."

89. See Moshe Halamish, *An Introduction to the Kabbalah*, trans. Ruth Bar-Ilan and Ora Wiskind-Elper (Albany: State University of New York Press, 1999), 285; J. Abelson, *Jewish Mysticism: An Introduction to the Kabbalah* (Mineola, NY: Dover, 1913), 164.

90. Lauren E. Glaze and Danielle Kaeble, "Correctional Populations in the United States, 2013," Bureau of Justice Statistics (BJS), December 19, 2014; purl.org /ccar/pa-06.

90a. The biblical term in question is *chata-im* ("sinners"). According to Rabbi David E. S. Stein (personal communication), B'ruriah is drawing upon a subtle distinction within the semantics of two related grammatical parts of speech (as discussed in cognitive linguistics by Ronald Langacker). She is playing on the fact that the biblical designation employs an adjective form that's being used as a label—as opposed to the obvious alternative, namely the noun form *chot-im*. Of these two ways to designate "sinners," the adjectival form regards its referent in terms of a single attribute, whereas the noun form would regard its referent in terms of intrinsic character. B'ruriah observes midrashically that the verse by its choice of label leaves open the possibility that these "sinners" are only temporarily so; they can shed that negative attribute, because it's not their essence.

91. Nachmanides, Commentary on Leviticus 19:2.

92. Cf. Marx, *The Communist Manifesto*; Freud, *Totem and Taboo*; and Spinoza, *Ethics*, respectively.

93. See Richard J. Leider, *The Power of Purpose: Find Meaning, Live Longer, Better* (Oakland, CA: Berrett-Koehler, 2015), 50.

94. Lillian Wald, Speech before Women's Peace March organizing committee, 1914.

95. Kook, *Midot HaR'iyah*, "Love," section 11, 27.

96. Ibid., 32.

97. *Avot D'Rabbi Natan*, version A, 11a.

98. *Avot D'Rabbi Natan*, version B, 31.

99. Cf. BT *Shabbat* 112b; Shaul Maggid, *From Metaphysics to Midrash: Myth, History,*

and the Interpretation of Scripture in Lurianic Kabbala (Indianapolis: Indiana University Press, 2008), 224.

100. C. S. Lewis, *The Four Loves* (New York: Hartcourt Brace, 1988), 121.

101. Martha Nussbaum, *Hiding from Humanity: Disgust, Shame, and the Law* (Princeton, NJ: Princeton University Press, 2006), 17.

102. Parker Palmer, *Healing the Heart of Democracy* (San Francisco: Jossey-Bass, 2014), 15.

103. Kook, *Orot HaKodesh* 2:316.

104. Menachem Mendel of Kotzk, *Maggidei HaEmet*; see also the S'fat Emet commentary on mishnah 2:13.

105. See Arthur Kurzweil, *On the Road with Rabbi Steinsaltz* (San Francisco: Jossey-Bass, 2006), section 5.

106. James Baldwin, quoted in Jane Howard, "Doom and Glory of Knowing Who You Are," *Life* 54, no. 21 (May 24, 1963), 89.

107. Johann Wolfgang von Goethe, *Conversations of Goethe with Eckermann and Soret*, vol. 2, trans. John Oxenford (London: Smith, Elder, 1850), 93; emphasis added.

108. Oscar Wilde, *Lady Windermere's Fan*, act 3.

109. As quoted in Ida Husted Harper, *The Life and Work of Susan B. Anthony: Including Public Addresses, Her Own Letters and Many from Her Contemporaries During Fifty Years*, vol. 2 (Indianapolis: Hollenbeck Press, 1898), 859.

110. Maimonides, *Mishneh Torah, Hilchot T'shuvah* 1:3.

111. Joseph B. Soloveitchik, "The Community," *Tradition* 17, no. 2 (1978): 16.

112. *Zohar, Korach* 3:179a.

113. Quoted in the commentary of S'fat Emet.

114. Cordovero, *Tomer Devorah*, chap. 1, p. 5.

115. Elie Weisel, *The Town Beyond the Wall* (New York: Holt, Rinehart, & Winston, 1964), 9.

116. Mother Teresa, Nobel Peace Prize acceptance speech, 1979.

117. Isaac Luria, as cited in Meshullam Feibush Heller of Zbarazh, *Yosher Divrei Emet*, 33; Chaim Vital, *Shaar HaKavanot* 1.

118. Martin Luther King and Coretta Scott King, *Strength to Love* (Minneapolis: Fortress, 2010), 53.

119. Natalia Ginzburg, *The Little Virtues* (Manchester, UK: Carcanet Press, 1985), 102.

120. Maimonides, *Mishneh Torah, Hilchot M'lachim* 2:6.

121. The rendering of the "humility" quote actually appears first in a book by Pastor Rick Warren. In *Mere Christianity*, Lewis actually writes, "Do not imagine that if you meet a really humble man he will be what most people call 'humble' nowadays: he will not be a sort of greasy, smarmy person, who is always telling you that, of course, he is nobody. Probably all you will think about him is that he seemed a cheerful, intelligent chap who took a real interest in what you said

to him. If you do dislike him it will be because you feel a little envious of anyone who seems to enjoy life so easily. He will not be thinking about humility: he will not be thinking about himself at all.

"If anyone would like to acquire humility, I can, I think, tell him the first step. The first step is to realise that one is proud. And a biggish step, too. At least, nothing whatever can be done before it. If you think you are not conceited, it means you are very conceited indeed" (*Mere Christianity*, New York: HarperOne, 1952), 128.

122. Cesar Chavez & Ilan Stevens (ed.), *An Organizer's Tale: Speeches*, New York, Penguin, 2008, "Aphorisms."

123. Maimonides, *Mishneh Torah, Hilchot T'filah* 4:15.

124. Abraham Joshua Heschel, *Moral Grandeur and Spiritual Audacity: Essays*, ed. Susannah Heschel (New York: Farrar, Straus & Giroux, 2001), 257–67.

125. *Sifra*, Leviticus 19:18.

126. Ronald W. Pies, *The Judaic Foundations of Cognitive-behavioral Therapy: Rabbinical and Talmudic Underpinnings of CBT and REBT* (iUniverse: Bloomington, IN, 2010), 69.

127. Kook, *Concerning the Conflict of Opinions and Beliefs, Orot*, 130.

128. *Ruach HaChayim* to *Avot* 1:4.

129. Isaiah Berlin, "Does Political Theory Still Exist," in Isaiah Berlin, *The Proper Study of Mankind*, ed. Henry Hardy and Roger Hausheer (London: Chatto & Windus, 1997), 76 (essay orginally published in 1962).

130. This quote does not have a definite source, but has been sent to me by rabbinic colleagues.

131. Quoted in the *New York Times* obituary "Pete Seeger, Champion of Folk Music and Social Change, Dies at 94," January 29, 2014, A20.

132. Marcel Proust, *In Search of Lost Time*, vol. 5, *The Captive* (1923), 236–37.

133. *Kallah*, section 21 in the Soncino Talmud, Minor Tractates 51a.

134. Luzzatto, *Path of the Just*, chap. 7, p. 42.

135. Michael Walzer, *Exodus and Revolution* (New York: Basic Books, 1985), 58.

136. Dionne Brand, "Nothing of Egypt," in *Bread Out of Stone* (Toronto: Coach House Press, 1994), 138.

137. Quoted in Conrad P. Pritscher, *Learning What to Ignore: Connecting Multidiscipline Content and Process* (Rotterdam: Sense, 2013), 46.

138. Quoted in Bernard M. Curtis, *The Affirmation Principle: How Effective Leaders Bring Out the Best in People* (Xlibris, 2012), 75.

139. Maimonides, *Mishneh Torah, Hilchot T'shuvah* 3:4.

CHAPTER 3

140. For an overview of the two schools, see Benjamin Brown's entry in Jacob Neusner and Alan Avery-Peck, eds., *The Blackwell Companion to Judaism* (Malden, MA, Blackwell, 2000), 330.

141. *Kohelet Rabbah* 12.

142. Jonathan Sarna, "Praying for Governments We Dislike?," *The Lehrhaus*; purl.org/ccar/pa-32.

143. Elyse D. Frishman, ed., *Mishkan T'filah: A Reform Siddur* (New York: CCAR Press, 2007), 76.

144. Primo Levi told of a man in Auschwitz who found a sack of potatoes. Any starving man would isolate himself and consume them alone. But instead this individual ran to the square and passed them out. He later said that, in that moment, he felt—for the first time in years—like a human being again. Giving makes us human.

145. Martin Buber, *Between Man and Man*, trans. Ronald Gregor-Smith (New York: Routledge Classics, 2002; originally published 1947), 22.

146. *Avot D'Rabbi Natan* 7.

147. Quoted in Kerry Olitzky and Rachel T. Sabath, *Striving Toward Virtue: A Contemporary Guide for Jewish Ethical Behavior* (Hoboken, NJ: Ktav, 1996), 33.

148. *Sh'mot Rabbah* 14:1–2.

149. Rabbi Levi ben Gershon, Commentary on Exodus 10:21–23.

150. *Tanchuma, Parashat Bo* §4.

151. Pema Chödrön, *Comfortable with Uncertainty: 108 Teachings on Cultivating Fearlessness and Compassion* (Boston: Shambhla, 2003), 73.

152. *Zohar* 3:80b.

153. Plotzky, *K'lei Chemdah*, Commentary on Deuteronomy 25:26.

154. Barbara Sher with Barbara Smith, *I Could Do Anything If I Only Knew What It Was* (New York: Dell, 1994), 3.

154a. Mary Oliver, *New and Selected Poems*, Volume One (Boston: Beacon Press, 1992), 10–11.

155. *B'reishit Rabbah* 8.

156. Abraham Joshua Heschel, *Between God and Man*, ed. Fritz A. Rothschild (New York: Free Press, 1997), 41.

157. Maimonides, *Mishneh Torah, Hilchot Y'sodei HaTorah* 2:2.

158. Irving (Yitz) Greenberg, *Sage Advice* (Jerusalem: Maggid, 2016), 127.

159. Kook, *Orot HaKodesh* 3:11.

160. Evelyn Underhill, *Mysticism: A Study in the Nature and Development of Spiritual Consciousness* (New York: E. P. Dutton, 1930), xvi.

161. *Kohelet Rabbah* 1 on 7:13.

162. *Sh'mot Rabbah* 10:1.

163. Abraham Joshua Heschel, *The Sabbath* (New York: Farrar, Straus and Giroux, 1951), 28.

164. Deanna Kuhn, "Learning to Learn," in *Education for Thinking* (Cambridge, MA: Harvard University Press, 2005), 39–59.

165. Mark F. Frisch, *You Might be Able to Get There from Here: Reconsidering Borges and the Postmodern* (Madison, NJ: Farleigh Dickinson University Press, 2004), 53.

166. Mother Teresa, *A Simple Path*, compiled by Lucinda Vardey (New York: Ballantine Books, 1995), 79.

167. René Descartes, *Key Philosophical Writings*, trans. Elizabeth S. Haldane and G. R. T. Ross (Hertfordshire, UK: Wordsworth Classics of World Literature, 1997), 371.

168. Aharon Lichtenstein with Reuven Ziegler, *By His Light: Character and Values in the Service of God* (Jersey City, NJ: Ktav, 2003), 249.

168a. Rivkah Blau, *Learn Torah, Love Torah, Live Torah: HaRav Mordecai Pinchas Teitz: The Quintessential Rabbi* (Hoboken, NJ: Ktav Publishing House, 2001), 8.

169. Rachel Aviv, "The Philosopher of Feelings," *New Yorker*, June 19, 2017; purl.org/ccar/pa-07.

170. *Yalkut Shimoni Esther*, 954.

171. Pinchas Eliyahu Hurwitz, *Sefer HaBrit* II:13:1;6.

172. Joseph B. Soloveitchik, *Out of the Whirlwind: Essays on Mourning, Suffering and the Human Condition* (Jersey City, NJ: Ktav, 2003), 179.

173. Quoted in Kerry M. Olitzky, Rachel T. Sabath, and Ronald H. Isaacs, *Striving Toward Virtue: A Contemporary Guide for Jewish Ethical Behavior* (Hoboken, NJ: Ktav, 1996), 47–48.

174. See "Words of Wisdom," *New York Times*, June 11, 2011; purl.org/ccar/pa-08.

175. Donald C. Klein, "The Humiliation Dynamic," 23; purl.org/ccar/pa-09.

176. Kook, "The Pangs of Cleansing," *Orot*, 128.

177. *Avot* 3:11; Maimonides, *Mishneh Torah, Hilchot Choveil u'Mazik* 3:7, 5:9.

178. *Tanna D'Vei Eliyahu* 26.

179. Quoted in Harold S. Kushner, *Living a Life That Matters* (New York: Anchor Books, 2002), 4–5.

180. See Peter Gray, *Free to Learn: Why Unleashing the Instinct to Play Will Make Our Children Happier, More Self-Reliant, and Better Students for Life* (New York: Basic Books, 2015).

181. Cardozo was appointed to the Supreme Court by President Herbert Hoover, serving from 1932 to 1938.

182. Susan Neiman, *Moral Clarity: A Guide for Grown-Up Idealists* (New York: Harcourt, 2008), 217.

183. Quoted in Joyce Antler, *The Journey Home: Jewish Women and the American Century* (New York: Free Press, 1997), 106.

184. Eleanor Roosevelt, *You Learn by Living* (New York: Harper & Brothers, 1960), 30.

185. *B'reishit Rabbah* 14:10.

186. *D'varim Rabbah* 4:4.

187. Jonathan Sacks, *Lessons in Leadership* (Milford, CT: Maggid, 2015), 14–15.

188. Code of Hammurabi, Law 252.

189. *Sefer HaBahir* 172a.

190. Anne Lamont, *Bird by Bird: Some Instructions on Writing and Life* (New York: Pantheon Books, 1994), 22.

191. Warren G. Bennis, *On Becoming a Leader* (New York: Basic Books, 2009), 49.

192. Sacks, *Lessons in Leadership*, 295.

193. For an overview of Kantian ethics with regard to revelation, see Robert R. Clewis, *The Kantian Sublime and the Revelation of Freedom* (Cambridge: Cambridge University Press, 2009).

194. Emmanuel Levinas, *Nine Talmudic Readings*, trans. Annette Aronowicz (Indianapolis: Indiana University Press, 2003), 37.

195. John D. Rayner, *An Understanding of Judaism* (Oxford, NY: Berghahn Books, 1997), 41–45; *Midrash T'hillim* 114:8; *B'midbar Rabbah* 13:7.

196. Patricia Karlin-Neumann, "*B'haalot'cha* (Contemporary Reflection)," in Tamara Cohn Eskenazi and Andrea L. Weiss, eds., *The Torah: A Women's Commentary* (New York: URJ Press, 2008), 402.

197. Abraham H. Maslow, *The Psychology of Science: A Reconnaissance* (Chicago: Gateway, 1969), 15–16.

198. Quoted in Matt Tenney, *Serve to Be Great: Leadership Lessons from a Prison, a Monastery, and a Boardroom* (Hoboken, NJ: Wiley, 2014), xix.

199. James MacGregor Burns, *Leadership* (New York: Harper Perennial Classics, 2010), 455.

200. Quoted in Anil Dutt Misra, *Inspiring Thoughts of Mahatma Gandhi* (New Dehli: Concept, 2008), 36.

201. The first instance of this quote appears in Donald Keys, *Earth at Omega: Passage to Planetization* (Boston: Branden Press, 1982), 79.

202. Sacks, *Lessons in Leadership*, 267.

203. Quoted from Maimonides, "Introduction to the *Shemonah Peraqim*," in *Truth and Compassion: Essays on Judaism and Religion in Memory of Rabbi Dr. Solomon Frank*, ed. Howard Joseph, Jack Nathan Lightstone, and Michael D. Oppenheim (Waterloo, Ontario: Wilfrid Laurier University Press, 1983), 168.

204. Jacob Milgrom, *Leviticus 1–16*, Anchor Bible (New York: Doubleday, 1991), 744, 767, 950; as cited by Elaine Goodfriend, "*Tazria* (Central Commentary)," in Eskenazi and Weiss, *The Torah: A Women's Commentary*, 637.

205. Chafetz Chayim, *Michtevei Chafetz Chayim* 2:86.

206. Kook, *Ig'rot HaR'iyah* 1:163–64.

207. Ibid., 369.

208. Almoli, *Me-assef l'chol HaMachanot*.

209. Rabbi Pinchas of Koritz, *Midrash Pinchas*, 82. See S. Sperber, *Hemshech HaDorot*, in *HaRa'aya*, 45–46.

210. Abraham Joshua Heschel, *Heavenly Torah: As Refracted through the Generations*, ed. and transl. Gordon Tucker and Leonard Levin (New York: Continuum, 2006), 710.

CHAPTER 4

211. Cited in Martin Buber, *Or HaGanuz* (New York: Schocken Books, 1946), 144.

212. Irving Greenberg, *For the Sake of Heaven and Earth: The New Encounter between Judaism and Christianity* (Philadelphia: Jewish Publication Society, 2004), 196.

213. Ibid., 201–3.

214. Kook, *Orot HaEmunah*, 25.

215. Eleanor Roosevelt, *You Learn by Living* (Louisville, KY: Westminster John Knox Press, 1960), 63.

216. John Donne, *Devotions upon Emergent Occasions* (1624), meditation 17.

217. *Sefer HaChinuch*, mitzvah 1.

218. *MeAm Loez, Parashat B'reishit*.

219. Carol Dweck, *Mindset: The New Psychology of Success* (New York: Ballantine Books, 2006), 48.

220. Nachman of Breslov, *Likutei Moharan* 2:25.

221. Yisrael Salanter, *Or Yisrael*, letter 30.

222. Often quoted as "praying with our feet," but the original language was "Legs were praying." Susannah Heschel, ed., introduction to *Moral Grandeur and Spiritual Audacity: Essays*, by Abraham Joshua Heschel (New York: Farrar, Straus & Giroux, 2001), vii.

223. James MacGregor Burns, *Leadership* (New York: Harper Perennial Classics, 2010), 454.

224. Thomas Merton, *New Seeds of Contemplation* (New York: New Direction Books, 1962), 29.

224a. The expression *halachta bidrachav* ("you walk in God's ways") comes from Deuteronomy 28:9, "The Eternal will establish you as God's holy people, as was sworn to you, if you keep the commandments of the Eternal your God and [*you*] *walk in God's ways*."

225. Joseph B. Soloveitchik, *Halakhic Man* (New York: Jewish Publication Society, 1984), 107.

226. *B'reishit Rabbah* 3:7.

227. Nachmanides, Commentary on *Parashat B'reishit*.

228. Kook, *Orot HaKodesh*.

229. Israel Bar-Yehuda Idalovichi, *Symbolic Forms as the Metaphysical Groundwork of the Organon of the Cultural Science*, vol. 2 (Newcastle upon Tyne, UK: Cambridge Scholars, 2014), 532–33.

230. Quoted in Epi Mabika, *Success Gravity* (Peterborough, UK: Fastprint, 2013), 140.

231. Rabbi Chayim Vital, *Shaar HaMitzvos, Noach*. See Natan Slifkin, *Man and Beast: Our Relationships with Animals in Jewish Law and Thought* (Brooklyn: Yashar Books/Lambda, 2006), 53.

232. *Zohar* 2:68b.

233. Simcha Raz, *A Tzaddik in Our Time* (Jerusalem: Feldheim, 1976), 108–9.

234. *Sh'mot Rabbah* 19:1.

235. Simone Weil, "Reflections on the Right Use of School Studies with a View to the Love of God," *The Simone Weil Reader*, ed. George A. Panichas (New York: David McKay, 1977), 51.

236. See Adrienne Rich, *Later Poems: Selected and New, 1971–2012* (New York: Norton, 2013), 248.

237. See Martin Buber, *Tales of the Hasidim: Later Masters* (New York: Schocken Books, 1948), 249–50.

238. See Freud's essay "Beyond the Pleasure Principle (Jenseits des Lustprinzips)."

239. See James O'Reilly, Larry Habegger, and Sean O'Reilly, eds., *Travelers' Tales France: True Stories* (San Francisco: Traveler's Tales, 1995), 447.

240. Quoted in Erica Brown, *Happier Endings: A Meditation on Life and Death* (New York: Simon & Schuster, 2013), 17.

241. *Kohelet Rabbah* 5:14.

242. Maimonides, *Mishneh Torah, Hilchot Y'sodei HaTorah* 5:11.

243. Irving (Yitz) Greenberg, *Sage Advice* (Jerusalem: Maggid, 2016), 178.

244. Sheryl Sandberg, *Lean In: Women, Work, and the Will to Lead* (New York: Knopf, 2013), 5.

245. Judith Plaskow, *Standing Again at Sinai: Judaism from a Feminist Perspective* (New York: HarperCollins, 1990), xvi.

246. Maimonides, *Mishneh Torah, Hilchot Shabbat* 2:3.

247. Moshe Pearlman, *Ben Gurion Looks Back in Talks with Moshe Pearlman* (London: Schocken Books, 1970), 52.

248. Quoted in Shaun Breslin, ed., *East Asia and the Global Crisis* (New York: Routledge, 2012), 4.

249. Benjamin Franklin, *The Autobiography of Benjamin Franklin* (Bedford, MA: Applewood Books, 2008), 138.

250. See BT *Shabbat* 23b; BT *Sanhedrin* 76b; BT *Gittin* 6b.

251. "A Conversation with Doctor Abraham Joshua Heschel," interview by Carl Stern, *The Eternal Light*, NBC, February 4, 1973; reprinted as "Carl Stern's Interview with Dr. Heschel," in *Moral Grandeur and Spiritual Audacity*, ed. Susannah Heschel (New York: Farrar, Straus & Giroux, 1996), 395–412.

252. *Sifra, K'doshim.*

253. See *Magein Avraham* 608:3.

254. Maimonides, *Mishneh Torah, Hilchot Y'sodei HaTorah* 5:11.

255. Learned Hand, "The Spirit of Liberty" speech presented during "I Am an American Day" 1944, quoted in *Life* 17, no. 1 (July 3, 1944), 20.

256. David Hume, *Essays Moral, Political, and Literary*, vol. 1 (London: Longmans, Green, , 1875), 220.

257. David Landes, *The Wealth and Poverty of Nations: Why Some Are So Rich and Some So Poor* (New York: Norton, 1999), 524.

258. Albert Camus, *A Happy Death*, trans. Richard Howard (New York: Vintage Books, 1972), 74.

259. *Sh'mot Rabbah* 1:27–28.

260. Rabbi Ben-Zion Meir Chai Uziel, *Mishp'tei Uziel, Choshen Mishpat* 42:6.

261. Rabbeinu Yonah Gerondi, *Sefer HaYirah.*

262. See Viktor Frankel, *Man's Search for Meaning* Boston: Beacon Press, 1959), 133.

263. Max De Pree, *Leadership Is an Art* (New York: Doubleday, 1987), 9.

264. Ludwig Wittgenstein, G. E. M Anscombe, P. M. S. Hacker, and Joachim Schulte, trans., *Philosophical Investigations* (Hoboken, NJ: Wiley-Blackwell, 2010), ccxliii.

265. Nachman of Breslov, *Likutei Moharan* 64:4.

266. Yisrael Salanter, *Birurei HaMidot* 142; 147.

267. *Avot D'Rabbi Natan* A 6.

268. John Locke, letter to Anthony Collins, October 29, 1703.

269. A dramatization of Professor Lipstadt's legal journey can be seen in the 2016 film *Denial.*

270. Maimonides, *Mishneh Torah, Hilchot Dei-ot* 2:6.

271. David McCullough, *John Adams* (New York: Simon & Schuster, 2001), 68.

272. Quoted in Dale Carnegie, *How to Stop Worrying and Start Living* (New York: Simon & Schuster, 1948), 171.

273. Montesquieu, *The Spirit of Laws*, trans. Thomas Nugent, vol. 1, book 1, 1758.

274. *Tanchuma, Parashat Vayakeil* 1.

275. *Seder Eliyahu Rabbah* 23.

276. *B'reishit Rabbah* 44:1.

277. Claire Yang, Courtney Boen, Karen Gerken, Ting Li, Kristen Schorpp, Kathleen Mullan Harris, "Social Relationships and Physiological Functioning," *Proceedings of the National Academy of Sciences* 113/3 (Jan 2016): 578–83; purl.org/ccar/pa-33. Anna Almendrala, "Friends Are As Important To Your Health As Diet And Exercise," *The Huffington Post.* January 06, 2016; purl.org/ccar/pa-34.

278. Kook, *Ein Ayah, B'rachot* 9:340–41.

279. See Chaim Navon, *Genesis and Jewish Thought*, trans. David Strauss (Jersey City, NJ: Ktav, 2008), 308–9.

280. Isaiah Horowitz, *Sh'nei Luchot HaBrit*, 20.

281. See Immanuel Etkes, *Rabbi Israel Salanter and the Mussar Movement*, trans. Jonathan Chipman (Philadelphia: Jewish Publication Society, 1993), 289–90.

282. Baal Shem Tov, *Keter Shem Tov*, 37.

283. Eckhart Tolle, *A New Earth: Awakening to Your Life's Purpose* (New York: Penguin Books, 2005), 74–75.

284. Adin Steinsaltz, *Talks on the Parsha* (Jerusalem: Koren, 2015), 77.

285. Ibid., 4.

286. Moshe Idel, *Studies in Ecstatic Kabbalah* (Albany: State University of New York Press, 1988), 130n132.

287. Avraham Weiss, *Holistic Prayer: A Guide to Jewish Spirituality* (Jerusalem: Maggid, 2014), 10.

288. Simone Weil, *The Simone Weil Reader*, ed. George A. Panichas (New York: David McKay, 1977), 383.

289. Oscar Ybarra, Piotr Winkielman, IreneYeh, Eugene Burnstei, Liam Kavanagh, "Friends (and Sometimes Enemies) With Cognitive Benefits: What Types of Social Interactions Boost Executive Functioning," *Social Psychological and Personality Science* 2/3 (October 13, 2010), pp. 253–61; purl.org/ccar/pa-35. Brett Nelson, "Six Reasons Small Talk Is Very Important—And How To Get Better At It," *Forbes* (July 30, 2012); purl.org/ccar/pa-36.

290. See John Kenneth Galbraith, *The Great Crash of 1929* (New York: Mariner Books, 1954), 106, n. 7.

291. See *Midrash T'hillim* 90:13; BT *Sukkah* 52b; Commentary on Genesis by Rabbi Samson Raphael Hirsch.

292. See the first section of Bachya ibn Pakuda, *Shaar HaYichud*.

293. See Eliezer Berkovits, "God Encountered," chap. 6 in *God, Man and History*, ed. David Hazony (Jerusalem: Shalem Press, 2004).

294. Kook, *Ein Eyah*, 4:174; *Orot HaKodesh*, 1:275.

295. There is much information in academic literature about this connection. For a short introduction, see Eric A. Zillmer, Mary V. Spiers, and William Culbertson, *Principles of Neuropsychology*, 2nd ed. (Belmont, CA: Thomson Wadsworth, 2008), 260.

296. See Martin L. Hoffman, *Empathy and Moral Development: Implications for Caring and Justice* (Cambridge: Cambridge University Press, 2000), 221–49.

297. See Jennifer Kahn, "Can Emotional Intelligence Be Taught?," *New York Times*, September 14, 2013; purl.org/ccar/pa-10.

298. Quoted in Gershom Scholem, *D'varim B'Go*, 326–27. See also Benjamin Ish-Shalom, *Rav Avraham Itzhak Hacohen Kook: Between Rationalism and Mysticism*, (Albany, NY: State University of New York Press, 1993), 152.

299. Joseph B. Soloveitchik (David Shatz, Joel B. Wolowelsky, and Reuven Ziegler, eds.), *Out of the Whirlwind: Essays on Mourning, Suffering and the Human Condition*, (Jersey City, NJ: KTAV Publishing House, 2003), 179.

300. For example: "Orbital and ventromedial prefrontal cortices are implicated in emotionally-driven moral decisions"; Leo Pascual, Paulo Rodrigues, and David Gallardo-Pujol, "How Does Morality Work in the Brain? A Functional and Structural Perspective of Moral Behavior," *Frontiers in Integrative Neuroscience*, September 12, 2013; purl.org/ccar/pa-11.

301. This is part of a broader discussion about God not rejoicing at the downfall of the wicked. See BT *M'gilah* 10b.

302. Meir Simcha of Divinsk, *Meshech Chochmah*, *Sh'mot* 12:16.

303. See BT *Chagigah* 15b.

304. "Investing in Education Crucial for Timor-Leste's Development—Ban." *UN News Center*, August 16, 2012; purl.org/ccar/pa-12.

305. *Shulchan Aruch, Yoreh Dei-ah* 245:5.

306. "Secretary-General's Remarks at the Oslo Summit on Education for Development Secretary-General," United Nations, July 7, 2015; purl.org/ccar/pa-13.

307. Maimonides, *Mishneh Torah*, introduction to *Hilchot Talmud Torah* 2.

308. EFA Global Monitoring Report, *The Hidden Crisis: Armed Conflict and Education* (Paris: UNESCO, 2011), 3; purl.org/ccar/pa-14.

309. Maimonides, *Mishneh Torah, Hilchot Talmud Torah* 6:9; see also *Shulchan Aruch, Yoreh Dei-ah* 244:1.

310. Editorial Board, "Getting Older, Growing Poorer," *New York Times*, October 5, 2013; purl.org/ccar/pa-15.

311. Alexandra Cawthorne, "Elderly Poverty: The Challenge Before Us," Center for American Progress, July 30, 2008; purl.org/ccar/pa-16.

312. "Fall Prevention in the Elderly," Caring for Aging Parents; purl.org/ccar /pa-17.

313. Nachman of Breslov, *Sefer HaMidot* §34.

313a. The editor of our Hebrew text, Rabbi David E. S. Stein, observes that the attribution for this saying has been a matter of longstanding uncertainty. According to Shimon Sharvit, who edited a critical edition of the *Pirkei Avot* text in 2004, the majority of reliable early Mishnah manuscripts, Geniza fragments, and rabbinic witnesses state this passage simply in the name of "Rabbi"—that is, Rabbi Y'hudah HaNasi. Other such sources state it in the name of Rabbi Meir, as shown here; and still others in the name of Rabbi Y'hudah (bar Ilai). My interpretation below makes the assumption that Rabbi Meir is indeed the source of this teaching.

314. Kook, *Orot*, 125.

315. Plato, *The Republic*, book 4.

316. *Kohelet Rabbah* 6.

316a. Rachel Emma Silverman, "Workplace Distractions: Here's Why You Won't Finish This Article," *The Wall Street Journal* (December 11, 2012); purl.org /ccar/pa-37.

316b. Bob Sullivan and Hugh Thompson, "Brain, Interrupted," *The New York Times* (May 4, 2013); purl.org/ccar/pa-38.

317. Friedrich Nietzsche, *The Gay Science: With a Prelude in Rhymes and an Appendix of Songs*, trans. Walter Kaufmann (New York: Vintage Books, 1974), 322.

317a. Gene Weingarten, "Pearls Before Breakfast: Can one of the nation's great musicians cut through the fog of a D.C. rush hour? Let's find out." *The Washington Post* (April 08, 2007); purl.org/ccar/pa-39.

318. Nachmanides, Commentary on Exodus 3:2.

319. Rabbi Amital said this in a video interview conducted to honor his eightieth birthday in 2004.

CHAPTER 5

320. Joseph B. Soloveitchik, *Worship of the Heart: Essays on Jewish Prayer*, ed. Shalom Carmy (New York: Toras oRav Foundation with Ktav, 2003), 21.

321. Rabbi Shneur Zalman of Liadi, *Tanya, Likutei Amarim* 1:4, 34.

322. Adin Steinsaltz, *Talks on the Parsha* (Jerusalem: Koren, 2015), 195.

323. Kook, *Orot HaKodesh* 3:285.

324. Alan Dershowitz, *Taking the Stand* (New York: Crown, 2013), 156, 158.

325. See *Sh'mot Rabbah* 26:2.

326. Rainer Maria Rilke, *Letters to a Young Poet*, trans. M. D. Herter (New York: Norton, 1993), 35.

327. Nachmanides, Commentary on Genesis 22:1.

328. See Bryna Jocheved Levy, *Waiting for Rain: Reflections at the Turning of the Year* (New York: Jewish Publication Society, 2008), 26.

329. Kook, *Igrot HaR'iyah* 2:43.

330. Zadok HaKohen Rabinowitz, *Sefer Tzidkat HaTzadik* 154.

331. Cited in the name of the Maggid of Mezritch by Avraham Chayim of Zlotshov, *Orah LaChayim* (Jerusalem, 1960), 25a.

332. *B'reishit Rabbah* 9:7.

333. Nachman of Breslov, *Sichot HaRan* 308.

334. Meir Leibush ben Yehiel Michel Wisser, Commentary on Genesis, *Parashat Vayeira*, the *Akeidah*.

335. See Viktor Frankl, *Man's Search for Meaning* (Boston: Beacon Press, 1959).

336. Levi Yitzchak of Berditchev, *K'dushat Levi, Va-et'chanan* 1.

337. See Marc Angel, *Maimonides, Spinoza and Us: Toward an Intellectually Vibrant Judaism* (Woodstock, VT: Jewish Lights, 2009), 10–12.

338. See Abraham Joshua Heschel, "Reason and Revelation in Saadia's Philosophy," *Jewish Quarterly Review*, n.s., 34, no. 4 (April 1944): 394.

339. Levi Yitzchak of Berditchev, *K'dushat Levi, Parashat Yitro*.

340. S'forno, Commentary on *Parashat Sh'mini*, Leviticus 11:1.

341. While it might seem contradictory for an omnipotent Being to not create something perfect or as intended, the presence of free will within humanity means there is always a degree of separation between God's intentions and humanity's inclinations.

342. Kook, *Orot HaTorah* 11:3.

343. An overview of near-death experience aftereffects can be found in P. M. H. Atwater, *Near-Death Experiences, The Rest of the Story: What They Teach Us about Living and Dying and Our True Purpose* (Charlottesville, VA: Hampton Roads, 2011), 72–73.

344. See Exodus 32:10–12.

345. Yochanan Muffs, *The Personhood of God: Biblical Theology, Human Faith and the Divine Image* (Woodstock, VT: Jewish Lights, 2005), 184.

346. Nachmanides, Commentary on Exodus 13:16.

347. Jonathan Sacks, *The Dignity of Difference: How to Avoid the Clash of Civilizations* (New York: Bloomsbury, 2002), 54.

348. Michael Walzer, *Spheres of Justice: A Defense of Pluralism and Equality* (New York: Basic Books, 1983), 193.

349. Abraham Joshua Heschel, *The Sabbath* (New York: Farrar, Straus and Young, 1951), 28.

350. See Joseph P. Hester, *The Ten Commandments: A Handbook of Religious, Legal, and Social Issues* (Jefferson, NC: McFarland, 2003), 165–66.

351. For an overview of the Fair Labor Standards Act and its impact on labor law, see Wage and Hour Division (WHD), U.S. Department of Labor, "Handy Reference Guide to the Fair Labor Standards Act," revised September 2016; purl.org/ccar /pa-18.

352. Section 161 of the New York State Labor Law; purl.org/ccar/pa-19.

353. See Albert Mehrabian, *Silent Messages: Implicit Communication of Emotions and Attitudes* (Belmont, CA: Wadsworth, 1981).

354. See Rabbi Nachman of Breslov, *Likutei Moharan, Kama* 64.

355. Shimon Gershon Rosenberg, *Faith Shattered and Restored: Judaism in the Postmodern Age* (Jerusalem: Maggid, 2017), 110.

356. Ibid., 111.

357. See Aristotle's *Nicomachean Ethics*, book 4.

358. *Avot D'Rabbi Natan*, version A, 11a.

359. *Tomer Devorah* 1:3.

360. Eliyahu de Vidas, *Reishit Chochmah, Shaar HaAhavah*.

361. For more about Carnegie's life and philanthrophic endeavors, see Laura Bufano Edge, *Andrew Carnegie: Industrial Philanthropist* (Minneapolis: Lerner, 2004), chap. 9.

362. See John Cassidy, "Mark Zuckerberg and the Rise of Philanthrocapitalism," *New Yorker*, December 2, 2015.

363. One of the most influential yeshivahs in pre–World War II Europe.

364. Yerucham Levovitz, *Daat Torah, B'midbar*, 94.

365. Avraham Weiss, *Spiritual Activism: A Jewish Guide to Leadership and Repairing the World*, Woodstock, VT: Jewish Lights Publishing, 2008), 137.

366. *Tosefta, B'rachot* 7:2.

367. Maimonides, *Mishneh Torah, Hilchot Deiot* 1:5.

368. Jeffrey Stout, *Blessed Are the Organized: Grassroots Democracy in America* (Princeton, NJ: Princeton University Press, 2010), 64.

369. Ibid., 65.

370. Based on Stout, *Blessed Are the Organized*, chap. 5.

371. Ibid., 66.

372. See Albert Camus, *The Rebel: An Essay on Man in Revolt* (New York: Vintage International, 1956), 250.

373. Joseph B. Soloveitchik, "A Theory of Emotions," in *Out of the Whirlwind: Essays on Mourning, Suffering and the Human Condition* (Jersey City, NJ: Ktav, 2003), 183–84.

374. Abraham Joshua Heschel, "A Prayer for Peace" (1971), in *Moral Grandeur and Spiritual Audacity*, ed. Susannah Heschel (New York: Farrar, Straus & Giroux, 1996), 231.

375. This phrase is the opening line to chapter 1 of *The Social Contract*. See *Rousseau: The Social Contract, and Other Later Political Writings*, ed. and transl. Victor Gourevitch (Cambridge: Cambridge University Press, 1996), 351.

376. Jean-Jacques Rousseau (Christopher Kelly and Allan Bloom, trans.), *Emile, Or, On Education: Includes Emile and Sophie, Or, The Solitaries* (Lebanon, NH: Dartmouth College Press, 2010 ed.), 342.

377. Alan Paton, *Ah, But Your Land Is Beautiful* (New York: Scribner Paperback Fiction, 1981), 66–67.

378. See Michael Leo Samuel, *Rediscovering Philo of Alexandria: A First Century Torah Commentator*, vol. 5, *Deuteronomy* (Sarasota, FL: First Edition Design Publishing, 2016), 64.

379. See Fishel Schachter and Chana Nestlebaum, *Loving Kindness: Daily Lessons in the Power of Giving* (New York: Mesorah, 2003), 208; Chayim Halberstam, *Darkei Chayim*, 37.

380. See Schachter and Nestlebaum, *Loving Kindness*, 209.

381. Chip Heath and Dan Heath, *Switch: How to Change Things When Change Is Hard* (Toronto: Random House Canada, 2010), 183.

382. Y'hudah HaLevi, *Kuzari*, 2:48.

383. Ibid.

384. Kook, *Orot HaTorah* 12:2–3.

385. See earlier comment from Rabbi Aharon Lichtenstein on pages 154–155.

386. David DeSteno, "Opinion: Stop Trusting Yourself," *New York Times*, January 17, 2014; purl.org/ccar/pa-20.

387. Joseph B. Soloveitchik, *Family Redeemed*, ed. David Schatz and Joel B. Woloelsky (Jersey City, NJ: Ktav, 2000), 40.

388. Jonathan Sacks, *To Heal a Fractured World: The Ethics of Responsibility* (New York: Schocken Books, 2005), 51.

389. Ibid., 54.

390. See Schachter and Nestlebaum, *Loving Kindness*, 95.

391. Ibid.

392. Elyse D. Frishman, "A Voice in the Dark: How Do We Hear God?," in *Duties of the Soul: The Role of Commandments in Liberal Judaism*, ed. Niles E. Goldstein and Peter S. Knobel (New York: UAHC Press, 1999), 115.

393. BT *Sanhedrin* 27b; BT *Rosh HaShanah* 29a; BT *Sotah* 37b.

394. Aharon Lichtenstein, "Mutual Responsibility in the Jewish State," trans. David Strauss, Virtual Beit Midrash, September 21, 2014; purl.org/ccar/pa-21. (Rabbi Lichtenstein based his conclusion on JT *Sotah* 7:5.)

395. Avraham Weiss, *Principles of Spiritual Activism* (Hoboken, NJ: Ktav, 2002), 66.

396. The phrase appears in the *Shemoneh Esreih* prayer. I heard of this commentary from the Bach during my time learning in a yeshivah in Israel. Also see Rabbeinu Yonah's commentary on *Pirkei Avot* mishnah 1 (*chelek b'chochmah*).

397. See David Wolpe's entry in *Rosh Hashanah Readings: Inspiration, Information, and*

Contemplation, ed. Dov Peretz Elkins (Woodstock, VT: Jewish Lights, 2006), 133.

398. See Alan Brill, *Thinking God: The Mysticism of Rabbi Zadok of Lublin* (New York: Yeshiva University Press, 2002), 181n41.

399. See Joan Borysenko, *Fire in the Soul: A New Psychology of Spiritual Optimism* (New York: Warner Books, 1993), chap. 8.

400. Kook, *Midot HaR'iyah, Kavod* 4.

401. This excerpt is from the "I've Been to the Mountaintop" speech given at the Bishop Charles Mason Temple in Memphis, TN, on April 3, 1968; purl.org/ccar/pa-22.

402. Quoted in Joan Borysenko, *Fire in the Soul: A New Psychology of Spiritual Optimism* (New York: Warner Books, 1993), 4.

403. Martin Buber, *Tales of the Hasidim, Early Masters* (New York: Schocken Books, 1947), III.

404. Jonathan Sacks, *A Letter in the Scroll: Understanding Our Jewish Identity and Exploring the Legacy of the World's Oldest Religion* (New York: Free Press, 2000), 84–85.

405. Nachmanides, *Sefer HaMitzvot*, mitzvah 16.

406. Maimonides, *Commentary on Pirkei Avot*, 5:6.

407. Nachmanides, Commentary on Leviticus 26:11.

408. *Kesef Mishnah, Hilchot Rotzei-ach* (1:14); *Shulchan Aruch, Choshen Mishpat* 426.

409. Shlomo Zalman Auerbach, *Minchat Sh'lomo*, vol. 2, 86:4.

410. For more, see Peter Singer, *The Life You Can Save: How to Do Your Part to End World Poverty* (New York: Random House, 2010).

411. Joseph B. Soloveitchik, "A Theory of Emotions," in *Out of the Whirlwind: Essays on Mourning, Suffering and the Human Condition* (Jersey City, NJ: Ktav, 2003), 200.

412. See earlier passage from BT *Shabbat* 54b.

413. *Shulchan Aruch, Yoreh Dei-ah* 93:4.

414. Moshe Sofer, *Chatam Sofer, Yoreh Dei-ah* 234.

415. *Arukh HaShulkhan, Yoreh Dei-ah* 151:4.

416. See BT *Shabbat* 112b; BT *B'rachot* 35b; BT *Sanhedrin* 11a.

417. "A Conversation with Doctor Abraham Joshua Heschel," interview by Carl Stern, *The Eternal Light*, NBC, February 4, 1973; reprinted as "Carl Stern's Interview with Dr. Heschel," in *Moral Grandeur and Spiritual Audacity*, ed. Susannah Heschel (New York: Farrar, Straus & Giroux, 1996), 395–412.

418. Martin Luther King Jr., *Strength to Love* (Philadelphia: Fortress Press, 1981), 25.

419. Oliver Wendell Holmes, Jr., Memorial Day Address, May 30, 1884, in speeches I, II (1913).

420. Levi Yitzchak of Berditchev, *K'dushat Levi, Parashat Ki Tavo* 28:7.

421. Immanuel Kant, *Critique of Practical Reason*, 5:161–62, 1788.

422. Yaakov Tzvi Mecklenburg, *HaK'tav V'haKabbalah*, Exodus 24:17.

423. Lawrence Kushner, *God Was in This Place & I, i Did Not Know: Finding Self, Spirituality, and Ultimate Meaning* (Woodstock, VT: Jewish Lights, 1991), 13.

424. Jonathan Sacks, *A Letter in the Scroll: Understanding Our Jewish Identity and Explor-*

ing the Legacy of the World's Oldest Religion (New York: Free Press, 2000), 52.

425. See Rabbi Y. Emden's introduction to his siddur; Schneur Zalman of Liadi, *Tanya* (New York: Kehot, 1965), chap. 38.

426. See Marc Angel, *Maimonides, Spinoza and Us: Toward an Intellectually Vibrant Judaism* (Woodstock, VT: Jewish Lights, 2009), 36–37; *Mishneh Torah, Hilchot T'filah* 4:15–16.

427. Mary Oliver, *Thirst* (Boston: Beacon Press, 2006), 37.

428. Max Planck, *Scientific Autobiography* (New York: Philosophical Library, 1949), 91–93.

429. Susan Neiman, *Moral Clarity: A Guide for Grown-Up Idealists* (New York: Harcourt, 2008), 159.

430. Theodore White, *The Mountain Road* (New York: William Sloan, 1956), 340–41.

431. See Locke's *Essay Concerning Human Understanding*.

432. See Rousseau's essay *Émile*.

433. This thought is usually rendered as: "If I am I because I am I, and you are you because you are you, then I am I and you are you. But if I am I because you are you and you are you because I am I, then I am not I and you are not you." See Martin Buber, *Tales of the Hasidism*, vol. 2, trans. Olga Marx (New York: Shocken Books, 1948), 283.

433a. The rendering of the passage from Samuel is adapted from the NJPS translation.

434. See Avi Sagi and Daniel Statman, eds., *Religion and Morality* (Atlanta: Rodopi, 1995), 120–21.

435. See Saadyah Gaon, *The Book of Doctrines and Belief*.

436. Kook, *Orot HaKodesh* 4e.

CHAPTER 6

437. Kook, *Orot HaKodesh* 2:314.

438. From "Reframing the *Sh'ma* to Repair the World," presented at Limmud New York, 2013. A video of this talk can be viewed at purl.org/ccar/pa-23; transcript at purl.org/ccar/pa-24.

438a. See Lawrence Kushner, *The Book of Miracles: A Young Person's Guide to Jewish Spiritual Awareness* (Woodstock, VT: Jewish Lights Publishing, 1997), p. 35; *Zohar* 2:85b.

439. *B'reishit Rabbah* 11:6.

440. Pew Research Center's Religion & Public Life Project, *A Portrait of Jewish Americans: Findings from a Pew Research Center Survey of U.S. Jews* (Washington, DC: Pew Research Center, 2013); purl.org/ccar/pa-25.

441. Pew Research Center's Religion & Public Life Project, "Religious Landscape Study," May 11, 2015; purl.org/ccar/pa-26.

442. P. A. Boelens, R. R. Reeves, W. H. Replogle, and H. G. Koenig, "A Randomized Trial of the Effect of Prayer on Depression and Anxiety," *International Journal of Psychiatry in Medicine* 39, no. 4 (2009): 377–92; purl.org/ccar/pa-27.

443. Ibid.

444. David Ramsay Steele (ed.), *Genius—in Their Own Words: The Intellectual Journeys of Seven Great 20th Century Thinkers* (Chicago: Open Court, 2002), 159.

445. President Obama's 2012 Democratic National Convention acceptance speech; full transcript at purl.org/ccar/pa-28.

446. Robert St. John, *Ben-Gurion: Builder of Israel* (Washington, DC: B'nai B'rith Books, 1986), 112.

447. Kook, *Arpilei Tohar*, 2.

448. See Fishel Schachter and Chana Nestlebaum, *Loving Kindness: Daily Lessons in the Power of Giving* (New York: Mesorah, 2003), 52.

449. Maimonides, *Guide for the Perplexed* 2:42.

450. *Tanchuma, Mishpatim* 19.

451. See Schneur Zalman of Liadi, *Tanya* (New York: Kehot, 1965), chap. 39.

452. Dov Baer ben Avraham, *Magid D'varev l'Yaakov, Likutei Amarim*, 198.

453. Cited in *Hayom Yom*, 17 Adar 1.

454. Anna Howard Shaw, *The Speeches of Anna Howard Shaw* (Madison: University of Wisconsin-Madison, 1960), 44.

455. Quoted in Martha Watson, *Lives of Their Own: Rhetorical Dimensions in Autobiographies of Women Activists* (Columbia, SC: University of South Carolina Press, 1999), 116.

456. Abraham Joshua Heschel, *God in Search of Man* (New York: Octagon Books, 1976), 216.

457. *B'reishit Rabbah* 69:7.

458. Jonathan Sacks, *To Heal a Fractured World: The Ethics of Responsibility* (New York: Schocken Books, 2005), 27.

459. See Steve Covey's foreword to Erik Weihenmayer and Paul Stoltz, *The Adversity Advantage: Turning Everyday Struggles into Everyday Greatness* (New York: Fireside Books, 2006).

460. See the webpage from the Viktor Frankl Institute, based out of Vienna: purl.org/ccar/pa-29.

461. Kook, *Orot HaKodesh* 3:349.

462. See Lynne Olson, *Freedom's Daughters: The Unsung Heroines of the Civil Rights Movement from 1830 to 1970* (New York: Scribner, 2001), 159.

463. See Taylor Branch, *Parting the Waters: America in the King Years, 1954–63* (New York: Simon and Schuster, 1988), 295.

464. For more, see Clive Webb, *Fight against Fear: Southern Jews and Black Civil Rights* (Athens: University of George Press, 2001), 63–66.

465. Luzzatto, *M'silat Yesharim* 7:42.

466. Alexandria Sage and Pauline Mevel, "Lauded as Hero in Paris Attack, Malian Man Made French Citizen," *Reuters*, January 20, 2015; purl.org/ccar/pa-30.

467. Maimonides, *Mishneh Torah, Hilchot M'lachim* 12:2.

468. Elijah ben Solomon Zalman, Commentary on *M'chilta*, Exodus 14:20.

469. Deepak Chopra, "Thinking About the End of the World," *Huffington Post*, June 6, 2011; purl.org/ccar/pa-31.

470. *PBS NewsHour*, March 9, 1998.

471. BT *Shabbat* 151b–152a; *Eichah Rabbah* 2:19.

472. *P'sikta D'Rav Kahana.*

473. Chanan Morrison, *Gold from the Land of Israel: A New Light on the Weekly Torah Portion – From the Writings of Rabbi Abraham Isaac HaKohen Kook* (Jerusalem: URIM, 2006), 113.

474. Martin Buber, *Tales of the Hasidim*, vol. 2, trans. Olga Marx (New York: Schocken Books, 1948), 86.

475. Jonathan Sacks, *A Letter in the Scroll: Understanding Our Jewish Identity and Exploring the Legacy of the World's Oldest Religion* (New York: Free Press, 2000), 186.

475a. *K'dushat Levi* on Lamentations 1:1.

476. Also known as *Bellum omnium contra omnes*, which in Hobbesian ethics regards the state of humanity against nature. Hobbes expanded on this thought in his works *Leviathan* (1651) and *De Cive* (1642).

477. Rachel Elior, *The Mystical Origins of Hasidism*, trans. Shalom Carmy (Oxford: Littman Library of Jewish Civilization, 2008), 150.

478. Ibid., 183.

479. Ibid.

480. See ibid., 208.

481. See *Tzidkat HaTzaddik*, last paragraph of section 202.

482. Batya Gallant, *Stages of Spiritual Growth* (New York: Devora Publishing, 2010), 11.

483. *Midrash Aggadah*, *Parashat Chukat*, chap. 2.

484. For Maimonides's affirmation of religious compromise, see *Mishneh Torah*, *Hilchot Sanhedrin* 22:4.

CONCLUSION

485. Ahron Soloveichik, *Logic of the Heart, Logic of the Mind: Wisdom and Reflections on Topics of Our Times* (Jerusalem: Genesis Jerusalem Press, 1991), 67.

486. Maimonides, *Mishneh Torah*, *Hilchot Sanhedrin* 21:6; *Shulchan Aruch*, *Choshen Mishpat* 15:2.

487. Ahron Soloveichik, *Logic of the Heart, Logic of the Mind: Wisdom and Reflections on Topics of Our Times* (Jerusalem: Genesis Jerusalem Press, 1991), 7.

488. Shlomo Ganzfried, *Kitzur Shulchan Aruch* 29:14.

489. See *The Essays of Henry D. Thoreau*, ed. Lewis Hyde (New York: North Point Press, 2002), 133.

490. Rashi, Commentary on Genesis 1:1.

491. See Ahron Soloveichik, *Logic of the Heart*, 67, citing *Yalkut Shimoni*.

Index of Sources

About *Pirkei Avot: A Social Justice Commentary*

PIRKEI AVOT is the urtext of Jewish practical wisdom. In many ways, the words of *Pirkei Avot* were the first recorded manifesto of social justice in Western civilization. This commentary explores the text through a lens of contemporary social justice and moral philosophy, engaging both classical commentators and modern thinkers.

RABBI DR. SHMULY YANKLOWITZ is the President & Dean of Valley Beit Midrash, Founder & President of Uri L'Tzedek, Founder & CEO of The Shamayim V'Aretz Institute, and Founder & President of YATOM: The Jewish Foster & Adoption Network.

Rabbi Yanklowitz's writings have appeared in outlets as diverse as the *New York Times*, the *Wall Street Journal*, the *Washington Post*, the *Guardian*, and the *Atlantic*, among many other secular and religious publications. Rabbi Yanklowitz is a sought-after educator, social justice activist, and motivational speaker, as well as the author of eleven books on Jewish spirituality, social justice, and ethics.

Rabbi Shmuly earned a masters degree from Harvard University in Leadership and Psychology, another masters from Yeshiva University in Jewish Philosophy, and a doctorate from Columbia University in Moral Development and Epistemology. He obtained rabbinical ordination from the Yeshivat Chovevei Torah Rabbinical School and two additional, private ordinations in Israel. He has twice been named one of America's Top Rabbis by *Newsweek*. In 2016, the *Forward* named Rabbi Shmuly one of The Most Inspiring Rabbis in America. In 2016, the *Forward* named Rav Shmuly one of the 50 most influential Jews. In the same year, Yanklowitz was selected for the Ariane de Rothschild Fellowship in Cross-Cultural Leadership and Innovative Entrepreneurship at the University of Cambridge.

Rabbi Shmuly, his wife Shoshana, and their three children live in Scottsdale, Arizona. They are also foster parents.

CPSIA information can be obtained
at www.ICGtesting.com
Printed in the USA
BVHW092234200722
642674BV00010B/90